Please renew/return this item by the last date shown.

So that your telephone call is charged at local rate, please call the numbers as set out below:

	From Area codes 01923 or 020:	From the rest of Herts:
Renewals:	01923 471373	01438 737373
Enquiries:	01923 471333	01438 737333
Textphone:	01923 471599	01438 737599

L32   www.hertsdirect.org/librarycatalog

D1491707

TELEGRAM FROM GUERNICA

by the same author

Dead Man's Chest: Travels after Robert Louis Stevenson

TELEGRAM FROM GUERNICA

The Extraordinary Life of George Steer,
War Correspondent

Nicholas Rankin

faber and faber

First published in 2003
by Faber and Faber Limited
3 Queen Square London WC1N 3AU

Typeset by Faber and Faber Limited in Minion
Printed in England by Clays Ltd, St Ives plc

The illustrations in the plate section are reproduced by kind permission of:
The Times (1); Jerry Weibler (10); ADAGP, Paris and DACS, London 2002 (14);
Imperial War Museum (15); PvKK / Kuvaosasto (18).
While every effort has been made to trace copyright holders, in some cases
this has not been successful and should anyone get in touch about permissions
we will be happy to emend further editions.

A CIP record for this book
is available from the British Library

ISBN 0–571–20563–1

10 9 8 7 6 5 4 3 2 1

for
GEORGE BARTON STEER
remembering the dead

I distrust patriotism; the reasonable man can find little in these days that is worth dying for. But dying against – there's enough iniquity in Europe to carry the most urbane and decadent into battle.

Geoffrey Household, *Rogue Male* (1939)

I must go out tomorrow as the others do
    And build the falling castle;
Which has never fallen, thanks
    Not to any formula, red tape or institution,
Nor to any creeds or banks,
    But to the human animal's endless courage.

Louis MacNeice, *Autumn Journal* (1939)

Contents

List of Illustrations, xi
Map of Africa in 1939, xii
A Note on Names, xiii

	Prologue, 1
ONE	In Abyssinia, 7
TWO	Death from the Air, 45
THREE	Torn Apart, 78
FOUR	Men at War, 104
FIVE	Gernika, 114
SIX	Axis in Africa, 148
SEVEN	Winter War, 164
EIGHT	Khaki, 172
NINE	Into Ethiopia, 188
TEN	Special Operations, 213
ELEVEN	Forgotten Army, 227
TWELVE	Home, 241
	Epilogue, 253

Acknowledgements and Sources, 255
Index, 265

List of Illustrations

1   George Lowther Steer with wildfowl bag, Lake Hayk, Ethiopia.
2   Ethiopian warriors in *shammas* with bolt-action rifles.
3   Hubert Fauntleroy Julian with his wife Essie at a Delaware airport.
4   Sir Sidney Barton, British Minister at Addis Ababa, Ethiopia.
5   Dr John Melly, Head of the British Ambulance Service in Ethiopia.
6   Ethiopian cavalry in Belgian uniforms.
7   Margarita de Herrero and George Steer on their wedding day.
8   George Steer and his second wife, Esmé Barton Steer, with his parents.
9   Condor Legion Heinkel 51 'chaser'.
10 Reichsführer Adolf Hitler with General Wolfram von Richthofen.
11 Father Carlos Morilla dead in Santa María church at Durango.
12 German-made thermite incendiary bombs picked up at Guernica.
13 Gernika after the bombardment and fire, 27 April 1937.
14 Pablo Picasso's *Guernica,* painted May–June 1937.
15 Orde Wingate leading 2nd Ethiopian Battalion, Gideon Force into Addis Ababa, 5 May 1941.
16 Dan Sandford and Haile Selassie, 15 April 1941.
17 Haile Selassie with Captain George Steer, 3 June 1941.
18 A Soviet SB bomber, shot down by Finns during the Winter War.
19 Indian Field Broadcasting Unit officers, 1944.
20 Covers of four books by G. L. Steer published by Hodder & Stoughton, 1936–9.
21 George Steer at East London airport, 2 November 1938.

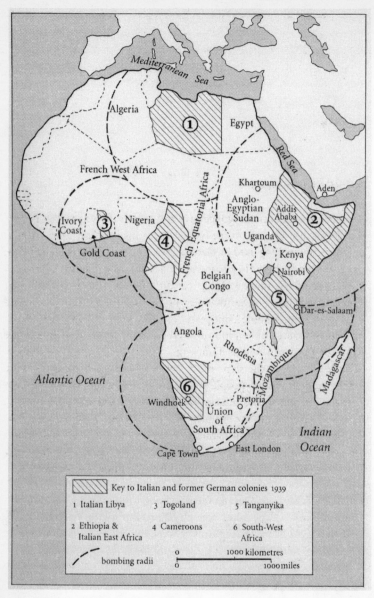

Map for chapter six, Axis in Africa, showing potential ranges of German and Italian bombers, 1939.

A Note on Names

Amharic is a Semitic language and there are different ways of transcribing it into English. At the risk of offending scholars, I have chosen to follow the spelling used by George Steer and *The Times* newspaper in the 1930s, and where they sometimes disagree (e.g. Djibouti/Jibuti) I have selected the more familiar variant and stuck to it consistently. Thus Haile Selassie rather than Hayla-Sellase. Born Tafari Makonnen in 1892, this remarkable Ethiopian became *Ras* or Duke in 1916, *Negus* or King in 1928, and then in 1930 was crowned *Negusa Nagast*, King of Kings or Emperor. So Ras Tafari, the Negus, the Emperor and Haile Selassie all refer to the same man. I have also retained the name Galla for the modern Oromo people because that was the term everyone used in the 1930s and 1940s, and no insult is intended. However, I use the Basque (Gernika) and the Spanish (Guernica) spellings of the town that George Steer witnessed in flames because he himself used both. Pablo Picasso's painting is forever *Guernica*, but G. L. Steer called his book *The Tree of Gernika* out of solidarity with the Basques under attack.

Prologue

Five foreign correspondents covering the civil war in Spain drove out to see the atrocity. Beyond the Basque hills the night sky glowed fleshy pink. As they drew closer, the clouds seemed obscenely alive, wobbly red bellies of billowing smoke. Then Gernika came into view: a meccano framework with flames at every hole. It was Monday night, 26 April 1937, and the town had been fire-bombed.

Dusty survivors told the journalists about the three-and-a-half-hour air raid: how aeroplanes with a black cross on the tail had dropped blast bombs on market-day afternoon, slaughtering people and animals; how fighter planes had dived to machine-gun others fleeing into the fields or along the roads; then how more planes had tumbled out thousands of shiny incendiary bombs, as long as forearms, that fizzled and spurted fire, making a conflagration of the historic town. In the hot rubble of Gernika's collapsed streets there was now a gagging smell of charred meat. Hundreds were dead. 'The Most Appalling Air Raid Ever Known' was the *Evening News* headline on the Reuters dispatch printed in London on Tuesday afternoon.

One of the reporters, an intense twenty-seven-year-old called George Lowther Steer, held back for a day. He questioned more Basque refugees who had reached Bilbao, and drove out again to see the destroyed town by daylight before sending a long cable with his copy. George Steer's story appeared on Wednesday, 28 April 1937 on the foreign news page of *The Times* of London and the front page of the *New York Times*, the most important newspapers on either side of the Atlantic.

George Steer identified the aeroplanes as German. He revealed to the world the dirty secret that Nazi Germany was deeply embroiled in the Spanish Civil War, hugger-mugger with General Franco's 'insurgents'.

Times correspondents were not named then, so few in England knew who told them about the destruction of the town that the Basques spell 'Gernika' and the Spanish 'Guernica'.

THE TRAGEDY OF GUERNICA
TOWN DESTROYED IN AIR ATTACK
EYE-WITNESS'S ACCOUNT

From our Special Correspondent. BILBAO, April 27

Guernica, the most ancient town of the Basques and the centre of their cultural tradition, was completely destroyed yesterday after-noon by insurgent air raiders. The bombardment of this open town far behind the lines occupied precisely three hours and a quarter, during which a powerful fleet of aeroplanes consisting of three German types, Junkers and Heinkel bombers, did not cease unloading on the town bombs weighing from 1,000 lbs. downwards and, it is calculated, more than 3,000 two-pounder aluminium incendiary projectiles. The fighters, meanwhile, plunged low from above the centre of the town to machine-gun those of the civilian population who had taken refuge in the fields.

The whole town of Guernica was soon in flames except the historic Casa de Juntas with its rich archives of the Basque race, where the ancient Basque Parliament used to sit. The famous oak of Guernica, the dried old stump of 600 years and the young new shoots of this century, was also untouched . . .

At 2 a.m. to-day when I visited the town the whole of it was a horrible sight, flaming from end to end. The reflection of the flames could be seen in the clouds of smoke above the mountains from 10 miles away. Throughout the night houses were falling until the streets became long heaps of red impenetrable debris . . .

CHURCH BELL ALARM

In the form of its execution and the scale of the destruction it wrought . . . the raid on Guernica is unparalleled in military history. Guernica was not a military objective . . . The object of the bom-bardment was seemingly the demoralization of the civil population and the destruction of the cradle of the Basque race. . . .

One reader would make the story immortal.

*

In Paris, Pablo Picasso was already appalled by the Civil War in his homeland. The fifty-five-year-old artist supported the Spanish Republic and loathed Franco and his followers, who had murdered so many when they took over his birthplace, Malaga, two months before. This new massacre from the air was a horror that rivalled anything in Goya's *Disasters of War*. The fascist planes had attacked the town on market day, when it was full of *campesinos* with their animals, and local women and housewives come to sell and buy food.

Stocky, bullish, his grey hair combed over his bald patch, Picasso angrily read the newspapers and was galvanized into work. 'Painting is not just done to decorate apartments,' Picasso later said. 'It is an instrument of war . . . against brutality and darkness.' Since January he had had a commission to fulfil for the Spanish Republic, and now the subject found him. Picasso imagined the town's agony, its weeping women and wounded animals. As the left-wing May Day parades through Paris chanted 'Guernica! Guernica!', the Spaniard began charcoal-sketching in his high-windowed studio on the top floor of 7 rue des Grands Agustins.

On 11 May Picasso started to draw the outlines on his giant canvas. Only his current mistress, the Surrealist Dora Maar, was allowed to photograph the work in progress. On 4 June the enormous painting – 12 feet high, 25 feet long – went to the Spanish Pavilion of the *Exposition Internationale des Arts et Techniques Appliqués à la Vie Moderne*, the 1937 Paris World's Fair, which was visited by over 30 million people that summer.

Picasso's *Guernica* is such a well-known image of the twentieth century that nowadays we forget its original impact as the shock of the new, the shock of the *news*. The graphic canvas is black and white, stark as a crime photo lit by a glaring bulb. The creatures are screaming like headlines. The horse's body is made of mashed-up newspaper.

George Steer's story caused a global outcry. Herbert R. Southworth, who wrote the classic fortieth-anniversary study of the 1937 events, called Steer's dispatch 'the basic document in establishing world public opinion about the destruction of Guernica'.

In England, there were questions in the House of Commons. The TUC and the Labour Party condemned 'the merciless and inhuman spirit which animates the rebel forces and their Nazi and Fascist accomplices'. The Bishop of Winchester denounced in a sermon 'a cruel, deliberate, cold-blooded act against the laws of God and against every law of civilization and of man'.

In the United States of America, both houses of Congress were outraged. Senator William Borah of Idaho denounced the 'Fascist strategy' as 'the most revolting instance of mass murder in modern times', and hundreds of prominent Americans signed an 'Appeal to the Conscience of the World', condemning this act of terrorism, or 'frightfulness'. The American Ambassador in London said that news of the forty-two-plane attack on the Basque town 'had been received with the utmost horror in America, where it was regarded as a practice for the bombing of London and Paris'.

The bombing of Guernica brought the brutality of colonial warfare home to white people. Since the First World War, when a few European civilians had been bombed, the tactic had mostly been used in faraway places to punish tribal dissidents. This warfare abolished geography. Death could drop from the air, at any time, to destroy a town without warning and to burn women and children at home in their beds. In this kind of war, civilians *were* the front line. Guernica, like Hiroshima, like 9/11, marked a terrible new order of things.

The Germans were furious at George Steer's story. Adolf Hitler had vowed in 1935 never to bomb open towns, and Nazi Germany had publicly agreed in the Non-Intervention Pact not to get involved in the Spanish Civil War. Now the Nazis were revealed to be field-testing *blitzkrieg* in Spain, on behalf of Franco's Nationalist insurgents, fighting against the democratically elected Spanish Republic. Germany denied everything, and loudly denounced *The Times*.

Adolf Hitler cancelled an interview he was due to give the newspaper on 4 May. Nine days later, Steer's story, 'Bombing of Guernica: German Airman's Statement', caused the German Secret Police to confiscate all copies of *The Times*. On 16 May 1937 the correspondent who was meant to have interviewed Hitler wrote to his editor from Berlin: 'the German papers have been very savage about *The Times*, in fact worse than at any period I remember. The latest discovery is that if you spell it backwards it spells SEMIT, which leads them to deduce we are a Jewish–Marxist organisation.'

The name 'Steer, G. L.' was on the Gestapo Special Wanted List of 2,820 people to be arrested when the Nazis invaded England in 1940. After the war, when Rebecca West found herself on that list with Noel Coward, she quipped to him, 'My dear – the people we should have been seen dead with.' By then George Steer was among the 50 million dead of the Second World War.

Steer's early witnessing of the use of bombing and chemical weapons against the civilian population gave him a unique perspective on twentieth-century history, and made him one of the first to understand the psychological effects of air power. His second book, *The Tree of Gernika*, explored what he called 'the mystique of the air' – the way in which aerial bombing, so often incompetent in practice, would magnify in the imagination, becoming the presiding terror of the twentieth and twenty-first centuries.

Who was George Steer? Almost nothing remains of his personal letters and papers. His widow destroyed much in the 1940s before remaking her life; his parents' executors destroyed the rest in the 1950s. But his six published books (two other manuscripts were lost) and his dispatches and articles allow us to piece together a quite extraordinary life. In the run-up to the Second World War, the greatest and most transforming conflict in human history, George Steer was the only journalist to report from three precursor places – Ethiopia, the Basque country and Finland – where small nations fought for their lives against great powers, and lost. He is among the select band of intrepid reporters and war correspondents (mostly outsiders from the Dominions and Colonies) who invigorated 'the first draft of history' in the 1930s and 1940s. In the clash of totalitarianisms, Steer was resolutely anti-Fascist without ever being compromised as a Communist. He was to the right of George Orwell but well to the left of Evelyn Waugh. (Both writers reviewed him, and Waugh was jealous of him.)

When Steer gave up journalism in 1940 to become a British soldier himself, he helped liberate Ethiopia in the first Allied victory of the war, and drove at the front of the column that brought the Emperor Haile Selassie back into Addis Ababa. He applied his sharp formal intelligence to new kinds of 'psychological warfare' in Africa and Asia, designed to persuade enemy soldiers to surrender. Steer also pioneered the dangerous art of field propaganda, broadcasting in Burma, yards from the Japanese front line.

George Steer was small, brave, fiercely clever, red-haired and amusing. His *Who's Who* entry said, 'Hobbies: *Archery*. Clubs: *Avoided*.' An American diplomat in Ethiopia described him as 'boyish, small-bodied, fox-faced with a mischievous glint in his eyes.' George Steer called himself 'a South African Englishman', and came to etiolated, war-exhausted England with all the energy and irreverence of a young springbok. Raised in a Christian, liberal household amongst black, white and brown people in the Eastern Cape, he was a natural ally of the underdog. English education sharpened his mind, but sun-burnt Africa was his home and his first love. It is in the continent of his birth that George Lowther Steer's adventures begin.

ONE In Abyssinia

1

Addis Ababa, July 1935. With a shriek on his whistle and a yell of 'Kas-bil! Kas-bil!' the black policeman slows Steer's canter down to a trot. No galloping is allowed in the sprawling African city whose name means 'New Flower'. The Addis Ababa police have bare feet, khaki puttees, blue tunics and white sola topis with red bands. There are more donkeys and cows than cars, but there is a new breed of insolent taxi driver who ministers to European needs. There is only one tarmac road, to and from the railway station. The mud-walled streets are full of cheerful young men, walking or lounging in white cotton togas or *shammas*. By day, vultures and crows sit on the corrugated-iron roofs, and hyenas slink through the streets at night.

Steer found Addis Ababa filthy but exhilarating. 'Nine thousand feet up, a sparkle in the air, clear sunlight between leaves and storms of rain. And after rain, the smell of dripping eucalyptus, which made me feel careless and fresh as a child; for it brought back memories of young years in the Cape.'

George Steer's happy butterfly-hunting boyhood had been in South Africa's sunlit Eastern Cape. At eleven he had been sent away for a conventional schooling in England, winning open scholarships to both public school and university. However, he had never forgotten his African beginnings. At Winchester College in the 1920s he reportedly 'showed a colonial disregard for the conventions of this country', and in early 1931 he helped to found Oxford University's Africa Society, dedicated to studying 'the native peoples of Africa, their present condition and future development'. Steer covered the sofa of his rooms in Christ Church with the skin of a lion his father had shot with a bow and arrow.

Straight after Oxford he returned to South Africa for a journalistic apprenticeship on the *Cape Argus*, before working in the London office of the *Yorkshire Post*.

In January 1935 Steer reported on the rigged referendum where the people of the disputed Saar borderlands voted overwhelmingly to join Nazi Germany, and the dirty snow of the cobbled tramlines at Saarbrucken had made him dream of sun on yellow grass and long again for the Africa that he loved. Now, at the age of twenty-five, he had become the Special Correspondent of *The Times* in Ethiopia, pipping Evelyn Waugh to the post in the only medieval Christian kingdom in Africa, the land where the mighty Blue Nile began.

As Steer rode around the Ethiopian capital early in the rainy season of 1935, he could see the tatty remains of the arches put up for Emperor Haile Selassie I's coronation in 1930. Evelyn Waugh had covered the event for *The Times* and satirized it in his 1932 comic novel *Black Mischief*, where Oxford-educated Seth becomes 'Emperor of Azania and Lord of Wanda'. Unlike Waugh, Steer was sympathetic to the Emperor. Haile Selassie was slowly bringing his ideas of neatness and order to the Ethiopian capital, but Steer felt the shapeless pell-mell African city owed most to Haile Selassie's predecessor, Menelik.

2

The dream of the later emperors of Ethiopia was to restore what had once been the greatest empire between Rome and Persia, and to integrate the entire Horn of Africa from the Nile to the Red Sea and the Indian Ocean. The mountains at the north of the Great Rift Valley were Ethiopia's heart, but the swamps of the west, the fertile lakes of the south and the deserts of the east were all parts of the ideal kingdom.

Emperor Menelik II, who claimed descent from the wise King Solomon and the Queen of Sheba, was a dark-skinned dreamer with a grizzled, straggly beard and sad eyes. He loved machines and liked the foreign traders to get them for him. Armenians and Frenchmen like the renegade poet Arthur Rimbaud sold him guns from 1887 onwards. Menelik II expanded the Ethiopian Empire during his reign from 1889 to 1913, conquering and absorbing many states and their peoples. He also authorized the building of the railway from the coast, which was completed in 1917.

In the scramble for Africa that followed the opening of the Suez Canal in 1869, European powers began seizing East African coasts, thus blocking Ethiopia's access to the sea. In the north, Italy took and named Eritrea, with the ports of Massawa and Assab on the Red Sea. To the east, across the Danakil Desert, the French stole French Somaliland with the port of Djibouti. East of Harar were the piratical British in British Somaliland, whose capital Berbera faced Aden and Arabia across the Gulf. Then in the south-east, running down the Indian Ocean coast from the tip of the Horn, there was Italian Somaliland. How were Ethiopians to deal with this oppressive ring of three, who ganged up on them in the Tripartite Treaty of 1906?

One way had always been by fighting them. Emperor Tewodros could not overcome General Napier's huge British force at Magdala in 1868, and shot himself rather than surrender. (The British liked to say he put the barrel of a pistol given him by Queen Victoria in his mouth.) Three decades later, though, in 1896, Menelik II had a great victory over the Italian General Baratieri, who had marched an army of 14,500 men from Eritrea and struck at Adowa, the capital of Tigre. He was surprised by a massive Ethiopian army of foot soldiers and cavalry, equipped with 100,000 new rifles and 40 cannon, including a battery of Hotchkiss quick-firing mountain guns, the kind the US 7th Cavalry had recently used on the Sioux at Wounded Knee. It was the biggest defeat of a European army by Africans since the time of Hannibal of Carthage: 8,000 Italians and 4,000 askaris were killed outright. Because it happened on St George's Day (he is the patron saint of Ethiopia as well as of Catalunya, England and Portugal), the Ethiopians interpreted their victory as divine. Only when Italy recognized the sovereign independence of Ethiopia were 1,865 Italian prisoners returned. Thirty of them had been castrated.

The prestige of Menelik II increased. Diplomats came to pay court from Austria, Belgium, France, Germany, Russia and the United States – and, of course, from Great Britain. In August 1898, the year after her Diamond Jubilee, the Empress of India, Queen Victoria, sent her personal greetings, recorded in her own rather squeaky-sounding voice. The Ethiopian Imperial couple listened respectfully to the recording several times, before the British agent, Lieutenant Colonel John Lane Harrington, solemnly destroyed the phonograph cylinder to keep Her Majesty's voice from profaner ears.

Menelik's succession was a problem. Ethiopia was a Christian empire just across the water from the heart of Islam, and many of its subjects were Muslim. Menelik's grandson, Lij Iyasu, thought he could unite the black Christians and Muslims of Ethiopia and drive the whites from the coast. This was during the First World War, when the Allies did not want an anti-colonial Islamic revolt in Abyssinia that might hand over control of the Gulf and the Suez Canal to the Ottoman Turks and their allies the Germans. Lij Iyasu wooed the Somali Muslims and set learned men to trace his own descent from the Prophet Mohammed. This outraged the conservative, status-conscious Ethiopian Orthodox Church; Lij Iyasu was deposed, and Menelik's daughter Zauditu was made Empress. The British and French covertly supported the man who became her regent, Tafari Makonnen. His aristocratic title was *Ras* Tafari (a *Ras* is like a Duke); the name would become known round the world through the Jamaican-based cult of Rastafarianism, which began in the 1930s.

Ras Tafari was a modernizer like Menelik; a child of the railway age, educated by French priests. He admired new technology, like his father, the Governor of Harar, who had returned from Edward VII's coronation in 1902 with a motor car, two motor-tricycles, a timepiece with moving figures and the very latest firearms. Machines were becoming all the rage in Ethiopia. A month after Arthur Rimbaud first arrived in Harar as a trader in December 1880 he sought 'to obtain manufacturer's catalogues of mechanical toys, fireworks, conjuring tricks, working models, miniature constructions, etc.'.

In November 1922, when Ras Tafari was still regent, he fell in love with aviation on his first flight in an RAF biplane at the British military base at Aden, and became an apostle of air power. In March 1930, when Empress Zauditu's husband, Ras Gugsa, rebelled, Ras Tafari sent the French pilot André Maillet to make three bombing runs to scatter the insurgents, allowing marksmen to pick off the isolated leader.

A young British acting vice-consul happened to see Maillet's small biplane returning to the Addis Ababa racecourse. A grizzled Ethiopian general clambered out of the back of the open cockpit, holding aloft in triumph the rebellious Ras Gugsa's severed head.

Ras Tafari, the educated modernizer, was a gentleman with whom the West could do business. A strategic thinker, in 1923 he took Ethiopia into the League of Nations, promising to abolish slavery. Ras Tafari modelled his 1930 coronation as Emperor Haile Selassie I of Ethiopia on Emperor Hirohito of Japan's 1928 symbolic ceremony, inviting high-ranking dignitaries and the international press. Tafari made use of foreign advisers, but played them off against each other. As a prototype 'non-aligned' leader, he put his faith in paper protocols and the chimera nowadays called 'the international community'. He needed to clarify the exact limits of his land. The Anglo-Ethiopian Boundary Commission first sorted out the borders of British Somaliland and Italian Somaliland, and then the line demarcating British Somaliland and Ethiopia; but the trickiest frontier was the one that divided Ethiopia from Italian Somaliland, running across the Ogaden Desert.

Nationalists in Fascist Italy still nursed a grievance against Ethiopia after their massive defeat by Menelik II in 1896. In 1934 *Il Duce* Benito Mussolini was not looking forward to the shame of the fortieth anniversary; he dreamed instead of a new Roman Empire, joining Ethiopia with Eritrea and Italian Somaliland into *Africa Orientale Italiana*. The Treaty of Friendship between Italy and Ethiopia was already foundering when the 'Walwal incident' occurred on the border.

In the desert, water is vital, and the Somali clans of the dry, thorny Ogaden moved along river beds and between oases to water their camels and cattle. At Walwal there were over a thousand waterholes. When the Anglo-Ethiopian Boundary Commissioners arrived on 23 November 1934, their 600-strong armed Ethiopian escort found Walwal occupied by Italian irregular forces, 200 white-turbaned Somali frontiersmen. The camps dug in facing each other.

Walwal was sixty miles inside Ethiopian territory, but an Italian captain soon arrived with further reinforcements, and the Boundary Commission found him 'disobliging'. Two Italian aircraft buzzed the British camp, and the Boundary Commission withdrew five miles to Ado. For ten days the armed men growled at each other, until 5 December, when someone fired the first shot.

Within minutes three Italian aircraft with bombs were overhead and two armoured cars were pushing through the thorn hedges, spraying machine-gun fire. The Ethiopian military leader was shot dead through the forehead. An Ethiopian rearguard fought on, led by Ali Nur, late of the King's African Rifles, but fell back after midnight with 107 dead and 45 wounded.

Ethiopia made diplomatic protests, and asked for international arbitration. Italy demanded instant reparations, apologies and salutes to its flag. Ethiopia appealed to the League of Nations. Italy rattled sabres and frightened the democracies into appeasement.

Robert Vansittart, Permanent Under-Secretary at the British Foreign Office, saw with hindsight the fundamental importance of the failure of French and English politicians to resolve the Walwal dispute. 'Thus, because a few askaris had died by brackish water-holes in an African waste, was taken the first step to the second German Holocaust.'

3

George Steer had grown up with newspapers. His father Bernard Steer was the Managing Editor and future Chairman of the East London *Daily Dispatch*, the best paper in South Africa's Eastern Cape. (The *Dispatch* later became famous under the editorship of Donald Woods, when he became friends with the Black Consciousness activist Steve Biko.) Steer learned to read and write by lying on the floor and copying out words and headlines from sheets of newspaper, and then running to his mother Emma to ask what they meant. At school in England in 1928 he edited the Winchester College magazine *The Wykehamist*. He served his basic apprenticeship in journalism on Cape Town's afternoon paper the *Cape Argus* from 1932 to 1933, where he learned 120 w.p.m. shorthand and fast, clean typing, and then doing the 'London Notes' from the Fleet Street office of the *Yorkshire Post* from 1933 to 1934.

In the months after Walwal, George Steer was ready to step up to *The Times*. 'The Thunderer' could cherry-pick candidates. Ex-staffer Claud Cockburn parodied the *folie de grandeur* produced by so many clever and eager applicants: 'Brilliant and sound I grant you. But brilliant and sound enough for *The Times*? This one mentions his triple First, his double Blue and his uncle the Bishop. Estimable, but the dear good chap does only speak four languages . . . Is, indeed, anyone, anywhere, truly worthy of *The Times*?'

Steer had an excellent establishment education as a Wykehamist and a scholar of 'the House'. He stressed his knowledge of Africa, and bluffed his way through an oral in Amharic, Ethiopia's main language. But one of his referees, Arthur Mann, Editor of the *Yorkshire Post*, warned that his political judgement might be 'quixotic'.

Nevertheless, Ralph Deakin, the Imperial and Foreign News Editor of *The Times*, eventually hired George Steer as a Special Correspondent in Abyssinia on £60 a month (about £2,100 in today's money), which included travelling expenses. In his letter of confirmation of 21 May 1935, Deakin spelled out Steer's duties: to supply 'cablegrams and special articles recording the main developments in the Italo-Abyssinian dispute . . . on an average, two or three cables a week, the best length for

which would be between 200 and 400 words'. The special articles would
be sent by mail, each about 1,600 words long.

Steer had his tonsils out and his teeth filled. With a sola topi in
Winchester colours given him by *Yorkshire Post* colleagues, a typewriter
and a copy of the *Times* booklet *Aids to Correspondents*, a Mauser
sporting rifle and a shotgun, khaki shorts and tropical kit, the twenty-
five-year-old set off from London on 27 June 1935. Today you can fly to
Addis Ababa in under half a day; then it took a fortnight. The route was
by boat-train to Paris, by train to Marseille, then five days by ship across
the Mediterranean to Port Said and four days down the Suez Canal and
the Red Sea to Djibouti in French Somaliland.

On 5 July 1935 the *Spectator* published his unsigned article 'The
Abyssinian Adventure'. 'There are now well over 100,000 – some say as
many as 150,000 – Italian troops in East Africa,' it begins. 'Materials of
war, lorries, tanks and armoured cars, gas and barbed wire, are poured
into the Italian colonies every day.'

Steer's mention of 'gas' is a shrewd guess or good intelligence. Italy
had already broken the 1925 Anti-Gas Treaty, both before and after
ratification in 1928, by bombing Senussi Arabs in Libya with phosgene
and yperite. To be fair, they were not alone in this practice. The
Spanish military secretly used a vast amount of chemical weaponry
against the tribes of northern Morocco between 1921 and 1927. Before
the international treaty, the British had used mustard gas in
Afghanistan and on the North-West Frontier in 1919, and against Arabs
in Iraq in 1920. Winston Churchill, then Secretary of State for War and
Air, declared he was 'strongly in favour of using poisoned gas against
uncivilised tribes'.

In his *Spectator* article Steer pointed out: 'Ethiopia is the last African
Empire to be invaded by a white Power, when feeling against the colour
bar is rising all over Africa. The war . . . for the subjugation of Ethiopia
may well light a fire throughout the African bush.' Steer concludes with
a prophetic sentence: 'Victory, eventual victory, will remain with the
Ethiopian if he remembers one lesson – never to mass against mechanized forces, or when he is within air range from the Italian side.
Bombs or mustard gas on a massed Ethiopian army, like that which
fought at Adowa, might break its heart and with it the resistance of
Ethiopia.'

4

Amid the sweltering heat, flies and smells of Djibouti, Steer gathered
some local opinions about the fate of Ethiopia. 'They are not our
religion,' said the Somali Muslims, 'but they are black like us.' Then
Steer made the three-day journey by puffing steam train up the Awash
river valley to Addis Ababa.

At Diredawa, the railway town near Harar, the rail travellers ate outside in the evening, between rustling orange trees, with the scent of
bougainvillea. The days were brilliantly clear; he saw white-rumped
antelope under 'mimosa trees in green parasol'. On the second night at
Awash (where bones of the earliest humanoids have since been found),
Steer stumbled to bed over dead whisky bottles and lean cats.

They reached Addis Ababa on the third night, shivering at the rise in
altitude and drop in temperature, to be met by red-turbaned Arab
porters, a mixture of Europeans and a crowd of curious Ethiopians in
their jodhpurs and white cotton *shammas* (derived from the ancient
Greek word for toga, *himation*). Buffeting and barrelling through them
came a modern Greek, George Mendrakos, the manager of the Imperial
Hotel, looking through horn-rimmed spectacles for new guests to
collar. Built in 1907 by the wife of the Emperor Menelik II, the
Imperial is known today by her name, Taitu, or her title, Etegui. The
travel writer Charles Rey in 1923 commended the Imperial's views
but advised 'a liberal sprinkling of Keating's powder'.

On Steer's way in to dinner, 'grease and artichokes and Greek sweet-
meats', he passed two melancholy journalists hunched over a dusty chess-
board: Will Barber would die of malaria three months later and win a
posthumous Pulitzer Prize; and the other was a young goatee-bearded
Greek lawyer called Akeos Angelopoulos, reporting for Hearst newspapers. Ten months later, with the war over, Steer and Angelopoulos
would be the last reporters out of Addis Ababa, expelled by the Italians on
the same train.

'I woke up early, jumped out of bed and waited for the dust to settle.
Then I moved onto my wooden balcony and looked at Addis – superb.'
Looking north from his window on his first morning in Addis Ababa,
Steer could see Mount Entoto, where Menelik II had first begun the
capital of his empire-state. (Arthur Rimbaud, on an arms-trading trip,
saw Menelik's people felling the cedars there.) It was too cold to live
permanently up high, so the Empress Taitu moved lower down to settle

on a big hilltop near some hot springs, where she built a palace, or *gibbi*, and after Adowa in 1896 the settlement really started to grow. Steer could also see the cathedral of St Giorghis on another big hill with Arada, the commercial centre, around its flanks. Ethiopian nobles put their *gibbis* on other hilltops, and their spreading encampments solidified into neighbourhoods. After they planted quick-growing Australian eucalyptus trees that could be regularly coppiced for firewood and poles, the court and capital did not move again.

5

Clopping round Addis Ababa on his pony, one of Steer's first ports of call to drop off his card was the large compound housing the British Legation. There he met the British Minister (the equivalent of an ambassador) who, after many narrative twists and turns, would eventually become his father-in-law. Sir Sidney Barton, appointed to Addis Ababa in 1929, had been caricatured in Evelyn Waugh's *Black Mischief* as the languid and ineffectual Envoy Extraordinary Sir Samson Courteney, who occupied his time when Third Secretary in Peking building 'a cardboard model of the Summer Palace'. This parody was far from the truth. A testy Irish Protestant, Barton had risen to the top of the Chinese consular service, after winning a medal and a mention in dispatches during the 1900 Boxer Rebellion. He dealt vigorously with warlords and gave away Chiang Kai-shek's bride, Mei Ling, at the Chinese Nationalist leader's wedding. He was nicknamed 'Gunboat' Barton after cabling: 'Trouble at Weihaiwei. Send two cruisers', but he also managed to revise the standard Chinese–English dictionary. Barton's obituary in *The Times* recorded: 'In Abyssinia his diplomacy was blunt and forceful, but he won the high regard of both Government and people. He supported with characteristic enthusiasm the Emperor's efforts to modernize his country.'

Steer's account of his first meeting with Barton contains the words 'brisk', 'short', 'snap' and 'sharp'; but Sir Sidney may have felt more vulnerable than usual at the time, because his elder daughter had fallen in love with an Italian diplomat.

Marion Barton and her sister Esmé were fun-loving girls who kept a 'poppet list' of eligible young attachés to flirt with, but Marion's passionate relationship with a virile Italian horseman, Filippo Muzi

Falconi, was a *coup de foudre*. When his Protestant daughter eloped and married Filippo in a Roman Catholic ceremony in Rome in 1933, Sir Sidney, haunted by Ulster's religious conflicts, refused to attend.

Falconi was one of the Italian consuls in Ethiopia, based at Debra Marcos, a fortnight's travel away from Addis Ababa. Marion had her first child, Alessandro, there in late 1934. The political situation worsened in the middle of 1935 and, probably at the insistence of the worried Barton grandparents, the Emperor sent his plane to take the unweaned baby and nanny away. Marion, left on her own, begged Ethiopian mothers to lend her their babies to relieve her aching breasts, but they did not want her 'white milk' for their black infants.

As war fever mounted in 1935, Marion had a romantic involvement with the Italian Legation's Second Secretary, Filippo de Grenet, and her husband shot himself.

ACCIDENT TO ITALIAN CONSUL

From our own correspondent. ROME, Aug. 22

Baron Filippo Muzi Falconi, Italian consul at Debra Marcos, has been accidentally injured while out shooting in Abyssinia.
A rumour that he was wounded by Abyssinians is denied here . . .
According to a Reuters telegram, the Consul, who was shot in the chest, but not dangerously hurt, explained that he had fired his pistol at some game, and that it went off accidentally while he was replacing it in its holster.

The Times, 23 August 1935, 9g.

What really happened? Half-mad with jealousy, Muzi Falconi muffed the shot. Had he hoped to throw suspicion for the deed on 'Abyssinians', thus creating an incident that would provoke a war with Ethiopia? If he wanted to die a Fascist martyr, his timing was wrong: the Italian invasion was not due until the rains ended in late September.

Back in Addis Ababa, Marion had a *mauvais quart d'heure* in her father's study. He received her coldly, tapping the Foreign Office cable on his desk, asking if the incident was serious. Marion did not speak to her father again until he was on his deathbed. Thus Sir Sidney Barton came to rely on his younger daughter, the vivacious redhead Esmé, who would eventually marry George Steer. Esmé enjoyed the socializing of diplomatic life more than her mother, Lady Winifred; a newspaper photograph shows her accompanying her father in his morning coat to a reception in Addis Ababa, with a tiny boat-brim hat tilted over her marcel wave. She has a strong Irish face. In another picture (the *Daily Telegraph*, 14 September 1935) she's smiling in jodhpurs, jersey and beret, reining in a powerful grey horse. The Barton girls adored riding, and Addis Ababa was a great place for it because the Ethiopian nobles and warriors valued good horses. (Muzi Falconi had been wooing aristocrats to the Italian cause with bloodstock.)

Esmé had flirted with lots of men; one she fell in love with was the idealistic medical missionary Dr John Melly, MC, who first appeared in Ethiopia at the end of July 1934, wearing a double-breasted suit, Monte Carlo sneakers and a blue hat, carrying an ivory-handled fly-whisk. With his elegant mien and the poems of Algernon Swinburne in his luggage, the blond, blue-eyed Melly seemed like an Oxford dandy; but he was a devout Christian and trained surgeon who wanted to found a hospital and medical school in Ethiopia where the staff would swear loyalty to Jesus. Melly believed the Lord would provide the £200,000 funding required. 'Conditions here are appalling,' he wrote. 'The country is way back in the 15th century – ruled over by feudal lords – with sanitation unheard of . . . and . . . riddled with disease.'

Melly wrote to his friend Kathleen Nelson in April 1935:

> Kathleen, they have *no Red Cross whatsoever*. If you want a sleepless night, picture to yourself the indescribable horror and suffering behind the Ethiopian lines when Italian planes . . . have been dropping bombs on the Ethiopians for twenty-four hours . . . I hope to come back to England armed with the Emperor's authority, and persuade the British Red Cross – failing them, to Paris to the International Red Cross – failing them to Geneva to the League Red Cross – failing them, I shall have a great Press campaign and raise what money and volunteers I can, and have my own bally Red Cross.

When he was still in London preparing to go out to Ethiopia in June 1935, George Steer met the newly returned John Melly at lunch with Majors Lawrence Athill and Arthur Bentinck, who were helping start Melly's scheme for a British Ambulance Service in Ethiopia. The Archbishop of Canterbury blessed their convoy of sixteen thirty-hundredweight Bedford lorries in mid-November, and the British

public responded with money. A single BBC radio appeal by Dick
Sheppard broadcast on Sunday, 5 January 1936 raised a record-
breaking £27,408 (over £1.6 million in today's money). Steer said he
'liked Melly immensely'.

6

Steer was summoned to interview Haile Selassie I, the Emperor of
Ethiopia, on Tuesday, 16 July 1935. Through Barton, European court eti-
quette had become *de rigueur*. Steer had to borrow the elements of
morning dress (white shirt, top hat, black tail coat, pinstripe trousers)
from members of the British Legation before he set out with his interpreter for the palace at the north of the city. Not huge and sprawling like
Menelik's Great Gibbi, the unpretentious Little Gibbi was modelled
on the Norfolk country house of Lord Noel-Buxton, which Ras Tafari
had visited on his European tour in 1924. Past the sentry boxes with
diagonal green, yellow and red stripes and the Imperial Guardhouse,
the gravelled drive curved through formal gardens, past the tinkling
fountain, up to the portico of the palace.

> A servant of the court, his white *shamma* tied respectfully across his
> chest, his sword arm covered and his trim beard pointed, greeted us
> and led us into the Emperor's study . . .
>
> Directly facing the door by which I entered his study, and with
> his back to a window, the Emperor of Ethiopia sat behind his heavy
> gilt table dispatching business. Two little dogs lay at his feet and a
> big fire of eucalyptus crackled in a grate at his side.
>
> He bowed gravely and waited for me to open the conversation,
> which lasted for an hour and a half.
>
> Other people have remarked the Assyrian perfection of his fea-
> tures, the delicacy and length of his hands, the serenity of his eyes
> and the great dignity of his bearing. The first thing that I noticed
> was the extreme rapidity of his mind . . .
>
> He spoke without hesitation and without any correction: quickly,
> with the authoritative voice of a logician. He had an immensely able
> mind, and he knew his own views to the last detail . . . Throughout,
> the Emperor economized gesture and sat perfectly straight in his
> seat. Only the jewelled hand moved a little from under his black
> cloak. A man of great intelligence, completely controlled by himself.

The dogs lay by his feet for an hour and a half with the same motionless obedience.

The Emperor wanted *The Times* to put across his position. Ethiopia needed a seaport on the Red Sea, and would cede part of the Ogaden to Italy in return for a corridor to Zeila in British Somaliland; but if Italy declared war, or her troops dared to cross the frontiers, Ethiopia would immediately respond in kind and appeal to the League of Nations.

Steer conveyed the points cleanly in his first piece in *The Times* of 18 July 1935.*

On 30 July Steer got his first 'turnover' in *The Times*. This was the special article on the right-hand edge of the editorial page. 'The Emperor's Army' was illustrated by photographs headlined 'The Abyssinian Dispute: Military Preparations', with Mussolini Fascist-saluting, a troopship leaving Naples, and piles of Italian military stores at Massawa quayside. Steer supplied four Ethiopian photographs. One showed eight relaxed soldiers of the Imperial Guard wearing khaki uniforms with peaked caps, puttees and bare feet. Three of them are leaning on their Lebel Mausers like shooting sticks, with their muzzles jammed into the mud. Steer pencilled on the back: 'good treatment for rifles'.

Steer estimated that Ethiopia had 30,000 modern rifles, maybe 1,000 light machine guns and at most 15 million rounds of small-arms ammunition (about twice the amount the Italians shot off in one three-day battle). They had no artillery to speak of, only eight planes that could fly, and thirteen Oerlikon anti-aircraft guns; but they had edged weapons, and guts.

In July 1935, Great Britain and France imposed an arms embargo. This, in fact, favoured the aggressor nation, since Italy was already an arms manufacturer and exporter, while Ethiopia had to get the rifles, machine guns and ammunition it needed from countries such as Belgium and Czechoslovakia.

Belgian officers were training the Imperial Guard, whose neat khaki made good publicity photos; but the real Ethiopian army was passing

---

* In his well-known book about war correspondents, *The First Casualty*, Philip Knightley repeats the story by the *Daily Express* journalist O. D. Gallagher about how he faked a fulsome telegram of congratulation to G. L. Steer from the owner of *The Times*. Gallagher's punchline was that its interception by the Ethiopian authorities led to Steer's first getting the exclusive interview with the Emperor. This is unlikely, as Gallagher only reached Addis Ababa a week after Steer met Haile Selassie.

through Addis Ababa on its way to the north. Other contemporary
news agency photographs show crowds of barefoot black men in white
shammas shouldering muskets, marching along muddy streets.
Traditional mounted warriors wearing bristly lion's-mane headdresses
escort cloaked and turbaned chiefs on velvet-caparisoned mules.
Behind them are ragged veils of eucalyptus, corrugated-iron veran-
dahs and adobe walls. The occasional motor car, stopped to let the
medieval horde pass, seems as incongruous as a shiny Ford V8 saloon
among Sir John Falstaff's men. These sudden movements of armed
retainers through the streets were as mysterious as Amharic grammar
to Europeans.

7

Steer was just ahead of a flood of foreign journalists into Ethiopia.
Akeos Angelopoulos, wearing his opera cloak, met two new arrivals at
the railway station. O'Dowd Gallagher of the *Daily Express* was accompanied by a big ruddy-faced Australian freelance called Noel Monks,
who was carrying a Bible because somebody had told him there was a
lot about Abyssinia in it.

'There is only one man ahead of you,' 'Angel' told the Fleet Street
men. 'He is little George Steer of *The Times*.' In his 1955 autobiography,
Eyewitness, Monks recalled:

A short, slight man with an impish face came up to us and said:
'I'm George Steer, of *The Times*. Welcome to Sheba's land.' Then:
'Did you bring your Bibles?' We said we had.

'Is there going to be a war?' we asked.

'There's going to be a massacre unless the League of Nations get
off their bottoms and stop Mussolini. These people are still living in
the spear age. That's all they've got, spears.'

In the years ahead, this brilliant little man and I were to be
colleagues in much bigger wars than this one.

Noel Monks found it hard to sleep in Addis Ababa. It was not just
barking dogs and yowling hyenas; the twenty lions the Emperor kept
also roared all night. And they would be woken early by the stentorian
voice of 'Colonel' Julian drilling barefoot Ethiopian recruits on the
wasteland next door.

*

Hubert Fauntleroy Julian was a tall and handsome Trinidadian adventurer with a monocle and a British accent who had been obsessed with flying since the age of twelve, when he had seen the first aeroplane flight in the West Indies, in May 1909, end with the pilot crashing to his death near Port of Spain. Taught to fly in Canada by the air ace Billy Bishop VC, Julian was introduced to a New York crowd by the Jamaican black-consciousness activist Marcus Garvey in 1921 as 'the first Negro in America or in the British Isles or Commonwealth to qualify as a pilot, and his example should inspire us all'. After he did several crazy public parachute jumps into the north end of Manhattan, the *Herald Tribune* dubbed him 'the Black Eagle of Harlem'. On 4 July 1924 Julian attempted to take off for Africa in a Boeing hydroplane with 'Dedicated to the advancement of the Negro race' painted on the side. As he aimed to fly to Liberia, the only Negro republic, he thought it right to call the plane *Ethiopia*, in honour of the only black kingdom; but a pontoon full of water made him crash into Flushing Bay, New York.

Ras Tafari sent an emissary in February 1930, asking Julian to organize an Ethiopian air force and act as the Emperor's personal pilot, on a salary of $1,000 a month. Julian accepted. With two French pilots, he began training Ethiopian airmen and mechanics. In the run-up to the coronation they put on a little air display with the country's five planes: the Black Eagle did an unexpected parachute jump and landed near the Emperor, who awarded him the Order of Menelik and the rank of colonel in the Ethiopian forces. However, at the next air display, in front of foreign guests who had come for the coronation, Julian crashed his biplane into the eucalyptus. He told the Emperor that the wily French pilots had sabotaged his plane – either they or he must go. Julian travelled back to the States via Paris and London in November 1930.

When he returned to Ethiopia, in 1935, the Emperor asked him to take a critical look at his air force. Of the twelve planes, five were unfit to fly and the other seven were small, slow, obsolete and unarmed. So Haile Selassie asked him to train an infantry detachment instead. With no military experience, and speaking no Amharic, Julian set out to lick a motley band of clerks and shopkeepers into shape.

Noel Monks got to know Julian. He used to come into the journalists' room after a drill session and flop into a chair, saying in a voice hoarse from shouting: 'I'll teach those goddam black bastards to drill if it's the last thing I do.' Monks thought Julian himself was blacker than most Abyssinians.

Once again, things went wrong. Julian got into a fist fight in an Addis Ababa bar with a rival American Negro flyer from Chicago called Johannes Robinson. When 'the Brown Condor of Chicago' pulled a knife, 'the Black Eagle of Harlem' had to deck him with a chair. Banished to Ambo, Julian ran away in mid-November 1935, reaching Djibouti with only a few dollars and the uniform he stood up in.

'The Negro Lindbergh', as *Time* magazine once called him, may have failed in his mission, but he was part of the world-wide wave of sympathy and support for Ethiopia among black people. Rastafarianism, the Jamaican millenarian movement which sees Haile Selassie as a semi-divine figure who fulfils biblical prophecy, only began to spread in the 1930s, but all across the Caribbean Basin and the Atlantic coast of America there was a tremendous reaction to news of war coming in Ethiopia. Black people saw it as colonialism in action; as a race war; as a rallying point for the African diaspora. When heavyweight boxer Joe Louis fought the Italian circus strongman Primo Carnera on 25 June 1935, everyone read the fight as an augury. 'The Brown Bomber' won by a knockout in the sixth round.

In early August 1935, 20,000 attended a pro-Abyssinian rally in Harlem, New York City. Many African Americans signed petitions to be allowed to enlist in Ethiopia's armed forces. Racial tension ran high. A week later, riot police were called out in Jersey City to break up a clash between 'Negroes and Italians'. In South Africa, black harbour workers refused to do any work on Italian ships. In London, the Trinidadian socialists C. L. R. James, George Padmore and Eric Williams were all involved, together with the Kenyan Jomo Kenyatta, in the International African Friends of Abyssinia.

8

On 7 August 1935, at the same time as the Emperor instituted a government press bureau under Dr Lorenzo Taezaz, the former 'political director' of Harar, the journalists at the Imperial Hotel set up L'Association de la Presse Etrangère (Collins of Reuters was President, Steer was Secretary, and Evelyn Waugh would become Treasurer).

Taezaz, whom Waugh described as 'a suave, beady-eyed little Tigrean', had read law at Montpellier, been on the Boundary Commission before Walwal, and run the Emperor's counter-espionage service against Italy's many spies in Ethiopia. His impersonations of foreign journalists greatly amused Steer, and he was one of the new breed of Young Ethiopians whom the Emperor was encouraging. Evelyn Waugh mocked the *jeunesse éthiopienne* as half-baked in *Black Mischief*, but Steer was far more sympathetic to their predicament. Born in Eritrea, Italian-educated, very bright, Lorenzo Taezaz had risen to be secretary to the Governor of Asmara at a young age; but he was not white, and the humiliation of being hissed by Italians in a cinema made him flee to Aden, where the Emperor rescued him from poverty. People like Taezaz became the agents of reform in Ethiopia – sent abroad to learn and study with their fees paid by the Emperor, they owed him their new status in the civil service ministries, and shared with him the frustrations of trying to cajole the older and more conservative *rase*s into new ways.

Everyone thought the war would start in the south, with an Italian move across the Ogaden to cut the railway at Diredawa. Taezaz and Steer had several secret meetings, over maps of the Ogaden, and a trip was arranged for a look at the southern front; Steer agreed to report back personally to the Emperor. On 20 August, 'all muffled up in secrecy', George Steer took the train down to Diredawa, the nearest railway stop for the Ogaden. Lij Worku, head of the railway police, fixed him a place in the cab of the lorry to travel the thirty-five miles up to Harar. Two boys rode on the mudguards carrying stones to wedge under the rear wheels if they started sliding backwards on the slopes. The back of the vehicle was packed full of Ethiopians, chickens, mules and bundles. Then a huge chuckling Somali in a white coat turned up, carrying a black umbrella. Steer thought Haji Asfar Omar looked like the Aga Khan leading in a winner.

'So you going to Ogaden? You want informations? You want bedding?'

Steer wondered how the Haji knew where he was going, and changed the subject. Some weeks later, when Steer was shown the papers of a man arrested for spying for Italy, a sentence caught his eye: 'An old Somali says that an Englishman, St George, has gone down to the Ogaden.'

Out of dusty Diredawa the lorry began to climb through spiny cactus and grey-green euphorbia, all knots and crazy candelabra, on the 2,500-foot rise to the Harar upland. They saw herds of camels across the dry river bed, and troops of baboons parading rump-high. The maize stalks were yellow and dry in cracked fields as they left behind the fierce Danakil plains that Wilfred Thesiger had explored the year before. Higher up, the air was fresher, the earth redder, and fields of *Catha edulis* appeared, the tall shrub whose glossy smooth leaves with reddish stalks are chewed for the stimulant known as *qat*, *chat* or *miraa*. Bare-breasted Galla women with baskets of leaves on their heads stood aside to let the lorry pass. Then, outside Harar, two men standing by a car flagged down the lorry. Steer did not understand the conversation, but the grinning Somali Haji in the cab told him that he had to go with them. Gripping his rifle, Steer climbed into the old Ford. *Who were these bandits?* This is the moment on a hot afternoon when adventure begins.

One of the men had an athlete's rawboned face and wore khaki, with a fluffy feather on the side of his topi. Suddenly both were smiling. The man in uniform was Ali Nur, the hero of the Ethiopian rearguard at Walwal.

'I am to take you all over the Ogaden for the Emperor,' he said.

Steer was taken to a house a mile outside the mud-walled city that had once been home to Arthur Rimbaud. He slipped away briefly to borrow a camera from the Frenchman who ran the leper hospital under the city walls, shaded by pepper trees and pink oleander. That night Steer pencilled a letter to Ralph Deakin:

> There is no ink in this house in Harrar and I am forced to live in seclusion so that nobody shall know that a white man is going in a military lorry to JIJIGA . . .
>
> So far as I can see the best thing for me at the beginning at least is to stay with the Emperor, with whom I am now on more friendly terms than any other journalists. I am the only one since Sandford abandoned journalism to see him privately.

The letter, which suggested hiring planes and radios, ended like one from school: 'Please send gasmasks and buy me 200 rounds of MAUSER sporting ammunition . . . yours ever, G. L. Steer'.

They left the next afternoon in a lorry to Jijiga. Ali Nur's soldiers stuck ostrich feathers in their rifle barrels to stop them being choked with Ogaden dust. Ali Nur, an asthmatic Muslim who drank alcohol when he could and smoked Aden Gold Flake cigarettes, had once been interpreter to the British Consul at Maji, Captain Pennefather-Holland, who had shot crocodiles with his revolver and died of blackwater fever, as Ali Nur put it, 'in my hands'. Ali Nur had later organized a special corps of Somali scouts for the Emperor, an Ethiopian Foreign Legion, 'composed of all sorts of bandits, Somali roughnecks . . . elephant hunters and men thrown out of our own Camel Corps for drunkenness, theft, desertion, insubordination, not polishing their boots and all the other marks of a good soldier'. These men had not run away at Walwal, and became the backbone of the resistance in the months to come.

The lorry reached Jijiga, headquarters of the Ogaden, at night, after a purple sunset with flying foxes gliding across their headlights. Steer was taken into a two-roomed dwelling behind a palisade, the house of Gerazmatch Afewerk. He was half-Amhara and half-Kafa, historically 'a slave race', but for Steer this man of character and intelligence exemplified the changes that Haile Selassie was bringing to the Ethiopian provinces. In the dining room, Steer held up a paraffin lamp to look at the photograph of Afewerk, in court dress, with ferocious hair and forceful features, that hung on the wall together with Huntley and Palmer's almanac, an advertisement for Johnny Walker, and photographs of the Imperial family.

In the morning, in a dusty wind, Steer hitched a lift south to the wells of Jijiga, deep holes in the ground cradled with wooden frames, where it took as many as nine men to pass up one oval clay pot of water to pour into the cattle trough: 'An Ethiopian soldier knelt beside one of them washing his thick hair with lime to keep out the lice. All the Somalis do this: half the men that you see in the Ogaden saunter along on their slim easy walk, their hair copper with dried whitewash.'

Jijiga is at the top corner of the Ogaden, an almost flat, waterless plain 450 miles long and 250 miles broad. Roads were made by butting a lorry through a grey sea of mimosa and sharp camel-thorn, scattering the hornbills. At midday in the market square Steer saw his first mobilization of Ethiopian troops. Lorries were assembling to take sixty soldiers down to the frontier post at Tefere Katama, a three-day drive. All the soldiers were roaring drunk and fighting with the town police. Steer went to the assembly point outside town with a stout and jolly British Somali: 'A fearful volley resounded from the back of the lorry . . . In my extreme nervousness I reached for the door. "Don't worry," laughed the Somali, "they're only shooting into the air. That means 'Goodbye, I'm going to the war, may not come back Jijiga again, so here's how.'"'

They left the next day for Daggahbur, fairly sober: 'Fifty men and four lorries, one of which carried my fruit and another my whisky and soda water.' They drove for eight hours through thick bush and a hot wind that made the soldiers put on woollen balaclavas against earache, before camping for the night in the bush under the stars. Seven camp-fires of crackling thorn gleamed on the brass cartridges round men's waists. Ali Nur and Steer had a tent each; the other ranks slept on the ground without covering.

They entered Daggahbur just after dawn, and left at eight. Six old men were digging trenches. 'It was blistering hot.' They stopped for lunch at the muddy wells of Anale. The men mixed sun-dried crumbs of *injera*, millet-grain bread, with chillies and clarified butter in a wide bowl and ate with their right hands. 'One man kept watch in the sweltering sun. In their free hands, or in the crooks of their arms, they kept their rifles.' The soldiers offered him their food, 'gritty stuff with a sting in it', and told him to put on his riding boots against the Gordit camel tick, whose bite makes sores and fever.

Later they ran into the dandyish Governor of Harar, on a lightning tour in his car with an escort of ten lorries. Dedjazmatch Nasibu had a little moustache and was elegantly dressed in a khaki silk shirt with a light-mauve tinge that set off his dark skin, shorts and stockings. His topi bore the button of the Ethiopian state official, concentric rings of green, yellow and red. A silk neckerchief, fawn gloves and a riding switch completed the outfit.

Soon he and Steer were drinking coffee from gold-rimmed cups under a thorn tree. Governor Nasibu was pessimistic about the League of Nations and the arms embargo. 'How can we hold out against gas?' he asked. It was the first time an Ethiopian had mentioned gas to Steer. With his crop the Governor traced in the sand the plan that he and Afewerk had devised to defend the Ogaden, and how they would even-tually fall back before the Italians: '"They will beat us," said Nasibu, "but we will hold them as long as we can. We are supposed to be brave; our courage is our only weapon. It is no use attacking any of their posts – what can we do against their machine guns? Better for the camps in the Ogaden to hold out to the finish. Afewerk will see to that. His motto is – 'Over my dead body.'"'

Nasibu left Steer his reserves of champagne and Vichy water. That night Steer slept under six rifles hung on a wall at the hill fort of Gabridihari. An oval of mud huts for 300 men had no trenches, just a hedge and a shallow ditch. The telephone didn't work any more because the poles had fallen down. The man in charge was very thin and had no front teeth. Steer enquired about tank defences. '"Tanks won't climb this hill," he replied, with the startling assurance of the ill-instructed.'

Steer was not impressed until he came early next day to Gorahai. There was a radio mast, a flagpole, freshly made yellow beehive huts, and the perimeter was protected by a deep trench with a firestep, manned by Ethiopians in khaki. Ten men on either side of the road presented arms. Steer saw a small cannon under camel-thorn camouflage.

In the middle of the well-ordered camp, under a large brushwood canopy, very high and cool, sat Gerazmatch Afewerk. The African was wearing a Japanese sola topi, a 'British warm' overcoat, Ethiopian jodhpurs, Somali sandals, and a heavy revolver. At last Steer met the soldier he had heard so much about. 'And the first thing that he did, with a great courtesy I admit, was to place me under open arrest.'

Afewerk hated Europeans, but not mindlessly. He had sent half the Jijiga boys' school to follow the Anglo-Ethiopian Boundary Commission so that they could benefit from studying wireless, health and sanitation, camp and lorry maintenance. Afewerk liked cleanliness, order, technical ability, knowledge; but not at any price:

> Other Ethiopians who resisted European influences did so on the basis of conservatism. They wished to preserve ancestral usages. To Afewerk these meant little; the western accretions upon him were not superficial. A black man, he knew the value of thinking for himself outside the customary circle of the Ethiopian mind. The Italians he knew wanted to rob him of his country and basically, he felt, all these Europeans with their common tradition whatever their collective promises, would stick together . . . In all his dealings with Europeans, he saw their clannishness sticking out a yard. He detested them all.

Steer hated Afewerk at first too, for treating him as a foreign spy.

> But as I looked at his beautifully organised camp: the trenches against air-raids, skilfully built on the zigzag pattern, the placing of the guns, the huts distributed round the circle at spaces which would prevent a general conflagration: the measures of hygiene: the regular and detailed issue of orders, and his personal explanations to his troops: his rapid communications – for as well as his radio, his car and two horses stood by all day at the Mullah's Fort, ready.

And as I see his face now, full of force and sarcasm, heavy with authority, vigilant and steady, when he stood at salute with his troops before his country's flag at sunset.

And when I remember his contemptuous voice, 'The Italians can rob all my country – when I am dead. I shall not care. I shall not *know*.'

I thank God that made me and Africa, and bound us together in such a bitter union, that once in my life I met this man.

Steer's first book, *Caesar in Abyssinia*, is dedicated to Afewerk, whom he considered 'without exception, the most capable Ethiopian I ever met'. He also thought it a tragedy in Ethiopia that not enough of these dynamic new men had risen up the system to squeeze out the old politicians and fixers who squatted at the top.

As Steer and Ali Nur dined with Afewerk in the Mullah's Fort, on flabby rolls of *injera* with meat, onions and chillies, followed by mangoes and oranges, he talked with contempt about the League of Nations and British policy towards Ethiopia: "'I get it all on my wireless, and it makes me sick." As my own views were identical, but I was addressed as a specimen Englishman, I found it difficult to take up the dialogue. "Well," said he, relenting a little, "I've had a message from the Emperor this evening. He says you can be shown all our arms."'

Steer saw 300 men manning the trenches with modern rifles and eleven light automatics. He saw the bare-chested Somalis with fringed turbans, dust-coloured skirts, Lee Metford rifles and cartridge belts, the men whom Afewerk used for scouting and tribal espionage. He was shown the two heavy machine guns, and how they could be fired low at infantry, high at aviation; and then Afewerk led him into the fort's side turret. The moonlight gleamed on the barrel of the Oerlikon anti-aircraft gun. 'We have only this one against the planes,' he said, 'I handle it myself. The people who sold them to us said they were wonderful; but they were Europeans and probably cheated us.'

Afewerk received the wound that killed him while firing his Oerlikon, a lone weapon against twenty planes, two months later.

At six in the morning Steer left in a lorry for the all-day drive 150 miles south to the fort on the frontier in the Webbe Shebeli valley. The windows were closed, but dust poured in suffocating clouds through the holes for the foot pedals. Towards sunset they climbed a hill to Tefere Katama, which means 'Strong Village', garrisoned by 500

Ethiopian troops. Across the plain, downriver, was another hill with a fort on top.

The Italian garrison at Moustahil had about 700 Somali troops and two white officers. Through field glasses Steer saw men stirring and the Italian flag run up. A *donga*, or gully, the colour of dried blood marked the frontier between the two forts; the Italians would soon cross it.

At Gerlogubi, Steer was told he was four miles away from hundreds of Italian-armed Somali *bande*, and that behind them 3,000 more troops were guarding the fifty Italians who looked after the aeroplanes. When Steer was shown the Ethiopian defences of Gerlogubi that night, the trenches seemed very well manned; but back at his tent the reporter found his fat, pockmarked cook roaring with laughter. Moosa revealed that there were only forty men at Gerlogubi and they were running around in the darkness to fill up the trenches, pretending to be more. In the morning, Steer went back to Gorahai and shook hands with Afewerk. He would never see him again.

On 1 September 1935 they drove through Daggahbur to Jijiga. It poured with rain, the first they had seen or smelled in the Ogaden. The whole bush, dull with dust, suddenly burst into greenness. Steer saw a party of Somalis dancing and clapping round a small water bottle on the ground that was overflowing.

Rain kept them a day and two nights in Jijiga, but Steer spent the time gathering details about a French spy, the Comte de Rocquefeuille, who had been sending information on Ethiopian troop movements to the Italian Consul in Harar. The Somali milkmaid who was his courier was among five chained prisoners in the back of Steer's truck that set off for Harar on 3 September. Heavy rain had swollen the rivers on the Karramarra Pass, and the singing prisoners helped push the lorry through rocks and mud towards the city where they would face execution.

Terrified Indian families with bright saris and wet eyes were fleeing from Harar to Jijiga. Bazaar rumours had said the Italians were going to bomb the city. Nightfall caught the party on the road with no tents. Steer put a mattress over three benzine boxes in the mud and slept, uncovered, through the downpour. He observed, laconically, 'Ali Nur and the boys were immensely impressed by this feat. I was rather impressed myself. It dried off under the Union Jack of the Harrar Consulate, and internally it was cured by Chapman-Andrews porridge.'

Steer discussed his tour with the Emperor soon after he got back to the capital on Sunday, 8 September. A third of the 7,000 troops he had seen in the Ogaden had modern arms. He had counted 8 heavy machine guns, 30 automatic rifles, one anti-aircraft gun, two small cannon and 140 lorries. This puny Ethiopian force was facing 50,000 Italian and native troops in Italian Somaliland under General Graziani, Italy's most famous colonial soldier, with thousands of lorries, scores of artillery batteries, tanks, aeroplanes with sixty landing fields, and almost unlimited ammunition and supplies. Mussolini had already spent two billion lire and wanted a lot of territory to show for it. The Italian Consul was boasting of victory 'in a few days'. In the event, it took them seven months to get past the Ethiopians.

9

Meanwhile more war-hungry journalists were flooding into Addis Ababa, and the system was creaking under the strain. There was no international telephone, no air mail, and letters took at least a fortnight. Cable and Wireless telegram prices could reach an incredible 2/6d a word. Half a crown in 1935 is perhaps the equivalent of £3.60 or US$5 in today's money, so a sentence as long as this would cost around £65 or $90.

Back in Addis Ababa from the Ogaden, Steer found his pay had risen to £80 a month, subsidised by the New York Times, which was now taking his stories. Deakin had sent a memo to the Editor at the end of August: 'Steer has worked hard and given The Times some pioneer dispatches. The Times service influenced numerous other agencies and newspapers, British and American, to send their own Correspondents. In several instances the discrepancy between our payments to Steer and the expenditure incurred by other papers is most noticeable. The Daily Mail has now sent Evelyn Waugh out with a big salary.'

Red-faced Evelyn Waugh and red-haired George Steer first met on an Ethiopian railway platform on 21 August 1935, when Steer was on his way down to the Ogaden and Waugh was on his way up to Addis Ababa. Their trains went in opposite directions, and so did their dispatches and their politics. Waugh was working for Lord Rothermere's pro-Fascist Daily Mail and, as a Roman Catholic convert, tended to see a benign civilization behind Mussolini's Fascism. Steer supported independent Ethiopia and was the kind of Anglican who thought Christianity meant sympathy with the underdog. Both men got memorable books out of the Italo-Ethiopian War. Waugh's novel *Scoop* saw the conflict as a comedy; Steer's *Caesar in Abyssinia* as a tragedy. 'Only a shit could be good on this particular job,' remarked Waugh. In 1930 the irascible writer had covered Haile Selassie's coronation as Negus for *The Times*, and now he was resentful that someone else was representing 'the most important newspaper in the world'.

Waugh condescended to Steer as 'a zealous young colonial reporter' – Steer, at twenty-five, was six years younger. Perhaps he was also irritated that Steer's public school and Oxford college, Winchester and Christ Church, were rather grander than his own, Lancing and Hertford, and that Steer's Double First in Classics was more distinguished than his own poor Third in History. This shows in Waugh's waspish review of *Caesar in Abyssinia* in the Catholic weekly *The Tablet* in 1937, where he wrote: 'Mr Steer . . . had great sympathy, I think it is not unfair to say affinity, for those nimble-witted upstarts who formed the Negus's entourage, like himself African born, who had memorized so many of the facts of European education without ever participating in European culture.'

Waugh did not court popularity in Ethiopia. 'My name is mud all round,' he confessed, and 'I am universally regarded as an Italian spy.' One evening, in September 1935, the novelist was nursing his peculiar concoction of brandy and crème de menthe in Le Perroquet, one of the two cinema nightclubs in Addis Ababa, when a young woman approached his table. Esmé Barton was angry. She and her family had fed and entertained Waugh when he had come for the coronation five years before, and Waugh had repaid their hospitality by parodying her parents as the ridiculous Sir Samson and Lady Courteney in *Black Mischief*: he was naïve, dim and incompetent and she was blithely vague about everything but gardening. Worse, Waugh had put Esmé herself in the novel as their daughter Prudence Courteney, a promiscuous girl in a red beret, ardent author of *The Panorama of Life*, whose RAF rescue plane crashes in the jungle. One of her lovers eventually locates her, after sharing a meaty stew of peppers and aromatic roots with a large African. ('"The white woman? Why, here," he patted his distended paunch. "You and I and the big chief – we have just eaten her."') When Esmé reached the nightclub table, she dashed a glass of champagne in Evelyn Waugh's pop-eyed face.

Waugh and Steer were wary colleagues. Waugh conceded that Steer 'exhibited in a high degree the peculiar gifts required for that kind of journalism – keen curiosity of mind, a retentive memory, enterprise, a devotion to duty even at the expense of personal dignity and competitive zeal that was notable even in the international cut-throat rough and tumble of his colleagues', but deplored Steer's conclusions.

Waugh wrote two non-fiction books featuring Ethiopia – *Remote People* and *Waugh in Abyssinia* – and two novels: *Black Mischief*, about 'Azania', and *Scoop*, set in 'Ishmaelia', books which have set the superior tone and absurdist attitude that the well-read English adopt towards places like Ethiopia. Steer represents the opposite pole. The 'serious war book' that Waugh told Laura Herbert in October 1935 he hoped to write was actually penned by the younger man, with *Caesar in Abyssinia*. No wonder Waugh's review of it in *The Tablet* was so barbed.

Their different cultural attitudes show in their descriptions of the same event, the King's Maskal, or Dance of the Priests, on 23 September 1935, when Steer and Waugh were probably standing next to each other among the pressmen. Steer's description in *Caesar in Abyssinia* accepts the ritual on its own terms.

> The dim *gebir* hall of the great palace was opened to foreigners. It is at this festival that the Emperor appears to his chiefs and priesthood, and admits the triumph of the Ethiopian Coptic Christian Church over African paganism.
>
> Haile Selassie presided on his bed-throne . . . The palace servants . . . in shimmering light green satin surcoats and jodhpurs, carrying their whipping wands and long red swords, ushered in a hundred priests. These, under faded Ethiopian flags and fringed silk umbrellas, sang in a chorus to five choirboy altos dressed in white robes.

For Evelyn Waugh, however, the priests' dance that followed was 'clumsy and rather lugubrious'. His much longer account in *Waugh in Abyssinia* describes the Ethiopian Coptic ceremony as a shoddy thing, inferior to his vision of European Catholicism:

> We had seen the highest expression of historic Abyssinian culture; this was the Church's most splendid and solemn occasion . . . It was natural to consider, as one drove back to one's typewriter, what a ceremony of the kind was like in medieval Europe; of the avenues of fluted columns, branching high overhead into groined and painted roof, each boss and capital a triumph of delicate sculpture . . . It was significant to turn from that to the artificial silk and painted petrol cans of Addis Ababa.

Waugh wrote to Diana Cooper that month, 'i have got to hate the ethiopians more each day goodness they are lousy & i hope the organ-men gas them to buggery.'

10

On Thursday, 3 October 1935, George Steer was sitting on a hippopota-mus skull in his bank manager's office. The skull, stuffed with cleaners' brushes and polishes, was nicknamed Vinci (after the Italian minister) because it was both comic and sinister. It adorned Wright's office at the Bank of Ethiopia, where Steer had come to cash a cheque into the big, high-silver-content *thaler* coins that Ethiopians preferred to paper money. Lorenzo Taezaz approached and, without taking the cigarette out of his mouth, informed *The Times*: 'The war began this morning.'

Everyone made for the Great Gibbi. The streets up to the palace were a flurry of *shammas*, bristling with rifles. In the courtyard, thousands of soldiers squatted before the *negaret*, a half-globe of dark brown lion skin, the great war drum of the Ethiopian Empire. Two silk flags, green, yellow and red, with the Lion of Judah, waved defiantly on long poles as, with a crooked stick, the drummer began the deep, lone beats that would call the men to arms.

> From the platform behind the drum I looked at Addis Ababa over miles of grey eucalyptus, dusty roads, dull brown *tukuls* behind wood fences, turbulent seas of corrugated iron . . . Amazing town – squalor and natural beauty sprawling side by side. For all its irregu-larity the African lived in Addis Ababa a happier, freer and cleaner life than in any other town of the continent. Accra, Freetown, the 'locations' of Cape Town and East London, Djibouti . . . all these gifts of the white to the black were far more crowded, stank more, more gravely offended the eyes than the gift of Menelik and Haile Selassie to unconquered Ethiopia.

Notables were gathering. The crowd watched the Court Chamberlain, Ligaba Tasso, read the Emperor's Mobilization Decree, standing on a rough kitchen chair. It ended: 'The feeling of the whole world is in revulsion at the aggression aimed against us. God will be with us. Out into the field. For the Emperor. For the Fatherland.'

The crowd went wild and rushed forward, waving rifles, knocking Varges the cinematographer over. Steer's interpreter, Joseph, having no weapon, brandished the reporter's typewriter. Lorenzo Taezaz, reading the decree in French, was mobbed by a scrum of squabbling European press and diplomats. When Taezaz read out a telegram about the Italian bombing of Adowa and Adigrat, and told them that thousands of Italian troops had crossed the Mareb River from Eritrea into Tigre, the enraged Ethiopian crowd pulled out their knives and ran, yelling, 'Death to the Italians!', to the north tower, where the Emperor was standing calmly. Haile Selassie gently commanded silence with his hand, and then spoke from the balcony, counselling them to fight a guerrilla war: '"Do not take white clothes, do not mass, as now. Hide, strike suddenly, fight the nomad war, steal, snipe and murder singly. To-day the war has begun, therefore scatter and advance to victory."

'The whole wild assembly clapped sharply three times, shouted "Glory to the Emperor" and plunged away through the narrow Palace gates.'

By lunchtime, however, the idlers were in the same places on the pavements of Addis again, and the press were back in the hotels. And there for almost two months they mainly stayed, up to 130 journalists, stewing in anticlimax, back-stabbing and hysterical competitiveness for non-existent news stories. There were panics about air raids that never happened and futile attempts to get to where the fighting might be. Patrick Balfour of the *Evening Standard* said it was like trying to report Bonnie Prince Charlie's 1745 rebellion in Scotland, while stuck in London. ('Charlie' became a press nickname for the Emperor.) *Scoop* shows how the bored and frantic press turned on each other for amusement. Evelyn Waugh bought a baboon, which masturbated; Steer found himself nailed into his room at the Imperial Hotel, had to be rescued by an Indian carpenter and moved out to a private house with a government phone. There were fist fights and even a shooting among the desperate journalists. On 13 October 1935 the enterprising George Steer got his name into the *New York Times* in a Reuters report:

> Mr Steer was scaling an unguarded wall of the Italian Legation to get inside when some Ethiopian soldiers came along. The correspondent slipped to the ground and made off, with the soldiers in hot pursuit, and they finally overtook him. En route to a military post a struggle ensued and Mr Steer was slightly injured.
>
> The incident was ended by an order from the palace freeing Mr Steer.

Evelyn Waugh wrote: 'A zealous young colonial reporter climbed the wall; was captured and frogmarched, rather roughly, to imprisonment in the telephone hut.' Later Waugh saw Steer outside the Legation front gate, where scuffles continued. 'The colonial had been released and was now alternately protesting and apologizing.'

On Remembrance Sunday 1935, both Evelyn Waugh and Patrick Balfour recorded seeing Steer kick and belabour an Armenian spy who had got into the cable office after hours to read or steal his copy. 'The *Times* correspondent a very gay South African dwarf – is never without a black eye', Waugh wrote to Diana Cooper on 12 November.

In October and November 1935, Steer thought the Italians were handling the media far better, and winning hearts and minds abroad. Italian propaganda 'flickered dully across sham-pacific newsreels' showing the war 'as a series of submissions, non-resistance, ceremonial occupations, road building . . . a political parade without horrors'.

In this unreal atmosphere Sir Samuel Hoare, the British Foreign Secretary, and Pierre Laval, the French Foreign Minister, drew up a peace plan that tried to buy Mussolini off with a huge chunk of Ethiopia, while allowing Abyssinia a thin sliver to the sea. When this craven pact was leaked, in December 1935, public indignation led to both Hoare's and Laval's resignations, but the damage was done. Great Britain and France, who had spoken so heart-warmingly of standing together in 'collective security' at the League of Nations, were shown to be shamming. Mussolini could do what he wanted.

11

The Italo-Ethiopian War began slowly and cautiously in 1935, because Emilio de Bono, the Italian general in charge, was determined not to repeat Baratieri's humiliating defeat in 1896. Even though they had massive technical and numerical superiority, the Italians had to gather themselves first. From Eritrea 38,000 Italian labourers made the roads, bridges and water supplies 'which enabled an army of 170,000 Europeans and 65,000 natives with 60,000 pack-animals to live, move and fight with modern weapons'.

At the end of November 1935, de Bono would be replaced by the more brutal General Pietro Badoglio. His counterpart on the southern front in Italian Somaliland, General Rodolfo Graziani, shared his reputation for ruthlessness. Both Badoglio and Graziani were veterans of colonial

war in Libya, which Italy had seized from the crumbling Ottoman
Empire in 1911–12. The leader of the Libyan resistance, Omar el
Mukhtar, was seventy-three years old when Graziani had him hanged in
Benghazi in 1931. Graziani, nicknamed 'the Butcher', filled the wells of
the Bedouin with concrete, hanged or shot thirty rebels a day, and
deported 80,000 Arabs to concentration camps or slavery in the salt
lakes. The atrocities only strengthened resistance. In May 1930, some
Bedouin in Libya told the young Danish adventurer Knud Holmboe:
'We do not fear death from their machine guns . . . We shall fight to the
last man. We all love God, but we hate the white devils who cause us
more harm than anyone can imagine.'

By then the Italians were already regularly bombing villages and
oases with mustard gas. According to Sven Lindqvist's *A History of
Bombing* (2001), an Italian in Libya, Lieutenant Giulio Cavotti, was the
first man to bomb from an aeroplane, dropping four Danish Haasen
hand-grenades on two oases near Tripoli on 1 November 1911. Bombing
became the Italian speciality, exulted over by Fascist poets and artists
such as D'Annunzio and Marinetti. This was how 'Butcher' Graziani
did his business in the Ogaden.

On 4, 5 and 11 October 1935 the outpost round the Mullah's Fort at
Gorahai was bombed and machine-gunned by six Caproni CA133
bombers. Of the 300 or so bombs dropped in the second day's raid,
one-third failed to explode. Afewerk, who was now eating his food with
a knife made from a bomb-splinter and trying to get his men to treat
aeroplanes with contempt rather than panic, stood to his Oerlikon gun
and maintained morale. Steer noted the psychological impact on the
Ethiopian soldier: 'First, a belief at the back of his mind that the aeroplane was a devilish instrument, uncannily accurate when it was
directly on top of you . . . Second the failure of all Ethiopian arms to
bring a plane down. Bitterest of all, the feeling that one could never
send *one's own* planes back to strike the Italians.'

The southern border outposts were bombed and overrun by the middle of October. Twenty Italian planes attacked Gorahai on All Souls' Day,
2 November, relentlessly bombing the Mullah's Fort and its circle of
zigzag trenches, a target with a diameter of 150 metres. It took the planes
half an hour to reload and return, reload and return, reload and return.

Afewerk was struck in the leg by a heavy splinter. It was a serious
wound, but the nearest Red Cross unit was at Daggahbur, 140 miles

north, and Afewerk knew that if he left, all his men would follow, because the Ethiopian way is to stay with the chief, and if he falls, to carry him back to consecrated ground. So Afewerk remained at his post without medical aid. Only a select few knew he was wounded. The planes bombed the fort again on the 3rd, and the waterhole half a mile to the west, killing a hundred cattle, thirty Somali women and fifteen children. Afewerk kept firing.

On November 4 the twenty planes returned to their fearful work of devastation. Ali Nur, who is a brave man, told me it could no longer be borne. The whole earth heaved about and rocked under explosions which seemed to break the ears. One could not see to shoot under the deep pall of sand. Nothing but sand, flashes of red lightning, thundercrack explosions, more sand, groans and shrieks of wounded men, the earth heaving in foul yellow obscurity and a noise like the falling of mountains.

And all at once the Oerlikon, whose repetition had kept them steady in their places, ceased to fire.

Afewerk had fallen unconscious. He was sprawling over the breech of his gun, his hands tumbled to the ground. His wound was beginning to gangrene.

When the planes had gone, they carried Afewerk out of the fort and put him in the back of a lorry. The garrison had twelve killed outright and seventy dying or seriously hurt, for Ethiopians do not count light wounds. Fitorari Simu ordered the retreat, even though Afewerk had commanded him to hold Gorahai. (Simu was sentenced to death for this, later commuted by the Emperor to thirty lashes and two bayonet stabs in the back.) They torched their yellow beehive huts and left the Mad Mullah's Fort. Afewerk died on the way to Daggahbur. All his men wept.

The Italians sent a column in pursuit of the retreating Ethiopians. On Armistice Day, 11 November 1935, near the wells of Anale, the pursuers ran, quite by chance, into 500 Ethiopian reinforcements. The Italians had unloaded their little two-man Fiat-Ansaldo tanks with double machine guns to chase some retreating Ethiopians away from their broken-down lorries. Seeing nothing in the dusty bush, the driver and machine-gunner of one Italian tank both got out of their scorchingly hot metal box. Twenty Ethiopians were lying in the roots of thorn trees forty yards away. Their officer whispered, 'Kill them.' Twenty shots rang out. 'They fell very slowly to the ground, like sand off riverbanks,' the Ethiopians later told Steer. Another Italian tank came to investigate, with the same result. A third tank driver, getting out to fit tow-chains, was also felled. The Somali *dubats* were shot up and fled south to Gorahai. The Ethiopians bolted north for Daggahbur with their wounded, leaving the Ogaden to the hyenas and the vultures.

And that, according to Steer, was the end of General Graziani's vaunted offensive in the south. Graziani, with his Roman emperor's profile, could easily have pushed on to Harar and the railway, and seized a crown of laurels; but for five months ghosts held him back. 'He dared not,' wrote Steer. 'He thought that the Ethiopians were a hundred thousand strong.'

12

Steer got these stories from Ali Nur when he returned to Jijiga in the middle of November 1935. He travelled down on the train to Diredawa with the walrus-moustached British Assistant Military Attaché, Captain R. H. R. Taylor, nicknamed 'the Firkin' for his girth. Collins of Reuters, with his pet monkey Angko, was aboard; and among the other journalists was a very special foreign correspondent who had arrived the day the war started: the cosmopolitan and darkly attractive Margarita de Herrero, born in France to an English mother and a Spanish father, educated in England, and now working for *Le Journal* in Paris, where they called her Marguerite. She was thirty-six, ten years older than Steer, and he was falling in love with her.

The great age of women war correspondents was only just beginning, and people like Virginia Cowles and Martha Gellhorn were yet to make their names, so it was unusual for someone like Margarita de Herrero to make her way to Addis Ababa in 1935. She was independent, intelligent, enterprising and she had courage – in Hemingway's definition, 'grace under pressure'. What could be more appealing to an excitable man like Steer?

Margarita de Herrero was smaller than he was and had a strong face, strong hands but a sensual mouth. She was curvaceous and sexually attractive, with soft, wavy shoulder-length hair, but there was something in her determined jawline that seemed reminiscent of Steer's mother Emma, the dominant influence in his boyhood. Emma, whose own mother had founded the South African Women's Industrial Union, had accustomed George to the idea of active, forceful women. Little wonder that he fell in love with *Le Journal*'s female correspondent in a war zone and that Emma Steer (who never met her) always spoke very approvingly of Margarita de Herrero.

She had been born in Pau, in the south-west of France, and when she was eighteen had buried her father in Biarritz. Margarita de Herrero knew the Basque country and people and she may have been partly Basque herself. Certainly, in that sharing of pasts that people getting to know each other do, they would have talked of the region that would later come to play such an important part in George Steer's life.

Steer first met Margarita, and her friend Dolores de Pedroso, not long after the two women arrived on 2 October. A pair of attractive and sophisticated women would have stood out in the journalists' small circle; apart from the Imperial Hotel, there were really only two places of entertainment for them in Addis Ababa, both cinemas with a night-club/bar attached. There was Le Perroquet, run by Madame Idot, and Mon Ciné, run by Madame Moriatis. Idot's was coarser and cheerier; Mon Ciné had pretensions to respectability and a gloomier proprietor. 'Both prospered on the contrast,' wrote Evelyn Waugh, 'because, after an hour in either place, you longed for the other.'

Le Perroquet was where Esmé Barton threw her drink in Waugh's face. The principal witness to this essay in practical criticism was a young reporter from the *Morning Post* called William Deedes, generally held to be the basic model for William Boot of the *Daily Beast*, the innocent protagonist of Waugh's 1938 novel *Scoop*.

W. F. Deedes is a legendary figure in British journalism. After the *Daily Telegraph* absorbed the *Morning Post* in 1937, he stayed put and has been there ever since. He was elected Conservative MP for Ashford in Kent, and rose to Minister of Information under Macmillan, where he had to deal with the Profumo scandal. In 1973 he became the editor of the *Telegraph*. *Shome mishtake shurely?* – an imitation of Deedes's clenched-teeth speech – became a famous bracketed catchphrase for editorial puzzlement in the British satirical magazine *Private Eye*.

Lord Deedes, at eighty-five plus, is still a reporter. He goes often to Africa, where he campaigns against landmines. He was just back from East Timor when I went to see him in the *Daily Telegraph* editorial offices at Canary Wharf, sixty-five years after he saw Esmé Barton throwing a drink in Evelyn Waugh's face. Bill Deedes was sitting in striped shirtsleeves, grimacing at a computer screen.

'You're asking me to rake back sixty years, you know. George Steer I hadn't connected with the staff of *The Times* until I met him in Addis Ababa, and I think he had been recruited *ad hoc*. He wasn't one of us hacks, but a different kettle of fish: Steer was more adventurous. I didn't see a lot of him because we all worked in different compartments, doing our own thing with our boys and our spies. Apart from remembering what George looked like with his little ginger moustache and his short stature, there's also the fact that he was extremely enterprising.

'It was a bit of a Fred Karno's army, all those journalists. You've read *Scoop*? I don't think George appears in *Scoop*. I think George escapes the satire because he's so efficient; he was a very efficient correspondent.'

(The only likely candidate for Steer in *Scoop* is Pappenhacker:

Mr Pappenhacker of *The Twopence* was playing with a toy train – a relic of College at Winchester, with which he invariably travelled. In his youth he had delighted to address it in Latin alcaics and to derive Greek names for each part of the mechanism. Now it acted as a sedative to his restless mind.

The Twopence did not encourage habits of expensive cabling. That day he had composed a long 'turnover' on Ishmaelite conditions and posted it in the confidence that, long before it arrived at London, conditions would be unrecognisable.')

'Now the only really close connection I had with George Steer was at the end of that year, 1935, when one or two of us thought that the south would be a better bet than the northern front. I think I travelled down on the train with Steer and another correspondent. Was it Sheepshanks of Reuters? Dick Sheepshanks was a bit of a hero to me as he'd scored a century at the Eton–Harrow match at Lords. Anyway – and this is the real point – with us came two ladies who were representing Spanish newspapers. I don't know how well Steer knew the Spanish ladies then, but not very. Possibly the romance with Margarita started then.

'The four or five of us went south to Harar, when Graziani had attacked the Ethiopians with mustard gas. The local hospital became a very disagreeable place, with these ulcerated wounds, and the two Spanish girls, to the best of my recollection, put their Spanish newspapers on hold, and went into the hospital to work on these casualties.

They were overcome by the extent of the Ethiopian casualties. We all stayed in the same hotel, and I can remember a jolly evening with them all. It was the only time really I was close to Steer. I went back in time for Christmas, but he stayed on until the end.'

The freelance Noel Monks also came south before Christmas 1935:

> I heard the first angry gunfire of my life in the Ogaden desert in Abyssinia. It sounded like thunder, and it wasn't until a day later when I saw the victims of the gunfire that I had my first realisation of the horrors of war. Men without arms or legs; with holes in their heads or chests. Some just a mass of red pulp. That they were black men somehow made it seem all the more horrible.

The Emperor flew down to Ogaden HQ at Jijiga on 19 November to hear how his men had fought on the southern front. Simu, who had surrendered, was publicly flogged. Ali Nur was promoted. And for doing his duty and dying so heroically, Afewerk was honoured by becoming the first man in Ethiopia to be given a posthumous title: Dedjazmatch, or High Commander, of the Ogaden.

13

On 28 November 1935 the Emperor flew north to Dessye. Haile Selassie I went to war like a European gentleman, with his four-course meals, his wine cellar, his sola topis and walking sticks, his Arab horses and his motor cars. 'The Emperor of Ethiopia', wrote Steer, 'had the gift of appearing at all times, even in the middle of war, completely detached and poised above the mêlée, pursuing his quiet, rather delicate and well-dressed life without noting overmuch the noise which surrounded him.' But behind his house was a dugout full of ammunition, and camouflaged under mimosa and blue gum stood the Swiss-manufactured Oerlikon anti-aircraft gun the Emperor had learned to handle. 'The Emperor had a liking for arms of precision; accuracy, the neat bull's eye, were to his taste.' He would need them, for now a more terrifying kind of war was starting.

On Friday, 6 December 1935, St Nicholas' Day, six Italian aeroplanes bombed Gondar, killing four women and six children, and burning many *tukuls*, or huts. On the same day, just after a quarter to eight in the morning, twelve Italian aeroplanes attacked Dessye. The first forty bombs were dropped on the Red Cross dressing stations and the Seventh Day Adventist Mission, which was clearly marked with a large red cross. The instrument room and a surgical tent were destroyed, two wards damaged, and the head nurse Mademoiselle Havig wounded with an open fracture of the left leg.

In the one-hour raid, the planes also dropped incendiary and explosive shrapnel bombs on the crowded town, killing 53 and wounding around 200. Every Ethiopian with access to a firearm, including the Emperor, blazed away furiously, and a stray bullet in the knee felled the Havas agency man. The six doctors did thirty amputations that day and then all signed a letter of protest to the League of Nations. The uniformed Emperor posed with his foot on a large unexploded bomb for nervous photographers.

The Emperor's army in the north did not sit on their hands. On 15 December 1935, 4,000 Ethiopians in two columns crossed the Takazze River south-west of Axum and, moving at night, avoiding planes, punched forty-five miles through the Italian right. They took 10 tanks and 28 machine guns, killing 150 Italian and 200 Eritrean soldiers. Exactly a week later, in the Tembien on 22 December, the same number of Ethiopians took Abbi Addi in a nine-hour fight, killing twenty Italians and many Eritreans, and taking twelve machine guns, hundreds of rifles and much ammunition.

Steer thought that Ethiopians in smaller, more flexible and surprising units could beat the Italian forces hands down; but sneaky guerrilla warfare did not accord with Ethiopian aristocratic traditions of mass attack and conspicuous personal courage. When Ethiopian armies got bigger, 'they became static and unwieldy . . . clogged by their cumbrous train of mules, women, servants, children, pots and pans'; and they became larger targets for artillery and planes.

14

The day of the Abbi Addi attack, 22 December 1935, was a pivotal one of the war for George Steer. It was a Sunday, when the journalists usually worked until the Cable and Wireless office closed at midday, and then liked to drive out of Addis Ababa up Entoto or along the Dessye road to somewhere green and pleasant to eat and drink; Steer would show his skill at catching butterflies without harming them. That Sunday, 22 December, Steer was packing a picnic into a disreputable Ford when two Ethiopians turned up, one fat, one thin. The thin, sly one was Ato Makonnen Habtewold, the Emperor's Director of Commerce, who, with his small straggly goatee, looked like a mild Leon Trotsky. He drew Steer aside, and said: 'An aeroplane will be ready for you at four. Tell nobody that you are going, not even your friends. Say that you are going to a funeral.'

Steer packed a small suitcase, and dolefully told his acquaintances he was off to the cemetery. At Akaki aerodrome he found an Armenian mechanic hauling a ten-year-old Potez two-seater biplane out of the hangar. The grey-uniformed Ethiopian pilot smiled cheerily and said, in French, 'We haven't had a fatal accident yet.' Swaddled in an oversize Ethiopian flying suit with an Italian parachute he had no idea how to use clamped round his waist, Steer was hoisted into the rear seat, and handed a machine gun. In three minutes he was soaring high over the eucalyptus, looking down on the circular Coptic churches of Entoto.

The air grew cold, and the leather helmet, made for big Ethiopian hair, blew loose at once. Steer sat bareheaded, clutching a hat that did not fit and a gun he could not fire, gazing down at the map made real. His flight to see the Emperor at Dessye was a lesson in geography. He had thought of Ethiopia as a solid mountain fastness ringed by dry deserts, but he soon saw from above how the rivers had cut and carved the land: 'As far as the eye could reach to the north were other yawning cauldrons where the confluents of the Nile were boiled, and other giant trenches of rock through which the waters poured west. We soared high, the sun flashing upon the threaded streams and showing the towering walls of mountains alternately grey and rose.'

Each cultivated mountain-top plateau, or *amba*, was ringed with cactus euphorbia to stop the cattle falling over the cliffs. Steer could see no paths down, and imagined passages between the massive mountain fastnesses along razor edges that would frighten even an Abyssinian mule.

He had thought that Ethiopia was divided into Amhara upland above and Danakil desert below. Now he saw hundreds of miles of green foothills between these ecologies that had been settled by the Galla people (now better known as the Oromo), who had moved north from Kenya. When the Ethiopian Empire had expanded, the Amharic speakers had conquered the Galla and treated them as vassals; the Galla of Wollo would later take their revenge on the Emperor when he was in trouble.

Steer flew across the fantastic gorge that divided Shoa from Wollo. This was just the country for the press to get airborne to see what was going on. Afterwards, Steer kept urging *The Times* to share a plane with other papers or with Planet News photographers, but it was always too expensive or too difficult to arrange.

Curiously, in Dr Samuel Johnson's novel about life's forking paths, *The History of Rasselas, Prince of Abyssinia*, written in January 1759, the eponymous Ethiopian hero meets an artist who is building a flying machine, and asks him about the mystery of flight. Johnson's inventor is secretive about the bat-wing design of his aircraft. His answer seems ominously prophetic.

If men were all virtuous . . . I should with great alacrity teach them all to fly. But what would be the security of the good, if the bad could at pleasure invade them from the sky? Against an army sailing through the clouds neither walls, nor mountains, nor seas, could afford any security. A flight of northern savages might hover in the wind, and light at once with irresistible violence upon the capital of a fruitful region that was rolling under them. Even this valley, the retreat of princes, the abode of happiness, might be violated by the sudden descent of some of the naked nations that swarm on the coast of the southern sea.

TWO Death from the Air

For I dipped into the future, far as human eye could see,
Saw the vision of the world, and all the wonder that would be;

Saw the heavens fill with commerce, argosies of magic sails,
Pilots of the purple twilight, dropping down with costly bales;

Heard the heavens fill with shouting, and there rained a ghastly dew
From the nations' airy navies grappling in the central blue . . .
    Alfred Tennyson, 'Locksley Hall' (1842)

1

The Italo-Abyssinian War was the laboratory of air power. In his classic 1921 book *Il dominio dell'aria* (*The Command of the Air*), the Italian Colonel Giulio Douhet said that the air force had to 'inflict upon the enemy attacks of a terrifying nature to which he can in no way react'. On the day that Steer flew to Dessye, the Italians began to put the theory into practice.

In the north, on 22 December, Ras Imru led a fast column of 8,000 Ethiopians hooking round the Italian right to attack their undefended supply base at Adi Quala. If he had succeeded, he would have cut off the entire Italian Second Army Corps from its base. In desperation, Badoglio asked the Italian air force to defend Adi Quala *at all costs*. They used their yperite bombs.

Yperite, named after Ypres in Flanders, where it was first used on 12 July 1917, is called a mustard gas because it smells of garlic and horse-radish, though part of its stinging action is to kill the sense of smell. Dichloro-ethyl-sulphide, chemical formula $C_4H_8Cl_2S$, is an oily liquid that is hard to wash off. Yperite blisters skin, injures moist lung tissue and eyeballs, and is now classified as a carcinogen. Kept stable in steel

cylinders, it can be sprayed, fired in artillery shells or dropped in
bombs. The Italian air force, Regia Aeronautica Italiana, used a heavy
bomb, the C500T, which carried 467 pounds of yperite. It was meant
to detonate 250 yards off the ground and could spray an area of about
thirty football pitches in extent.

On Sunday, 22 December 1935, the Italians dropped six of these
bombs on the Ethiopians; the next day, thirty-six more. 'For the first
time in the history of the world, a people supposedly white used poison
gas upon a people supposedly savage . . . Some were blinded. When
others saw the burns spread upon their arms and legs and felt the
increasing pain . . . Imru's men broke and fled.'

News of the victory spread quickly through the Italian forces.
Graziani's air force in the south first started using poison gas on
Christmas Eve, and went through forty-four tons of chemical warfare
agents by the end of April 1936. The Italians used six times as much to
break the Ethiopian armies in the north.

2

Meanwhile, Abyssinia was causing political turbulence in Britain. In
September, the Foreign Secretary Sir Samuel Hoare had made a ter-
rific speech in Geneva about Britain doing its bit to support 'collective
security'. At the end of October the political parties prepared to fight
the General Election of 1935. Stanley Baldwin's National government
also campaigned for 'collective security'. Its election poster: 'Grip The
Key To Peace – Vote National' shows, punching through the paper, a
strong right fist holding an elaborate key whose head reads 'League'
and whose handle 'of Nations'. The government's policy looked like
complete British support for the League, and the Nationals duly won
the election; but on 10 December 1935, British newspapers caused
uproar by printing leaked details of the notorious Franco-British
Hoare–Laval pact, which would concede to Italy a large chunk of
Ethiopia, leaving the Ethiopians only 'a corridor for camels' to the
sea. The public outcry forced Sir Samuel Hoare to resign, and on 19
December 1935 Anthony Eden became the new Foreign Secretary. In
his resignation speech, Hoare, his nose broken in a skiing accident,
painfully explained that he had been 'terrified with the thought that we
might lead Abyssinia on to think that the League could do more than
it can do'.

The impotence of the League of Nations was humiliatingly exposed, and other international organizations, such as the International Committee of the Red Cross, were found wanting too. In late October 1935, the ICRC sent two Swiss representatives, the lawyer Sidney Hamlet Brown and the surgeon Marcel Junod, to find out what the newly founded Abyssinian Red Cross needed. The President of the ICRC, Max Huber, told them they were not going as investigators or judges, but to relieve the distress of all war victims.

Brown and Junod arrived in Addis Ababa on 8 November, to discover that the Ethiopian armies had gone north with no doctors, no nurses and no bandages. The Ethiopian Red Cross Committee had two ambulances in the field, and had raised supplies for ten more, but they could staff only four. There was only one trained Ethiopian doctor in the entire country. So a Greek and a German ran the first ambulance; an Austrian Nazi and an Indian the second; two Poles the third; and the last was given to a Jewish doctor, who insisted on taking his violin along. In charge of the mule transport unit was a sixty-two-year-old English master of foxhounds (who had quietly taken ten years off his age), Major Gerald Achilles Burgoyne.

More foreign help was on the way. The national Red Cross societies of twenty-eight nations responded with money and medical supplies, and Egypt, Finland, Holland, Great Britain, Norway and Sweden sent well-equipped field units. Marcel Junod's job was co-ordinating them, while Sidney Brown dealt with the politics. First, he had to sort out the problem of the Red Cross icon. In Ethiopia, the sign of the red cross on a white ground traditionally hung outside a *tej* house, which was often a knocking-shop as well as a bar. Brown wanted the brothels' signs removed, to avoid confusion with hospitals. He also had to explain to the Emperor that the ICRC represented not the Pact of Geneva, where member states stood shoulder to shoulder against aggression, but the Convention of Geneva, which simply tried to make war fair play. They were not allies, but linesmen.

3

This war was no game. The Abyssinians killed all their enemies with guns, swords and spears: they took only five Italian prisoners in seven months. Their old *fusil gras* muskets fired a large soft-lead bullet whose appalling exit wounds led the Italians to claim they were dum-dum bullets, outlawed by international law for their explosive effect, and which the Italians alleged were being supplied by Great Britain.*

The Italians themselves fouled, by bombing ambulances. The destruction of the Red Cross hospital at Dessye on 6 December 1935 was just the beginning. In reprisal for the torture, mutilation and beheading of an Italian pilot at Daggahbur on 24 December, seven Italian planes deliberately bombed the Swedish Red Cross ambulance at Dolo on 30 December, killing twenty-seven patients and a Swedish medic.

In January 1936, the Italians bombed three more Ethiopian Red Cross camps. The master of foxhounds, Gerald Burgoyne, had pitched his red tent with its flaps open to make a red cross at Waldia on Wednesday, 15 January, when three planes appeared from the north. 'They're going to bomb,' said the vet who was with him; 'better come away.' Burgoyne wrote to his wife that there followed 'half a dozen thunderous claps. "Your tent's gone," said the vet. It had too. A real good shot. The Iti seeing the red roof put six big bombs carefully round it, the furthest 20 yards away – holes 15ft in diameter and four or five feet deep . . . It was too evident that he deliberately bombed my tent . . . Can't understand the idea.'

Another British officer attached to Number 3 Ambulance of the Ethiopian Red Cross was Captain Marius Brophil, a veteran of the First World War who had seen mustard gas used before. In the *Spectator* of 24 April 1936, Brophil wrote:

> On the morning of January 14th I was standing at the centre Red Cross of our ambulance . . . Three Red Cross flags were displayed very prominently at three points of a triangle. While standing in the middle of them I noticed an Italian 'plane flying very low at a height of about two hundred feet. It then came swooping over. On looking up I saw that the side door of the 'plane was open and I could see the pilot . . . I waved to him, pointing to the Red Cross flag at my feet and giving the 'wash-out' sign. He acknowledged these signals of mine. I stood there whilst he circled over me four more times. Then he went away.

Next morning, however, three tri-motor aeroplanes appeared, and bombed the camp for forty-five minutes, killing two women and

---

* Anthony Eden informed the House of Commons in May 1936 that the 'Colonel Pedro Lopez' who had tried to buy dum-dum expanding bullets in Birmingham for 'big-game hunting' was actually an Australian called Henry Lawrence Bernstein, working for the military attaché at the Italian Embassy in London.

wounding eight. At 1.30 p.m. more planes came back. 'We were not only bombed but machine-gunned for two and a half hours . . . I counted thirty direct hits around the Red Cross and the ground around was torn by machine-gun bullets.'

G. L. Steer saw exactly why all the British, Dutch, Swedish, Ethiopian and Egyptian Red Cross ambulances were attacked: 'It was meant to clear foreign witnesses out of the way while illegal methods of war were being used by the Italians.'

4

On Christmas Day 1935, Steer drove north from Dessye with the two stringers, Holmes of *The Times* and Lowenthal of Reuters, in the lorry that advertised their trade. At Lake Hayk in the Wollo region Steer shot for the pot, and Holmes took a picture that *The Times* ran five months later: several brace of duck hanging on the left side of the truck over the painted sign '*The Times*', and Steer smiling with the shotgun in the crook of his right arm (see plate 1). They met an aged Muslim who was full of curiosity. In *Caesar in Abyssinia* Steer says this man 'wanted to know everything about the tent, the truck, the clothes, the soap and water. What was it all *for*? He asked questions like my old tutors at Oxford.' Steer thought of Maurice Bowra and Gilbert Ryle.

North and west of where the journalists had reached, the three Ethiopian armies led by Ras Seyyum, Ras Kassa and Ras Mulugeta were assembled. The grizzled Minister of War Ras Mulugeta had left Addis Ababa in November and marched north to find a five-mile-long platform of rock south of Makalle, which was nearly 10,000 feet up. This mountain was called Amba Aradam, and the army of 35,000 filtered up into its stronghold. There was water; grain could be supplied from Dessye, and meat and chickens from local tribes. An old-style sword-and-shield warrior, hacking his way to victory, Ras Mulugeta was out of his depth here. He was as harsh to his own people, flogging and branding them, as he was ignorant of the modern enemy flying above him. From the air the Italians could clearly see his supply lines and bomb and gas his mule-trains.

Ras Mulugeta's men huddled behind rocks and in caves high up on the mountain under a punishing barrage of high explosives and shrapnel from 200 field guns and squadrons of aircraft. Ras Mulugeta stubbornly sat through it while four Italian divisions encircled his mountain below, and only managed to escape the trap because another chief, Bitwoded Makonnen, sacrificed himself to save him. Makonnen led his sons and 4,000 of his best warriors straight into the Italian machine guns on the east side of the mountain. He later died in a cave at Mahara on the River Buie, after being shot several times through the waist and hips. Major Gerald Burgoyne, who had delivered a mule-train of Red Cross supplies to Amba Aradam, washed and dressed Makonnen's wounds late on Thursday, 13 February, but the chief had already been bleeding for twelve hours. Makonnen died in the morning, and his Wollega officers, distraught, cut his body in two and packed the halves in a pair of sealed war drums to carry back home.

On Thursday, 27 February they were limping south towards Kworam when the Italian planes caught them between a cliff and a ravine. A bomb destroyed the mule carrying one of the drums. The Wollegas buried the shattered drum under an acacia, and the other in the church of St George in the next village. Bitwoded Makonnen's mangled body mirrored the severing of social relations. Steer wrote:

> Italian air supremacy made of the Ethiopians a rabble which could not think for itself. It demolished, in fearful explosions and vibrations of the solid earth, the aristocracy which was the cadre of their military organisation. The people's support of that framework was very physical. It kissed its feet, hung on to its mule, crowded behind it in the streets, touched it when it walked, helped its limbs in every activity. The aerial supremacy of Italy abolished all these contacts in war for ever.

Thanks to Bitwoded Makonnen's courage, Ras Mulugeta and many of his men got out from Amba Aradam on 13 February. The 6,000 Ethiopians left behind were all killed by grenades and machine guns when the Italians took the mountain. The retreat south was nightmarish. Italian planes pursued the Army of the Centre, dropping a hundred tons of high explosives in two days, machine-gunning and gassing, while the Galla sniped from either side of the track. Only a few thousand ever reached Lake Ashangi.

Ras Mulugeta had crossed the ford at Ahayo when a servant with torn clothes ran to overtake him. Back down the corpse-strewn road, his son, Colonel Tadessa Mulugeta, had been walking with Major Gerald Burgoyne and their mules and soldiers, when three Caproni bombers had appeared. The Englishman and the Ethiopian had been running for cover under a big cypress tree when a bomb had exploded between them, killing them instantly. Now the Galla *shiftas* were attacking.

In his last black rage the old Ras turned round to avenge his son. The Galla surrounded him, and planes, recognising the khaki in the middle of their allies, flew low to bomb. Mulugeta fell near his son: his bodyguard carried him off the field, over the rocks and short grass which concealed their enemies. So died the last of Menelik's high officers, the man who stopped more lead in his rhino-skin shield and killed more men with the sword than any in Ethiopia.

5

On 28 February 1936 Steer wrote to thank the Editor of *The Times*: 'The work has often been tiring, the search for truth fantastically difficult, and many colleagues in the search highly dishonest. But I like the country and the story: physically I have never felt so fit in my life: and the fact that you and Mr Deakin have always supported me, with occasional useful reproof, has given me the greatest satisfaction.'

Steer still thought, erroneously, that the south was the front where the main Italian thrust would come, and his letter is full of possible strategic moves in the Ogaden that the Italians never made. Steer admitted later he had 'a particular weakness' for the Ogaden army, in 'their queer little camps from Jijiga down to the Webbe Shebeli', and he remembered the land with nostalgia. 'The wide open thorn among occasional long low hills, the brightly feathered birds and herds of buck, the sun in the waterless stretches, the Ogaden mimosa in white flower made me love the place.' Perhaps the glare of what he knew dazzled him to the disaster already happening in the north. He did not then believe the news of the huge defeat of Ras Mulugeta at Amba Aradam, nor foresee that the Emperor's army would be destroyed at Mai Ceu.

On 2 March *The Times* cabled urging Steer to go to Dessye to find out about the trapped armies and Steer replied: 'EYE STRIVING UTMOST NORTHWARD SEDCOMMUNICATIONS DIFFICULT'.

Walter Holmes, the *Times* stringer, was still in the north and on Friday, 6 March 1936 the paper carried his dramatic news that the British Red Cross ambulance unit had been attacked from the air, with three patients killed and four wounded. The camp was in the middle of a flat plain about three miles in diameter, laid out in a square, with two very large Red Cross flags pegged out on the ground. On two flagpoles flew the Red Cross flag and the Union Jack. At midday a single Italian plane, marked S62, dropped forty bombs on the unit. One bomb fell right in the middle of the forty-six-foot square Red Cross. Another destroyed the tent where the doctors, Melly and Macfie, had been operating, wounding the anaesthetized patient in the leg. The *Times*/Reuters lorry was blown up, and Holmes lost all his kit. The plane pursued the doctors, patients and dressers who fled to hide in ditches, and the remains of the camp were bombed again on 5 and 6 March. The doctors had to set up in a cave overlooking the Alomata valley to carry on treating the wounded.

Yet torn tents, blackened craters and a few British medics stumbling after their mules, far away in Africa, were not an important story compared to the dramatic news from Europe, where 22,000 mechanized German troops, under Luftwaffe air cover, were smoothly reoccupying the Rhineland.

The Times started reporting heavy use of gas in the north of Ethiopia from 17 March 1936, noting both phosgene and mustard gas dropped on Kworam, and the gassing of peasants, who were being sprayed from planes used like crop-dusters.

Haile Selassie's daughter, Princess Tsehai, sent a telegram of protest to the Women's Advisory Council of the League of Nations, based on information from her father: 'This suffering and torture is beyond description, hundreds of country-men screaming and moaning with pain. Many of them are unrecognisable since the skin has been burned off their face.'

From Paris, the Ethiopian minister Ato Wolde Mariam sent a note to the League of Nations: 'Italy is making use of asphyxiating gases and raining down hyperite [*sic*] . . . and over immense areas is massacring the population of women, children and aged people. She is destroying the churches and holy places.'

The Ethiopian Red Cross appealed via the International Red Cross Committee for 'large quantities of gas masks and manuals dealing with technical protection against asphyxiating, poisonous and other gases', a request that the International Committee 'did not feel justified in acceding to in the form presented'.

Two days later, on 25 March, *The Times* printed an emotional telegram received from the Executive Secretary of the Ethiopian Red Cross:

The bombing of country villages around Kworam and Waldia, the permanent blinding and maiming of hundreds of helpless women and children, as well as the infliction of similar injuries on soldiers with that most dreadful of all agencies, yperite or so-called mustard gas, should cause us to ask ourselves the question – whither? . . .

To-day a few thousand peasants in Wallo will be groping their way down the dark years because of a dictator, whose name they have never heard of, but whose decree of ruthlessness has put out their eyes. Wallo is a long way from Charing Cross – yes, but not for aeroplanes.

On 26 March, the day when he also reported the bombing of Jijiga, with 33 killed and 140 wounded, Steer wrote in *The Times*: 'This is the first time in history that a white Power has used gas upon a black people.'

On 29 March Italian planes bombed Harar, and General Valle boasted that the Italian air force had racked up 20,000 flying hours in Ethiopia, dropped 2,000 tons of bombs, and fired 300,000 rounds of machine-gun ammunition.

The House of Lords in London debated 'Air Bombing in Ethiopia, Italy and Poison Gas' on Monday, 30 March. Viscount Cecil opened by quoting Princess Tsehai's telegram and referred to Sir Hesketh Bell's lead letter that morning in *The Times*, which warned of 'a terrible Nemesis in the days to come' from 'the coloured peoples throughout the continent of Africa'. The Archbishop of Canterbury said, 'I hear from every quarter of Africa how natives are watching the conduct of the war.' Lord Mottistone said that using poison gas was 'a crime against humanity'. Lord Rennell, however, was sure the Italian people were naturally humane and kindly: 'I do not believe that the Italian people can share in the guilt.'

Viscount Halifax, Lord Privy Seal in Baldwin's government, reported to the House that the British government had received a formal protest from the Ethiopian government to them as a contracting party to the 1907 Hague Convention and the 1925 Geneva Protocol against the use of poison gas. Because these attacks affected the civilian population, the Ethiopian government reserved the right to claim compensation under the Hague Convention, and asked for action to stop the violations.

Lord Halifax, however, infuriated George Steer by saying that 'he had no information . . . It would be quite wrong and quite unjust to prejudge a matter so grave and so vitally affecting the honour of a great country.' On 1 April the Diplomatic Correspondent of *The Times* wrote: 'The use of poison gas has not been witnessed by an authoritative British observer.'

As Steer pointed out in *Caesar in Abyssinia*, the British government already had irrefutable evidence. On 31 December 1935, three months before the debate in Parliament, 'Firkin' Taylor, the British Assistant Military Attaché, had collected fragments of bombs from the Ogaden which had been sent to the Gas Experimental School at Porton Down in England and found to contain mustard gas. The British government also had evidence from Sir Sidney Barton, who had talked with Dr J. W. S. Macfie of the British Ambulance Service on 27 March.

In *An Ethiopian Diary*, the doctor recorded his experiences: 'An old man sat moaning on the ground, rocking himself to and fro, completely wrapped in a cloth. When I approached he slowly rose and drew aside his cloak. He looked as if someone had tried to skin him, clumsily; he had been horribly burned by "mustard gas" all over the face, the back and the arms. There were . . . many blinded by the stuff, with blurred crimson apologies for eyes.'

On 30 March 1936, the highest-ranking group ever from the International Committee of the Red Cross met with Benito Mussolini in Rome. Il Duce stiffened when Max Huber mentioned the word 'mustard gas' in his introduction, but nothing more was said about what everyone knew was the most important issue of the day. The ICRC had reports of poison-gas use from its own people, yet the organization chose to say nothing.

'What happened in Rome has never really been explained,' wrote Caroline Moorehead in her authoritative book *Dunant's Dream: War, Switzerland and the History of the Red Cross* (1998). The Italians received no international rebuke and continued their covert use of gas. The 'impartiality' and 'neutrality' of the ICRC amounted, in the end, to good men doing nothing, and allowing evil to triumph.

The *Times* stringer Walter Holmes got back to Addis Ababa late on 2 April with John Melly and the remnants of the British and Dutch Red Cross. 'This isn't a war,' Melly wrote to Kathleen Nelson, 'it's the torture of tens of thousands of defenceless men, women and children with bombs and poison gas . . . and the world . . . passes by on the other side.'

Steer and Holmes did their best. On Friday, 3 April 1936, the *Times* article 'Italian Use of Poison Gas' said: 'Your Correspondent and another British Press representative have seen and photographed gas cases in the Kworam area . . . The Emperor cannot sleep at night for misery at the screaming and groaning of his fighting men and his country people who have been burned inside and out by mustard gas.'

In *The Times* of Saturday, 4 April, Holmes's lead story on page 13 was: 'Poison Gas in Ethiopia: Eye-Witness's Account':

On arriving here from the northern front last night I was astonished to read a report that members of the House of Lords had expressed the hope that the allegations of the use of poison gas by the Italians might prove untrue . . .

My first personal experience of the use of gas bombs in this campaign occurred on Sunday, March 1, in the bush between Alomata and Kobbo, about 10 miles south of Kworam. Italian machines flew over this area and dropped several mustard-gas containers . . . [They] fell in dense bush, thus producing an effect which . . . is particularly barbarous. The corrosive liquid lies on the foliage, retaining its potency for two or three days, and passing Ethiopians received terrible leg burns . . .

During the subsequent three weeks which I spent in the neighbourhood of Kworam and Lake Ashangi, I saw, almost every day, bombing and spraying of mustard gas by Italian aeroplanes.

6

Lady Barton's Ethiopian Women's Work Association had been making canvas gas masks based on an old First World War design. These had mica eye-slits, a flannel breathing filter, and covered the head and shoulders. By 6 April they had made nearly 2,000 of them for the Emperor's northern army. Major Arthur Bentinck volunteered to take the twenty large sacks up in an Armenian truck, and Steer went along for the ride. On this eleven-day African safari they shot their own food, and dug themselves out of mud at least thirty times.

They left on 7 April. That day *The Times* reported that students from thirteen British universities, and representatives of twenty-three women's organizations, had protested against Italian aggression, and in Parliament the Liberal leader, Sir Archibald Sinclair, called for sanctions and a shipping embargo against Italy, saying, 'it was shameful that the Government should stand idly by while Italy machine-gunned Red Cross workers, killed and maimed Abyssinian peasants with a deadly and tortuous gas, and piled lawless outrage on ruthless aggression. (Hear, hear.)'

The lorryload of gas masks rolled across the Shoan plain, which was full of horses, wheat fields ringed by pink lilies, and grey stone houses with thatched roofs. As they climbed up into the mists of the Jib Washa range, Steer noted the wild flowers: white thyme, yellow daisies, 'a blue flower with a stem like burrage and a bloom like forget-me-not'. It rained so hard that they had to camp for a day and night. They carved runnels round the tent to draw off the water, and Steer went down through bright, wet flowers to bucket water from an icy stream that 'sprinted narrowly' below. 'We had our comforts. Every herb on that mountain smelt sweetly and the Ethiopians gathered them in armfuls to make a springy carpet for the tent. Nothing to do but lie in bed eating wild duck with our hands from the pot, soothing ourselves with rum.'

When the skies cleared, they walked ahead of the truck down the Tarmaber Pass, filling and levelling a roadway scored by watercourses, edging down the hairpin bends of the 4,000-foot escarpment, with the wreckage of a Greek lorry far below. At Shola Mieda they dug themselves out of mud by torchlight. It was Good Friday, 10 April 1936.

They dropped down towards the Danakil borderlands at Mahfud, with Mount Agelu to the east over the yellow desert, driving through hot, dry country with dusty mimosa, scarlet finches and white swallowtail butterflies flouncing through the bush like torn-up paper. All Easter Day, with a single rush tied round their heads in Coptic Christian manner, they drove through brown hills. They were stuck in a marsh full of small coloured butterflies, when a column of twenty Ethiopian lorries with 200 soldiers came the other way, retreating towards Addis Ababa. Fifteen miles from Dessye they drove into the side of the hill and bent the steering tie-rod. Madros, the Armenian driver, cold-hammered it straight again in the glare of the headlights, and they slept out in the open. The next day they entered the war zone.

Flights of bombers overhead meant they had to hide their lorry by the river. They drank *talla* (native beer), watching naked women and children splash in the hot springs. Two Ethiopian Red Cross lorries were heading back to Addis. 'They're all going back,' whispered the Hungarian Dr Ngjaros. Two little boys, hand in hand, walked along the road. They said they had been with their fathers in the Tembien, and that one father had been gassed. At the sound of a plane, the boys broke apart and dived for cover. To the west a long line of men and animals was heading south along the mule track.

At the gates of Dessye Steer talked to some retreating Ethiopian soldiers. 'Their wounded hobbled along . . . women in crude splints covering bomb wounds . . . immense suppurating swellings on the skin they said was gas . . . others lay face forward upon their mules covered with a worn shamma.'

Steer and Bentinck entered Dessye at 4 p.m. on Easter Monday and drove into the Sudan Interior Mission compound. The missionaries had all been ordered to leave by the Ethiopian Crown Prince, but had no transport. Six thousand Galla were reported not far to the north, and Dessye was about to be sacked.

Steer and Bentinck went to a hillside cave to give the Crown Prince their letters of introduction and to deliver the twenty sacks of gas masks. Amid his shrieking soldiers shouting for food, money, arms, cartridges, permits, the dignified eighteen-year-old son of Haile Selassie, Asfa Wossen, refused to let the foreigners take the risk of staying with him. 'You must go back *at once*,' he said.

They were crossing the bomb-pitted Dessye marketplace when a red-faced white man came running out of a hut. 'Take me away this evening,' he pleaded. 'Save my life!' It was Captain de Norman, the last survivor of the Belgian Military Mission, gabbling about the screaming and killing at night as the Galla edged in. By dusk, more people were leaving, and desultory shots echoed from the hills. The Dutch Red Cross were breaking camp to retreat.

Steer quarrelled with Captain de Norman, who wanted to take not just his clothes but all his supplies of food; Steer threw them off the lorry. The last Ethiopian truck out of Dessye left at midnight, with Galla shooting from both sides of the road. Steer lay on the cab roof with his Mauser loaded and the safety catch off. Far ahead on the dark road he could see the Dutch ambulance headlights on the mountain's hairpin bends. The missionaries in the back sang hymns under the Southern Cross. Troops from Italian Eritrea took Dessye early the next day.

7

The British government could no longer ignore what was happening in Ethiopia. On 8 April a British memorandum on 'Alleged Italian Use of Poison Gas' was handed over at Geneva, with evidence from, among others, Drs Melly and Macfie. On 10 April the Foreign Secretary told the House of Commons that Italy could not protest innocence when it had declared 259 tonnes of gas in transit through the British-run Suez Canal.

The League of Nations Committee of Thirteen was now investigating Italy's use of poison gas in the Horn of Africa, and asked the International Committee of the Red Cross for its evidence; but ICRC President Max Huber would not hand over any eyewitness testimonies, saying that it would breach the trust of both warring parties.

On 20 April 1936 Anthony Eden spoke in person to the League of Nations, saying it was

> impossible not to take account of the evidence which . . . goes to show that poison gas has been used by the Italian armies in their campaign against Abyssinians, themselves utterly unprovided with any means of defence against this method of warfare . . . Not only the two belligerents, but nearly all the nations of the World, are parties to the Gas Protocol of 1925 . . . If a convention such as this can be torn up . . . how can we have confidence that our own folk . . . will not be burned, blinded and done to death in agony hereafter?

Yet all these urgent questions fizzled out a fortnight later when Addis Ababa fell on 5 May. Four days later Ethiopia was annexed by Italy. No one in the great League of Nations would go to war for little Abyssinia, and on 18 June 1936 Anthony Eden told the House of Commons that Great Britain was lifting all sanctions against Italy. The *Cape Argus* pointed out that the date of this retreat was the anniversary of the Battle of Waterloo.

8

On Monday, 27 April, the aeroplanes dropped flares at first, red, white and green, the colours of the Italian flag. Then there were leaflets fluttering down from the sky, on to the eucalyptus trees and *tukuls* of Addis Ababa, with a message printed in Amharic on red, white and green sheets of paper.

'People of Shoa, listen! I am the head of the victorious Italian Army, and will enter Addis Ababa with the help of God. The Emperor and his First Army are useless and defeated,' they began, and 'I do not want the Christian Ethiopian people destroyed. We bring peace and civilization . . . But if you try to prevent the advance of our army, then the Italian Army will destroy and kill without pity, the aeroplanes will massacre from the air and destroy everything that exists.'

The Ethiopian government propaganda department rushed to print 5,000 copies of its own leaflet denouncing the Italians as liars. 'If they come here by guile, they will rob you first of your rifles then of your lives. They will give your land to their own people and your little children will work upon it as slaves.' The leaflet urged resistance. 'We shall say to ourselves every day, "Never submit" . . . The Lion of Judah has conquered for 1,000 years. If we stand together like men, he will conquer again.'

A seventeen-year-old girl spoke up. Princess Tsehai summoned the foreign press to the Ethiopian Women's Work Association, where she and the other aristocrats in their white overalls were finishing another batch of 1,000 gas masks. The journalists were handed copies of her last, desperate appeal: 'For God's sake help us . . . Rally your husbands, brothers, sons, and force them to use their massed strength to force the Parliaments and rulers to take action . . . I know, as you know, that if mankind lets armies and gas destroy my country and people, civiliz- ation will be destroyed too. We have common cause, you and I . . . If you fail to help us now we shall all die . . .'

April 29th 1936

Dear Mr Deakin

Sorry this article is in pencil . . .

I shall stay here as long as possible. After that, if any government remains in being outside the town (supposing the Italians come in) I shall go wherever it goes. I shall stay with them until the end . . . I shall find ways to get my stories out.

Best wishes

Yours ever

George Steer

9

On Thursday, 30 April 1936 the Emperor was driven back to Addis Ababa down the mountain road from Fitche. He had the blasted look of a man who had seen the end of the world. His armies were broken – bombed, gassed and machine-gunned to shambles. The faces of the dead haunted him. He had prayed in the holy churches of Lalibela after Easter, lifting up his eyes to the hills. Conciliation had failed at Geneva. Where were the allies? When would help come?

His defeat was a constitutional crisis, because the Emperor Haile Selassie *was* the state. There were no political parties or elections. It was built around his decisions, his policies, his patronage. The dance of *shum-shir*, the Ethiopian political musical chairs of balancing rivalries and rewarding favours, was orchestrated by him. He was the head of the executive and the judiciary, held the keys to the exchequer, and was the fount of honours. He was Prime Minister, effectively all ministers. Now a technically superior foreign army and air force were hammering him. This was Haile Selassie's Hiroshima. As Emperor Hirohito would say in 1945, 'the war has developed not necessarily in Japan's favour'; but Haile Selassie, unlike Hirohito, would not be staying on to finesse a transition to the new order. For him it was nearly over. *Après lui, le déluge.*

The Press Secretary Lorenzo Taezaz met the Emperor with plans to move him and his capital to Goré in the west. Then the Emperor, looking exhausted, met the heads of foreign missions. Haile Selassie asked Sir Sidney Barton for assurances that Great Britain would support more sanctions at Geneva. Barton said he could not give them. The French minister urged the Emperor not to defend his capital, because Italian artillery would damage the property of the Greek and Armenian shop-keepers currently sheltering in a huddle of worry at the French Legation. The new American minister presented his credentials and observed through horn-rimmed spectacles that the Emperor was in need of a haircut. The Emperor went back to his Council.

There was no defence of Addis Ababa. With the Emperor away in the north, squabbling and chaos had supervened. Neither truly feudal nor efficiently modern, Ethiopia's administration slipped gears in between. Instead of the 6,000 soldiers that were needed, only 350 young cadets were sent to hold the route from Dessye. The escarpment road was not blown up. A well-trained brigade of 2,000 men with 36 superb new German anti-tank guns was paralysed because an Ethiopian chief

commandeered all their transport; the rubber-tyred guns that cost a
million marks never fired a shot.

The four of them spent Thursday evening together: George Steer and
Margarita de Herrero, and her friend Lolita with Don Lee of the British
Legation. They were talking about weddings. George and Margarita
were in love and were due to be married by the British Consul on the
following Monday. They had known each other for barely seven
months, but war hastens weddings.

Steer expected it would soon be over; the Emperor would go to the
west of Ethiopia, and the Italians would enter Addis Ababa on Saturday.
The rains from June to September would stop the war and diplomacy
would proceed in Geneva. A more pressing question was whether Steer
should seek the protection of the British Legation on the outskirts of
Addis Ababa. The Italians had apparently denounced his reports as
'grotesque' and 'ignoble', but would they do anything about it? He
decided to stay in town. It was a clear night, echoing with occasional
shots as citizens welcomed back returning defeated soldiery. The men
were splitting apart from their units in twos or threes, or bands of ten
and fifty, demoralized, uncertain, but carrying their weapons. There
were menacing beggars on the streets, demanding *birr, birr* – money,
money.

The Emperor slept at the Little Gibbi with the Empress. The plan was
that he would go to Goré in south-west Ethiopia to muster his forces
and regroup, and she and the children would leave on Saturday on a
special train to Djibouti, where a British warship would take them into
exile; but the Empress, who still felt fresh and strong, was determined
that the tired Emperor should come with her to Jerusalem, the Sacred
City, to invoke the aid of God and then the help of Geneva.

Steer thought all the influences working on the Empress were
defeatist. The palace women were terrified of planes and gas, and 'the
Wooha-Boha, weird pagan priest of the Abyssinian lower classes', a dirt-
encrusted sooth-sayer adorned with leather amulets and lion's claws,
splintered bone and afterbirth, was a witch doctor whose prophecies of
doom and failure 'crept through the servants and shivered their masters';
the Coptic Church repeated a Christianized version of his warnings.

Marcus Garvey, writing in the *Black Man* journal in 1936, also dis-
liked the religious atavism surrounding Haile Selassie:

He resorted semi-mentally to prayer and to feasting and fasting, not consistent with the policy that secures the existence of present-day freedom for peoples whilst other nations and rulers are building up armaments of the most destructive kind . . . The Italians triumphed by the use of mustard gas. Surely God was not on the side of the Italians helping them to disload the gas of death. The Abyssinians lost. God could not have been on their side either. It is logical therefore that God didn't take sides, but left the matter to be settled by the strongest human battalion.

On Friday, 1 May the Emperor continued to prepare for the move west to Goré. His archives were packed in lorries, mules and tents read-ied. The Italians were a day away; but then the most powerful chief, Ras Kassa Hailu, advised in the Council of Ministers against the move west. It would do no good if the Emperor were killed now. Better to go via Djibouti to Europe to appeal to the Great Powers under the Covenant of the League of Nations. There were grunts of approval.

Dedjaz Igezu, the military governor of Addis Ababa, an old-fashioned Menelik-ish figure with his muslin-bandaged head and a blue cloak, opposed Kassa. He said, 'Goré,' with great determination, stamping his black-buttoned boots on the Council floor. So did Blatta Takkala Walda Hawaryat, who later became an implacable enemy of the Emperor. A proper Ethiopian emperor should die in battle, he declared, brandish-ing a pistol and stating that he would rather shoot the Emperor himself than see him desert his country and his people. It was no good. On Friday afternoon the Council itself decided to leave for Djibouti by twenty-one votes to three.

The Emperor could see the merits of both courses of action. If he stayed, he could lead the resistance; and yet only Europe could restrain the Italians, so he must make a personal appeal to the Powers.

Haile Selassie ordered the drums of the Great Gibbi to be beaten for an hour and a half. The flags flew, and Shoan chiefs and armed men made their way to hear the Imperial Awaj read as the sun was setting. Steer saw that the decree was written in the Emperor's own handwrit-ing. It rejected the advice of the Council. The Emperor was going west to Goré. Three Ethiopian armies were ordered out to the east of Addis Ababa to delay the enemy while he did so.

Ministers and Young Ethiopians gathered at the Little Gibbi. Steer saw the Foreign Minister's sons, Sirak and George Herrouy, one an

Oxford graduate, wearing his Brasenose College muffler, the other a Cambridge graduate, in riding breeches. Benjamin and Joseph Martin, the two sons of the Ethiopian Ambassador in London, were there in khaki with their motorbikes. Mischa Babitcheff, the half-Russian, half-Abyssinian pilot, stood with Ayenna Birru, the young Wallega engineer, trained at Camborne School of Mines in Cornwall. He had made the road from Dessye, and all the young boys he had taken along to learn road-making were dead from bombs or exhaustion. The hope of Ethiopia stood quietly waiting. Then palace servants ran out, clearing the way, and the Emperor followed, in a general's uniform. 'His aspect froze my blood. Vigour had left the face, and as he walked forward he did not seem to know where he was putting his feet . . . his shoulders drooped: the orders on his tunic concealed a hollow, not a chest.' The Emperor was in shock. The chiefs had just told him they would not go out east to delay the advance of the Italians, because they could not muster their troops.

In the gathering dusk, Steer looked in through the doors of the pavilion. The Emperor was lying back in a deep sofa, exhausted, as the Empress lectured him with a finger raised. When he said wearily that he would fight on, she insisted he should fly. Ras Kassa came in and settled into a chair to begin talking. The Young Ethiopians outside grumbled that they would never see the Emperor now that the old bore had arrived, and began to drift away. They would continue to do their duty in the Patriot Resistance.

Steer went to the Spanish girls' flat. There was a lot of shooting at the stars in the city and the odd spent round plinked on the tin roof and rolled into the gutters. Idot's next door was shut, like the other bars, though Steer could see Madame Idot taking her last or last-but-one stiff whisky. Steer got a taxi back to his house through ominously calm streets. The *zabanias*, or guards, who sat wrapped in blankets in their corrugated-iron shanties all seemed to have gone. Lorries with blazing headlights came and went from the Upper and Lower palaces, moving heavy boxes from the Bank of Abyssinia to the railway station.

While Steer slept, at four in the morning, the Imperial family arrived at the station, with all the little princes and princesses, ministers, courtiers, servants and dogs. Their luggage, their silver thalers and a couple of Imperial lions were already aboard.

The Emperor himself went quietly by car to Akaki at 4.20 a.m., and boarded the train into exile.

10

Steer woke at 7 a.m. on Saturday, 2 May 1936 to the sound of shooting. Bayenna, his new interpreter, came in and said that both palaces had been left wide open. The Emperor had given orders that all his possessions should be distributed among his people. Steer and Harrison of Reuters drove over to have a look. There was no bored lounging in the streets now, no Amharic slumber; everyone was scrambling to see what they could get. At first, the atmosphere was like a festive holiday, with mafficking, laughing people firing off new rifles in the air to see if the ammunition fitted. They arrived at the New Gibbi, furnished by Waring and Gillow of Oxford Street only two years before. 'Waring and Gillow were coming out by instalments. A chair here, a carpet there, an electric bulb in one hand and a book from the Emperor's library in another. A woman passed staggering under a roll of tapestry. Another gainful woman kicked her behind, rolled the tapestries off her back, and ran off with the brightest one.'

They drove past the prison to the caves where the arms and ammunition were kept. The chief of police, Balambaras Abeba Aragai, had tried to keep order with a few tough blue-coated *zabanias*, but the crowd took no notice, so he took most of the machine-gun rifles, and left them to fight over the weapons with fists and knives.

They drove to the railway station for the 09.20 departure for Djibouti. Lorenzo Taezaz was on the station platform, with a revolver in his pocket in case he met Italians on the line. No one had told him the Emperor was leaving. The Swedish military mission was retreating, and there was a last-minute rush of Greeks and Armenians, sniffing a change in the atmosphere.

By the time the train left late at 10 a.m., hell had started to break loose in Addis Ababa. The traffic police started it. Because they were on duty, they had missed their fair share of the loot. The smartest grocer's shop in the Arada district, Ghanotakis, owned by a Greek from the Italian-occupied Dodecanese Islands, had been closed and sealed up since the beginning of the war. The traffic police broke open the heavy doors of the enemy property and went straight for the fine wines, shattering the bottlenecks on the pavement edge and draining the contents through the jags. 'In the flash of an eye, shop-breaking and looting became general. The poorer pillaged the richer and shot if they resisted. The class war, without distinction of colour and spontaneous as an African thunderstorm, broke with a crackle of rifles all over Addis Ababa.'

Steer went to the *Times* office, at the back of the Imperial Hotel. Some Ethiopians who had looted the Goanese tailor's were running up the street in top hats and tailcoats, followed by a blind-drunk woman in a bowler, with a knife in her hand. Steer went upstairs to collect cash and valuables and to burn a few carbon copies of messages he did not want the Italians to see, and forgot to take the seven bottles of champagne he was saving for his wedding.

He took Bill Collins's old closed Ford with the dirty Reuters flag on it and made for Margarita's flat. The streets were full of mobs returning from the palaces, drunk and carrying rifles. Mon Ciné, the elite Greek cinema-bar, had been smashed in, and chairs were coming out through the windows. People were drinking from bottles, stealing the pictures of film stars, and playfully unspooling the movies from their canisters all over the road. George and Margarita had booked seats for that night's showing of *Hell Below*, the First World War submarine drama with Robert Montgomery and Madge Evans. It crunched as Steer drove over it.

The crowd was looting car parts from Paleologue's garage, and chucking foreign newspapers out of the bookshop. All the Greek wine shops and hotels that had imported vast amounts of Chianti to sell to the victorious Italian soldiers were having their profits liquidated by thirsty gangs.

The car pulled up near Idot's, which was being looted to the sound of gunfire. Steer did not want to leave the money unguarded in the car, so he sent Selassie, Harrison's interpreter, up the stairs to look for the Spanish girls. Steer himself sat unarmed in the car, half-hiding under the broad brim of his felt hat, watching Marcel Junod of the Red Cross laughing on his wooden balcony across the street as the Ethiopians machine-gunned the doors of the travel agency. (Junod laughed on the other side of his face when the mob came for him later, and he had to fight for his life.) Selassie came back. 'They're not there,' he said. Steer was distraught. He ran up the stairs, which were splashed with fresh blood, to find a servant beating an intruder with a sword.

The women were hiding in the loft. Lolita was frightened, Margarita calm but amused.

(The whole scene recalls chapter 6 of *Black Mischief*, in which William Bland and Percy Anstruther rescue Dame Muriel Porch and Miss Sarah Tin of the League of Dumb Chums from their roof during an Azanian riot.)

Outside, the roads were packed with drunken, armed people, and the old Ford had unreliable steering and brakes. Steer knew that if he hit someone the crowd of rioters might turn on them. Over the four miles to the British Legation, people fired haphazardly across the bonnet, battered the roof with swords and sticks and made threatening faces, but Steer kept driving. The crowd was attacking the offices of the Ethiopian Red Cross as they passed by, and 'the streets were rolling with dollars, bandages and postage stamps'. As the crowds thinned, the yellow-red-eyed drunks looked hungrier and crueller. 'We thanked God when we saw the barbed wire and the fringed turbans of the Sikhs, entered the neat gateway and climbed the cool, empty drive of the British Legation, under the eucalyptus trees planted in Menelik's time.' Sir Sidney Barton's precautions were paying off. The eighty-acre Legation compound was now ringed by twenty miles of barbed wire, and patrolled by 130 Sikhs of the 5th Battalion of the 14th Punjab Regiment.

Steer went out again in the Ford, alone. The drunkenness was getting worse. He hooted and accelerated his way to his house near the Armenian church. His servants proudly came to show off their loot; Wodaju the cook had taken 500 thalers from the Red Cross; Wolde Giorghis the *syce*, or groom, had a splendid old gun, Bayenna a rope-handled box with 750 rounds of government rifle ammunition. Steer packed tent, beds, shirts, shorts and the most valuable notebooks in the back of the Ford. He gave his Mauser rifle and dead Burgoyne's shotgun to Wolde and told him and Wodaju to guard the house till he came back. Foolishly, he also handed them a bottle of whisky to keep their spirits up under fire.

Bayenna asked if he could come to the Legation. As they left, the klaxon horn fell off and one of the tyres, punctured by broken glass, quietly flattened. Steer drove one-handed, using the other to bang on the door, shrieking, while Bayenna bashed his metal side with a stick, to make people get out of the way. Wobbling comically on the flat tyre, they clanked their way into the British Legation just before lunch.

By then it was starting to fill up with escapees from the looting. Old Dr Hanner, the Swedish surgeon, had deterred the rioters in his hospital dispensary from opening the medicines and sniffing them, by saying gloomily, 'That is gas.' Hanner drove an ambulance full of Swedish nurses to the British Legation; there was a cheer when the blondes arrived at the gate. The place was beginning to turn into the League of Nations.

Americans, Armenians, Greeks, Syrians, Swiss poured in. Cypriots and Jews, Portuguese and Sudanese, Egyptians and Somalis: it was like Pentecost, all of them praising the wonderful works of Barton. There were French and Germans who did not wish to go to their own Legations. There were Indians of every creed known to Abyssinia, Hindus, Sikhs, Muslims, Bohras, Parsees, and Goan Christians. All the revisionist powers were represented, bar Italy. Here a Turk prowled, there a Jamaican. Latvia was not forgotten.

Everyone who arrived was registered and given a coloured ticket for their camping area in the big paddock. All firearms were taken away and locked in the guard room; automatic pistols and pouches of ammunition were found in the voluminous skirts of the Greek clergy.

Robert J. 'Wordy' Stordy, an eloquent and elderly Scottish vet who had come out to Ethiopia for the RSPCA, was in charge of the camp. He soon had 1,520 people in his refugee paddock, doled out careful rations of rice, flour, dhal, ghee, lentils, sugar and salt and, according to Steer, was never happier.

Steer and the three remaining journalists pooled themselves as British United Press and sent out joint messages through the Legation radio. The ten-strong British Red Cross unit had turned the Empress's Menelik Girls' School into a hospital, and the Red Cross trucks went out in pairs, with two men in each, to rescue Europeans and to care for all other wounded. On the wrecked streets, however, drink was inflaming hatred of foreigners. Dr Empey of the Red Cross was bending over a wounded man in the gutter when a drunken Ethiopian thrust a gun barrel into his ribs, grunting *'Ferenj'* (foreigner). He was fumbling for the trigger as he was knocked away by other Ethiopians. 'You fool, you bastard! *Chay Maskal*, Red Cross!'

Another Red Cross representative, the tall, grey-haired sportsman Frank De Halpert, who was in his sixties, seemed to Steer 'the coolest of the Europeans who patrolled Addis, at frightening risk, trying to see whether the people lying in the street were dead, drunk, or *bona fide* wounded . . . Dressed precisely as a member of the IRA, with long grey overcoat, sinister grey Homburg over one hawkish eye, and a pilfered British rifle slung across one shoulder, he never had to take a bead on any *shifta*. He only looked at them in a hostile manner and the criminal intention evaporated.'

Steer went out after lunch on Saturday with the military attaché Taylor, in John Melly's car, through streets 'sprinkled with dead'. An old, bearded Armenian lay in the roadway, shot in the head, his feet still tied from when he had been dragged out of his shop.

Steer and Taylor drove hooting up to Mohammed Ali's store, and were let in through the iron gate to the huge goods yard. Half a dozen dead 'streaked the cobbles' outside. Mohammed Ali's was a Muslim family trading business that had first come into Ethiopia from Bombay in Menelik's time. They had become important bankers, car dealers and high-class grocers. Their solid stone store (which still functions as the Arada Post Office) had all its windows smashed by bullets, but the canny shopkeepers had installed iron bars behind the shutters and now bags of bran and flour were packed behind them, with rifles poking out ready to repel more attacks. Steer and Taylor found the bearded British Consul, Hope-Gill, cheerily supervising the defence. Fresh gunfire broke out as they talked to him. Steer ducked; Taylor knocked out his pipe dottle irritably. The Arabs and Hindus living either side of Mohammed Ali's were keeping up a continuous fire from their balconies, trying to pick off the best-armed looters so that they could nip out and get their weapons. Soon it became a market: *shiftas* with excess guns and ammo offered to sell them for cash; Basra's, the store next door, eagerly bought light automatics.

Then Steer and Taylor went out in Melly's car to rescue Matthews the padre from the English church behind the Imperial Hotel. The fires were spreading, and the benzine at Paleologue's garage was beginning to catch light. Driving through drunken looters near the Makonnen Bridge they passed a stumbling, semi-hysterical, thin Greek woman with streaming reddish hair and a fur-collared coat, clutching three icons under her arm. They pulled her into the car, shaking, mad with fear. All she could say was: 'Smyrna, Smyrna.' Steer wrote: 'Poor wretch! It was her second massacre.' In September 1922, Turkish soldiers had razed the mainly Christian port of Smyrna, raping and robbing. They had killed 150,000 Greeks and Armenians while twenty-seven Allied warships looked on impassively.

The pharmacist L. J. Bunner was in the second of two British Red Cross rescue lorries when he saw rioters surround the vehicle in front. He drove his truck straight at the crowd, and jumped out to find Dr John Melly bleeding copiously through his jacket. The British Ambulance Service leader had stopped to treat a wounded man in the street outside Idot's when a drunk in khaki had walked up with a revolver and shot him point-blank through the right lung.

Bunner liked and admired his commanding officer. He remembered one night at Alomata when they were all exhausted and one final patient had been brought in with a bullet in his skull. The doctors had agreed he would die, but Melly had said he had a thousand-to-one chance if they operated at once. It had taken two and a half hours, but the man had lived.

Bunner wrote: 'Dr Melly was lying wounded on the running-board and although badly shot prevented us shooting at the blackguards in return, saying, "They're drunk. They don't know what they're doing. Don't cause more bloodshed than there is."' Melly the surgeon knew he was mortally wounded and insisted on being moved from the hospital to the Legation so that the other patients would get more attention. 'His last words to us before he was taken away were, "Don't stop the good work because of this."'

The benzine store at the Addis Ababa railway station went up in a roaring funnel of flame, scaring the camels being loaded with loot. By Sunday evening the centre of the town was burned out. Next it would be the turn of the hospitals and the legations. The Turks asked for help, and then the Americans. The US minister made an early-morning radio appeal for 'a few Sikhs and a Lewis gun'. An American warship in the Gulf picked up the message, and relayed it to Washington, DC, where it was transmitted to the Foreign Office by transatlantic telephone, cabled to Aden and then radioed to Sir Sidney Barton at the British Legation. Three lorry-loads of Sikhs were eventually sent out in the dark to rescue the women and children. Steer found himself sitting at the back of the rear lorry with an automatic in each delighted hand. The young Sikh who crouched at his side said, softly: 'We won't fire first, but won't we just shoot second.'

There were hyenas flitting along the roadside. Addis was a gaunt, empty shell, tangled with steaming rubbish and stifled with hot, hanging air. Smoke blotted out the stars. At a forced stop, Steer saw a heap beside the wheel. He jumped down into a sickening smell of stale wine, rotten corpses, unswept offal. The heap was a dead boy of about fourteen, beautiful, of pale-brown complexion, with once lively features and a purple gunshot wound in his forehead. In his hand was a blue *zabania*'s cap that he must have taken for fun.

11

On Monday, 4 May 1936, as Léon Blum savoured the anti-fascist Popular Front electoral victory in France, George Lowther Steer got married. He wondered what to wear. A khaki shirt and trousers and a pair of old boots were the best he could muster; but he noticed an Ethiopian at the Legation gate with some peculiar headgear, the DLV (*Deutsche Luft Verband*) cap that had once belonged to Ludwig Weber, Haile Selassie's pilot, so he took it from him to crown his wedding.

Steer drove to his abandoned house to see if there were any more respectable clothes *chez lui*. Fired with whisky, his servants had helped the rioters loot the place. The front steps were strewn with hay, two bullet holes were drilled through the glass, and it was bedlam inside. All his clothes and possessions had gone, except some broken boot-trees. The mud-tracked floor was littered with unopened copies of *The Times*. All the furniture had vanished, except the broken dining-room table and his ransacked desk. His loofah and sponge still floated in his Saturday morning bathwater, 'ineffective as the Mediterranean Fleet'. He got back to the Legation late for the marriage ceremony.

The bride wore three casually looped strings of pearls over her polka-dot blouse and long skirt. She had a trilby tilted dashingly over her right eye, and carried a bouquet of arum lilies and enormous Ethiopian daisies pinched from Lady Barton's flower beds. They stood on the sunny lawn outside the Residence, with Lolita de Pedroso y Sturdza as bridesmaid and Don Lee as best man. First Hope-Gill, the Consul, and then Matthews, the padre, joined them in civil and religious matrimony. (There was amusement in the congregation as 'all the worldly goods' of the looted couple were endowed.) The ceremony and the register-signing were punctuated with odd shots from all around the

Legation, which gave the Reuters story its headline in the *New York Times*: 'Reporters In Addis Ababa Wed To Tune Of Rifle Fire'. Then they drank champagne at the Bartons' and drove round the grounds in the pick-up, blowing on the hunting horn that belonged to the Legation's 'Plug-hole' paper-chase hunt. The other refugees in the Legation must have thought they were mad.

The afternoon was fuddled. Steer went by lorry to Mohammed Ali's to get food for the refugees and feed for the horses, and the place came under attack again while he was there. Steer remembered, vaguely, gripping the iron bars with one hand while emptying a revolver with the other at a lot of *shiftas* in the smoking marketplace across the road. When he grew tired of standing, he shot from a chair, white carnation in buttonhole. Steer is frank about his less sanitized instincts:

> I found that I was enjoying the idea of killing people. It was interesting to note in myself one of the normal processes of colonial warfare. The smell of bodies, the burning of houses, the breakdown of every social restriction was a part of it. You can't get away from it. Destruction and its physical attributes, putrefaction, arson, pillage, a demeanour of menace are things that attract one when they are really let loose.

The First Secretary Patrick Roberts was giving the newly-weds a cocktail party in his bungalow when about thirty *shiftas* attacked the Belgian Legation, which lay across a wooded gully from the British compound. The Commanding Officer, Major Charter, sent a platoon of Sikhs to clear them out. Steer had just walked into the drawing room when the British Vickers gun started loudly firing at the *shiftas*. 'The girls slipped in a supple manner which did them credit on to the floor.'

Volunteers manned sentry posts all round the British Legation after dusk. The rescued Turks drank all Lady Barton's coffee and fired hundreds of excited rounds at everything that moved. This was George and Margarita's wedding night.

12

On Tuesday, 5 May the riotous excitement was finished. The hung-over town was emptying to the west. More Italian planes appeared, heralding the Italian advance. Around four in the afternoon Steer and his companions stood about the Legation gates, waiting. Down the road from Dessye came the roar of Italian engines, the grinding of Italian tracks. As the noise grew louder, the Britishers drew out the folds of the limp Union Jack and Steer slung his Thompson sub-machine gun across his shoulder and folded his arms grumpily, trying to hide his sense of humiliation under haughty *froideur*. Behind them, the refugees were beginning to cheer, and across the road expedient Ethiopian arms were going up in the Fascist salute. The noise was overwhelming.

All night the Italians came in, past the British Legation, 1,600 lorries with thousands of Italian troops, Eritrean askaris, a bus-load of new journalists. There was no booze or fags for them in the smouldering city. As the lorries rumbled in on Tuesday evening, John Melly died in a Legation bedroom, conscious and in pain till the end.

Naomi Mitchison wrote a thirty-eight-line poem, 'Dr A. J. M. Melly', which the *New Statesman* published on 16 May. It began:

> We are ashamed for Europe. You only escape.
> Because of you we may yet perhaps be forgiven
> By those with cause to hate Europe.
> The soldier, the destroyer, has power now;
> Europe raves hideously through his distorted mouth.
> The doctor, the healer, is murdered;
> Our Europe of kindness and decency is murdered with him.
> We are ashamed.

John Melly was posthumously awarded the Albert Medal in Gold, which his friends liked to think of as the civilian equivalent of the Victoria Cross. Though the House of Commons had done nothing, they rumbled 'Hear, hear' when Anthony Eden told them that Indian infantry had helped guard many lives. They waved order papers when he said members of the British community had rescued Europeans, regardless of nationality; and they rousingly cheered the name of Sir Sidney Barton, 'whose conduct of affairs throughout has been beyond all praise'.

The Italian authorities now instituted the death penalty for looting and/or possession of weapons. Eighty-five Ethiopians were formally tried and executed but the carabinieri shot 1,500 in groups of forty on the spot to encourage the others, according to the *New York Times*. Among them was the tallest man in Ethiopia, Belahu, who was seven feet five inches tall. He had killed a man in Jimma in 1934, but the Emperor had paid 1,000 thalers blood money to free him so he could be first his umbrella-carrier, then the drum major of the Imperial Band. Now Belahu was summarily shot for 'espionage and brigandage'.

They buried John Melly at 4 p.m. on Wednesday, 6 May. The Sikhs formed an honour-guard on the Legation steps and half a dozen more of them carried his coffin, draped in the Union flag. Barefoot hospital dressers in big overcoats carried a wreath made of a cross of red roses on a field of white lilies and Ethiopian daisies. The English community stood grim-faced in black brassards. From that day on, all Legation correspondence – On His Britannic Majesty's Service – would use black-bordered writing paper and envelopes. At the small cemetery an Indian bugler rang out 'The Last Post'. The missionary Alfred Buxton said that John Melly was a brave man and a good Christian. Then Sir Sidney Barton nodded, and another bugler blew 'Reveille'.

The Times tried to get Steer re-accredited as a journalist with the new authorities in Ethiopia. Ralph Deakin telephoned the Rome Correspondent on 7 May, and he messaged back that evening: 'We are in touch with the people here about Steer and they have promised to put the matter in hand at once.'

On Monday, 11 May Steer's turnover article 'The Ethiopian Tragedy, Final Phase in Addis Ababa' appeared in *The Times*. It was datelined 'Addis Ababa, May 8 (delayed)', but seems to have been written on 5 May.

On Wednesday, 13 May two Italian carabinieri and a pair of Eritrean askaris tried to get Steer out of the British Legation to go for a little drive. He refused. The Italians, apparently, were preparing a warrant for Steer's arrest on charges of transporting gas masks to Ethiopian troops and assisting in blowing up a road between Dessye and Addis Ababa. Steer said he had accompanied the gas-mask convoy in his capacity as a journalist, and that there was no evidence for the second charge. The warrant was never executed.

The same day in London, the Foreign Office contacted *The Times* with a message from Sir Sidney Barton: 'Mr G. L. Steer, *The Times* correspondent, is at present staying with me here, as his house has been gutted. He wishes the following message to be conveyed to *The Times*: *Am I to leave here for Jibuti by train on May 16? I have many articles.*'

The Times replied through the Foreign Office to Legation Addis: 'THINK
YOUR BEST PLAN WOULD BE TO RETURN TO LONDON'.

This reached Steer on Thursday, 14 May, not long before the official
Italian communiqué ordering him and his family to leave 'the
Viceroyalty of Ethiopia' on the Saturday train: '*Vi notifico che siete stato
espulso da tutto il territorio dei Vice-reame d'Etiopia. Voi e la vostra
famiglia davrete pertanto lasciare Addis Abeba il mattino di Sabato ven-
turo, Maggio 16, con il treno in partenza per Gibuti.*'

Steer rode in the last of his paper-chases with the Legation's 'Plug-hole'
hunt, jumping walls and galloping under eucalyptus. There would be
no more beer and gramophone records at the British Embassy after
such meetings: now it was time to sell Flick and his other ponies; it was
the end of the happy days. Margarita had a going-away khaki ensemble
made at the Lebanese couturier's by the station. All of their possessions
fitted into a small sack and a benzine box.

On Saturday, 16 May Steer sat on the steps of the railway coach with his
typewriter on his knee, typing out recommendations for his faithful
servants Bayenna and Igezu, and a letter authorizing Bayenna to keep his
remaining horse, saddle and tent, since the Italians might otherwise
shoot him for looting. Forty-five had been shot on Thursday night,
twenty-three on Saturday morning. These black men, Igezu and Bayenna,
had lost all their savings because they had been steady and true, and had
not pillaged like the other servants. He was full of gratitude to them, but
it was they who held his hand and kissed it. 'I could have cried,' Steer
wrote. The whistle blew, and the train pulled out, with all their friends
waving on the platform. George and Margarita put on a brave face,
pretending it was great fun being expelled, but in reality it felt terrible.

According to a Reuters telegram of 17 May, the expelled journalists
were all accused of 'anti-Italian propaganda and espionage'. (After this
information appeared in the *Daily Telegraph*, the British Secret
Intelligence Service, MI6, checked their cards to see if G. L. Steer was, in
fact, one of theirs. He was not.) When the Foreign Secretary was asked
in the House of Commons on 20 May how many British subjects had
been directed to leave by the Italians and why, Mr Eden replied only
one. 'This is Mr Steer, *The Times* correspondent in Addis Ababa, who
had already decided to leave, and who actually did so on May 16. The
official order directing Mr Steer to leave the country did not give any
reason for his expulsion.'

13

When their plane landed at London airport, Croydon, in the late afternoon of 2 June 1936, George Steer had been away from England for
almost a year. He was home in time to be among those meeting the
Emperor Haile Selassie when he arrived by special train at Waterloo
Station at 4.30 p.m. on Wednesday, 3 June.

After a fortnight in Jerusalem, the Lion of Judah had travelled on
HMS *Capetown* from Haifa to Gibraltar, from where the Orient pas-
senger liner *Orford* had taken the Imperial party to Southampton.
There was no question of a ceremonial reception, Mr Eden told the
House of Commons, as the Emperor's visit was private. In fact, the
government were declining to show full support. Thus, on the station
platform, *The Times* wrote, the monarch was 'greeted officially by Mr
O. C. Harvey, private secretary to Mr Eden, the Secretary of State for
Foreign Affairs. This is in accordance with the ordinary practice when
a Royal visitor comes to this country *Incognito*.' But the Abyssinia
Association delegation was there in strength, including the Labour
MPs Vyvyan Adams and Eleanor Rathbone, the scholar Margery
Perham, who had once lectured to Steer's Africa Society at Oxford, and
the suffragette and artist Sylvia Pankhurst, who had started her anti-
racist and anti-fascist newspaper *New Times and Ethiopia News* earlier
that year. The Emperor said he was touched by the welcome: 'We feel
that you share our sorrow, for Ethiopia is the victim of a war which was
forced upon her . . . the aggressor poured gases upon our children and
all our people, and so we are come to appeal, to ask for judgment from
Europe.'

The huge crowds waiting outside Waterloo Station carried banners
with messages like 'Welcome to the Emperor', and people shouted, 'Well
done, Abyssinia,' and 'Down with Fascism and war.' The congestion was
so great that Haile Selassie had to take a different route to get to the
Ethiopian Legation at Princes Gate, Kensington, where more cheering
crowds greeted his arrival. (On Saturday, 6 June Sir Oswald Mosley's
Blackshirts, the English fascist party, held a protest meeting in Hyde
Park against his presence.)

Back at *The Times*, Steer had to justify some hefty Ethiopian expenses: a
total of £1,165 since July 1935, with chits last sent in on 10 March 1936;
but he seems to have accounted satisfactorily for the remaining

£468/8/7d (around £15,000 in today's money), because *The Times* agreed to continue his salary for another month from 15 June.

This was also the day on which G. L. Steer signed a contract with the American publishers Little, Brown & Co. for a book on Abyssinia with a US$1,000 advance. His agent Curtis Brown also sold the book, *Caesar in Abyssinia*, to Hodder and Stoughton in the UK, who would eventually publish five of Steer's books.

Under the auspices of the Abyssinia Association, Steer also spoke to Members of Parliament at the House of Commons on the evening of 16 June. His talk, 'The Truth about Abyssinia', attracted such interest that they had to move to a larger committee room. The Emperor dined with them that night at the House of Commons.

Popular sympathy for the Emperor in England continued. His dignity and courage moved ordinary people, who turned out in thousands to see the 'frail but indomitable' figure, or hear Princess Tsehai's eloquent denunciations. Despite the tiny glow of pride in the British Ambulance Service, and their Legation's protection of foreigners, some British people felt ashamed of their own country's role over the last eighteen months. Didn't Britannia rule the waves any more? Couldn't Italian troopships and armaments have been blocked in the Suez Canal? Peace at any price was shaming to a martial nation. 'Is it really coming to this,' asked Lloyd George on 24 June, 'that Britain will not do its duty for fear of a black eye?'

The Derby by-election on 8 July 1936 seemed to prove the point. The government candidate argued it was common sense to abandon sanctions, but the Labour candidate, Olympic athlete Philip Noel-Baker, denounced 'the betrayal of the pledges made to Abyssinia'. Noel-Baker, who was to become a friend and ally of Steer's, overturned a 12,000 government majority and won by 2,753 votes.

14

Before retiring to exile at 'Fairfield', his house in Bath, the Emperor made an appeal to the world. On 30 June 1936 he addressed the League of Nations at Geneva. As the Emperor rose to speak, Italian journalists in the press gallery began whistling, booing and catcalling. Delegates stood up in protest, and the lights went out. '*A la porte les sauvages!*' said Nicolas Titulescu of Romania, and on the order of the Assembly President, Belgian Prime Minister Paul van Zeeland, the police removed the Italians. The jackals did not stop the Lion.

Haile Selassie threw down the gauntlet before the League of Nations. He came to ask for justice and help from those who had promised it. He accused the Italians of genocide. (While it is true that the actual word 'genocide' was not coined in English until the 1940s, Professor Edward Ullendorff points out that the Amharic words used by the Emperor – 'to extinguish methodically and by means of cruelty the entire stock of another people' – correspond exactly. Perhaps they should be cited as a first usage.) The Emperor told the international delegates how it had been done:

> A mechanism spraying yperite liquid was installed in the aircraft, and it was arranged that a fine rain bringing death should descend over vast tracts of country. At one time, nine, fifteen or eighteen Italian aeroplanes were going to and fro bringing down an unceasing rain of yperite . . . This death-dealing rain descended uninterruptedly upon our soldiers, upon women, children, cattle, streams, stagnant waters as well as pastures . . .
>
> Those who drank the water upon which this poisonous rain had settled or ate the food which the poison had touched died in dreadful agony . . . It was to make known to the civilized world the torment inflicted upon the Ethiopian people that I decided to come to Geneva.

The Emperor warned that international morality was at stake. Were small states all to be subject to powerful ones? What were the assembled fifty-two nations willing to do for Ethiopia?

As he walked from the podium, the Emperor uttered a prophecy: 'It is us today. It will be you tomorrow.'

THREE Torn Apart

1

It was the summer of the Nazi Olympics. The giant airship *Hindenburg* hovered above the stadium in Berlin, trailing a five-ringed flag over the swastika-hung streets. In the first days of August 1936, as the black American athlete James 'Jesse' Owens was breaking records and taking golds to the immense displeasure of the *übermensch* Adolf Hitler, George Steer was on his way to the Franco-Spanish frontier as a Special Correspondent for *The Times*.

The paper agreed to pay twelve pounds towards his travelling expenses and £2 2s. a day or fourteen guineas a week for a period of 'temporary service', which lasted until 14 September. In this period Steer caught the end of the first act of the Basque campaign in the Spanish Civil War, a long-brewing conflict that had exploded the month before.

On Sunday, 5 July 1936, as the Steers were settling into their newly married life in a mews flat in Chelsea, another journalist in nearby Kensington had been busy on the telephone. Luís Bolín, London Correspondent of the Madrid monarchist daily *ABC*, was taking urgent instructions from his newspaper's proprietor in Biarritz. At Croydon aerodrome the next day Bolín hired a seven-seater de Havilland Dragon Rapide for a trip that would change European history.

Luís Bolín, like Margarita Steer, was the child of a Spanish father and an English mother. His politics were completely to the right, however, and he was now engaged in a plot to overthrow the Republican government in Spain. At Simpson's in the Strand, Bolín had roped in his old collaborator Douglas Jerrold, the Catholic right-wing editor of the *English Review* and a director of the publishers Eyre and Spottiswoode,

to help provide a cover story for the flight. Jerrold had suggested enlist-
ing a right-wing adventurer called Major Hugh Pollard, who brought
two young blonde women along for the air trip.

The party flew to Morocco on Saturday, 11 July, and then on to the
Canary Islands. The English disembarked for a 'holiday', but the plane
collected a mystery passenger. He was a Spanish soldier nicknamed
'Miss Canary Islands 1936' for his girlish reluctance to get involved in
earlier military plots. This time, however, he had been galvanized by the
assassination of the rightist politician José Calvo Sotelo in Madrid.
'Miss Canary Islands' was General Francisco Franco, and he was flying
to Spanish Morocco to head the right-wing military uprising against
the left-wing Popular Front Republic. That day, 18 July 1936, the Spanish
Civil War began. General Franco asked if the little de Havilland plane
could bomb a Moorish *harka*, or irregular unit, near by, but Bolín pointed out that this was not in his contract with Olley Air Service, Croydon.

Bombing was one of the satisfactions of colonial warfare. Franco had
seen aircraft flying for the French and Spanish punishing Moroccan
resistance in the Rif Mountains in 1925. He wrote a note authorizing
Bolín to 'purchase aircraft and supplies for the Spanish non-Marxist
Army' in England, Germany or Italy. A footnote in pencil added: '12
bombers, 3 fighters, with bombs (and bombing equipment) of from 50
to 100 kilos. 1,000 50-kilo bombs and 100 more weighing about 500
kilos.'

Bolín went to Italy where the Fascist government agreed to supply
Franco with a dozen Savoia-Marchetti SM81 'Pipistrello', or 'Bat',
bomber-transports, which could each carry up to 3,000 kilograms. The
planes landed in Spanish Morocco on 30 July. Luís Bolín, who had
flown with them, was made an honorary captain in the Spanish Foreign
Legion, and went on to handle Nationalist media relations in Seville.

General Franco urgently needed more aircraft to ferry his Moors and
Legionaries across the Straits of Gibraltar to the Spanish mainland, and
he appealed to Adolf Hitler for help. Two Nazi businessmen resident in
Morocco flew to Germany on 24 July carrying a letter from Franco. They
found Hitler in Bayreuth, Bavaria, attending the annual Wagner festival.
On 25 July they met Hitler at the Wagner home, the Villa Wahnfried,
after the Führer returned from a stirring performance of *Siegfried*.
Hitler worked himself into a frenzy of anti-Bolshevik enthusiasm.
Summoning his Ministers of Aviation and War, Hermann Göring and
Werner von Blomberg, he told them that Franco was initially to have

twenty planes, as part of *Unternehmen Feuerzauber*, or Operation Magic Fire (a code-name that is pure Wagner). This led to thousands of German troops going to Spain, where they called themselves *Legion Condor*, the 'Condor Legion'. Göring became enthusiastic for the idea when he realized that Spain could be an excellent training ground for his new Luftwaffe.

The first Junkers Ju-52/3m aircraft arrived in Morocco on 29 July, the last on 11 August. They helped ferry 14,000 men, 44 pieces of artillery, 90 machine guns and 500 tons of ammunition and stores from North Africa to southern Spain, in the first major airlift of troops in military history. It was these Italian and German aircraft that rescued the fascist rebellion against the Spanish Republic.

Franco's African army waged war by terror. In their march north from Seville, they massacred prisoners, raped women, left mutilated corpses. Their attack on the fortress city of Badajoz on 14 August 1936 replicated the Duke of Wellington's on the same city in 1812: severe casualties in the initial assault, followed by slaughter and looting. The defeated were rounded up and taken to the Badajoz bullring. Anyone with a rifle recoil bruise on his shoulder was shot.

2

The Spanish Civil War was not one simple war of the Left (the Republicans/the Loyalists/the Government) against the Right (the Nationalists/the Insurgents/the Rebels). It was many wars, of peasants against landowners, workers against bosses, anti-clericalists against Catholics, regionalists against centralists, and so on. The Spanish Republic said it stood for 'Democracy against Fascism', and censored press references to the Soviet Union and the International Brigades. The Spanish Nationalist junta said it stood for 'Christianity against Communism', and lied about its links to Fascist Italy and Nazi Germany. Journalism, in a war where some atrocities were invented while other, real ones were suppressed, often became more propaganda than a search for truth. Everyone took sides.

George Steer's first experience of the fighting in the Spanish Civil War was a grandstand view of a spectator sport. From the Bakea Hotel at Biriatou, foreign journalists, drinks in hand, could look from the French side of the Pyrenean valley across the frontier to the Spanish slopes where Franco's professional troops were pushing back the untrained Republican militias. At 11 p.m. on the night of Friday, 28 August, Steer watched a fire-fight.

> It raged for four hours. A night battle in forest is a magnificent sight to see. The unpleasant details of war are sponged away by night. No tired men, no wounded in sweat, no dead lying heavy on the dry uncomfortable grass. You are saved the view of the broken ammunition cases, the discarded tins and piled filth of the temporary camp. Quickly trowelled trenches do not gash the fern-banks and the roads and fields are not pitted with ugly irregular shell-holes under a pall of dust . . .
>
> It is ethereal, war by night . . . At the centre of Zubelzu, where a sable dome of hill cuts the light and starry night sky, tinsel sparkles back. Between, mortars discharge like red reflecting ornaments and their shells explode like candles lighting yellow. Tinsel, hangings, candles, glitter, the dark background: what is this but a giant Christmas tree . . .?
>
> Charming illusion to me, who sits wrapped in pyjamas and an infant wonder, gazing across the river . . . No killing and maiming, thirst, hunger and pain to be picked out through curious field-glasses. Only the prettiness of war, under the moon and against the sober foil of mountain and pinewood.

That weekend, Franco's aeroplanes began dropping leaflets saying the border town Irun would be bombarded unless it surrendered. 'The effect of this propaganda was astonishing,' Steer noted. Thousands of men, women and children began fleeing from north-west Spain across the border into France. Irun was bombed on the Tuesday and was about to fall to the Nationalist troops on the night of Thursday, 4 September 1936 when the last-ditch Anarchists went into action, blasting and burning the centre of Irun with dynamite and petrol. It was a perfect propaganda gift to the Nationalists. For the rest of the war, Franco's forces could blame the ashes of the Republican towns they bombed and devastated on the self-destructive behaviour of the Left.

3

George Steer's arrangement with *The Times* was ended at his own request in September 1936 to enable him to finish his first book, and

Caesar in Abyssinia was completed in Nationalist Spain. Its introduction is datelined 'Burgos, 1936'. This grey, conservative city, birthplace of El Cid, was the Spanish army's Divisional Headquarters in the North, and Nationalists held the place for Franco on the second day of his rebellion. ('The very stones are nationalist here,' said the Countess of Vallellano.) From 24 July 1936 Burgos was the capital seat of the *Junta de Defensa Nacional*, Directorate of National Defence, the group who elected Franco as *Generalísimo* in September 1936.

Steer's experience of the panic-stricken stampede at Irun adds an urgent emphasis to the last section of his introduction to *Caesar in Abyssinia*, which quotes the Italian propaganda pamphlets dropped on Addis Ababa, threatening that, if the Ethiopians resisted, 'then the Italian Army will destroy and kill without pity, the aeroplanes will massacre from the air and destroy everything that exists'. Steer thought this pamphlet started the breakdown of social cohesion that ended in the sack of Addis Ababa. The same demoralization could happen in a European city. 'War against the civilian population breaks it up into its warring parts,' he wrote, in a warning to 'our leaders'. 'Ethiopia is nearer to Europe than they think.'

It is very possible that Margarita Steer accompanied her husband on some of his travels around northern Spain in September and October 1936. She spoke the language and doubtless had relatives or friends there. The couple had money (Margarita was not poor; Steer had his book advance and his father had just become Chairman of the *Daily Dispatch*) and they had time to be together. Certainly, in October 1936, alone or not, G. L. Steer drove through Old Castile, the heart of Franco's territory, where he found that 'the punitive revolvers of the Guardia Civil and the military courts' were punishing Republican sympathizers in the small villages. In Venta de Baños he found there were 123 dead, and in Dueñas 105, some of them women. These small places are about 100 miles from what Steer called the 'smoky cafés of Salamanca', the old university city that became Franco's headquarters from October 1936.

Salamanca was the site of a Spanish debate that crystallized history. It happened on 12 October 1936, called *Día de la Raza*, Day of the (Spanish) Race, after the date when Columbus first sighted the New World in 1492. The sermon in the cathedral explicitly linked Generalísimo Franco (who was not present) to 'a united, great and imperial Spain'. A secular celebration followed in the Great Hall of the university. On the dais were General Franco's wife, Doña Carmen, the Bishop of Salamanca, Enrique Plá y Deniel, who had been calling Franco's uprising a 'crusade', and the new head of Franco's Office of Press and Propaganda, General José Millán Astray, founder of the Spanish Foreign Legion, who had lost his left arm and his right eye in the Moroccan wars. The man who took the chair in place of Franco was the seventy-two-year-old Rector of the university, the philosopher, essayist, novelist, poet and playwright Miguel de Unamuno, one of the great figures of the famous 'Generation of '98' who revitalized Spanish intellectual life after the country lost its colonies in Cuba, Puerto Rico and the Philippines to the Americans. Unamuno was a Basque.

A series of speeches was made, justifying the Nationalist rebellion, ranting about the true Spain of the eternal verities versus the false Spain of the Reds, the Catalans and the Basques. Millán Astray barked that fascism was the surgeon that would cut out these cancers. He had come with his usual escort of armed Legionaries, and one of these bellowed the Legion's slogan '¡Viva la muerte!' (Long live death!), inducing a Pavlovian response in the black-eyepatched Millán Astray. '¡España!' (Spain!) he roared three times, with the response '¡Una!' '¡Grande!' '¡Libre!' (United! Great! Free!) echoing from the audience, some of whom sprang up with the right-arm, palm-out Fascist salute.

Miguel de Unamuno, a quixotic, thin man with a grey pointed beard, rose to conclude the event. He had not intended to speak, but the life of the mind demanded it. 'Let us waive the personal affront implied in the sudden outburst of vituperation against Basques and Catalans,' Unamuno began. 'I was myself, of course, born in Bilbao. The bishop, whether he likes it or not, is a Catalan from Barcelona. He teaches you a Christian doctrine that you do not want to learn. And I, who am a Basque, have spent my life teaching you the Spanish language, which you do not know.

'I have just heard the senseless and necrophiliac cry of "¡Viva la muerte!" To me this is the same as crying "Death to Life!" I have spent my life creating paradoxes that annoyed those who did not understand them. But I have to tell you, as an authority on the subject, that this outlandish paradox seems repellent to me. I take it that it was directed to the last speaker, in testimony to the fact that he himself is a symbol of death . . . General Millán Astray is a cripple. It is nothing to be ashamed of. Cervantes was a war invalid too. But extremes cannot be taken as the norm. Unfortunately, there are too many cripples today. And soon there will be more, if God does not help us. It pains me to think that General Millán Astray should dictate the pattern of mass psychology. A cripple who lacks the spiritual greatness of a Cervantes (who was a complete man despite his mutilations) is often made to feel better by seeing the number of cripples around him grow. General Millán Astray would like to create a new Spain in his own image, a negative creation, a mutilated Spain.'

Apoplectic with fury, Millán Astray screamed: '¡*Muera la inteligencia*!' (Death to intelligence!). The right-wing poet José María Pemán shouted: '*No. ¡Viva la inteligencia! ¡Mueran los intelectuales malos!*' (Long live intelligence! Death to bad intellectuals!).

Unamuno managed to conclude: 'This is the temple of intelligence. I am its high priest, and you are profaning its sacred precincts. I have always been, no matter what the proverb says, a prophet in my own country. You will win [*venceréis*] but you will not convince [*pero no convenceréis*] . . . It seems to me useless to beg you to think of Spain.'

The Basque philosopher managed to leave the hall safely only because Doña Carmen Franco gallantly took his arm, amid boos, jeers and gun-pointing. Demoted and isolated, Miguel de Unamuno died two months later, in December 1936.

4

In November 1936, before the Francoists expelled him, Steer was seen by two British witnesses in Nationalist-held Toledo. One was Peter Kemp, a young English right-winger who fought for Franco's side, first with the Carlists and then in the Spanish Foreign Legion. He arrived in rainy Toledo, El Greco's old town, on 18 November 1936. The famous Alcázar fort stank of ordure and decay, and the city was full of Nationalist troops: regular army, Moorish soldiers in thin khaki with blue capes over red fezzes, Requeté and Falange. Among the journalists Kemp saw George Steer.

A temporary correspondent of *The Times* called William F. Stirling confirms this. Stirling was a young university lecturer hired by Ralph Deakin because he was fluent in Spanish. Sent to cover Franco's HQ at Salamanca, his first letter ascribed his reporting difficulties to 'an objectionable man called Bolín (½ English ½ Spanish) who suffers from acute anglophobia with *Times* complications'. On 18 November 1936 Stirling wrote to Deakin that the Francoist authorities 'resent Steer's arrival, for they consider him a "dangerous" person in view of his record in Abyssinia . . . and his articles on Spain. Steer is at present in Toledo and sometimes helps me when there is an extra amount to do. It is clear that the authorities are out for someone's blood.'

Stirling's letter also paints a bleak picture of the 'indescribably foul' town:

> Executions still take place every day . . . there are two a day, morning and evening at Toledo, but I don't know how many shot each time. There seems to be no sanitary corps to remove the filth and refuse of a battle . . . Even on battlefields, the bodies are sometimes left, sometimes burnt, some unburnt for more than a week after the army has advanced . . . The Moors commit few atrocities but pillage and plunder with complete freedom . . . The most objectionable people are the Fascists – Falange Española.

Steer thought the Falangists were no good as fighters. Some Germans told him that they had captured Pozuelo three times and three times the Falangists had lost it. The Requetés were better, seeing war rather as a sport. Steer had himself seen 500 German infantry at Salamanca, and estimated the total number of Germans in Spain in late 1936–early 1937 to be 13,000–14,000 men. (He said this in an interview with Lieutenant Colonel Arnold of MI3 in London on Thursday, 4 February 1937.)

In his second volume of autobiography, *The Thorns of Memory* (1990), Peter Kemp explains why he thought Steer was expelled from Franco's Spain.

> George Steer [was] a truly adventurous man of great initiative and charm, but a natural rebel whose utter contempt for authority and the pomposity that too often went with it was bound to land him in trouble. His perversity, inflamed by understandable fury at Spanish plumbing, was soon to lead to his expulsion by the Nationalists.

It seems that the military at last decided to listen to the journalists' pleas and arranged for them a conducted tour of the front, starting at 8.30 one morning from Toledo. All the journalists – British, American, French, Italian, German and even some Latin Americans – were assembled in the square outside the hotel, ready to leave on time. Only Steer was missing. After waiting more than half an hour in a jitter of impatience, the officers and newsmen were on the point of leaving without him when Steer appeared on the hotel steps, his expression grim, his face suffused with rage. He addressed the assembly, speaking slowly, loud and clear.

'You pull, you pull, and nothing happens. You pull again, and the shit slowly rises. There's Spain for you,' he roared, 'in a nutshell!'

In a post-war memoir, Bernard Steer suggested that his son was expelled because General Franco's staff had cross-checked Steer's name with Italian Military Intelligence. Steer himself believed that the newly published *Caesar in Abyssinia* made him unpopular with the Italians. The Spanish Nationalists were certainly keen to control the press after the *Chicago Tribune* had electrified the world with the story, on 30 August, that Franco's troops had slaughtered 4,000 Republicans in Badajoz.

Luís Bolín recommended that all journalists be vetted and escorted. Bolín had been a war correspondent with the British in the First World War and now imposed similar harsh restrictions in the press office he ran. 'It took time to sift credentials,' Bolín wrote; in fact he weeded out the critical journalists and encouraged the compliant ones. 'Captain' Luís Bolín was a bully who wore a revolver on a Sam Browne belt. Noel Monks of the *Daily Express* noticed his cruel streak. 'Whenever we saw a pathetic pile of freshly executed "Reds", their hands tied behind their backs . . . he used to spit on them and say "Vermin".'

Nationalist Spain was not the place G. L. Steer wanted to be. He needed another Ethiopia, with freedom of movement, access to the top, and a cause to believe in. It was time to find out more about the embattled Basque Republic on the north coast of Spain, then under siege by Franco's forces on land, at sea and in the air.

5

The Basques are an old, stubborn people ('the queerest and staunchest of Spain's minorities', says Jan Morris) with the highest frequency of the rhesus negative blood group gene in the world. The cluster of eight dialects that makes up their language, Euskera, is very old, pre-Indo-European. It might even be Cro-Magnon. They seem always to have lived in the same heart-shaped place, Euskal Herria, smaller than New Hampshire, in the green elbow of the Bay of Biscay. They were there before there was a France or a Spain, and to this day insist they are neither French nor Spanish. They saw the Romans and the Visigoths and the Arabs come and go, and fought them off when they had to. Basque arrows slew Charlemagne's Frankish army at Roncesvalles in 778. The first sea captain to sail around the world, in 1519–22, was a Basque called Elkano from Getaria. In his book *The Basque History of the World* (1999), Mark Kurlansky points out how Basques were 'the explorers who connected Europe to North America, South America, Africa and Asia. At the dawn of capitalism they were among the first capitalists ... Early in the industrial revolution they became leading industrialists: shipbuilders, steelmakers, and manufacturers.'

In his second book, *The Tree of Gernika* (1938), Steer adds that 'the Basque' was always a democrat.

> *Unlike every other western European people, he has never passed through the feudal stage.* He has always owned his land, and he has never known a landless class, either slave or villein. He has always been a member of a full democracy, in which every man has voted ... so fixed is the Basque in his land, that his surnames still mean Hillside, and Warm Valley, and Appletree, and New Plum, and Rock and Fast River.

Basques invented the vigorous game pelota (whose nineteenth-century name *jai alai* means 'happy game') and Steer remarked they were the only people in Iberia who had the conception of linking leisure with exercise. 'The Basques are industrious, and the Spanish are idle. The Basques are all yeomen, and the Spanish would all be gentlemen.'

These racial generalizations appear in the introduction to *The Tree of Gernika*. When George Orwell reviewed it for *Time and Tide*, in February 1938, he commented: 'Mr Steer writes entirely from the Basque standpoint, and he has, very strongly, the curious English characteristic of being unable to praise one race without damning another. Being pro-Basque, he finds it necessary to be anti-Spanish, i.e. to some extent anti-Government as well as anti-Franco.'

Orwell began his review: 'It goes without saying that everyone who writes of the Spanish war writes as a partisan.' The Etonian George Orwell and the Wykehamist George Steer carried different sets of prejudices. Steer found his decency among the Basque Nationalists; Orwell found his among the *groupuscules* of the non-Stalinist Left. Younger historians in the Basque Country today echo some of Orwell's criticisms: they say Steer identifies too closely with Basque nationalism and its myths and is unfair to the non-Basque Loyalist left-wing soldiers, who suffered more casualties.

Paul Preston has pointed out there was a third Spain, between right-wing extremists and left-wing fanatics. In his book *¡Comrades!*, Preston portrays intelligent men such as Indalecio Prieto, Manuel Azaña, Julian Besteiro and Salvador de Madariaga trying to deal decently with a nightmare. (He might have included the Basque President José Antonio de Aguirre y Lekube in that cast.)

Steer characterized the position of the moderate Basque nationalists, too, as being caught in the middle. 'The Spanish attack on the Basques came in the guise of military Fascism from without, and proletarian pressure from within.' Steer saw that the Basques wanted to be free, left alone, not regimented either way. '[T]he Basque fought for tolerance and free discussion, gentleness and equality.'

Their leader, José Antonio Aguirre, expressed the peculiar Basque National Party position in an address to the Spanish Parliament in 1931:

> If being on the right means defending any kind of regime, as long
> as it is identified with religion . . . then we are leftists. And if by
> being rightist, it is understood that . . . we oppose progress for the
> working class . . . then we are leftists. But, on the other hand, if to be
> a leftist means to be against family, against the holy principles of the
> Catholic Church, whose rules we observe, then . . . we are right-
> wingers.

6

Steer first arrived in Bilbao on a neutral British ship in January 1937. The Royal Navy destroyer lay just outside the five-mile limit, slowly dipping and climbing as the Atlantic swell rolled in to the abrupt Basque coastline. Over the rail Steer saw a hard, brown headland and green pyramidal peaks, with blue and grey mountains behind, blurred with drizzle. A big speedboat came foaming up alongside, and Basque sailors in blue berets helped down the few passengers and luggage. Steer shook hands with a big-nosed man called Joaquim Eguía, dubbed the 'First Lord of the Basque Admiralty' by the British Consul in Bilbao. As the 500-horsepower engines surged, the Basque flag, or *ikurriña*, at the stern unfurled and straightened. It was an attractive emblem, Steer thought, the same design as the British Union Jack, but with different colours and layers, an apple-green saltire with a white cross on a scarlet ground.

The flag was invented in 1895 by the founder of Basque nationalism, Sabino de Arana y Goiri, to symbolize Basque identity: red background for shared blood, green St Andrew's cross for the oak tree of Gernika, and a straight white cross for their Roman Catholic faith. Sabino Arana's original political vision for Basquedom was a theocracy – politics ruled by religion – but his was also an ethnic nationalism. Not untypical of his time, Sabino Arana was a racist and anti-Semite who mythicized his own people. As part of the 'invention of tradition' so inseparable from nationalist projects, he wanted to purify the language, trying to weld a common tongue from eight Basque dialects by forging new words. Arana coined a name for his new nation by simplifying the old geographical name *Euskal Herria* (Basque Country). His amateurish and incorrect philology led him to believe that the name for the language *euskera* was derived from the Basque word for the sun, *eguzki*, so he started seeding zeds into his re-ploughed language. Thus *euskera* (Basque language) became *euzkera*, *euskaldun* (Basque-speaker) *euzkaldun*, and the usual combining form *euskal* became *euzko*, to link it to *eguzkiko*, 'of the sun'. From dubious linguistic logic, Sabino came up with the name of his political nation-to-be: *Euzkadi* (still current, but nowadays spelled *Euskadi*).

On 1 October 1936, José Antonio de Aguirre had spoken eloquently to the hundred remaining deputies of Republican Spain at the Cortes in Valencia. He had said the Spanish Civil War was a war between democracy and fascism, but condemned the left-wing burning of churches and the killing of people for their opinions, ending, 'Until Fascism is defeated, Basque nationalism will remain at its post.'

Euzkadi was barely three months old when Steer arrived. On 5 October, in return for Basque loyalty to the Republic, the Republican government passed the Autonomy Law giving full powers over Euzkadi, for the duration of the Civil War, to a Basque provisional government. Two days later Basque municipal councillors met in Gernika to elect the leaders of that Basque government.

Gernika is a special place, 'the historic centre of Basque liberties', as Steer put it. 'The representatives of the towns and parishes of Vizcaya have met there since time immemorial, under the oak, which is sown again as soon as it dies.' Since the beginning of Basque written history, as Steer understood it, the Juntas de Gernika had met for a fortnight or more every two years. The representatives were elected by every man old enough to vote in every country parish. There was no upper chamber, and no class distinction. Every Basque was an aristocrat, and his *nobleza* was recognized also in the rest of Spain.

Basque special rights and privileges were embodied in municipal charters called *foruak* in Basque and *fueros* in Spanish, derived from Latin *forum*, the public square of municipal business. In the early Middle Ages these charters gave the Basques much local autonomy: lower taxes, avoidance of military conscription, freedom from rapacious nobility. The Spanish King of Castile swore to recognize these rights under the oak tree at Gernika and received in return the title Señor de Vizcaya (Lord of Biscay). The coat of arms of Vizcaya/Bizkaia shows the oak tree, and the famous song 'Gernikako Arbola' (Tree of Gernika), written in 1853, is a nationalist anthem. One of Sabino de Arana y Goiri's first symbolic actions in August 1894, the year before he founded the first Basque Nationalist Centre, was to burn a Spanish flag in front of the tree of Gernika.

So it was with some emotion that on 7 October 1936 the Basque councillors secretly gathered in the Basque Parliament, the Casa de Juntas, in Gernika and unanimously elected José Antonio Aguirre as the first President of an autonomous Basque Country. The delegates trooped outside and stood under the oak tree. A few leaves fell in the autumn sunlight as Aguirre took the oath in Basque: 'Before God, in all humility, standing upon Basque earth, under the tree of Gernika, remembering our ancestors, in front of you representatives of the people, I swear to carry out my duties faithfully.'

One of the first things the new government did was to scrap the existing security forces and set up a new Basque police force called the *Ertzana*, or People's Guard, under the Interior Minister, the young aristocrat Telesforo de Monzón. The 500 members of the foot section wore silver-badged berets and long blue greatcoats, and were trained to use rifles, machine guns and tear gas. The 400 men in the motorized section had fast cars and motorcycles, linked by wireless. They wore brown leather coats, knee breeches, uniform caps and high boots, and had revolvers on Sam Browne belts. Two of them became Steer's drivers-cum-bodyguards.

7

In January 1937, Steer was one of the first professional reporters into Bilbao, the capital of the besieged Basque Republic. Looking from the speedboat bringing him across the turbulent ocean, at first Steer could see farms and pastures, cows grazing on sharply angled fields, a vision of bucolic Basquedom. Then the helmsman turned the wheel, and the River Nervion opened up an utterly different landscape, in a narrow valley running between two lines of hills: 'an industrial ribbon packed with tall black chimneys, gasometers, foundries like giant dark pill-boxes, grimed steel stairs and bridges, clattering trains, soot, crumble-faced slums. Iron-ore tilts . . . steep brown peaks of mine-waste . . . [d]ozens of cranes . . . Shipping, Transatlantic and Continental, lay anchored side to side in rusty black as far as the eye could reach. Trawlers . . . in phalanxes of a hundred.'

Oak, cod and iron were the basis of Basque wealth. Basque cod fish-ermen had sailed to Newfoundland and back. Basques built and manned the Spanish Armada of 1588, a fleet made with oak off their own hills; hills made of iron. Bilbao forged pikes and anchors and gave its Basque name, Bilbo, to the English language with the well-tempered, flexible 'bilbo' swords of Shakespeare's day and the sliding-shackle leg irons known as 'bilboes'. Later they made muskets and cannon barrels. Bilbao's low-phosphorous iron was ideal for Bessemer's new steel-making process, and by 1910 almost a third of Spain's banking investment was in Basque iron and steel, chemicals, cement, paper and hydro-electricity. By 1930 Bilbao controlled 71 per cent of Spain's shipbuilding; a third of all savings and nearly half all bank deposits were in the Basque Country.

Now, though, as Steer sped up the nine miles of the Nervion, the industrial powerhouse was close to starving. Shabby clothes and gaunt faces among Bilbao's population of 300,000, swelled by 100,000 refugees from San Sebastian, showed the Nationalist blockade was pinching hard. Franco's warships patrolled the estuary mouth, and France and England were interpreting non-intervention zealously. Bread and milk had run out. Meat was rare: people were eating cats and seagulls. Rice, chickpeas and oil were meanly rationed. Over forty years later, one woman said her worst memory of the war was early in 1937 when, aged eight, she had accidentally dropped a half-litre bottle and seen her family's ten days' worth of olive oil smash and drain away on the cobbles of the Old Town.

Seagulls were mewing and planing through the misty late-afternoon drizzle when Steer's speedboat tied up by the eighteenth-century

St Nicholas' Church, where men doffed their berets and women put on black veils as they entered. Steer was invited to a bar for a *kopa*. It was not smoky, for there were few cigarettes; no beer, but ersatz whisky; no change, because coins were being smelted for war.

At the nearby Hotel Torrontegui, once the leading hotel of Bilbao, there was hot water only twice a week because coal was running short. Steer dined in silence in the top-floor restaurant on lentil and chickpea mash, fish and horse meat. As he made his way to an early bed down the corridor, he noticed many of the rooms had trays outside. Later, the air-raid siren tumbled out the inhabitants of these caves, 'many pale ladies and old gentlemen with distinguished sallow faces', the frightened bourgeoisie hiding in their rooms, afraid of the mob.

There had not been a social revolution in Bilbao. The Basques, with sensible hard-headedness, had tried to put a stop to the destruction of property and political murders (a maximum of 800 people and 50 priests were killed by leftists in the Basque Country). 'The only thing I am afraid of is fear,' said the Duke of Wellington once, talking about cholera; but in the six days he spent in Bilbao in January 1937 Steer would find out that not only epidemic disease could cause panic.

On his first morning Steer went along to the Carlton Hotel, which had become the Basque government HQ. The young chief of the Department of Foreign Affairs, a construction engineer called Bruno Mendigurren, took him in to see the President. José Antonio de Aguirre rose from his desk and came forward with his hand outstretched. Short and stocky, he still walked with the chesty swagger of the famous footballer he had once been, inside-right for Atletico Bilbao. The fineness and delicacy of his features struck Steer, and the humorous eyes under straight black brows. Steer saw Aguirre as essentially a conciliator.

Aguirre said he would fight on the side of the Republic till the finish because they had given their word. If they fought for the Republican government and won, he told the South African Englishman, they could negotiate for something like Dominion status. If, on the other hand, they fought for Franco, or lost to Franco, it would amount to the same thing: defeat of Basque hopes, and loss of Basque rights. Aguirre also talked about exchange of prisoners: he would give 2,300 Francoists to get 1,000 Basques back, but the insurgents would not play ball. Marcel Junod confirmed that the Basques always kept their word to the International Red Cross, but Franco's side did not. Aguirre's humanitarianism and openness impressed Steer. The President invited him to ask the police about political murders, and to see if the Basques kept women prisoners. 'Ask at your hotel how many wretched members of the Right we have saved from Asturias and Santander.' (Steer found out later that Aguirre's own mother ran the Escaping Club, which helped bourgeois Basques get away.) 'Ask your consul how many we have permitted him to carry away to France, and how many of the people we have rescued are now working against us for the rebels.' Steer found Aguirre rather sporting: 'He was captain of a soccer team again, and even if they lost they were going to obey the whistle and the rules. No biting; no hacking; no tripping.'

8

The Tree of Gernika is subtitled *A Field Study of Modern War*, as if Steer were an ecologist of combat. George Orwell complained that it was 'not at all clear what he has seen with his own eyes', echoing Evelyn Waugh's criticism of Steer's first book, that 'he does not give any reference for the majority of the facts he records, facts which could not be known to him by personal observation'.

George Steer wrote *The Tree of Gernika* not just as a newspaper reporter, but much more like a historian (Macaulay said that history was a blend of poetry and philosophy) who evaluates and assimilates from many sources and witnesses in order to construct a narrative. 'My habit is to prowl around a subject long before I write about it, preferring microscopy to scoops,' Steer wrote in a later book. His technique is clear in chapter 8 of *The Tree of Gernika*, describing the massacre of prisoners on 4 January 1937. Steer was not in Bilbao then – he was not an eyewitness – but, given permission by Mendigurren to go anywhere and talk to anybody, like a good reporter/historian he managed to pull together the story of how the atrocity had happened.

It all began with a completely unexpected air raid. Nine Junkers 52 bombers, protected by twelve Heinkel 51 fighters flying top cover, appeared over Bilbao. Young Felipe del Rio, the star pilot of the Republican air force, flew his snubnosed Russian Polikarpov I.15 fighter plane straight at one Junkers 52, four guns blazing. (The German bomber had no forward guns, so this worked if you got out of the way in time.) Del Rio shot down the bomber and, as two silk parachutes blossomed over Bilbao, the other Junkers junked their bomb loads randomly and flew away.

Lieutenant Hermann of Berlin, aged twenty-four, parachuted down on to the road up to Pasagarri. An angry crowd pressed in on him. A Basque militiaman fired at the German, missed and killed a woman behind him. Hermann promptly shot the militiaman with his pistol. The crowd then kicked Hermann to death. Some of his paperwork was still legible enough afterwards to show who else was helping Franco. A receipt for 2,284 litres of fuel for his German plane was written in Italian.

The Junkers 52 radio operator, a twenty-one-year-old member of the Nazi Party called Karl Gustav Schmidt, was luckier. He parachuted down on the other side of the river at Enecuri, and one of the Soviet pilots, whose plane had been damaged, landed close by him. The country people raced to get the German, but the Russian held them off with his pistol, because the boy was more useful alive than dead.

At dusk the Communist brought the Nazi down in a closed car. They could see a crowd along the riverside and the red-and-black flag of the Anarchists waving over wild, shouting faces. The landless, penniless, homeless refugee population, frightened and enraged by the bombing, was heading for the Larrínaga prison and the two nearby convents, all holding Nationalist prisoners. The crowd wanted revenge.

The prison governors telephoned the Ministry of the Interior urgently asking for troops to quell the mob. The Basque Nationalists did not want to send one of their battalions, because if they had to fire on the crowd it might cause a civil war among the political parties. The Socialists agreed to send one of their battalions, thinking the UGT (Union General de Trabajadores) could be relied on to restore order.

However, the UGT soldiers had also been infected with bloodlust by the bombing. They went up to the Larrínaga prison gate and asked to be let in 'in the name of the Government'. About a hundred UGT troops reached the central hall. Dormitories off the ground floor held thirty Nationalist prisoners to a room, and then there were three storeys of cells above joined by wrought-iron galleries, dimly lit by electric light high up in the roof. The UGT started throwing grenades into the crowded cells and shooting at figures scattering in terror along the walkways in the dim yellow light. Sixty-one were killed in the Larrínaga, thirty-three more in the Casa de Galera annexe.

Another UGT detachment led the mob armed with sticks and knives into the Convent of Custodian Angels. Many of the political prisoners here were elderly, but the crowd shouted, 'You are the men who brought the Germans to kill our children. You have lived your lives, and are fitter to die.' They killed ninety-six there. Some of the bodies were mutilated, and the stairs and floors were slippery with blood.

At Carmelo Monastery only a few prisoners died, because six armed Basque guards with some Francoist officers jammed the wooden staircase with beds, mattresses and doors and pelted the UGT militia with bottles of water. A misthrown grenade bounced back to explode among the attackers and the Basques fired a volley over their heads. The mob and the militia fled just as the Basque motorized police came up the hill to the prison, led by the Minister of the Interior, Telesforo de Monzón. Steer wrote:

> [Monzón] was a brave man, and he went straight into the Normal Prison without an escort: the militia were still chasing people up and down the dirty iron stairs and openwork galleries of the Central Hall, and battering at resistant doors with rifle-butts . . .
>
> Monzón took an officer by the shoulder of his revolver arm, and said: 'If you do not clear your men at once from the prison, they will all be shot inside it.' The shooting ceased to a shouted order.

The mob blackened out into the winter night. Some militia vomited at the outer gate, where the street lamps gleamed on the tall figures of the Basque police with their hands on their guns. As sober dread sank in, the pale-faced UGT troops were marched back to their barracks and disarmed. Their officers were placed under arrest. Steer thought that the way the Basque government handled the atrocity was exemplary:

> At this time, it should be remembered, true stories of the killings in Madrid could only be smuggled out as uncensored articles by unknown correspondents: with Franco the situation was even worse. If a foreign newspaper dared to publish any statement about atrocities in his territory, its correspondent – whether responsible or not – was immediately expelled.
>
> For the Basques, the word conscience was possessed of dynamic meaning. They had, as best they might, to expiate the horrible crime committed by the air-maddened population of Bilbao. Though they were at war, they gave orders to the censor to let all truthful descriptions pass.

The Ministry of Justice and Culture printed the names of the 224 dead, with eight marked as *mutilizados* (mutilated). The foreign press and the radio were allowed to broadcast all the facts, families permitted funeral processions through the town, as church bells tolled for the dead. The leaders of the UGT battalion were tried, and six of them sentenced to death, though none was executed.

Why had it happened? Steer saw worse bombings in April without atrocities following. The difference was as plain as bread: there was no food in early January. 'That month the concentration of hunger and bombs was too much for everybody.' But there were no more massacres and murders in Bilbao after that. The police now ruled the streets, and energies could be concentrated on the war. Yet fear of the mob's hatred remained. This was why the right-wing bourgeoisie were hiding in their rooms at the Torrontegui Hotel, waiting to be escorted by the Basque police out to the British destroyers that would take them to safety in France.

9

Then George Steer received bad news. His heavily pregnant wife Margarita was dangerously ill, and he had to get back to London immediately. The Basque government put a minesweeping trawler at his disposal. With running lights out to slip the blockade it took thirteen hours of zigzagging through the Bay of Biscay to get to Bayonne.

A journey of darkness, cold and dread.

Erica Wright was sitting at her desk in London, in the offices of Faber and Faber, where she worked as secretary to Geoffrey Faber and T. S. Eliot, when the telephone rang. She had often visited her brother Armin and met his friends when he was an undergraduate at Christ Church, Oxford; and now, suddenly, on the phone, out of the blue, was a man she had not seen since those days at the beginning of the 1930s, someone she knew as 'Lowther' Steer. He was sobbing, agonizingly. She never forgot the emotional impact of that telephone call: 'I was just a silly virgin then. He was hysterical, completely distraught. It was his wife. He said that when her waters had broken, they didn't do anything, and she and the baby had died. I don't remember what I said, what I could say. I had never heard a man crying like that.'

The Times of Saturday, 30 January 1937 reported the news.

DEATH OF MRS STEER

Former War Correspondent in Addis Ababa

We regret to announce that Mrs Steer, wife of Mr G. L. Steer, Special Correspondent of *The Times* in Abyssinia during the Italo-Abyssinian war, died in childbirth in London last night.

Before her marriage, Mrs Steer was Mlle Marguerite de Herrero, Special Correspondent in Addis Ababa of the Paris newspaper *Le Journal*. While acting as correspondent in Abyssinia she met Mr Steer and they were married in Addis Ababa last year, to the accompaniment of the rifle shots of marauding bandits. Their honeymoon was spent behind the barbed wire defences of the British Legation Park in paying visits to the refugees camp.

Mrs Steer, who was born in Pau, was the child of a Spanish father and an English mother. Her early education was received in France, but later she completed it in England. Her love of adventure took her to Abyssinia just before the war broke out there. She remained in Addis Ababa throughout the dangerous times that followed and proved herself to be a journalist of marked ability and a brave and fearless woman.

Margarita Steer died in the London Clinic, a private hospital at 20 Devonshire Place, W1. According to the registration of her death in Marylebone the causes were '(a) Toxaemia of Pregnancy (b) Foetal death (c) Influenza'. She was thirty-seven years old, and though her mother Hope Hassett had been thirty-nine when she gave birth to Margarita, she was not Hope's first child. Margarita's was therefore a higher-risk pregnancy. Her waters broke, and they did not induce, nor perform a Caesarean section. Steer later asked the lawyer Jo Stephenson, a friend at Winchester and Oxford, whether he should sue for negligence, but was dissuaded. Margarita's body was embalmed, and the funeral postponed until Emma Steer arrived from South Africa.

On 5 February, the day after his interview with Lieutenant Colonel Arnold of MI3 at the War Office, Steer replied to condolences from the manager of *The Times*, striving, with some pathos, to put a martial gloss on his private grief.

Dear Mr Lints Smith

Thank you indeed for your kind letter. I feel a lot the loss of my little fellow soldier. What a steady arm in a panic, what a pretty, fearless smile in a world of disorder. How cruel was the bullet that laid her in this muddy trench.

Yours

George Steer

The Tree of Gernika is dedicated TO MARGARITA, SNATCHED AWAY.

10

There was more bad news, this time from Ethiopia. The event that became known in Ethiopian history as Yekatit 12 began at the Little Gibbi on Friday, 19 February 1937. To celebrate the birth of a son to the King of Italy, Viceroy Rodolfo Graziani was to distribute two Maria Theresa dollars each to several thousand poor people from the front steps of Haile Selassie's former palace. Two Eritrean interpreters, who had been denied entrance to the cinema because the Fascists had introduced a colour bar, decided to assassinate Graziani there. They threw between six and twelve hand grenades, before escaping in the chaos. Graziani later said: 'Some "young Ethiopians" at the instigation of the British Intelligence Service ... hurled at least 18 bombs at me ... It did not, however, make me swerve by one millimetre. The attempt failed completely because repressive measures were taken with extreme promptitude and prevented a rising of the native population of Addis Ababa.'

A film cameraman rushed the bleeding Viceroy to hospital in his car. General Liotta, Commander of the Air Force, lost his right eye and right leg. The Italians went mad. In the smoking, screaming aftershock, the Federal Secretary, Guido Cortese, started emptying his pistol at the Ethiopian dignitaries around him. The carabinieri took their cue from him and opened fire on the beggars, the blind, halt, lame and old, the women and children who had come for alms. Cortese then went straight to Fascist HQ in Addis Ababa and told the assembled Blackshirts, 'For three days I give you *carta bianca* to destroy and kill and do what you want to the Ethiopians.'

A weekend of atrocities followed. All the fear and resentment in the Italian colonists' psyche came boiling out. Italian Blackshirts and civilians started clubbing, stabbing, shooting and burning Ethiopian men, women and children wherever they found them, and photo-

graphing the results. Nobody knows exactly how many died that weekend. Italians say 300; Ethiopians say 30,000.

Young educated Ethiopians, including Benjamin and Joseph Martin,
sons of the Ethiopian Minister to London, were photographed by the
portico pillars of the Little Gibbi, close to where the grenades had gone
off, before they were shot or hanged. All 297 monks and 129 deacons at
the monastery of Debra Libanos were executed by firing squad. Six
thousand Ethiopians were sent to camps in Somaliland, where more
than half died. In May, in the Debra Brehan sector, the Italians killed
2,491 'rebels' and torched 15,302 *tukuls*.

But Ras Abeba Aragai's Ethiopian patriot resistance army swelled by
10,000.

The *Spectator* of Friday, 12 March 1937 published Steer's elegy for the
dead. He had to come to terms with the massacre of young Ethiopia while
still in the acute stage of grief for his own dead wife and child. This
superb piece of writing is an *ubi sunt* lament that somehow enfolds the
dead body of his beloved Margarita into the wrecked city of his friends.

ADDIS ABABA – CIVILISED
G. L. STEER

In Addis Ababa there are 25,000 soldiers of Italy, Savoy Grenadiers,
Blackshirts and Eritrean Askaris. There are many aeroplanes at Akaki,
on the tawny plain outside: though the giant white bombers, the
three motored Savoia 81s, have rotted their lovely wings in the rains
of the plateau. So the Capronis have come into their own again, which
means that they drop corrosive gas on the unsubmitted population.
The little tanks which were such a failure in the Italo-Ethiopian war
are parked in dozens in Addis – little tanks, with linked machine-guns
to fire in a traverse of 15 degrees, enough to drill a man in two in one
short burst of logic and convince his widow for ever of the superiority
of the West. There are also 'buses in Addis now, separate 'buses for
Italians (whites) and Ethiopians (blacks): that is what I call *effortless*
superiority; it is so much easier to prove that the Italian is a nobler
creature if he travels in comfort alone. And the ruined streets are lit,
so that patrols shall not be shot at night.

Addis is a ruin still, the centre of Addis is still burnt to the
ground. But how curiously beautiful the greatest African city of the
East remains: what a strange bloom and sudden withering has

come to the New Flower of Menelik, through whose short span of
life Italian arms have hammered at her wild, garden gate. Addis
Ababa, founded with the disaster of Baratieri, burnt and looted
with the mechanical triumph of Badoglio. Like the cup of a flower,
she rises to her mountain rims – a disordered forest flower of the
tropics, she is splendid as a flag in her setting, quaint-speckled and
repellent in detail as the prosaic botanist dissects her. Go through
her. Here was the grocer's shop Ganotakis, built with thin stone
and gold letters, now a shell. Across the Central Square was the
wood-and-iron Post Office, a flimsy structure bound together by a
ramble of balconies and tied up with thousands of telegraph-wires,
now level with the ground. Facing the Post Office was Mon Cine,
where we saw Greta Garbo in an old but satisfying *Grand Hotel*,
and danced until the stars faded into their heavenly screen: then we
walked home past dark policemen muffled nose and ears in their
shammas against the dawn wind. All those houses are destroyed by
war. Tasfai Teguegne was at Mon Cine and Blatta Kidane Mariam,
and the British Legation and the Greek garage proprietors. The
young Ethiopians drank and laughed at the little chromium bar.
Now they have been murdered because they could speak French.
And we have gone.

Go through Addis and mark the towers thereof. Here was the Red
Cross, here the market, here the chemists, here the wineshops, here
the Syrian couturier, here the ramshackle hotels. All looted and
burnt. Nothing of it has been rebuilt. And the people? Under the
blue eucalyptus, which shales its dry skin and its scent from one
mountain to another, they have killed each other, they have been
shot by the Italians, they have fled to the hills, one and all they
hate the invading Frank. Thousands of them are dead, the lives of
thousands of families have been broken by the war.

Yet when I first came to Addis Ababa, it was a peaceful town.
There was a crowd of petitioners sitting quietly outside the Great
Palace, waiting for the Emperor's Justices. The market chaffered like
a swarm of brown bees, the Armenians hammered out their scarlet
leatherwork undisturbed on the hill of the Cathedral of St George.
The kites, wheeling tawdry in the sun's eye, picked no human bones.
The streets were full of talkative young men. A spray of African
dust, a sea of blue gums breaking softly on grey reefs: on the iron
sheeting of the Addis houses, on the pale grass roofs of the tukuls

which time had sombred into the colour of earth. In that forest
archipelago I could detect no burnt houses, no ruins of war. The
porters ran through the streets with meat on their heads. The young
Ethiopians took off their hats to talk as I rode past. Everybody was
friendly, the town was orderly, prosperous and happy: the huge
African population of Addis Ababa was healthy, for it had room to
spread and breathe the uncontaminated air. Ethiopia was still free,
and when the Emperor drove through the town the people
applauded him.

And think, if you can, of what Addis saw when the war-drum
beat for the defence of the empire under the red-yellow-green silk at
the Great Gibbi. Think of the tens of thousands who passed before
me on the long trek to the North; the grey-haired chiefs, rifles slung
across their backs, who sat the ambling mules while servants ran
shaking velvet flags behind; the riflemen who trotted along the
Dessie road in column of five, the pack-mules, the little serving-
boys, the women with the pots and gourds – till they were lost in
the mountain like the children whom the Pied Piper spirited away.
Think of the ochred tents in the plain, and the heaps of cactus and
russet forage before the cliff caves. Remember the bombs, the
sprayed yperite, the smoking circle of artillery and machine-guns
that burnt the blood out of the Ethiopians as they sat on their
mountains, defending their country and their women. Remember
the destruction of the Red Cross in the plains of the north and
along the sallow rivers of the south. Remember the revolutions, how
western money was used to turn Ethiopian against Ethiopian: the
villages in flames, the flies fat with man's putrefaction, the paths
stagnant with corpses, the caravans scattered and destroyed.
Remember the tens of thousands that died in battle and bombings
and the bitter retreat: these fell, remember, that civilisation should
prevail.

Civilisation! Last week I was going through some old papers of my
wife, and I found the declaration of Count Ciano at the League
Assembly in June, 1936. The famous Crazy Week at Geneva, you
remember, when the Italians whistled the Emperor and the Czech
photographer shot himself and Captain Greiser used his thumb
instead of a pocket handkerchief. Ciano set the pace; he promised that
Ethiopia would be governed on the most humane principles – just like
a League Mandate, I heard you say. Addis saw the humane principles

and the accomplished fact last month. Out of my local knowledge and
the reports of the French Minister, may I describe them?

Marshal Graziani, who executed so many men in Tripoli and
who allowed his native troops to massacre Harrar in May, 1936, is
distributing bonbons to the Ethiopians whom he has spared.
Somebody throws a hand grenade. Graziani survives. The Italians
are quickly pulled out the crowd of Ethiopians, and the Ethiopians
are machine-gunned to a man. Three hundred dead. I call that
smart work for civilisation. Graziani is carried off to a hospital.
The lovely planes take off from Akaki, over the sighing blue gum
into the brilliant air. The little tanks rattle through the still-ruined
streets. In the afternoon ammunition is handed out to the
Blackshirts, and the biggest massacre since Smyrna begins. They
kill all the Young Ethiopians, all my friends: not one they tell me
survives. They are dead because they spoke French, wore sometimes
European clothes, behaved decently, loved their country and wanted
to make it more efficient and more civilised. But unfortunately the
Italians beat them at that game.

The Blackshirts run with flamethrowers throughout the city,
from the American Legation south of the market to the French
Legation under Entoto. It is known, *known*, that they spared neither
man nor woman: that is what the French Minister, no friend of
Ethiopia, reports to the Quai d'Orsay, which would love to be the
friend of Rome. He names the figure. He says that 6,000 were killed,
with flamethrowers, grenades, machine-guns, rifles and the flashing
romantic knives which are the Blackshirts' especial fancy. The army
of murder continued their work until nightfall; the native huts
blazed into the star-pointed African night, as last year the European
shops were fiery pillars beckoning the Italians in to save the Addis
that they had destroyed.

The Northern war, where thousands died, was remote enough.
Even Afewerk at Gorahai may vanish upon the sad liaison of my
memory. But Addis, think of Addis, where I lived. The armies that
went out and never came back. The burning of the shops, the class
war. The bodies in the smoking streets. The Italian shooting parties
when they entered Shoa. The execution of the Amharan aristocracy.
The flight of the Shoans to the hills. The frightful massacre of all
my friends, the burning of the native huts and the killing of
thousands of the ignorant and unhappy. The New Flower is become

a butcher's shop, where Italy hangs Abyssinian flesh on hooks every day. The new abattoir is swimming with blood, the price of raw meat must be low indeed with such a glut in Shoa.

FUNERALS

MRS G. L. STEER

The funeral of Mrs G. L. Steer (Margarita de Herrero) took place yesterday morning at Farm Street Church, Mayfair. Father Bernard Butler, S.J., officiated. Among those present, besides Mr G. L. Steer and the family mourners, were Sir Sidney and Lady Barton, Miss Barton, and Mr A. E. Barker (representing *The Times* Publishing Company). Burial will be at Biarritz.

Sir Sidney Barton, the British minister, wearing a black armband for John Melly and the death of free Ethiopia, had come back a hero in the summer of 1936: 'Barton of Addis Ababa' – 'The Man Who Did His Bit', congratulated by King Edward VIII, and praised by Anthony Eden. Now living in Chelsea, the Bartons were retired from diplomacy, but not from the Abyssinian cause and its friends. Their daughter Esmé Barton was at the funeral on 4 March 1937. Though a social flibberti-gibbet, the flame-haired girl could see when someone needed looking after. She had felt the loss of John Melly, whom she had loved. She knew Addis, and understood what George was going through. Now it was time for her to comfort him.

On Thursday, 18 March 1937 another service was held in London in memory of the men, women and children slaughtered in Abyssinia, at St George's Church, Bloomsbury, in the presence of the Emperor of Ethiopia. The Dean of Winchester preached the sermon, quoting three passages from Steer's *Spectator* article. He predicted Mussolini's overthrow and urged penitence on England for its share in Abyssinia's affliction.

George Steer went back to the Basque Country in the spring. First he buried Margarita in Biarritz, in the family tomb at the grey Sabaou Cemetery, where they had buried her father Gustave in the summer of 1917. Now they committed two new coffins to the earth. Margarita Trinidad Herrero-Steer was in one, and her fifteen-year-old nephew Jean Gustave Labrely, who had died the year before in London, was in the other. The sun shone in the mourners' eyes as they stood at the graveside.

FOUR Men at War

1

The same day that he buried his wife, 2 April 1937, George Steer went
down to the Franco-Spanish border and phoned in a freelance story to
The Times about General Mola's new military campaign against the
Basques. One of Kipling's centurions remarks that work is the best sol-
ace for grief, and Steer really got stuck into the job that month. He was
not on the salaried staff, as he had been in Abyssinia, and consequently
was allowed no expenses. Instead, from 3 April 1937, he began to be paid
on the number of column-inches he got into the paper, marked up at
the rate of £5 a column.

Every day, a Contributors' Copy of *The Times* was 'marked up' in
different-coloured crayons with the names of who had written the copy
and what they were to be paid. A column in *The Times* was 32 inches, so
Steer was getting three shillings and three halfpence per inch. His first
little article, 'Advance against Basques', datelined, like the next two, 'on
the Franco-Spanish frontier', earned him £2 5s., about £65 in today's
money.

The Times already had a correspondent with Franco's forces on the
other side. James Holburn had arrived in Hendaye from Berlin on 16
February 1937. Filing copy in early March, he told Deakin: 'The censor
Captain Bolín did his part with the greatest dispatch.' But this story was
not one Bolín would want to suppress. The German General Faupel
brought greetings from Adolf Hitler to Francisco Franco and formal
recognition of Nationalist Spain by Nazi Germany. At the ceremony in
Salamanca, the swastika and the Spanish flag hung side by side, the
crowd shouted 'Viva Franco, viva Hitler' and the band played the 'Horst
Wessel Lied' as well as 'La Marcha Nacional'.

Bolín had been complaining bitterly to Holburn and *The Times* that the Nationalist side of the story was not getting through and that the newspaper's coverage was unfair. The problem was in fact a physical one – 'delay on the land lines' – but the Foreign News Editor was stung by the charge. On 7 March 1937 Ralph Deakin sent a memorandum to the Editor, Geoffrey Dawson, reminding 'the Night Staff': '*The Times* policy requires that the service from the two belligerent sides should be as nicely balanced as possible.'

2

Steer left the French Basque port of St-Jean-de-Luz early on Tuesday, 6 April, on board the British destroyer HMS *Beagle*, which promptly went into action. The Spanish Nationalist cruiser *Almirante Cervera* and the German pocket battleship *Admiral Graf Spee* had stopped a British cargo ship, *Thorpehall*, carrying food to Bilbao; HMS *Beagle* had armed its torpedoes and dashed to the rescue. *Thorpehall* had proceeded, but the consequences were dire.

The Nationalist fleet announced that no more supplies would be allowed into Bilbao, and the British Ambassador was warned that any attempt to break the blockade would be met by force. From Friday, 9 April the Royal Navy was effectively confined to French waters. When the British Cabinet met on the night of Sunday, 11 April, it formally decided to keep all British-flagged ships out of Bilbao and away from the north coast of Spain because it was too dangerous. Prime Minister Stanley Baldwin announced that both sides had laid mines, and Sir Samuel Hoare declared that Nationalist ships were operating inside the three-mile limit.

Both these statements were untrue and Steer's first job in Bilbao was to prove it. He discovered that from 15 March to date, no mines at all had been found by the Basques' two dozen trawler-minesweepers. Fifteen very large naval guns also kept any insurgent Nationalist ships at least eleven miles offshore. There was no reason why British ships could not bring food to the hungry people of Bilbao.

This was in some ways a rerun of the gas issue in Abyssinia, because reliable information like Steer's became ammunition for debate in the House of Commons. His dispatch 'Food Scarcity at Bilbao – Influx of Refugees', describing the scanty rations, chickens selling for £1 (£29 in today's money) and the soaring price of cat, came up when the

'Blockade of Bilbao' was debated in the House of Commons on Wednesday, 14 April 1937.

Clement Attlee for Labour spoke of government 'cowardice' in protecting British shipping. The Liberal crusader Sir Archibald Sinclair quoted Steer in his plea to get food through, and was supported by the Labour MP Philip Noel-Baker. (It is probable that Steer provided these two directly with information.) Then Winston Churchill stood up. A Tory in the wilderness, he had been aggressively neutral from the very beginning of the Spanish Civil War, and considered food as war *matériel*. He started dramatically: 'We seem to be steadily drifting, against the will of every race and people and class, towards some hideous catastrophe.' What followed was not the speech of the war leader of the future, standing up to dictators, but a rambling and irrelevant fantasy of utopian goodwill between nations. The *Times* editorial subsequently praised the government's policy of 'scrupulous impartiality', but the *Manchester Guardian* said it was a disgrace that British 'non-intervention' always intervened against the Spanish Republican government.

The press had a feeding frenzy on 16 and 17 April when they discovered there was a Welsh captain nicknamed 'Potato' Jones waiting to run the blockade with a cargo of tubers from St-Jean-de-Luz, but in the end 'Potato' Jones went nowhere. Steer's story on Wednesday, 21 April, however, was a great scoop.

Warned by Joaquim Eguia, the Captain of Bilbao Port, to be ready early on the morning of 20 April, Steer went out on the launch to meet the first British ship to run the blockade. *Seven Seas Spray*, captained by Mr W. H. Roberts of Penarth, South Wales, was carrying his twenty-year-old daughter Fifi as well as the wife of the Chief Engineer, Mrs B. M. Docker. The owner was also on board, with a 'cheerful, coloured crew'. They brought a general cargo of 3,600 tons from Valencia, including salt, wine, olive oil, hams, honey, flour, beans and peas. They slipped out of St-Jean-de-Luz around midnight on the Monday, ignoring frantic signals to stop. When semaphored by a British destroyer, *Spray* accepted full responsibility for going to Bilbao. 'Good luck,' said the Royal Navy.

At the mouth of Bilbao's River Nervion, a small flotilla awaited, and nine Republican fighter planes swooped low to welcome them. Steer went aboard the *Seven Seas Spray* for his first decent whisky in three weeks. The Captain took his position on the bridge, in a brushed uniform, with a clean white cover on his cap.

W. H. Roberts was ship-shape, a real master; we stood beside him trying hard not to let the ship down. And what a sight! . . . Mile after mile of the Nervion trough, the grey quays and waterside, was crammed with people. There were tens of thousands of them watching the English ship, with the Red Ensign that they knew so well in times of peace trailing at the stern, over green river . . . They cheered and shrieked, and ran out of houses to stand on waste blocks of stone and cement at the river's edge. It was not roses, but old handkerchiefs, twice-read papers and thousands of shreds of washing all the way, shaken from drab and grimy windows. Many raised the clenched fist, and the Captain and Fifi answered in our more English fashion . . . One could hear from the quays cries of *Vivan los marineros ingleses* and *Viva la libertad*; but the women were rather more carnal, and shouted *Vino y aceite*, wine and oil! So sharp was the lack of all things in Bilbao; there was nothing to cook with. Above it all, there came the guttural shout of a Basque sailor, in English, *well done*. The militia turned out of their barracks to salute the ship which had broken the paper blockade, and it was a great moment for the captain when he could take his megaphone at last, as we came among the high houses of Bilbao city, and the ship slowed down to the right-hand dock, and he called, with a quiet voice, '*Make her fast where she is now, Mister Bo'sun.*' What a comfortable journey; and the Basques had begun to believe that an English sailor would never take the risk.

Fifi and Mrs Docker stepped ashore to see if they could do any shopping.

The blockade was broken. *Macgregor*, *Hamsterley* and *Stanbrook* followed, protected by the 15-inch guns of the enormous battle cruiser HMS *Hood*. They arrived on the morning of the 22nd, carrying 8,500 tons of food, including 2,000 tons of wheat. Then came *Stesso* and *Thurston* on the 25th with more food and *Sheaf Garth* at noon the next day with coal.

Afterwards, pro-Fascist 'friends of reaction' said that British ships bringing food to Bilbao were an 'intervention' in the Spanish Civil War. Steer said that the Nationalists' untrue information, warning ships off Bilbao, was by far the bigger intervention. A solid blockade would have guaranteed defeat for Bilbao, whereas a broken blockade did not mean victory; it merely levelled the playing field on which the Basques would lose. Steer was proud of what he had done, and ran up a flag in *The Tree of Gernika*: 'A journalist is not a simple purveyor of news, whether sensational or controversial, or well-written, or merely funny. He is a historian of every day's events . . . and as a historian must be filled with the most passionate and most critical attachment to the truth, so must the journalist, with the great power that he wields, see that the truth prevails.'

3

Steer had returned to the Basque Country in April just as General Mola's Army of the North was turning its attention there. Madrid was proving a tough nut to crack, but Bilbao seemed easier because the military engineer in charge of building the Basque defences around Bilbao, the *cinturon de hierro*, or girdle of iron, had defected to Franco's side with the complete plans.

The Nationalists sought a victory within weeks. Bilbao was blockaded by sea, ringed from the south. They wanted to pound the Basque Republic into submission and commandeer its minerals to pay the Germans. They asked the German Air Force to use their Condor Legion planes like mobile artillery, blasting holes to let the Nationalist infantry through. General Mola dropped leaflets with the same type of threat that the Italians had made in Abyssinia: *If submission is not immediate I will raze all Vizcaya to the ground . . .*

Mola opened the campaign by bombing Durango on 31 March. At the mention of Durango many people think of northern Mexico and the making of Western movies. In fact, the Mexican Durango was founded by a Basque named Ibarra in honour of his home town in Vizcaya. The original Basque town, with its moated river and stone bridges, is medieval and picturesque. Once home to an interesting fifteenth-century heresy of communism and free love, Durango by 1937 was a light-industrial town with factories that made small arms; but these were not Mola's targets.

Early on a Wednesday morning, bombs from four Junkers 52s hit the nunnery of Santa Susana and two other churches in the middle of early mass. One photograph in *The Tree of Gernika* (see plate 11) shows Father Carlos Morilla lying dead in his robes in the dusty rubble of Santa María Church. Three Basque motorized police in leather coats and boots stand behind his corpse and the light is flooding through the blasted open roof on to the baroque altar. Another photo shows the great oak porch that skirts Santa María lying in wreckage and rubble. A view from the church tower looks down through the smashed tile roofs of four houses. A fourth photo shows five dusty men in berets digging a body out of the ruins of the Jesuit church, Corazón de Jesús. The raid lasted half an hour and killed scores of men, women and children. In *The Tree of Gernika* Steer called it 'the most terrible bombardment of a civil population in the history of the world up to March 31st 1937'. He says that they dug out 127 bodies and that 121 died later in hospital. A propaganda pamphlet published by the Spanish Embassy in Paris lists the names of 166 dead. Jon Irazabal Agirre's book *1937 martxoak 31 Durango 31 de marzo 1937* (2001) names 274 victims with 60 unknown.

A group from England that included the controversial 'Red' Dean of Canterbury, Hewlett Johnson, and John Macmurray, Professor of Philosophy in the University of London, author of *Reason and Emotion*, witnessed another attack on Durango on 2 April when fighters dived to machine-gun people fleeing for shelter, and they made a signed statement about it: 'The churches especially had been completely destroyed, as well as a convent, in which . . . a large number of nuns were killed.'

The deaths of fourteen nuns and two priests should have embarrassed the Nationalists with their 'Catholic Crusade for Civilization', but they flatly lied. Salamanca Press Office, Radio Sevilla and Radio-Club of Portugal put out the story that anarchists, communists and socialists had shot the priests and nuns, locked worshippers up inside the churches and then burned them.

On Sunday, 18 April the third air raid of the day on Bilbao took Steer out of the Torrontegui Hotel to see what was going on. Four Russian fighters were chasing three Dornier 17s, new Nazi fast bombers nicknamed 'flying pencils'. 'Suddenly across the hill of Begoña in front of me fell a line of bombs at top speed. Lightning, thunder, thunder, lightning, prolonged thunder, and smoke.' One of the bombers was shot down, and Steer went out to Galdakano to see where it had crashed.

The pilot, a twenty-seven-year-old German named Hans Sobotka, was half-burned, and his arms were still raised across his face from the last moment before he had gone into the hillside. The two other Germans had jumped from the Dornier, but their parachutes had not had time to open; they had hit the River Nervion so hard they had died of shock. One corpse was unusual. The plucked eyebrows, lipsticked mouth and manicured and pointed fingernails on the fine white hands appeared to show that the Germans were using women as war pilots; but the doctors at the Sanidad Militar in Bilbao were men of the world. They undressed the corpse and scrutinized it. The armpit hair had been plucked and it wore feminine pink silk underwear, but it was, biologically, a man. The underwear was hung on exhibition in the Basque Department of Defence, and the doctors jotted it down in their casebooks as 'one of the queerer incidents of the Civil War'.

This three-minute raid had killed 67 and wounded 110 people in a ribbon of destruction across the Old Town of Bilbao. The bombs tore open blocks of cheap flats, 'penetrated to underground lavatories, to railway tunnels, and to refuges marked secure by the Department of Passive Defence'. One of these was under a rubber and shoe factory, which caught fire. The fire brigade fought it for four hours before digging down into the air-raid shelter.

They worked all that evening; but the people were all dead, crushed, suffocated, drowned. Their pulpy bodies came up slowly. First a small child, of about five years; then a youngish man; then a pregnant woman. A whole family of the past and future wiped out by one bomb. Their hair lay wet and straggly over their bruised faces . . .
     On the woman they tried artificial respiration, why I knew not; she was long dead.

General Mola launched his land assault on Tuesday, 20 April. In Elgeta, south-east of Durango, Steer met the most competent of the Basque commanders, Beldarrain of the Basque nationalist Marteartu battalion. He was small, dark and shy-faced with fine brown eyes and a melancholy, unsmiling look; he wore shabby trousers, an old blue woollen jacket and a beret with no insignia of rank. Before the war, Beldarrain had worked a lathe as a turner-mechanic. Though he seemed inarticulate in his silences, he got things done properly, completely reorganizing the trenches on the Inchorta hills against air attack and infantry penetration, camouflaging his deep dugouts on the back of the hill, laying mines against tanks.

An aerial attack preceded Mola's ground assault. Steer thought that ignorant, babbling officers provoked half of their men's 'obvious and occult' terror of the aeroplane. Beldarrain, by contrast, stayed obdurately silent, and his men followed suit. Twenty-four bombers dropped their tonnage on Elgeta and plunging fighters raked the hill-top trenches with machine-gun fire, but not a man was killed. Then the land attack began. Mola's artillery opened up, firing hundreds of shells, killing about eleven people. A battalion of Moorish infantry in white turbans, fighting for Mola and Franco, moved forward to within 300 yards of Beldarrain's lines, confidently expecting the planes and guns to have done their work for them. This was exactly as Beldarrain had planned. His Basque troops now slid out of their dugouts, and their rifle fire flattened the attackers to the ground. Beldarrain's artillery, hidden in woods, dropped four shells at a time among the crouching Moors, who broke and fled.

Other units did not always match Beldarrain's stubborn inventiveness. Steer says that several left-wing battalions muddled about and retreated and gradually the southern front collapsed.

4

Steer saw much of this infantry war with a new friend. He first noticed him in the dining room at the Torrontegui Hotel, and thought that the stout, bald, pink-faced and thick-moustached man, dining alone with a map propped against his water jug like a newspaper, was Russian; but a sad waitress in a long black dress told Steer that this untidy chap was a French journalist who lived in the room next to his. The Frenchman, in a beret and a leather jerkin, used to come down to the Basque President's offices at the Carlton Hotel with the other journalists every day. He carried a Leica, which he never used, and facetiously claimed he was the Special Correspondent of the Salvation Army paper *Blood and Fire*. However, Corman, the Belgian journalist, found out that he had been a member of Maréchal Foch's staff, had the Légion d'Honneur and was presenting a handwritten military report to the Basque President, in person, every day. Noel Monks called him 'a little French Colonel fighting with the Basques'.

In *The Tree of Gernika* Steer calls the Frenchman 'Jaureghuy' all through until page 324, where he accidentally lets slip his real name, Monnier. In fact, Robert Monnier/Jaureghuy was a French secret service agent.

Delighted to believe that the first thing the enemy would do if they captured him would be to shoot him, J. learnt up the Basque cry, '*Gora Euzkadi Askatuta*' – 'Long live free Euzkadi' – for final comic use against the wall, and spent the rest of the offensive getting encircled and pistolling his way out again. The greater the risk the more crinkled and bluer the eyes of J. 'How the editor will praise my work! General Booth will give me a rise,' he used to say as he pushed another charge of thirty into his Astra machine pistol, made in Gernika, 1935.

On Saturday, 24 April Steer went on his first jaunt to the front with 'Jaureghuy'. General Mola was attacking Eibar and Berriz, so they went there. Steer soon learned that war was a game to the French officer, and the more dangerous it was, the more fun. They found chaos at night on the hilltop of Santa Marina Zar: inadequate trenches, no sandbags, no machine guns. The first attacks came in the early-morning mist. Steer saw a battalion commander shot dead and then saw Monnier return fire and accurately pick off the machine-gun post that had killed him. The Basques beat off three Nationalist attacks, exhausted their ammunition, and had to retreat. As Steer ran north with them, the mist lifted and they could see the enemy advancing on both flanks of the mountain. When General Mola's planes bombed Eibar, Steer noticed they were not using high explosives, but a new weapon, the incendiary bomb, which smudged the valley with smoke.

Going out with 'Jaureghuy'/Monnier was hilarious and hair-raising, and Steer stuck with the Frenchman for the rest of the campaign. Four years later Steer recalled: 'I used to follow Monnier around like a dog because he always knew the smartest sectors of the front. He led reconnaissances and arrested retreats, though he had no command. He exposed himself alarmingly.'

The two men left the Torrontegui Hotel in May and shared a flat together at 60 Gran Via, which was closer to the President's office at the Carlton. Steer was already trusted by the Basque government, but through Monnier he gained access to intelligence reports and wireless intercepts and was allowed to question enemy prisoners, especially captured German aircrew.

Monnier and Steer both figure as characters in the 1987 Basque feature film *To the Four Winds – Lauaxeta*, directed by José A. Zorrilla, which is in part dedicated to their memory. It's set in April 1937 and follows the

Basque poet Esteban Urkiaga, who wrote under the name 'Lauaxeta'. The opening shot is of men in berets digging trenches in the hills and filling bags with earth. A few scenes later we meet the poet, writing. He is told, 'Monnier's waiting,' and buckles on his uniform. We see him escorting a burly and moustached Monnier with beret and field-glasses as they drive in a black Mercedes to the front. A red-bereted Francoist ambushes them; Monnier's pistol jams; '*Tirez!*' he yells at the poet, who does not fire. Instead, the driver shoots the young soldier, who dies babbling and bloody. Next we see Monnier in a gun-and-grenade fight for a farmhouse, then ducking along trenches under artillery fire. A few scenes later the poet is in the newspaper office, his desk covered with photos of the bombing of Durango. A figure emerges from the blue shadows of the glass door. George Steer, back from the front, is wearing a pale trench coat over jersey and jacket. 'Hello, everyone. How is everybody? All right?' he asks in an educated English voice. There's a touch of Bogart's insouciant charm in Peter Leeper's portrayal of Steer, as he asks for a cigarette and urges Lauaxeta to come for a drink. The Basque poet says, 'George, you must stop taking unnecessary chances. We need what you write for *The Times*.'

Steer did take chances in the Basque war, running more risks than the other journalists because he felt he had less to lose than they did. Perhaps part of him wanted to die, because his wife and child were dead. There were many moments when mortality was horribly close.

On the road to Truende, Steer is in the cab of a lorry full of anti-tank grenades for the front. When the vehicle comes under shellfire and aerial machine-gunning, he endures imagining what will happen if the load is hit and the whole lorry explodes.

In Derio, bombs shatter the cemetery, splitting open tombs and coffins, scattering angels and crosses, turning the dead over in their graves.

Through field-glasses at Fruniz, Steer watches Italian bombers accidentally dropping high explosives on their own men sunbathing. They run about, frantically waving white sheets.

Steer is on Mount Urkulu when twenty Condor Legion aeroplanes drop incendiaries among the trees. Miles of pines become a single fiery scarf as the woods ignite in a picture of terror and beauty; enormous tongues of white smoke mouthing upwards, veils shot with broad sheets of dim fire, swirling ash flakes and the smell of flaming resin.

FIVE

Gernika

1

The twentieth-century German war machine almost conquered the world. Tacitus observed 2,000 years ago that Germans would sooner get things by blood than sweat, and Heine remarked that the ancient German eagerness for battle was only barely restrained by Christianity, and would one day break forth to eclipse the French Revolution. Wavell said Germans professionalized the trade of war. In Spain their brutal efficiency was clear.

Right-wing English apologists referred to the Germans in Spain as mere 'technicians'. They would never admit that German soldiers, sailors and airmen laid, loaded and fired the guns, primed, loaded and dropped the bombs, and flew the fighters down to machine-gun the panicking refugees. Yet in a sense it *was* all a technical rehearsal. The German Air Force, the Luftwaffe, developed in secret to outwit the restrictions of the Treaty of Versailles, had found in Spain a live testing ground. As soon as new bombers and fighters came off the production line, they went to Spain: the Messerschmitt 109, the Dornier 17, the Junkers 87 Stuka dive-bomber. The 18,000 men in the Condor Legion were all volunteers, young, fit, and keen as mustard, and their leaders were inventive. General Hugo Sperrle (code name 'Sander') was nominally in charge. However, the executive genius of this kind of warfare was his Chief of Staff, Lieutenant Colonel Wolfram von Richthofen, who would finish the war as Generalmajor Freiherr von Richthofen, Commander of the Condor Legion, and who stood next to Franco on the victory podium in Madrid on 19 May 1939.

A cousin of Manfred, the famous 'Red Baron' air ace who had commanded Göring's squadron in the First World War, Wolfram von

Richthofen was the first German fully to grasp Giulio Douhet's ideas of total war from the air. (He made a special study of them as unofficial air attaché in Italy, in the days when the Luftwaffe was still developing in secret.) After testing new aircraft models, von Richthofen went to Spain in January 1937 and put the ideas of terror-bombing into practice. Piecemeal air attacks on Madrid in autumn 1936 had not worked, but the Basque campaign was a new beginning. The Nationalist troops of Franco and Mola built a big new airfield at Vitoria, within easy flying distance of anywhere in Euzkadi, where the bombers and fighters of 'Geschwader 88' (the code name allotted to German air units) could return to refuel and rearm. The figure 88 has Nazi significance: the eighth letter of the alphabet is H, and HH stands for *Heil Hitler*.

The bomber force K-88 (*Kampfgruppe-88*) comprised three squadrons of Junkers Ju-52/3m bombers and one squadron of Heinkel He-111B-1 bombers, later joined by the 'flying pencil' Dornier Do-17E-1 bombers. The fighter force J-88 (*Jagdgruppe-88*) had three squadrons of Heinkel He-51 biplanes, later joined by Messerschmitts. All the aircraft had a white tailplane with a black saltire cross.

By the end of April 1937, the Condor Legion had almost total air superiority, and the fighters were used for ground attack and close support of infantry. The Heinkel 51s, with two rigid 7.92 mm machine guns and racks for up to six 22 lb anti-personnel fragmentation bombs, had open cockpits, which also allowed the pilots to carry on the First World War practice of taking grenades up to throw as bomblets. It is not hard to imagine this developing into a competitive game among the young pilots.

And when the Nazi hotshots were given the six very first, brand-new, box-fresh Messerschmitt Bf-109-B1s to experiment with on the Guernica raid of 26 April 1937, what red-blooded airman could have resisted showing off what the new monoplane could do, stitching up the tiny running figures below with beautiful lines of 13 mm ammunition fired through the wooden propeller, zipping down from the sky to dust them off the road?

2

Monday, 26 April seemed like a normal day in wartime Bilbao. An air-raid siren woke the Australian Catholic Noel Monks at 7 a.m. It was a beautifully sunny spring morning when he went out for eight o'clock

mass, remembering Anzac Day, the anniversary of the Australian
landing at Gallipoli in 1915. Breakfast in these lean times was black,
sugarless coffee and a piece of dry Bilbao ration bread, about which
there were many grim rumours. After lunch on a British ship, Monks
went down to the presidential office at the Carlton Hotel to find the
other journalists, but George Steer and Christopher Holme (the
Reuters man) had already gone to the front. Holme had also been in
Abyssinia, with the Italians, had reported the burning of Irun and been
expelled from inside Nationalist Spain, too. Monks wrote in *Eyewitness*:
'We were the only three British staff correspondents in the Basque
country. Each of us had spent six months with Franco's forces.' They
were British in the sense of 'British Empire', for all three reporters were
wild colonial boys: Christopher Holme had been born in Burma, where
his father had been in the Indian Civil Service, Noel Monks in Hobart,
Tasmania, and George Steer in South Africa.

Monks was offered a car with driver to follow the other journalists to
the front east of Guernica. 'I passed through Guernica at about 3.30
p.m. The time is approximate, based on the fact that I left Bilbao at 2.30.
Guernica was busy. It was market day. We passed through the town and
took a road . . . to Marquina.' Monks says they were 'about eighteen
miles east of Guernica' when the driver Anton jammed on the brakes,
shouting. A fleet of planes had appeared over the hills. There were a
dozen bombers higher up and half a dozen low-flying Heinkel fighters,
which wheeled to chase them. Monks and the driver left the car and
bolted for a waterlogged bomb hole twenty yards from the road and
crouched in the mud as the planes strafed the road. Only the day before,
George Steer had told him what to do: 'Lie still and as flat as you can.
But don't get up and start running, or you'll be bowled over for certain.'

George Steer was also in a hole. The way to the front at Bolibar and
Marquina had been blocked by wreckage at Arbacegui-Gerrikaiz.
Enemy bombers had just passed. There were four dead near the church,
two destroyed cottages, and several huge bomb craters, at forty feet
across the biggest they had ever seen, still warm and stinking from the
explosions. Steer, Holme and the Belgian journalist Mathieu Corman
climbed down into the field to look at them in the spring sunshine.
Suddenly, over the ridge, six Heinkel 51s appeared in battle formation
and swooped. 'Christopher, Corman and I thought that the bomb-hole
was the best place,' wrote Steer. 'We reached the bottom in two jumps.
It looked less safe from down below, for the sides were unusually wide

and one could see too much sky. But it was a hole, and we lay on the shady side face down in tumbled clay and jagged bomb splinters.'

The Heinkels circled. For fifteen minutes the German fighters dived over the crater firing their double guns from as low as 200 feet at the paralysed reporters.

It was difficult to think at all. As soon as the very material process known as the collection of one's thoughts was nearly complete another bloody little fighter was roaring down at us, and we were spread-eagled and passive again.

Of course it's all noise. The shooting was wild, and after a quarter of an hour of it we could not find a bullet in the bomb-hole . . . Terror and noise were their weapons, not death.

Their car was untouched, and they told the chauffeur to head straight back to Bilbao. On the way they had to stop twice and wait while enemy aeroplanes passed. They were Heinkel 111 light bombers flying in arrowhead formation to their right towards the Guernica inlet. They went on to Bilbao to write up their stories. It was about four-thirty by the clock of their car on Monday, 26 April.

3

Steer and the other journalists had witnessed only the fringes of a great air raid. All along the front east of Bilbao, road junctions in villages like Arbacegui-Gerrikaiz were smashed to impede and confuse any Basque retreat. At first it seemed that Guernica was just one among many villages hit that day. Indeed, subsequent pro-Nationalist accounts say that the strategic target of the attack on Guernica was merely the Renteria Bridge, which funnels traffic and troop movements to the east. But the Renteria Bridge was untouched by the bombing, as was the Astra gun factory. The real target was the town of Guernica itself, not only as a symbol of Basque nationalism but because it was close enough to Bilbao to stand as a warning to the people of that city of their fate if they did not surrender.

The first Condor Legion plane to attack Guernica on that afternoon was a Heinkel 111 piloted by Major Rudolf von Moreau. Having passed over the town and drawn no flak, he ran in again and dropped his six bombs around the railway station and the square in front. Market-day journeys and shopping exploded into carnage: a muddle of blood and bricks, severed limbs and broken glass, dust and screaming.

A quarter of an hour later the main force struck, in repeated successive waves, with more explosives and incendiaries. The Junkers and Heinkel bombers, Heinkel and Messerschmitt fighters that made up the forty-two-plane fleet had flown north from Vitoria to the coast. Guernica is not hard to find because it is a couple of miles from the sea up a wide green inlet, the Mundaka estuary, now a Global Biosphere Reserve. The planes wheeled over the sea and then came south on their bombing or strafing run, down the tree-lined road and the railway and the canalized river. Having dropped their bombs, the planes flew straight back to Vitoria to reload and refuel before repeating the process. The raid lasted more than three hours. There were no Republican planes to counter them, and no anti-aircraft fire. Guernica was a helpless target, and as its people ran into the sunlit green fields the fighters came dancing down after them. An honest Nationalist staff officer later told Virginia Cowles of the *Sunday Times*: 'Of course it was bombed. We bombed it and bombed it and bombed it, and *bueno*, why not?'

Back in Bilbao after his frightening experience in the crater, Steer cabled home a story about a British coal ship coming into port with the help of the Royal Navy, and reported, without much emphasis, that there had been bombing along the line. Around seven, the elegant press attaché Arbex told him that Guernica had been among the towns and villages hit that day, still without making much of it. At eight-thirty all the journalists went to dinner at the Torrontegui Hotel. The Welsh pioneer blockade-breaker Captain Roberts and his daughter Fifi were at the table. Other denizens of the wide and sombre dining room were elderly rightists waiting to be evacuated. Monks says they had finished their first course of beans and were waiting for their bully beef, at around nine-thirty, when a government official came into the dining room with tears streaming down his face saying, 'Guernica is destroyed. The Germans bombed and bombed and bombed.' Monks says Captain Roberts banged a great fist on the table and said, 'Bloody swine!' Steer remembered it differently. He said that Antonio Irala, Secretary-General of the Presidency of the Basque Autonomous Government, rang up around ten to say, 'Gernika is in flames.' The journalists threw down their napkins, and ordered cars. Steer thought that Irala had to be exaggerating. The whole town could not be burning.

The journalists (Steer of *The Times*, Holme of Reuters, Monks of the *Daily Express*, Corman of *Ce Soir* and the correspondent from the *Star*, possibly called Watson) followed the press attaché Arbex in his car, driving fast through the dark countryside on the same road they had taken that morning. Fifteen miles south of Guernica, the sky began to impress them as weirdly alive. It seemed to move and carry trembling veins of blood. It looked flushed, pink, fat; the fatness was bellying clouds of smoke and the pinkness the pulsing reflection of a great fire below. 'Out of the hills we saw Gernika itself. A meccano framework. At every window piercing eyes of fire; where every roof had stood wild trailing locks of fire.'

They drove up the road that enters Gernika from the south, past the untouched Astra gun factory, into black, burning beams, tattered telephone wires, leaping flames. Four dead sheep lay to their right in a trickle of blood. In front of the Casa de Juntas huge bomb holes with volcanoed fresh earth, and a score of Basque militiamen standing dazed. Hundreds of women were in the open space, lying on tables or wet mattresses. As the journalists moved among them the people tried to tell their story: 'They made the funny noises of bombers poising, fighters machine-gunning, bombs bursting, houses falling, the tubes of fire spurting and spilling over their town.'

4

The three British journalists were all experienced war correspondents and had seen horrible things and atrocious behaviour in Africa and Europe; but the impact of that particular night in the Basque Country was not something any of them would ever forget.

Christopher Holme's forty-four-line poem, 'Gernika, April 26 1937', begins:

> The world ended tonight.
> There in that unreal desolation
> Of molten tunnel, flame-arched passageway,
> House-hung setpieces dripping cement and bricks,
> A handful of dim creatures
> Are scratching for fragments of their slaughtered world.

Noel Monks went to look for a couple who had given him lunch the day before, and found his host a mangled, tangled mass of flesh. Pieces

of his wife were strewn over the cobblestones. Monks helped sobbing
Basque soldiers collect charred bodies. 'There were flames and smoke
and grit, and the smell of burning human flesh was nauseating. Houses
were collapsing into the inferno.'

George Steer watched men digging people out of ruined houses –
'families at a time, dead and blue-black with bruising. Others were
brought in from just outside Gernika with machine-gun bullets in their
bodies; one, a lovely girl.' The *gudaris* – Basque soldiers – were crying as
they laid her out in the grounds of the broken hospital.

Joseba Elosegi's company of soldiers had been billeted in the
Augustine Convent on the Bermeo road. In his remarkable autobiography *Quiero Morir por Algo* (*I Want to Die for Something*) he describes
people panicking and trying to shelter, then fleeing, mad with fear, into
the fields. He met a woman covered in dust who could only croak, 'My
son, my son.' Her house was a pile of rubble and he went at it like a
madman, lifting wood and stone, tearing his nails as he scrabbled
downwards. The boy was not yet three and his bloodsoaked clothes
were still warm. Joseba Elosegi gave the destroyed dead body to the
mother, who screamed and ran away with it. Her eyes haunted him.
And the bombing of Guernica haunted him all his life. On 18
September 1970, when Franco was watching the international pelota
final at Donostia, Joseba Elosegi set fire to himself. Shouting, 'Long live
free Euzkadi,' he jumped in flames twenty feet down into the court so
that the Generalísimo could see for himself what a burning person
looked like.

Steer went up to look at the Casa de Juntas. The gardens were torn,
windows broken, but the seventy-seven-year-old oak of Basque civil
liberty was untouched, and the other oak, the blackened three-hundred-
year-old one, still stood shielded by white stone pillars. The seats were
scattered with pink blossom, blown there in the blasts.

In the centre of the town the flames were gathering to a single roar.
Interior Minister Telesforo de Monzón stood helpless with his motorized police. Steer wrote:

> We tried to enter, but the streets were a royal carpet of live coals;
> blocks of wreckage slithered and crashed from the houses, and from
> their sides that were still erect the polished heat struck at our cheeks
> and eyes. There were people, they said, to be saved there: there were
> the frameworks of dozens of cars. But nothing could be done, and

we put our hands in our pockets and wondered why on earth the world was so mad and warfare become so easy.

We talked with the people round the great furnace for two hours. I smoked a number of cigarettes . . . drove back to Bilbao, and slept on my story.

5

'We had to destroy the village in order to save it.' In incendiary terms the bombing of Guernica was a brilliant success for the fliers of the Condor Legion, but the arrival of foreign journalists (which had not happened at Durango) made it a public-relations disaster for Franco's side. 'We did not like talking about Guernica,' said the German fighter pilot Adolf Galland. This was also a different kind of bombing. Steer held the evidence for that in his hands, picked up at Guernica and taken back to the Torrontegui: three shiny aluminium tubes, weighing about two pounds, as long as a tibia, with a silver powder inside. These thermite incendiary bombs were marked with the initials of the German Rheindorf factory and dated 1936. Above the name was stamped the German Imperial eagle 'with scarecrow wings spread'.

The Condor Legion ceaselessly experimented with different sizes and mixes of blast, fragmentation and incendiary bombs. Steer himself noted three different types of incendiaries in use. It is possible that the fire-bombing of Guernica really was a technical experiment, a test to see what would happen if a lot of incendiaries were used at once. It was von Richthofen himself who selected the mix of blast, splinter and fire bombs for this particular operation, agreed at a military conference in Burgos the night before. Von Richthofen wrote in his diary: 'As it was, a complete technical success of our 250 kgs (explosive) and ECB1 (incendiary) bombs.'

Steer's 28 April *Times* report makes it clear that thousands of incendiaries caused the fire that destroyed Guernica, an old, packed town built largely of wood. When the silvery-white incendiary bombs landed, a striker in the nose was meant to ignite the powder inside. Thermite is a trademark name for a mixture of two powdered metals, aluminium and iron oxide, which when ignited can reach a temperature of 2,500°C or more, producing a molten metal that can be used for welding. The magnesium igniters did not go off straight away on all the bombs; some fizzled and dribbled in roof spaces or flared up when heat reached them, so they kept restarting fires for hours; but more than enough ignited successfully to create a firestorm in the centre of Guernica, destroying all the buildings from Santa María Church east to the railway station and north-east to the Renteria Bridge.

6

Reuters was first with the news that bombs had destroyed a whole town. The readership was in some sense already primed to expect it. From Jules Verne on there had been fictions of air attack. Stanley Baldwin's notion that 'the bomber will always get through' had just been graphically translated into film: *Things to Come* (1936), written by H. G. Wells, showed a city called Everytown destroyed by a fleet of giant bombers. (Wells had also prophesied *The War in the Air* in 1908.) People knew it could theoretically happen but, as Sven Lindquist argues in *A History of Bombing*, bombing had till then been something mostly done in faraway places, often as a way of punishing rebellious colonial subjects. In civilized Europe, in 1937, the bombing, burning and machinegunning of white civilians shocked people.

Nowadays this is normal practice. Modern war is largely directed at civilians. In the First World War only 11 per cent of casualties were civilians; in the Second, 53 per cent. In the wars of the 1970s, 1980s and 1990s, the proportions were 68 per cent, 76 per cent and 90 per cent respectively. This may be the true legacy of Guernica and Durango in 1937. A vital line was crossed. From then on, war became total. The Japanese in China, the Russians in Finland, and the Nazis across Europe led the way; but the British and the Americans in the Second World War would inexorably follow with their 'strategic bombing', which would kill over half a million German civilians and 55,000 Allied air-crew. On 11 September 2001 two passenger planes were flown into the twin towers of the World Trade Center in New York City, killing some 3,000 civilians. Immediately, there was talk of war and retaliation.

George Orwell ended his 1938 review of *The Tree of Gernika*: 'The horror we feel of these things has led to this conclusion: if someone drops a bomb on your mother, go and drop two bombs on his mother. The only apparent alternatives are to smash dwelling houses to powder, blow out human entrails and burn holes in children with lumps of thermite, or to be enslaved by people who are more ready to do these things than you are.'

Lewis Mumford summed up what we owe to the Condor Legion in August 1945:

> The fascist theory of total warfare was first put forth by the Italian General Douhet . . . The believers in this theory held that wars could be won by unlimited aerial attack upon the civilian population. The demolition of Warsaw and the centre of Rotterdam brought this theory into action. Instead of recoiling against it and concentrating our whole might on the fighting area, we imitated our enemies. By the practice of obliteration bombing (alias strategic bombing) we lost any edge of moral superiority we originally held over the enemy . . . This general moral disintegration paved the way for the use of the atomic bomb.

And who bombed the centre of Rotterdam and demolished Warsaw, as well as Belgrade and Crete and Stalingrad? It was the future Nazi Field Marshal Freiherr Wolfram von Richthofen, the man who bombed Guernica. Perhaps he was only the 'technician'. The political decision to bomb Guernica – heartland of Basque freedoms – was made by Generals Mola and Franco.

7

George Steer of *The Times* waited longer than Christopher Holme of Reuters to write his story. On Tuesday morning Steer spoke with scores of refugees who had come in to Bilbao on government lorries or ox carts. Then he went back out to Guernica in daylight. Instead of taking pictures, his photographer joined the men and women desperately looking for their families in the wreckage. The British Consul in Bilbao, R. C. Stevenson, wrote to Sir Henry Chilton, the British Ambassador, two days after the bombing:

> On landing at Bermeo yesterday I was told about the destruction of Guernica. I went at once to have a look at the place and to my amazement found that the township normally of some five thousand inhabitants, since the September influx of refugees about ten thousand, was almost completely destroyed. Nine houses in ten are beyond reconstruction. Many were still burning and fresh fires were

breaking out here and there, the result of incendiary bombs which owing to some fault had not exploded on impact the day before and were doing so, at the time of my visit, under falling beams and masonry. The casualties cannot be ascertained and probably never will be, accurately. Some estimates put the figure at one thousand, others at over three thousand.

The piece that Steer sat down to write for *The Times*, 'The Tragedy of Guernica', shows a classical education. Its emotional impact comes from its refusal of overt emotion. In his analysis of the dispatch in *The First Casualty: The War Correspondent as Hero and Myth Maker from the Crimea to Kosovo*, Philip Knightley says that Steer was 'careful not to claim eye-witness status, a precaution that tends to encourage the reader's acceptance of firmer assertions such as . . . *Guernica was not a military objective . . . The object of the bombardment was seemingly the demoral-isation of the civil population and the destruction of the cradle of the Basque race* . . . Steer's story tallied substantially with those of his colleagues, but his interpretation and his accusations of a new kind of warfare were the most precise, the most thoroughly argued, and the most extreme.' Knightley nevertheless concludes that 'Steer, with understandable professional, political and personal ardour, overreacted to the story.'

Contemporary accounts do not support Knightley's conclusion. When the *Manchester Evening News* interviewed Captain Basil Liddell Hart, perhaps the foremost military thinker of his generation, for an article on 7 May 1937 called 'What We Have Learned From Guernica', he said, 'The object of raids like this is to smash at a blow the *morale* of a population . . . The spirit of the population is the military objective.'

The largely urban British grasped straight away what Guernica meant. A German fleet of aircraft could cross the North Sea and blot out Hull, pass over the Channel and obliterate Portsmouth. They could bomb London. The psychological effect of the story ran deep. A Conservative MP, describing the panoply of the coronation of King George VI on 12 May 1937 in the *Spectator*, wondered what would happen if bombs came through the roof of Westminster Abbey. George Orwell ended *Homage to Catalonia* in 1938 with an image of a lovely sleeping England, waiting to be woken 'by the roar of bombs'.

'The attack upon the civilian population leads to the retreat of the civilian population,' wrote Steer. This too was a legacy of Guernica: over 100,000 Basques were evacuated from the north Spanish coast between

May and August 1937. Steer reported an improvement in morale in Bilbao when men did not have to worry about women and children. Popular feeling in Britain forced the British government to admit nearly 4,000 Basque children. When they arrived in Southampton, all the coronation bunting had been left up to welcome them, on the Mayor's orders. They then went to a tent camp at North Stoneham, where they were given new clothes by Marks and Spencer and free chocolate by Cadbury's. The British government also offered Royal Navy protection to all ships taking refugees away from Bilbao. But by 1939–40 the tables had turned. Thousands more children were evacuated from cities under threat of Nazi bombing. This time they were British children, leaving London and Manchester and Birmingham and Liverpool, and chocolate on the ration was no longer easy to find.

8

In his 1943 essay 'Looking Back on the Spanish War', George Orwell wrote:

> The most baffling thing in the Spanish war was the behaviour of the great powers. The war was actually won for Franco by the Germans and Italians, whose motives were obvious enough. The motives of France and Britain are less easy to understand. In 1936 it was clear to everyone that if Britain would only help the Spanish government, even to the extent of a few million pounds' worth of arms, Franco would collapse and German strategy would be severely dislocated. By that time one did not need to be a clairvoyant to foresee that war between Britain and Germany was coming: one could even foretell within a year or two when it would come. Yet in the most mean, cowardly, hypocritical way the British ruling class did all they could to hand Spain over to Franco and the Nazis. Why? Because they were pro-Fascist, was the obvious answer. Undoubtedly they were, and yet when it came to the final showdown they chose to stand up to Germany. It is still very uncertain what plan they acted on in backing Franco, and they may have had no clear plan at all. Whether the British ruling class are wicked or merely stupid is one of the most difficult questions of our time.

There were two wars for Steer from May 1937 onwards: the infantry war on the ground, which he covered at great physical risk to himself, and the media war of propaganda, often waged in the pages of his own newspaper. The destruction of Guernica was not only a horrible thing to have seen, Steer remarked, but also led to some of the most horrible and inconsistent lying in modern history, much of which is exhaustively tracked in Herbert R. Southworth's remarkable book *Guernica! Guernica! A Study of Journalism, Diplomacy, Propaganda, and History*.

What seems to have happened is that the international reaction to the bombing of Guernica panicked the Nationalists. Instead of brazening it out, their first reaction was to deny the bombing utterly and say that no planes had taken off because of the weather. Then they said a few planes (but not German ones) might have bombed Guernica intermittently. As all liars know, the trouble with changing your story is that contradictions become impossible to manage. The Nationalists wobbled between stories until the right lie could be agreed on. Some argued that Guernica was a military target, an important crossroads with a militia barracks and the Astra gun factory. When Hugh Pollard (the man who had flown to the Canaries with Bolín to bring Franco to Morocco) wrote to *The Times* on 3 May 1937, his robust view was that Guernica was a perfectly legitimate target. When he suggested that small arms of Spanish make had reached terrorists in India and Egypt, he implied that the Nazis were doing the Constabulary of the British Empire a favour. But the trouble with acknowledging *any* bombing was that it led to awkward questions about German and Italian participation, so that avenue was blocked off.

They settled on the standard atrocity retort: 'Blame the victim'. The story was first born on 28 April 1937, the same day as George Steer's dispatch appeared in *The Times* and the *New York Times*. James Holburn, the *Times* correspondent with the Nationalists in northern Spain, was among the first to deliver it, along with Berlin Radio at 10 p.m. Holburn was thirty-six, and had been Assistant Correspondent in Berlin for sixteen months before coming to Spain in mid-February 1937. He returned to Berlin in July 1937 for another two years, before moving to Moscow at the time of the Nazi–Soviet pact. Holburn telephoned *The Times* from Salamanca HQ, where Bolín was in charge of the press, and his story was in the paper on Thursday, 29 April: 'In Nationalist circles it is asserted that the enemy fired Guernica as they did Eibar, where, according to Nationalist sources, the enemy before evacuating the town sprayed petrol on the buildings. A few incendiary shells . . . inferno . . . It is stated also that mines were exploded.' Holburn was working under strict censorship and the story is clearly flagged three times as a Nationalist assertion; but to the faithful, these words became gospel facts. The Reds had burned their own town and blamed the other side.

The Times had already cabled George Steer at the Torrontegui: VIEW OTHER SIDES DISMISSAL YOUR GUERNICA STORY FURTHER JUDICIOUS STATEMENT DESIRABLE. Steer replied on 28 April:

> The denial by Salamanca of all knowledge of the destruction of Guernica (in Basque, Gernika) has created no astonishment here, since the similar but less terrible bombing of Durango was denied by them in spite of the presence of British eye-witnesses.
>
> I have spoken with hundreds of homeless and distressed people, who all give precisely the same description of the events. I have seen and measured the enormous bomb-holes at Guernica, which, since I passed through the town the day before, I can testify were not there then.
>
> Unexploded German aluminium incendiary bombs were found in Guernica marked 'Rheindorf factory, 1936'. The types of German aeroplane used were Junkers 52 (heavy bombers), Heinkel 111 (medium fast bomber), and Heinkel 51 (chasers). I was myself machine-gunned by six chasers in a large bomb-hole at Arbacegui-Gerrikaiz, when they were returning from Guernica. According to a statement made by the German pilots captured near Ochandiano early in April at the beginning of the insurgent offensive, they are manned entirely by German pilots, while nearly all the crew are German, and the machines left Germany in February.
>
> It is maintained here that the entire insurgent air force used in this offensive against the Basques is German, except for seven Italian Fiat fighters and three Savoia 81 machines.

The original telegram (which Steer copied to Philip Noel-Baker, asking him to use it in the House of Commons and get the information to Lloyd George and Anthony Eden) ends:

> THAT THEY BOMBED AND DESTROYED GERNIKA IS CONSIDERED JUDGEMENT YOUR CORRESPONDENT AND MORE CERTAIN KNOWLEDGE IF THAT POSSIBLE OF EVERY WRETCHED BASQUE CIVILIAN WHO FORCED TO SUFFER IT MESSAGEND = PLEASE PUBLISH WHOLE THIS MESSAGE WHICH UNDERSTATEMENT OF TRUTH STEER +

Guernica became the ground of a propaganda battle fought in print and on the wireless. Steer took part in a broadcast from Bilbao Radio on 4 May that described and condemned the bombing. Father Eusebio Arronategui of Santa Maria Church took part, as did the Mayor of Guernica, Jose Labauría Porturas. There's a photo of them standing together: Steer is on the right in his sports jacket, clasping his hands in front of him. He looks startled by the camera flash and his hair is wild and rumpled.

General Mola's troops – Italians, Moors, Navarrese *requetés* and a few Germans – occupied the town three days after the bombing, around midday on Thursday, 29 April. (From near by, Steer watched the Spanish Nationalist forces enter Guernica from the east; there was no fighting.) With them were some journalists, four Italian, two French and a German. The only English reporter was Pembroke Stephens of the *Daily Telegraph*. In print the next day, he gave a non-committal report of damage; but Stephens also went to see the British Ambassador, Sir Henry Chilton, in Hendaye on Sunday, 2 May. In confidence, asking for the information not to be traced back to him, because he had to return to Nationalist Spain, the reporter told the diplomat that he had no doubt the air raid had taken place. The remaining inhabitants described it for him. 'He also saw many unmistakable bomb-holes. He has no evidence that damage was done by Government forces.' Stephens believed that 'the main object of the raid (which was probably unauthorized by Salamanca) was to make a warning demonstration of frightfulness'.

Nationalist press officers closely escorted all subsequent tours of Guernica. James Holburn was shown round the town on Monday, 3 May, and the report of his visit was in *The Times* on 5 May 1937. Holburn remarked on the absence of blast damage, and said of the holes in the ground that he was shown that it was 'a fair inference that these craters were caused by exploding mines which were unscientifically laid to cut roads'. This delighted the Right, who cited it thereafter as conclusive proof, but infuriated Steer. 'The statement issued from Salamanca that Guernica was destroyed by "Red" incendiaries is false,' Steer replied in *The Times* of 6 May 1937. And so it went on.

The Basque Foreign Affairs and Propaganda Department published a sixty-eight-page pamphlet about Guernica in English and Basque, with sixty photos. The English text is attributed to Canon Alberto Onaindía, a crucial eyewitness of the bombing, there by accident on a visit to his mother. Onaindía, a progressive Basque nationalist priest, was sent by the Basque President Aguirre to Paris soon afterwards to tell French Catholics what he had seen and to try to reach Rome to inform the Pope. He never made it to the Vatican but he did persuade intellectuals such as François Mauriac and Jacques Maritain that Franco could not possibly justify his attack on the Basques as a 'Holy War', since the Basque people were as Catholic as he was. (The Right then said Maritain was a Jew.)

At a League of Nations Union rally in London's Albert Hall on 30 April, the French Minister of Aviation, Pierre Cot, a radical professor of international law and a convinced anti-fascist, was among those who condemned the bombing of Guernica. Two days before, Steer had urged Noel-Baker to see Cot if he was in London, 'and emphasize needs of Basques as described my letter to you'. On 10 May 1937 Noel-Baker forwarded a letter and telegram from Steer via 'the sure hand of a friend from the Spanish embassy' to Pierre Cot. 'Steer is very strongly of our views on the whole issue, and about the League and everything else,' Noel Baker wrote. 'He is a remarkable man: the most brilliant scholar of his year at Oxford, and now a very keen student of war, who has been in the front-line throughout the whole of the Abyssinian conflict and throughout most of the fighting in Spain. He communicates with me through the Basque Government, who send his telegrams in code.'

If Bilbao could be held, Steer reckoned, Franco would be defeated and the war finished quickly; but Bilbao could only be held if there were more aircraft to help the defending forces. Hence the appeal to the French Minister of Aviation, who, through his *chef de cabinet* Jean Moulin (the future resistance hero) and the adventurer André Malraux (who formed and flew in the 'Escuadrilla Espana'), had covertly provided about five dozen new French bombers and fighters to the Spanish Republic in July and early August 1936. That, however, had been before non-intervention became official French policy. Pierre Cot could often turn a blind eye, but his hands were tied.

On 29 May 1937 the Council of the League of Nations passed a unanimous resolution calling for the withdrawal of all non-Spanish forces from the Civil War, and condemning air attacks on open cities in Spain. Steer was in Geneva for the vote, and had a long conversation with a man called Roberts who ran the Spanish desk in room 100 at the

Foreign Office. The day before, Stanley Baldwin had been succeeded as British Prime Minister by Neville Chamberlain, set on a course of appeasement of Germany and Italy. Steer told Roberts that Aguirre and the Basques had no intention of surrendering; indeed they wanted even more autonomy. He said the Basques did not like the Asturians, who let them down in the line, and that he intended to return at once to Bilbao.

9

Saturday, 12 June 1937 dawned with a blue sky. Steer rose early, and was driven by police escort to Urrusti on the *cinturón*, the iron ring around Bilbao. He walked along the trenches with men who were carrying up some of the new olive-green Czech machine guns that had been smuggled in by sea.

The ridge of Gastelumendi, at the middle of a straight line drawn between the centre of Guernica and the presidential offices in Bilbao, was the weak section of the iron ring, and the enemy was now turning its attention there. Below Steer was a plain, stretching away at the left to Munguia. Right before him was the front from Fika to Vizkargi. At 8.30 a.m. Steer started noting down, on the side of his Basque army map, the first of the fifty-five bombers and fighters he was to count that morning. At ten o'clock the enemy shelling began to step up its rate, as dozens of artillery batteries began to pound the line, while the planes zoomed overhead to bomb the reserves behind them. Steer found an alcove of sandbags two deep that would protect his head, then he settled down to smoke and to read the calming poetry of the seventeenth-century Anglican parson George Herbert. 'It was like stripping on scorched rocks at an African lakeside and plunging into clear pebbled water without risk of *bilharzia*.'

(The Metaphysical Poets meant a lot to the martial modernists of the 1930s. Ernest Hemingway – who asked his editor Max Perkins to send him three copies of *The Tree of Gernika* – chose a line from John Donne for the title of his 1940 Spanish Civil War novel *For Whom the Bell Tolls*.)

Then bombs began falling near, dust rattled on the page, and it was impossible to read 'The Church Floore' or 'Vertue' any more. A man swore: *I shit on God*. Steer felt incredibly thirsty. He moved out of his alcove, and had not gone ten yards when a shell hit it, blowing the sandbags to pieces. The artillery was firing eighty rounds a minute. The only water he could find was a puddle in an old shell hole. He dipped into it with a torn sardine tin. The enemy tanks were moving up, followed by hundreds of men. Thick smoke blew across from Gastelmundi as the Basques fired their small arms down the hill. Tank shells started hitting their parapet. One exploded through the brushwood canopy to Steer's left and blew the faces off two young men in the firing line. 'Many kinds of wound and death would not revolt me; but the human face, source of all visual charm and meaning, versatile, clever and affectionate, smiling and determined – not that – that made me sick. These were, one minute before, decent lads; and now they were dead, with blank red shreds of faces, moving only with blood, which pulsed out of them as their bodies still stirred gently.'

More shells were falling, and everything was jumping up and down with dust. An officer came running from the right to say that the enemy had got behind them. Bullets sang through the trees on the top. They stumbled and scrambled up the hill through littered trenches in clear hot sunshine. Planes machine-gunned, artillery shelled, but the Basques went back steadily to the top of the brown ridge. Steer's tongue was dull and dry, his eyes filmy. He felt like a horse in blinkers, plodding back to Bilbao through dozens of exploding shells. 'We were not demoralised. We were not retreating in disorder. We were not retreating in order. We were retreating.'

A few men fell; the rest went on, deafened, uncaring. It was quieter and cooler among the pines on the back of the hill, until the planes found them and streamed down with rattling guns while they sheltered behind zinging, chipping stones. Steer walked to Brigade HQ at Zamudio, where they plied him with an enormous quantity of wine. Larrañaga, the communist political commissar, was going back to Bilbao to report the loss of Gastelumendi, and gave him a lift in his car. The portico of the Carlton Hotel was another world, with the British Consul and Vice-Consul standing well dressed and friendly on the white steps. They went upstairs.

I was still unbelievably thirsty, and as I drank Mendigurren's sherry, sallow stuff, I thought of dust, brittle aeroplanes, tanks like crackling beetles, smart artillery and dead faces, dry bombs, tank dust and stones scattering and scratching as sharp as metal. I was in three worlds, that of the real war with its moves and counter-moves, submissive to minds, propositions, conditions . . . in that of Mendiguerren's office, with his sallow sherry, looking at his pale, thin, over-young face as he asked me, 'What's happened, really, what has happened?' and in my immediate memory, which was peopled with these shining objects and the stupid, tumbled dead, and reminded me for all the world of a jackdaw's garden, full of hard, sharp things that reflect light and of the wretched dead worms and grubs and broken insects that serve him for fodder . . . I sat down in a soft chair and went to sleep.

An explosion startled him awake. The enemy was shelling the centre of Bilbao with twelve-inch armour-piercing shells. He turned over in the chair and went back to sleep.

10

The next day, Sunday, 13 June, Steer was retreating again, this time from Santa Marina, the last hill before Bilbao. Enemy soldiers, advancing from Lezama, were swarming over the eastern and south-eastern *cinturón* like bees. Steer stopped to pick cherries in a garden pocked with fresh bomb holes. In the afternoon the long, lean-bodied Heinkel 111s turned like sharks in the air above Bilbao as they machine-gunned the city for the first time, 'a metal hail from under their rigid, gliding fins'.

Suddenly, everyone knew Bilbao was falling. People prepared to flee for France. There was a conference under the glass candelabra in the President's long saloon at the Carlton towards midnight. Generals, ministers and foreign advisers sat on gilt chairs around a polished table. Aguirre looked older and paler. He asked whether Bilbao could be defended. Generals hummed, demurred.

Press attaché Arbex made an emotional speech that almost implored surrender. He was a handsome lightweight who had been in films before he got into public relations. Steer wryly judged his 'close-up shot' of despair to be quite affecting.

The Russian Gurieff said Bilbao could be defended if they had the will, but Steer's friend Monnier added, delicately, that only the Basques could decide if they were ready to see Bilbao destroyed, which it surely would be in three weeks of fighting.

The Cabinet eventually decided that Bilbao would be defended, but the civilian population would be evacuated *en masse* to the west.

The British government would be asked to secure guarantees from General Franco that he would not bomb or shell the city.

From that night on, Steer started sleeping in his clothes. Monnier, changing as ever into his elegant pyjamas, complained that the Englishman would now begin to smell.

The great evacuation of Bilbao began. Trawlers, steamers, lorries were pressed into service to go to Santander in the west. Two warships, *Ciscar* and *José Luis Diez* were designated to take women and children to France; the 'unstoppable mob' that clambered on board included several senior figures in the Basque civil and military establishment. For five nights the evacuation went on, carrying 200,000 to Cantabria.

Simpler soldiers abandoned their posts, too. On Monday night, 14 June 1937, Steer went with Monnier up to the Divisional HQ which was occupying the church of Nuestra Señora de Begoña. They found the tough new French commander, Colonel Putz, sleeping in his riding boots, wrapped in his overcoat beneath a crucifix with hand grenades ready under his bench. They left the dim church to go up to the front line, which the Asturian soldiers had deserted that night. Steer always hated night manoeuvres, and the cool, empty darkness, with faint firing to the north, was frightening.

There was now a 2,000-yard gap in the defensive line around Bilbao. Monnier alerted the Basque government, who left for western Vizcaya, leaving a four-man Junta de Defensa behind. With the rat-like cunning of the scoop-minded reporter, Steer warned the other journalists that the enemy was on the brink of pouring through, and the others all sped off in a powerful car. That left Steer and *The Times* in sole possession of the story of the fall of Bilbao. It would test all his powers of endurance.

He was brushing his teeth on Tuesday morning when the water failed. Then the lavatory would not flush. They tramped out with buckets to get scummy water from a fountain in the park. The last drive of the enemy on Bilbao began. On Thursday, 17 June they started shelling. Ten thousand shells were thrown at the Basque front line. A pause; and then ten thousand more. Then every type of plane coming in to bomb.

> White towers arose in Deusto across the river, climbed at a mad
> speed by scarlet creepers of fire . . . I went across to the other side of
> the river . . . Looking up from the bridge through the fires of Deusto
> I could see the last battle rage upon Arxanda.

At eight-thirty in the evening, Steer was at the Deusto drawbridge over the Nervion, a few hundred yards west of where the Guggenheim Museum now stands. Shrapnel was bursting overhead and men were firing uphill at the enemy. Their commander ordered the Asturians back into the line, but a man stepped out of the ranks and shot him dead. Steer was among a company digging up cobblestones to make trenches and barricades when six Heinkel 51s came over the ridge and plunged full throttle at them.

In his introduction to *The Tree of Gernika* Steer says he uses 'we' and 'our' because it was usual for journalists in Spain so to refer to the side they were working on, adding: 'It is not to be inferred from my use of these terms that I participated in any way in the struggle.' What we know about his character suggests that this statement is disingenuous. As the Heinkels swooped by the Puente de Deusto, George Steer was utterly at one with the Basques, and having the time of his life.

> In line, they dived upon us, firing devilish fast. But somehow, after the day's bombardment, it seemed a feeble rattle that they made. We had grown obtuse to things that would have driven us to cover before. Standing up on the hard wide road, we loosed off two hundred rifles and machine guns at them. Ah, what a memory. The mountain ridge spouting smoke like the spines of a pachyderm, fire raging across the river, everywhere the crack of artillery, the shrapnel mixed in a savage disorder with the plunging fighting planes ... The air sang with ill-directed bullets. And what sport! ... They made the cobbles round us rattle like dice.

And so, as night fell over the flames and firing, the last doomed fight for Bilbao went on. Three of the best Basque battalions made their final throw – the Kirikiño, the Itxas Alde and the Itxarkundia.

> In the history of the sacrifice of human blood for democracy may their names live for ever! As long as laurels spring out of the generous ground, there will be leaves to crown their memory. Heroes, salute! A forlorn hope, and knowing it, they went up the line singing the solemn songs of Basque Nationalism, songs like the Gaelic laments of prehistory to be accompanied upon the bagpipes and the xistu. Their deep voices were lost in the dark.

The last battalions of Euzkadi went up the slope with rifle, machine gun, mortar and grenade. They fought their way back into Fuerte Banderas,

Berriz, Arxandasarri and the Casino at Arxanda. They killed many, and many of them were killed. By 4 a.m., after the Casino had been mortared and shelled, taken and retaken, they pulled back to the river: half of them were dead or wounded.

11

The morning of Friday, 18 June found Steer, 'the bonehead Englishman' who had slept in his clothes again, breaking up the flat's furniture for Monnier, 'the continental', to cook on. Their castellated building had been shelled, because there was a machine-gun nest under the roof. At the General Staff HQ, maps were being taken down and trucks loaded with secret papers. When Steer and Monnier drove to visit the Basque commander Beldarrain, the Italians shelled their car from across the river, which they found hilariously funny.

After a day visiting unfed troops in disintegrating lines they ate tinned army food in the Presidency, washed down with pints of champagne. After supper Steer looted the empty Basque government offices. He pocketed two photographs, President Aguirre's pen and his last notepad, on which he would start writing *The Tree of Gernika*.

Steer admired Basque fortitude. The leonine lawyer Jesús María de Leizaola had been left in charge of the Defence Junta when Aguirre and his Cabinet had gone to the west. The Anarchists would not be allowed to blow up churches and set fire to university buildings; Basque nationalist battalions were stationed along the river bridges to stop any more damage to their dirty but dear city. Despite all they had gone through, Leizaola was anxious to release all the Francoist prisoners, and see them escorted safely back to their own lines.

> It would be difficult to exaggerate the courage and the calmness of Leizaola this evening. He was not, like the rest of us, a fighting man, or a man whom risks amused. At the bottom of his heart he detested war; we liked or accepted it. . . .
>
> After all, the Basques were a small people, and they didn't have many guns or planes, and they did not receive any foreign aid . . . but they had, throughout this painful civil war, held high the lantern of humanity and civilisation. They had not killed, or tortured, or in any way amused themselves at the expense of their prisoners. In the most cruel circumstances they had maintained

liberty of self-expression and faith. They had scrupulously . . .
observed all the laws . . . which enjoin on man a certain respect
for his neighbour. They had made no hostages; they had responded
to the inhuman methods of those who hated them by protest,
nothing more . . .

Now Bilbao was beaten, but the sad-faced Catholic lawyer in the
thick black suit who was ruling Bilbao was determined to see his
city's record clean to the finish . . .

He was the finest type of Christian. Faithful to the end to his
church and social conscience, he alone can have known how hard it
was to serve these two masters in Bilbao, June, 1937.

At two in the morning the Basques blew up the bridges across the
Nervion River and all the lights went out, because someone had forgotten that the power cables also ran across a bridge. By moonlight
Steer wandered the deserted streets of Bilbao alone, like 'a small fidgety
animal'. At the riverside the Basque nationalist militia waited silently
behind sandbags, with guns pointed, or huddled in blankets. They had
no fires and there was no shooting in the darkness.

In the cold before dawn on Saturday, 19 June Steer felt it was time to
say goodbye to Bilbao. The river was the colour of steel as he walked the
long road west. He sheltered in a tunnel for a while with some militia
when a Francoist machine gun opened up. When the firing stopped, he
left the road, clambered over garden fences, and ran past houses for a
mile until he reached safety at the girder bridge. Queueing drivers said
the road ahead was impassable, but Steer persuaded an old chauffeur of
his to take the risk. They went very fast, took two bullets from the
machine gun on Cobetas, but got out of Bilbao.

At midday Steer found Monnier in the gas-mask factory at Retuerto,
and wolfed down his leftover fish and dregs of wine. They drove west
through hot and dusty mining villages, where thousands of militia were
retreating but still marching in order. That hot afternoon they drove
through Somorrostro towards Santander, carrying an epileptic to the
Red Cross; he shook convulsively and slobbered on his collar, and the
trees looked dead and dull with dust. The drivers sweated in their iron
tanks behind the great retreat.

In the hills behind them, Peter Kemp and his Nationalist comrades were preparing to march down into Bilbao for Sunday mass.
!Contra Dios No Se Puede Luchar! (You Can't Fight God) was the

moral of the sermon, and General Franco himself was there to enjoy his triumph.

On Monday, 21 June, G. L. Steer telephoned his last piece to *The Times*, and they gave it the turnover on Tuesday. 'Bilbao's Last Stand – An Eyewitness In The Trenches – Heroism Versus High Explosive' is a grim litany of names and places, a tired tale of the who, what, when and where of defeat. It was too boringly factual to make *The Times Weekly Edition*, but James Holburn's paean of Francoist triumph did.

Franco's intelligence officers began going through Basque government files and Cable and Wireless copies looking for incriminating material. The cable to Steer from *The Times* requesting more details about Guernica was first published, with insinuations of inaccuracy, in an International Catholic Truth Society pamphlet 'Why The Press Failed On Spain!' in Brooklyn, New York. The extreme right-winger Major Francis Yates-Brown was shown some correspondence between George Steer and Philip Noel-Baker MP 'found by Franco's people at Bilbao, which showed conclusively that both were very much mixed up in Basque affairs, too much so in fact'.

12

In Paris on 1 July 1937, Thomas Tucker-Edwardes Cadett was a few days away from being promoted to Chief Correspondent of *The Times*. He heard a ring at the front door of his elegant flat, opened the door himself and recoiled from a tramp, 'a scruffy little man with wild eyes, tousled hair, dressed in a filthy canvas jacket, nondescript trousers, and wearing those rope-soled canvas shoes known in France as *spadrilles*. A mousy-coloured stubble on his chin completed the elegant ensemble. Incidentally, he stank. As I stared, wondering who the devil it was, there came a high-pitched giggle and the fantastic creature said, "It's all right, Tom, it's George Steer."'

Cadett saw that he was feverish, 'pretty well at the end of his tether', poured him a 'veterinary' dose of brandy and, forbidding him to sit on the furniture, went off to run a deep bath. They later burned Steer's clothes, and the reporter began writing *The Tree of Gernika* in the Paris apartment.

Tom Cadett, who was in SOE's French section in the Second World War and afterwards Chief Correspondent of the BBC in Paris, became George Steer's best friend. They had first met when Steer was on his

way to Abyssinia in the summer of 1935. Nearly ten years later, in an
obituary note, Cadett mentioned Steer's lesser-known activities in the
1930s:

> To the outside world, his newspaper despatches and his books
> naturally took first place, though even from them it was possible to
> glean an idea that the lost – temporarily lost – causes that he
> followed had, perhaps, received from him something more than
> verbal support. Only his friends could know at the time how far he
> possessed, and had already been exercising, those qualities of the
> guerrilla leader that he was to show later in full-dress warfare.

So much for Steer's suggestion that he took no part in the struggle.

13

George Steer saw the Basques once again. On Wednesday, 18 August
1937, he flew in a small Beechcraft from Biarritz to Santander, and
stayed three days in a city besieged by General Davila's troops.
Santander, further west on the north coast of Spain, was differently run
from Bilbao. The Santander Chief of Police had been a leftist thug
called Colonel Neila, who ruled by terror. His gunmen liked to leave the
corpses of those they executed propped up at café tables in the street;
but when they murdered their first Basque, an innocent chauffeur, the
two errant policemen were shot dead and Colonel Neila himself was
bundled on to a plane to France.

The Basque Presidency was in a white villa near the lighthouse at
Cabo Mayor.

'¡Saleva!,' said President Aguirre, raising his fist to Steer in a comic
salute. It was the new joke greeting, a cross between ¡salud! and evac-
uación. Since July, the hard-working Basque government had got
another 50,000 Basques out of Spain to France. Steer drove twenty
miles east with Leizaola to see the last peaceful evacuation the Basques
would make. A little tramp ship called Bobie lay anchored at Santoña
quay, her Greek captain 'obese and damp with anxiety' about whether
the Royal Navy would protect him at the three-mile limit.

Bobie was full of wounded men. Here were the cripples that Miguel
de Unamuno had prophesied in the debate at Salamanca in October
1936. Steer's description in The Tree of Gernika no longer uses 'we',
because healthy visitors like him did not belong in that community of

pain. He does not use 'I' either, since he does not want to intrude personally, but he respects, or holds back, as 'one'.

Here and there lamps half-lit the decks of *Bobie*, and the rough
wooden ladders and trestles that led down to the hold of the tramp.
They half-lit the faces, bandages, crutches, and gaps for legs and
arms of the Basque soldiers who lay on the decks or down below.
    There were five hundred of them. From the gaiety of their
conversation and the youthfulness of the looks of those on deck one
could scarcely guess that none would ever be able to fight again;
that many would never be able to earn a living, or walk about any
more. They were the *grands blessés* of Bilbao, the Blighty wounds of
the Basques, the first five hundred of several thousand. One kept
one's face in the dark shadow as one watched them drag their way
along the deck to get soup and candles, matches and cigarettes, in
the light of the flickering lamps. The boards where they lay were like
earth sprinkled in winter with light snowdrifts, with the great white
expanses of bandage that pied the ship and relieved the darkness
from end to end. Below other wounded lay in crude shelves along
the bottom of the ship; these were strapped in and were suffering
more sharply. When they turned their hollow faces to the smoky
twilight, one could see in the interplay of fire and shadow on the
bone-frames of their cheeks and eyes that all their features were
peaked with pain. They wanted not to be noticed, to be forgotten,
and plucked their blankets uneasily over their heads.
    One could smell the burnt wick as the lamps went out, like their
youth, and one's eyes became accustomed to the gaunt skeleton of
their hospital in the ship's hold, as hollow and dead as their future.
It was a solemn and terrible cave in which we stood, banked high
with wasted lives, hollow sockets of eyes that looked at us, bodies
lying like corpses under blankets that could conceal their pain but
not their thinness. Water from the bilge trickled under our feet as
the ship slid up and down on the night tide; nobody spoke and one
felt nobody wanted to.

On 26 August 1937 (a year after the battle for Irun had begun), the
remains of the Basque army laid down their arms to the Italian Black
Arrows division in Santoña. The Basques had negotiated and signed a
separate peace with the Italian General Mancini that guaranteed their
lives if they surrendered peacefully. Two ships, both well known to

Steer, the *Bobie* and the *Seven Seas Spray*, arrived to evacuate Basque notables, as agreed. They eventually sailed empty. General Franco overruled the Italian Fascists' agreement to a separate peace, and Euzkadi ended in betrayal.

The Basques were taken away in Roman lorries to captivity and concentration camps or to the execution wall, *al paredón*. The poet Lauaxeta, hero of the film that featured Monnier and Steer, was shot on 25 June 1937. At Bilbao, Franco's tyranny began its reign of judicial murder over the civilian population. But as one generation went to their deaths or into exile, dragons' teeth were being sown for the next, for Basque hearts were not defeated.

> [The Basque] is proud, too, of the year in which he governed himself . . . Alone in all Spain he showed that he was fit to rule; where others murdered and butchered, terrorised the working class and sold their country to foreigners, the Basque bound together his little nation in strong bands of human solidarity . . . His was a real People's Front . . . Its roots were very deep, and its lineage very old, but its leaves are full of a greenness and virtue that are renewed every year . . . and they stand unshaken in the fire and the explosions to give shade to future law-givers who are the people's choice. Their symbol, and their history, is Gernika's Tree.

14

So ended Steer's finest book. When he began writing it in Paris that summer, he could venture out from Tom Cadett's flat and see the clash of ideologies at the 1937 World's Fair. The totalitarian kitsch pavilions of the Soviet Union and Nazi Germany squared up to each other across the Seine, the huge communist hammer and sickle facing the naked Teuton caryatids with their big genitals. The British arts and crafts pavilion was tweedy and rustic, the French had Elsa Schiaparelli, and the Italians bullfrog portraits of Mussolini. On the ground floor of the Spanish 'Espagne' pavilion, however, was Pablo Picasso's enormous canvas *Guernica*.

The Spanish Republic had been preparing for this for four months, in the midst of a civil war. They considered it vital to present their cause as modern, progressive and civilized, but direly threatened by fascism. In January 1937, one of the Catalan architects who designed the pavilion, José Luis Sert, had commissioned Picasso to do the giant picture for the wall behind Alexander Calder's *Mercury Fountain* sculpture. Picasso's fee was 200,000 francs, about 10 per cent of the whole budget. We cannot be certain if George Steer ever went to see Picasso's *Guernica*, but they were in Paris at the same time and it seems very unlikely that he would not.

Picasso accepted the commission in January 1937 but was paralysed for months. He had done a strip cartoon called *Dream and Lie of Franco*, a repellent portrayal of the Spanish general, but when he went to visit the pavilion building site on 19 April, he was still toying with the idea of 'The Studio: The Painter and His Model' as the subject. The last of his fourteen drawings also sketches the position where the new painting will hang on the wall, seen from front and side, together with an upraised arm holding a hammer and a sickle. The pavilion organisers told Picasso that Joan Miró was doing the painting on the pavilion's staircase wall: Miró had chosen to do a Catalan reaper with his sickle and the red *barretina* cap of the French Revolution. Picasso realized that 'the artist's studio' was not quite political enough.

The shocking news of the bombing of Guernica thus came at an opportune moment for Picasso. Steer's dispatch, the fullest account of the bombing, was translated in the French papers. Rage galvanized Picasso. On 1 May 1937 he began painting and drawing the first composition and figure studies. Eight of them feature a wounded horse. On 11 May he started sketching silhouettes of figures on the canvas, and Dora Maar began her series of photographs of him and the work. In three weeks, he transformed it into the famous picture we know today. The dying warrior's upraised fist became a sun, then a disc, then the glaring light bulb. Next to it from the beginning had been the oil lamp held outstretched from an upper window. They are at the top of the picture's central triangle, the source of light in the middle, angling down towards the woman fleeing from right to left across the picture. Looking along the top of the picture, on the far left the bull's tail is like a plume of smoke; on the far right flames fret the top of a black building. In the middle is the light from the street lamp and the lantern. *Guernica* does not depict a bombing literally, but we get a single flash of chaos and terror. It is violently different from the orderly world of Raoul Dufy's pretty and luminous *La Fée Electricité*, a huge mural painted for the same Expo.

Picasso's *Guernica* became world famous and began travelling the globe. In 1938 it went to England and Scandinavia. On 1 May 1939, exactly two years after Picasso had started it, the rolled-up canvas arrived on the liner *Normandy* in New York City. It toured the USA and Mexico during the Second World War and in 1944 the artist himself installed it in New York's Museum of Modern Art. (It is said that Picasso was asked by a German officer in Paris during the war, 'Did you do *Guernica*?' and he replied, 'No, you did.') The painting went to Europe and South America in the 1950s and 1960s. In 1974 the canvas had to be repaired after the graffiti artist Tony Shafrazi spray-painted on it in red, 'Kill Lies All'.

Pablo Picasso died in 1973. He swore that *Guernica* would never go to Spain while Franco lived. The Generalísimo died in 1975, and after many negotiations, in 1981, Picasso's centenary year, the picture the Spanish Republic had commissioned finally arrived in Madrid. On 10 September 1992, the restored King and Queen of Spain inaugurated the museum in the Spanish capital where the painting is now the centre-piece. Most Basques would like *Guernica* to hang in the Guggenheim in Bilbao, but that would require a process of political evolution in Madrid that is at present inconceivable.

15

In England, the propaganda battle over the bombing of Guernica raged through the summer of 1937. The wave of indignation that Steer's report aroused had panicked both the Nationalist command in Spain and their supporters in England, and they went on the offensive to gain hearts and minds. Luís Bolín urged Franco to appoint the Duke of Alba and Berwick as Nationalist representative in London, and himself spent 'three weeks' leave' in London in June 1937, during which time, as he put it in his autobiography *Spain: The Vital Years*, 'I was not idle'. His mission was to get people to believe that the Reds burned Guernica themselves. Bolín worked in tandem with the more secretive British-born Marquis del Moral, who had passed forged anti-Red documents to the Foreign Office in 1936 and who, fresh from a visit to Franco and a dash through the occupied Basque Country, briefed a group of British MPs about Guernica on 26 May 1937.

Luís Bolín badgered Ralph Deakin at *The Times*, doubtless blackening Steer's name in the process. 'We have had two or three visits from Bolín,' Ralph Deakin wrote to *The Times*' Madrid Correspondent Ernest de Caux on 13 June. 'He has evidently come here to show a certain sweet reasonableness ... he has raised the question whether a senior member of *The Times* staff could not pay a visit to General Franco and his territory.' (De Caux, who had earlier been threatened by Bolín, declined this offer.)

'In England the Catholics were on our side,' Bolín wrote in his autobiography. He inaugurated 'The Friends of National Spain' to persuade Middle England that 'Asturian dynamiters' and 'Basque incendiaries' were responsible for the destruction of Guernica. He buttered up Tory MPs such as Sir Henry Page Croft of Bournemouth, who called Franco 'a gallant Christian gentleman', and gingered up ex-military men of a right-wing bent. His allies in this propaganda battle included Douglas Jerrold and the historian Arthur Bryant, whom Andrew Roberts in his essay 'Patriotism: The Last Refuge of Sir Arthur Bryant' calls 'a Nazi sympathizer and fascist fellow-traveller'. They were all encouraged to write books, introductions, articles or letters to newspapers and magazines.

Douglas Jerrold led the way with a long piece in the Catholic weekly the *Tablet* on 5 June 1937, which prompted a series of letters in the *Spectator*. Jerrold made much of the fact that Steer had made 'a hurried visit in the middle of the night', and claimed that the 'real examination', done by reporters who went in after the Nationalist forces, had revealed 'an absence of all traces of bombs, whether explosive or incendiary'. This he felt was 'evidence that the destruction by fire of the whole town was the work of some other agency'; and he cited the former *Daily Mail* reporter Cecil Gerahty as a witness that there were no planes.

Steer demolished that point by citing evidence from Gerahty's own book *The Road to Madrid* that he had seen fifteen bombers flying from Vitoria on 26 April. Cecil Gerahty was also partisan; the Right Book Club published his second book on Spain, *The Spanish Arena*, in 1938. Chapter 14, 'The Fiction Factory', mentions George Steer as a purveyor of 'false news', but itself begins absurdly: 'We have shown that Spain was the victim of a vast Communist plot, inspired and controlled by continental Freemasons, largely Jewish, and international agitators, working with certain Spaniards as their tools and assistants, to establish a world domination for the Comintern, which at present is identified with Stalin and Russia.'

Several letters helped refute Jerrold's case. D. W. Stather-Hunt wrote from Oxford in the *Spectator* of 9 July, drawing attention to an article on the Spanish Civil War, signed by Colonel Rudolf Xylander, in the 25 June edition of the *Militär-Wochenblatt*, the official German army paper. Xylander said, 'Thermite incendiary bombs generating a heat of more than 3000° Centigrade have proved particularly useful in causing conflagrations on the Basque front.'

G. L. Steer's own scathing riposte to 'Mr D. Jerrold' was in the *Spectator* on 30 July, headlined 'The Bombing of Gernika': 'I saw three immense bombholes in the open space immediately east of the Casa de Juntas; about forty feet wide and twenty deep, they were of precisely the same kind as that in which I and other correspondents sheltered that afternoon in the village of Arbacegui-Guerrikaiz. The metal fragments were exactly the same type.' He stated for the record that Guernica had never been bombed before 26 April, and he suggested that the reason the journalists had had to wait three days to go into the town after Franco's troops occupied it, was that the Nationalists had been busy panel-beating the evidence to suit their case.

16

Steer became a target for the Catholic Right. In Spain he was told there was a price on his head and he received death threats. In England and America he was calumniated. One example is the book *Spain's Ordeal: A Documented History of the Civil War* (1938) by Robert Sencourt, which devotes twelve and a half pages to niggling at supposed discrepancies in Steer's accounts of Guernica before concluding that arsonists burned the town. Sencourt (real name Robert Esmonde Gordon George) was a Catholic monarchist, and his version is full of errors ('crews cannot lean out of aeroplanes, and have never before or since been known to use hand-grenades') and has a sly, snide tone. 'The account that horrified England, and much of the world, is that of Mr George Lowther Steer. He was not a staff correspondent of *The Times*, but a free-lance journalist who offered it contributions' . . . 'He no longer makes contributions to *The Times*: nor is he in Spain. It had been felt that, already in Ethiopia, he had been unduly partial to the Negus.'

This annoyed Steer. Early in 1939 he instructed his solicitors Rowe and Maw to 'commence proceedings for damages for libel', and they wrote to Geoffrey Dawson for 'confirmation as to Mr Steer's position when he was working for *The Times*'.

The Manager's Department of *The Times* replied on 6 April 1939:

Dear Sirs,

In reply to your letter of April 4, addressed to Mr Geoffrey Dawson, *Mr G. L. Steer* was engaged as special correspondent of *The Times* from May 1935 to September 1936. He was representing *The Times* in Spain in August and September 1936.

Yours faithfully

May 1, 1939 to Rowe and Maw from Manager's dept.

Dear Sirs

In reply to your letter of the 27th ult. *Mr G. L. Steer*, besides representing *The Times* in Spain in August and September 1936, also acted on his own initiative as an occasional correspondent from April to June, 1937.

Yours faithfully

July 7, 1939 Manager's dept to C. H. Culross, Esq., Messrs Culross & Co, 65, Duke Street, Grosvenor Square, W1 [*The Times*' solicitors]

My dear Culross,

I enclose herewith the correspondence relating to Steer's action.

What we think we might say to them is that Mr Steer's report of the bombing of Guernica had no connexion with the cessation of his service with *The Times*. If you will be good enough to put this in proper legal and innocuous fashion I will send it.

With many thanks

Yours sincerely

July 11, 1939

Dear Sirs,

We write to inform you that the report of our former occasional correspondent, Mr G. L. Steer, on the bombing of Guernica had no connection whatever with the cessation of his service with *The Times*. He gave up the temporary work he was doing in Spain for *The Times* entirely on his own initiative and for personal reasons.

Yours faithfully

Manager

*

In July 1939, Steer was just about to marry for the second time and go on honeymoon to South Africa, so the court case went nowhere; but his relations with *The Times* had become chilly after the summer of 1937. There was an argument about money – Steer was sent 1,000 pesetas, or £25, to cover expenses in Bilbao, and was 'aggrieved' when it was later deducted from his payments; but squabbles over expenses are normal in journalism, and *The Times* seems to have paid him £35 to cover this. There was also a dispute about status. The 1 July 1937 memorandum from Michael Burn, Editorial Assistant in Ralph Deakin's Foreign and Imperial Department, to *The Times'* Manager, said:

> Steer himself appears to have assumed that he was on salary at Bilbao and acting as our accredited Correspondent. This is not quite correct. He was appointed our Correspondent on the frontier, but not at Bilbao, whither he went on his own suggestion. Deakin's letters to him show that we did not send him there deliberately, particularly a letter dated April 9. He did, of course, send us some very useful messages while he was there.

The real reason for the chilliness was that Steer's messages, however 'useful', had embarrassed *The Times*. Respectable opinion – and no one could be more respectable than Geoffrey Dawson, Editor of *The Times* – supported the British government's policy of non-intervention, but at the end of the day would rather have had Franco's side win.

More important than Spain, however, and far more threatening to Britain, was Nazi Germany. Britain's newly arrived Ambassador to Germany, Sir Nevile Henderson, had pressed to know on 4 May 1937 'whether *The Times* report [on Guernica] is correct or incorrect', and recommended that, if incorrect, '[it] should be frankly admitted by a Government spokesman in the House of Commons'. As for *The Times*: 'Should it be established that they have been misled by their correspondent they would be well advised in their own interests to make a handsome retraction'. (No mention of Guernica appears in the Ambassador's self-serving memoirs, *Failure of a Mission*.) Nazi Germany was the state that Geoffrey Dawson and his deputy Robin Barrington-Ward were also most anxious to appease. Dawson wrote an extraordinary letter to H. G. Daniels, the Berlin Special Correspondent, on 23 May 1937:

> it would interest me to know precisely what it is in *The Times* that has produced this antagonism in Germany. I do my utmost, night

1. George Lowther Steer with wildfowl bag in Ethiopia, 1935, beside the *Times*/Reuter truck later destroyed by Italian bombing.

2. Ethiopian warriors. Photo by W. Robert Moore from 'Modern Ethiopia', *National Geographic Magazine*, June 1931.
3. Hubert Fauntleroy Julian with his wife Essie at a Delaware airport, c.1929.

4. Sir Sidney Barton, British Minister at Addis Ababa, Ethiopia, 1929–36.
5. Dr John Melly, head of the British Ambulance Service in Ethiopia, 1935–6.

6. Ethiopian cavalry in Belgian uniforms, from *Abyssinia on the Eve* by Ladislas Farago, 1935.

7. Margarita de Herrero and George Steer on their wedding day, 4 May 1936, with caption from the *East London Daily Dispatch*.

8. George Steer and his second wife, Esmé Barton Steer, behind his mother, née Emma Cecilia Armitage Nutt, and his father, Bernard Augustine Steer, in the garden of their home in East London, South Africa, November 1939.

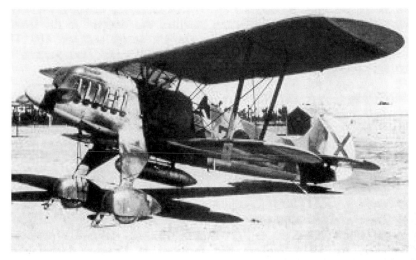

9. Condor Legion Heinkel 51 'chaser', the type that machine-gunned Corman, Holme and Steer at Arbacegui-Gerrikaiz on 26 April 1937.

10. Adolf Hitler with General Wolfram von Richthofen, whose planes bombed Guernica, at the Condor Legion victory parade in Berlin on 6 June 1939.

11. Father Carlos Morilla dead in Santa Maria church at Durango, 31 March 1937.

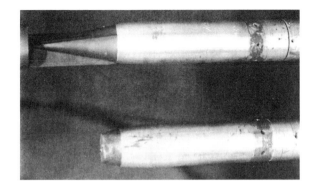

12. German-made thermite incendiary bombs picked up at Guernica, 26 April 1937.
13. Guernica bombed and burning, on the night of 26–27 April 1937.

14. Pablo Picasso's *Guernica,* photographed by Dora Maar in the studio, May 1937, before exhibiting at the Paris World's Fair.

15. Colonel Orde Wingate leading 2nd Ethiopian Battalion of Gideon Force into Addis Ababa, 5 May 1941.

16. Brigadier Dan Sandford and Emperor Haile Selassie, 15 April 1941.
17. Emperor Haile Selassie with Captain George Steer, 3 June 1941.

18. A Soviet SB bomber, shot down by Finns during the Winter War, November 1939–March 1940.

19. Indian Field Broadcasting Unit officers. Six unidentified Japanese-speaking Koreans with, from left, Captains Preston, Mollison (with dog) and Canadian missionary Roland Bacon at right. Lt Col Steer is seated below left.

20. Covers of four of G. L. Steer's books published by Hodder & Stoughton 1936–9.

21. George Steer at East London airport, 2 November 1938.

after night, to keep out of the paper anything that might hurt their susceptibilities. I can really think of nothing that has been printed now for many months past which they could possibly take exception to as unfair comment. No doubt they were annoyed by Steer's first story on the bombing of Guernica, but its essential accuracy has never been disputed, and there has not been any attempt here to rub it in or harp upon it. I should be more grateful than I can say for any explanation and guidance, for I have always been convinced that the peace of the world depends more than anything else on our getting into reasonable relations with Germany.

Iverach McDonald of *The Times* points out that George Steer was valued as a first-rate, bold correspondent, but he was fatally 'viewy', and his views were not Dawson's. The man and the institution parted. G. L. Steer never wrote for *The Times* again, and does not stress his involvement with the newspaper in *The Tree of Gernika*.

Reading fast through a run of newspapers is like flipping through those little books of stills in sequence that quicken into motion pictures against your thumb. In *The Times* of April, May, June 1937 you see interest in the Basque Republic flare up and die away. In the last days of free Euzkadi, Steer's dispatches decrease in size, while those of James Holburn with the Nationalists (including a triumphalist piece about the corporate fascist state Franco was planning) grow. Then comes the fall of Bilbao and Steer does not write any more.

From 25 June, it is Holburn's replacement, Kim Philby, who starts sending back pieces to *The Times* about Franco abolishing ancestral rights, the *fueros*, while the Basques retreat – articles from a journalist whom we now know was toadying to the fascists while secretly working for his communist masters in the forerunner of the KGB. The better man did not win.

six Axis in Africa

1

In early 1939, General J. C. Smuts, the Prime Minister of the Union of South Africa, ordered the arrest of over 2,200 Nazis after an undercover policeman managed to purloin all the membership cards of the South-West Africa Nazi Party. The authorities were finally taking George Steer's warnings of the German threat to the Union of South Africa very seriously indeed.

In 1937 Steer had come back by sea to South Africa sick of Europe, and ill with hepatitis picked up in Santander. The twenty-eight-year-old widower recuperated in the sunshine of the Eastern Cape. Esmé Barton had sent him a wire, which he would recall when they parted for the last time five years later: '*Mon coeur vole à te rappeler*' (My heart flies to call you back); but as 1937 dwindled, he was not yet ready to give up his grief.

Nazi Germany annexed Austria in the *Anschluss* of March 1938, and Steer's friend Christopher Holme of Reuters fled Vienna in a green Lagonda. In April, Britain offered Italy recognition of its sovereignty over Ethiopia in return for withdrawal of Italian troops from Spain. In early May 1938, Hitler visited Mussolini in Rome. The Germans were using a new Junkers plane in Spain, a whistling dive-bomber called a Stuka. The Japanese had learned the lesson of Guernica and were bombing more Chinese cities.

Down in the Cape, George Steer opened up the map of Africa, parti-coloured with different empires. Pink and green dominated: the green parts were French, the pink British; but four areas had once been German colonies, including South-West Africa (now Namibia), and they might be again, if Hitler had his way. And what about the two large yellow Italian sectors in north-east Africa, ominously close together? The Nazis in Germany and the Fascists in Italy were forming the coalition known as the Axis, getting ready to make war on the Allies. Steer saw that Europe was becoming 'the beehive of bombers', and the threat of Italian and German swarms over Africa became the subject of his next two books.

2

In August 1938, Steer was in French Somaliland, staying at Le Grand Hôtel des Arcades in the capital, Djibouti. Refused entry into Ethiopia, he gathered information on what was happening inside the country. Steer wrote articles about it for the *Manchester Guardian* and the *Spectator*, and in January 1939 gave a speech at a public meeting at the Central Hall, Westminster, which became the Abyssinia Association pamphlet 'Abyssinia Today'. Anthony Mockler has suggested that at this time Steer 'played a role as a sort of unofficial spymaster for the exiled Emperor.'

Certainly Steer received a lot of interesting information from a French intelligence officer in Djibouti called Troquard. The French diplomatic establishment was well informed about Ethiopia because the Ethiopian railway was still French-run. Steer learned there was 'bitter resistance' to Italian rule inside Ethiopia, with 'continual fighting'. In July 1938, 27 wounded Italian officers and 700 wounded Italian soldiers were shipped out through Djibouti; 36 Italian officers had been killed in one month. The most active Ethiopian resistance leader was Balambaras Abeba Aragai, the former Addis Ababa Chief of Police, whom Steer had last seen salvaging machine-guns from the mob at the government armoury in May 1936.

The Italians called the resistance 'bandits', but Steer wrote, 'These are . . . men from the greatest and richest Amhara families, accustomed to a life of ease and comfort, who . . . found guerrilla warfare all but intolerable, but go on fighting.' At the Ethiopian Consulate in Djibouti, Steer saw a list of 8,000 'great men' killed since the beginning of 1937.

Italy's Ethiopian empire was a failure, brutal, expensive and corrupt. There was no Italian economic miracle; the promised minerals and oil had not been found. Coffee exports were down by 75 per cent; food crops were failing; few came to settle. But Steer feared that Italy had further territorial ambitions.

*

The British Foreign Office, on the other hand, would not talk about Ethiopia for fear of damaging Anglo-Italian relations. Britain and Italy's 1936 'gentleman's agreement' had warmed into the policy of '*bon voisinage*', or 'good neighbourliness', under the new Foreign Secretary, Lord Halifax. From April 1938, Britain, France and Italy agreed not to carry out intelligence activity or support rebel movements in one another's territories.

In November 1937, the tall and charming Amedeo Umberto Isabella Luigi Filippo Maria Guiseppe Giovanni di Savoia, Duke of Aosta, cousin of the King of Italy, had replaced the psychopathic Graziani as Viceroy of Italian Ethiopia. Soon he had the British in the next-door Anglo-Egyptian Sudan eating out of his hand, flattering them by emulation. Always a generous host, with well-cut tweeds and a good seat on a horse, the Duke seemed the perfect gent.

Intelligence officers were bowled over by him. Douglas Dodds-Parker adored the way he was treated on a six-week visit. Another report, 'Recent Impressions of Italian East Africa', which was circulated widely in May 1939, whimpers with pleasure about the 'frank and friendly' ducal Viceroy: 'He speaks our language faultlessly and fully realizes the mutual advantages of good neighbourly relations between Sudan and Italian East Africa and desires to foster this friendship.'

Steer recognized 'wishful thinking'. When war came, the Italians could use their good roads in Eritrea and, with 40,000 troops from their 200,000-strong army of occupation, easily drive west to take Khartoum 'by charabanc'. The Italians had up to 300 fighters and bombers, the British only a squadron of elderly Vickers Valentias. 'The defencelessness of the Sudan has to be seen to be believed,' Steer wrote in the *Spectator*. With Italian forces also massing in Libya, they could threaten the Suez Canal and Upper Egypt from both south and west. *Reinforce the Sudan*, the young journalist urged His Britannic Majesty's Imperial Government.

3

During the alarming war-scare days of September 1938, when Neville Chamberlain was on an aeroplane for the first time in his life, flying off for talks with Herr Hitler, Steer was aboard an 8,000-ton German passenger ship sailing from Aden to Mombasa. It was 'a great moment for anthropological research'. On deck sat the Nazis, 'blond as brass', as Steer put it with beautiful economy. Also on deck were the more aristocratic German nationalists, 'once a party and now a grumbling club'. Behind 'the portcullis of second class, the Jewish émigrés sat in shabby clothes'. All the passengers, including settlers and missionaries, gathered for the evening tannoy broadcast of German radio. 'We hearkened in awe. Fearful things were afoot in Czecho-Slovakia. Germans had been murdered, tortured, robbed, and expelled in tears. Herr Dr Goebbels had made a speech (in full) and Field-Marshal Göring had boasted that Germany had food and arms for seven years (in full).'

German passengers all wanted to talk about their former African colonies, taken away after the First World War. Steer disputed with a German shipping agent who loudly demanded their return; but when 'the hypnosis of the German radio had lifted', he had a long talk on deck, afloat on the Indian Ocean under the brilliant African night, with a young German businessman. Would the Germans disarm and help organize a system of collective peace, if they got their colonies back? asked Steer. 'I think we would accept the first,' the businessman said, 'but Hitler will never stand for the second' – meaning 'a system of collective peace'. Steer was delighted with the answer, because the young German's tone of voice showed he disagreed with Hitler. 'He saw the real danger of world war; he did not live entirely in a guttural society . . . he persuaded me that the way to talk with Germany to-day was with arms . . . on guard, but without hatred in my heart.'

By 1939 Steer well understood how space and time were shrinking:

> If you open the small blue covers of the stamp books on sale in English post offices, you find that it costs no more than one penny halfpenny to send a letter weighing half an ounce by air to South Africa. Only two years ago it cost sixpence, and only half a dozen years ago one shilling; while less than twenty years back you could not do it for love or money.
>
> If you visit the offices of Imperial or South African Airways, you will be told that it takes five days in the European summer, six in the European winter, to travel between Southampton and Durban. Only two years ago it took eleven days; less than twenty years ago the quickest transport was by Union-Castle mail steamship, which took seventeen days to the Cape.

It had all happened in his lifetime. He had been born in 1909, the year that Blériot flew the Channel, but his earliest journeys to and from South Africa had all been by sea. Steer had been a reporter in Cape Town in early 1933 when Imperial Airways had first begun its eleven-day passenger service from England to South Africa. Now he went home by Empire flying boat from Mombasa down the East African coast to Durban. The lovely white craft all had names that began with C: *Caledonia, Camilla, Canopus, Cassiopeia, Cavalier*, etc., and could carry twenty-four passengers in green leather seats at up to 200 m.p.h.

They flew via Dar es Salaam, 'a tropical garden city standing to attention', planted by Germans as the capital of colonial Tanganyika, and south of Zanzibar the ex-Cunard steward drew Steer's attention inland, out of the starboard window through flecks of cloud: '"Up the Rufiji river – do you see, sir? – yes, in the fourth bend of the river to the left – yes, they all look very much the same, sir, in these mangrove swamps – there it is! What is? *What* is? – why the *Königsberg*, sir, where we ran her aground and knocked her to bits"'; and Steer looked down on a rusting relic of the First World War in Africa, the German light cruiser spotted from the air and sunk by British naval gunfire in 1915.

George Steer was at home in East London during the Munich Crisis. Czechoslovakia was traded away; and in order to appease Hitler further, Chamberlain started considering the return of Germany's former colonies. This caused consternation in southern Africa. Steer threw himself into the controversy. He wrote five articles for the East London *Daily Dispatch* in October 1938, published in pamphlet form the next month as 'Germany in Africa', negotiated with the London *Daily Telegraph* to do a series of features on the subject (which appeared in March 1939 and as a pamphlet in April), and readied Hodder and Stoughton for a book.

On 2 November 1938 Steer went to the airport at East London. A photo (see plate 21) taken against the ribbed fuselage and open door of the aeroplane shows a Chaplinesque figure with a small moustache and unruly hair in pinstripe trousers and a buttoned white jacket that go together oddly. His dark tie is awry on a crumpled shirt, and he is holding a book and a cigarette. Wrinkling his eyes against the sun, he looks far older than twenty-eight. George Steer is about to continue his flight round the old German empire in Africa:

a superb journey of over 10,000 miles by air – from the Union to South-West and back; thence to Tanganyika, Kenya, the Sudan, Nigeria and the Cameroons . . . In the pages that follow, there will only be suggestions of the sunlight of that experience; of the tonic air, stripped mountains, and rolling high veld of our South-West, the thorn and coffee plantations swathed in Tanganyika mist, the motionless darkness of the Cameroons forest, tiled with red leaves as thick as terra-cotta.

Judgment on German Africa – 'G. L. Steer on the New Colonial Question' – is described on the dust jacket as 'The Book That Was Written On The Spot'. It examines three countries, asking: 'Where are they? What do they produce? How are they run? How did the Germans run them? Of what strategic value are they? Could they solve Germany's economic difficulties? Do they offer any evidence on how colonies should be governed?' This look at South-West Africa, the Cameroons and Tanganyika is also a superbly marshalled anti-Nazi polemic. Steer's tutors at Winchester and Oxford would have been proud of the man whom the book jacket described as 'the most brilliant of the younger Foreign Correspondents'.

George Steer was almost in competition with Evelyn Waugh again. The National Book Association, a Tory book club founded in 1937, wanted Waugh to write a book about Germany's lost colonies in Africa, but he passed the commission on to Patrick Balfour, his old friend from Abyssinia. Balfour's book *Lords of the Equator: An African Journey*, published in the same year, 1939, reaches different conclusions from Steer's about the old pre-war imperial system. Neither writer expected full independence in Africa for generations, but Steer at least was clear about the path ahead, arguing idealistically that the purpose of colonial government should *not* be

raw materials for the mother country (seeing that all the colonies in the world produce only 3 per cent of the world's raw materials), or pockets for European investment (seeing that the beneficiaries can only be the few), or strategic power (seeing that if war is permanent life is not worth living). No . . . If we are to remain in tropical Africa we are there for the benefit of the people whom we rule; and their benefit is not only to learn and be healthy, have peace and produce; the greatest gift we can offer them is the opportunity to manage their affairs.

Patrick Balfour's book, on the other hand, saw Africans as children and asserted, 'there is much to be said for the German system of corporal punishment as applied to primitive peoples'. Steer's book concluded that the former German colonies in Africa, taken away after the First World War, should not be handed back, because under the Germans they had been run ineptly and brutally. General von Trotha's extermination of three-quarters of the Herero and Nama peoples in German South-West Africa in 1904–5 had been one of the most shameful episodes in African colonial history.

The former German colonies in Africa had not been annexed by France or Britain but were held in trust, 'in mandate', on behalf of the League of Nations, and Steer thought the system worked. The Mandatories had to give an annual account of their stewardship to Geneva, which Steer thought encouraged more progressive policies than in those European colonies that never had to report on their activities. In fact, he favoured the extension of the mandate system 'throughout black Africa'. (Patrick Balfour, however, saw these League of Nations reports as mere time-wasting bureaucracy.) Steer said international monitoring was needed more than ever at a time when the Nazis at home had gagged the press, the political opposition and the churches.

Chapters 8, 9 and 10 of *Judgment on German Africa*, headed 'Agreement', 'Fire, Flags, Initials' and 'Still Digged the Mole', investigate the almost complete success with which the Nazis had penetrated South-West Africa, despite the banning of the party in July 1934. They merely changed their names: the Hitler Youth became the Pathfinders. 'Away from the police, their leaders wear SS uniforms.' Germans were buying more land in South-West Africa and preparing to re-establish German rule. If that happened, Steer feared 'the Union would pass rapidly into the German orbit. Anti-Semitism would be the moral weapon of penetration.' At the moment when, in Europe, the pogrom known as *Kristallnacht* was shattering Jewish shop windows, Steer cast a cold eye on Nazi racial thinking:

> The German has been taught by Herr Hitler, of anti-Semitic Vienna, to hate and molest the Jew, not because he belongs to an inferior race (in that case, why worry?) but because he is on average more intelligent, more quick and more individual than the German; particularly than Herr Hitler himself. The whole corpus of anti-Semitic propaganda sweats with fear of the Jew. He is the scheming and

spiderish enemy of all pure, dumb Germans, and they must keep a blue weather eye open to see that he is not catching them on the hop.

No such subtlety is attributed to the African, in the German view a good-humoured tough who squanders his wellnigh inexhaustible muscles in sexual dances, and can by discipline be brought to divert this energy on honest work – honest work meaning, as always, work for somebody else.

The difference between Nazi views on Jews and Africans can best be expressed in a military parable. Consider high officers of the army, how they fret at civilian 'interference'; they hate politicians, because they fear that politicians may carry a superior mental equipment to their own. So it is with Germans and Jews. And consider the sergeant-majors of the army, how they shout and swear at recruits; they don't hate them; they rather like them, taken as tools and no more; they want to knock discipline into them and make them willing to fight without forethought. So it is with Germans and Africans.

Steer's most devastating argument in the book is about air power. 'The aeroplane reverses the colonial position of 1914, on which Hitler based his theory in *Mein Kampf*. Every colony is no longer a position lost in advance, but a fortress defended, in the African mind, by dragons of fire.' This is illustrated in two folding maps of southern and northern Africa. Both show in black the colonies that Germany wanted restored – South-West Africa, Tanganyika, Cameroons and Togoland – and black arrows and pebbly circles of black dots also show the range of long-distance bombers radiating from each Axis colony, and where surface ships and submarines could reach. Over each map, on a separate see-through sheet of greaseproof paper, is laid a diagram of the main international civilian airline routes and airports. The sinister Axis black arrows threaten all the Allied territories in Africa, including South Africa itself, as well as all their vital Atlantic and Indian Ocean sea lanes and air routes. Steer's maps (see page xii) show the extent of the danger if the German colonies were restored.

4

When *Judgment on German Africa* was published in early May 1939, George Steer was in the middle of a two-month trip to Tunisia and

Libya, looking at military preparation in the French and Italian colonies. On 3 May 1939, he wrote to his friend the Labour MP Philip Noel-Baker that the French in 'impregnable' Tunisia 'are *very* worried about our slackness in Egypt and the Sudan, and . . . wish to God that we would reinforce'. An Italian attack on Egypt would overstretch the French in Morocco and leave Gibraltar vulnerable. Steer was about to spy out the land in Libya, where the Italians had amassed three army corps, 10,000 white men working on military fortifications and 300 planes, nearly half of which were fighters. 'I shall of course have to be very careful, take no notes or photographs, and mark no maps; but I think it will be fun.'

A Date in the Desert, the book that Steer wrote after this trip, is, unlike *Judgment on German Africa*, much more of a travel book 'in which a present-day journalist drifts like a jellyfish along the sea of the Little and the Great Syrtes to see how they have changed since Ulysses made landfall'. In this unbuttoned book we see Steer's inability to get up in the mornings, his grumpiness and bad temper, sometimes due to hard drinking and heavy smoking. We learn of his lack of interest in classical music, his boredom and irritation with 'society', but he writes about his faults with humour and self-knowledge. He likes many of the characters that he meets, too: the engaging Mr Hamadi Smida, the principal *parfumier* of Tunis, the bearded gnomelike jeweller Yakob bin Cohen on the island of Djerba, and Mr Photis Papavassiliou, the 'plump and pacific' king of sponge-merchants in Sfax.

However, Steer's *Desert* is also a political landscape: 'I saw the preparation of another desert made by men. Here were troops and fortifications in Tunisia, here were troops and fortifications in Libya, and here they were in Egypt too; and over them all flew the same stiff-winged vultures propelled by petrol – the same petrol.' A civil war was brewing between white men of the same civilization. 'They are all more or less clean, wear ties, read books, enjoy the same kind of music, part their hair and drink whisky when they have the chance'; and soon they would be making an artificial desert, 'salted with blood'. Once North Africa had been rich, now it was poor, not just because barbarians had broken through in the past, but because the new European empires spent their money preparing for war.

Steer the classical scholar is fascinated by the Roman Empire's policy of 'absorption through imitation', the way it managed to include and embrace other peoples, cultures and colours. (Only Greeks could join the Greek world.) Steer believed the ancient North African barbarians were 'only too gratified' to join Roman civilization, whereas modern Western civilization was being rejected by a growing Arab nationalism. The Roman Emperor Septimius Severus (who spoke Punic, was of Berber blood and banned gladiatorial combat) was Steer's invisible companion on his journey: 'We are both Africans, Septimius and I.'

North Africa was a cultural layer cake. 'There were seven civilizations before me: Carthage, Rome, Byzantium, Arabia, Spain, Turkey and France.' In the holy city of Kairouan, south of Tunis, Steer laments the collapse of the well-settled and well-farmed post-Roman world, when soft Latin 'Africa' turned to gritty 'Ifrikiya' in the language of Berbers who brought a desert of destruction behind them, a 'sea of sand, of filth and ignorance and poverty blessed by fatalism; the soil erosion of intelligence as well as mountain sides'.

Sitting in the ruined theatre in Dougga, the largest and most dramatic Roman remains in Tunisia, Steer could see from the inscriptions that in the past Rome had absorbed the religion of the natives, and the Numidian natives themselves. 'They were swallowed up in Rome, names, customs, religion, dress, minds.' Perhaps it was easier to rub along when there were many gods: 'We have been able to give to the Arab certain forms of our own: the radio, the press, the political party, ties, and the cinema. But the mosque is still the real obstacle to the conquest of their hearts. Monotheism is as difficult to handle as the only child.'

A Date in the Desert begins in the *souk* at Tunis, capital of French-held Tunisia, at Easter 1939, exactly a year after leaders of the independence movement, including Habib Bourguiba, had been jailed. Steer's principal mission was military. The *Daily Telegraph* wanted two articles on war preparations in Africa, so Steer travelled south to the heavily defended Mareth Bastion, the African Maginot Line being built by the French to defend their colonies in Tunisia, Algeria and Morocco against a possible Italian invasion from western Libya. Steer liked and admired the French military. He talked to fort commanders and drank with soldiers in the evening. In Foum Tathouine he went with them to the brothel: 'I can conceive no better method, given the French character, to find out what regiments are at any single post . . . Prostitutes and spies are part of the same underworld; Mars always takes his armour off in the presence of Venus.'

(Steer thought the public considered journalism 'a rapid assembly of inaccurate statements, best forgotten'. They did not know 'the sweat and the discomfort nor the low and unembellished places where the facts are best sought', nor did they understand 'how atmosphere is drafted by running from the highest to the humblest, and being no less or more than the equal of each'.)

Steer took a ship to Tripoli, the capital of Fascist-held Libya. There he watched the German Mercedes-Benz team win the 1939 Tripoli Grand Prix. Marshal Italo Balbo, famous for having led a fleet of Italian flying boats across the South and North Atlantic in propaganda coups of 1931 and 1933, had replaced General 'Butcher' Graziani as Governor of Libya. When Steer arrived in early May, Balbo was entertaining the German Commander-in-Chief, Colonel General Walter von Brauchitsch, with some massive military exercises near Tobruk. Many Nazis were about: 'The muscular but awkward young men in spectacles, verging on early hairlessness, dressed in white linen suits tailored more woodenly than their Italian prototype; and the grim young women without make-up and with magnificent, earnest, hippopotamus teeth – these were Germans.'

About thirty blond German policemen in green uniforms were studying colonial police methods in preparation for the day when Germany would regain her old colonies. Steer thought they were spying. 'Once, when I charitably offered one of them a drink, the little fellow dropped his glass with fright and ran right out of the bar. Fancy a decent self-respecting member of the Gestapo being seen talking to a journalist who reported the German bombardment of Gernika. Oh horror!'

The German influence in Libya was strongest in the air. There was a squadron of Messerschmitt trainers, with German crews and maintenance staff, at the airport south of Tripoli. Hermann Göring himself had recently visited Libya, staying with his fellow flier Italo Balbo, and later sent him a Fieseler Storch monoplane as thank-you present.

Captain Bellini, an Italian cavalryman turned propagandist, escorted Steer on a fortnight's military tour of Libya. In a succession of late nights and early starts from a series of good hotels, they travelled to Nalut in the eastern part of Libya called Cyrenaica. They drove on fine Italian roads, and Bellini taught Steer how to eat spaghetti properly. On 12 May, 'Day of the Soldier' – celebrating the date when Mussolini had proclaimed the Italian Empire in 1936 – they saw many battalions on parade. The reporter kept his eyes peeled, without openly taking notes.

Steer reckoned there were about 120,000 fighting men in Italian Libya, motorized and mobile, supported by the most powerful aviation in Africa, and Steer knew they would one day attack British Egypt.

Steer went to the town of Sidi Bou Zid in central Tunisia 'to roast off the fat . . . won from the journalistic fleshpots' of Tunisia and Libya. The *Caid*, or judge in charge, was a melancholy aristocrat called Salah ben Khelifah, whose wife had died of pneumonia the previous year. He lent his fellow widower Steer a strong grey horse to help him lose weight and get fitter exploring the old Roman towns.

In string gloves and jodhpurs, Steer rode about 200 miles in six days. It was hard work for the unfit, and he reached Sbeitla looking 'like that picture of the sole survivor of an Afghan War arriving at Peshawar'.*

The next day, he wandered through the Roman ruins of Sufetula, once a city of 25,000, now a large village of 2,000. He thought, 'History is the most reputable form of nostalgia.'

He rode on to Kasserine and what once had been the Roman settlement of Cillium, and found 168 former sailors of the Spanish Republican navy, who had surrendered to the French in March 1939 and were now colonists, trying to grow vegetables and restore the ancient irrigation of Roman Tunisia. David Gasca and Enrique Perera sadly showed him some Spanish Republican postage stamps and photographs of their families, left behind in Spain. 'It made one sick to sit there and sum all the personal sorrows of the civil war: the executions, the broken families, the rich who had become poor, the poor who had become corpses, the headlong ruin of a whole people. How much the foulest of all things was war.'

Steer got horribly sunburned on the next stretch, a twenty-four mile ride north to Sbiba. With bandaged and greased arms he went on to the triumphal arch at Maktar, dedicated in AD 116 to the Roman Emperor Trajan, 'conqueror of the Germans, Armenians and Parthians'. Steer was getting fitter, and found he could tighten his trouser belt on a diminishing pot belly. As he rode in the clear sunlight and cool wind among the poppies and thistles, fritillaries, campions and anemones, he remembered the days with Margarita in a less harrowing way. Old dance tunes from Addis Ababa came into his head. He hummed happily in the saddle.

* *The Remnants of an Army*, by Elizabeth Butler, RA.

Steer admired the *Pax Romana*, the peace that came with Roman rule. In Roman days 27,000 men had guarded the whole of North Africa from Morocco to Libya. In 1939 there were 270,000 soldiers, with a tenth of the wealth to defend. Steer thought Rome 'beat us every time'. Their buildings had lasted 1,700 years; ours would not endure 170. 'Rome was our better because she was the expression of international order, and of the assimilation of the lesser races that she conquered . . . Rome enlarged her limits by the sword. To create the pattern of a civilisation, she dominated before she absorbed. We might have to take the same road . . . By peace or war, one idea would have to win and the other to go down.'

A Date in the Desert was published in December 1939, during the so-called 'phoney war' stage of the Second World War; but within a year of Steer's leaving Tunisia, France surrendered, and not long after, the armies of ten nations started battling back and forth over the lands he had traversed. The Desert Campaigns of 1940–43 marked the end of European control of the Middle East, and were the last great act of the united British Empire. In February 1943, listening to the BBC radio news, far away in Burma, Steer was amazed to hear of 'particularly violent fighting' between 130 tanks at Sidi Bou Zid where he had stayed in Tunisia. (The American Ernie Pyle later reported the complete destruction of the town.) Steer wondered what might have happened to his grey mare.

5

Back in Paris, in June 1939, Steer tried to knit together the strands of his life. First he fell into the arms of Esmé Barton. They were engaged to marry, and planned the wedding the following month in London together with their urbane best man, Tom Cadett. Then Steer engineered a lunch for his Ethiopian friend, Lorenzo Taezaz, so that he could meet his French friend from the fall of Bilbao, the secret agent Robert Monnier. Taezaz, ex-Press Secretary to Haile Selassie, and former Ethiopian representative at the League of Nations, wanted to know how the patriotic resistance to the Italian occupation of Ethiopia was going. Monnier was looking for a new adventure. So the three men combined forces.

Monnier took Steer to the French Ministry of Colonies in Paris and introduced him as 'the principal surviving expert on Abyssinia and an intimate (which I have always longed to be) of the shadier characters of the British War Department'. Monnier got permission and francs from Georges Mandel, the French minister, for a secret sortie by him and Taezaz into occupied Ethiopia to contact the Patriot Resistance, in defiance of the *Bon Voisinage* Accord between Britain, France and Italy. Steer was meant to pull wires and purse strings in London and follow them later. Instead, he got married.

On 14 July 1939, four years to the day since they had first met at the Bastille Day party in Addis Ababa, George Lowther Steer and Barbara Esmé Barton were married by the Bishop of London at the chic King's Chapel of St John Baptist of the Savoy, tucked just south of the Strand.

The smart establishment wedding was reported in *The Times* and the *Telegraph*: 'Given away by her father, the bride wore a gown of blue crêpe, narrow panels of the reverse side of the material decorating the shoulders and skirt. A blue bead headdress held in place her tulle veil, which was tinted to match the gown.'

Tom Cadett could not make it at the last minute, so Archie Rice of the *Yorkshire Post* stood in. A photograph shows the bridegroom and best man outside the chapel, both in cutaway morning coats, pinstripe trousers, white waistcoats and grey ties, with Steer holding a shiny top hat. Archie Rice is big, bald and grinning; George Steer has pomaded hair and a toothbrush moustache. They look like Mussolini and Hitler.

Among the guests was the Emperor Haile Selassie, in an elegant high-collared black cape, accompanied by his two oldest children, Prince Asfa-Wossen and Princess Tsahai-Worek, and his secretary Tafere Worq. Others with an Ethiopian connection were Major Lawrence Athill, the missionaries Mr and Mrs Alfred Buxton, and John Melly's mother and sister. Among the friends and relatives, publishers, painters and pressmen, and thin girls in smart dresses with big hats, there were also naval and military types and the head of MI5, Colonel Sir Vernon Kell, accompanied by his wife. They were invited because Esmé was then working as Kell's secretary. ('I like my girls to have good legs,' Kell once said.) Family rumour has it that Esmé looked up Steer's MI5 file before marrying him, and commented, 'At least it showed he was a man.'

Esmé and George were honeymooning in South Africa when Germany invaded Poland on 1 September 1939. W. H. Auden in New York City wrote his poem lamenting 'the low, dishonest decade', ending with the declaration, 'We must love one another or die.' President Roosevelt asked the combatants not to bomb civilians or undefended towns. Two days later Great Britain, France, Australia and New Zealand declared war on Germany, and on 6 September General J. C. Smuts took the Union of South Africa into the Second World War, narrowly outvoting the Afrikaaner Nationalists, who preferred neutrality or Nazidom. Smuts now led an army of 3,350, with no extra rifles or uniforms, two First World War tanks, one engineless ship and a few dozen obsolete planes.

The newly-weds were still in East London (which did not have a single naval gun to defend itself) in November 1939. On the 27th someone took a photo in the garden at 'Barnack' that Emma Steer captioned lovingly on the back: 'we four' (see plate 8). The parents are in Lloyd Loom armchairs, with Bernard or 'Bunny' looking patrician in a white suit, holding his trilby, and Emma in a cotton print dress and a broad-brimmed straw hat. George (who looks very like her) is standing behind his mother's chair wearing a light jacket and dark tie; the moustache has gone, never to return, most likely at the wife's insistence. Esmé stands behind Bunny, pushing against his chair with her arms, staring at the camera chin down, her hair wavy, looking flushed, petulant, wilful. Her husband was just about to leave her to go off to war again.

6

Robert Monnier and Lorenzo Taezaz reached Khartoum, in the Sudan, in September 1939. They took a train to Gedaref, hid from the British District Commissioner and rode on camels to the Ethiopian frontier. The River Atbara was high; they quarrelled about where to cross it, and parted. Taezaz crossed further south into Gojjam and then wandered round that upland province, stirring up the fragmented resistance, sometimes in uniform, sometimes disguised as a priest or a peasant, getting pledges of loyalty to the Emperor. He returned to Europe in March to brief both Steer and the Emperor.

Anopheles mosquitoes gave Robert Monnier malaria before he crossed the river into Armacheho, west of Gondar. He managed to handwrite a few reports on Italian dispositions on the same flimsy paper Steer had seen him use in the Basque Country two and a half years before; but the man that Steer affectionately dubbed 'the robin fighter of Bilbao' got terribly thin, and died in Aussa on 11 November 1939. A Coptic priest buried him there, 'crusted in the decorations that they found in his luggage'. Steer wrote about his valiant friend in the introduction to his 1942 book about the revolt and reconquest of Ethiopia, *Sealed and Delivered*:

> He must have been furious that he had to die of a fever. It cannot have done his temperature any good at all. Monnier, wherever I go, I think of you. You pretended to have no political morals, and yet you stood, laughing, for the most moral of causes. Your talent could have made you pots of money fighting for our common enemy; but you proffered your life away for the good of the common man, whom most of the time you ridiculed. Above all, you were unquenchably brave and cheerful. When I look at . . . the Petainist of today, I wonder how you could have been a Frenchman. They must have been a great race. Adventurer, this book in which our first plan is shown to be executed is dedicated to you.

SEVEN Winter War

1

After war broke out in the frozen north, Steer left warm Africa for sub-arctic Scandinavia, reporting for the *Daily Telegraph*.

Finland, 'the land of 60,000 lakes', was part of Sweden until 1809 when, in a secret deal with Napoleon, the Tsar made it a Grand Duchy of Russia. In the Russian Revolution of 1917, Finland fought its way to becoming an independent republic, and joined the League of Nations in 1920. But in the secret protocol of the cynical Nazi–Soviet pact of August 1939, Finland was earmarked as a potential spoil of Soviet Russia (along with Latvia and Estonia). The Soviet Union pretended to guarantee Finland's neutrality, but then demanded large concessions of land. Negotiations broke down. Then gigantic Soviet Russia (population 183 million) claimed it had been attacked by tiny Finland (population under 4 million). On 30 November 1939, a quarter of a million Russian troops began crossing the frontier and the Finnish capital Helsinki was bombed and machine-gunned by Russian planes.

Martha Gellhorn was in Helsinki when the bombs exploded. The feet of the first dead man she saw reminded her of the bombing of Madrid three winters before. 'In Spain the small, dark, deformed bundle wore the rope-soled shoes of the poor, and here the used leather soles were carefully patched.' Other familiar stories reappeared from Spain: after the Russians dropped blast bombs and incendiaries they said the Finns had burned down their own wooden homes (in winter) to discredit the innocent USSR. The Finns shot down a Soviet plane that had machine-gunned civilians and were surprised to find that the pilot was a woman. Evacuees began to flee south and west.

The League of Nations Assembly condemned the Soviet Union's

aggression and, for the first and only time in its history, used Article 16 of the Covenant to expel a member. Stalin's attack also convulsed communists worldwide. Singers of the 'Internationale', once loud in condemnation of the bombing of Guernica by Nazi Germany, or of Chinese cities by Imperial Japan, had to switch on 'double-think' at full power to justify the Soviet bombing of Finnish towns as 'liberating the people of Finland'.

The British government, which had sat on its hands over Ethiopia and Spain, now pledged arms to Finland. They had havered over helping black men or socialists, but 'patriots' fighting communism were acceptable. Thousands of volunteers from all over the world came to join a foreign legion in the Finnish Army. The British Vice-Consul in Helsinki, Mr Allen, resigned his post in order to help raise a British brigade. Nearly 9,000 people in Britain volunteered to fight the Russians in Finland and over 200, granted a special royal dispensation from the Foreign Enlistment Act of 1870, arrived before the fifteen-week war ended. Their buttons and badges, originally made in 1936 for the International Board for Non-Intervention in Spain, were rescued from a warehouse in Poole, Dorset. The main cap badge was a chromium-plated rose two inches across, bearing the letters 'NI' for 'Non-Intervention'. The volunteers wittily turned them upside down so that they read 'IN' for 'International'.

2

The Russians sent waves of tanks across the Karelian isthmus in December 1939. The Finns picked them off with their 20 mm anti-tank rifles, which could punch a two-inch hole through the armour. They blew them up with mines, and with 2- or 3-kilo sticky-back satchel charges that they slapped to the metal. The imaginative Finns destroyed many more with an ingenious development of the petrol bomb. Captain Eero Kuittinen's design went into production at the Finnish Liquor Board factory at Rajamäki, and it was mockingly named the 'Molotov cocktail' after the Russian Foreign Minister, a master of propaganda who swore blind to President Roosevelt that no Russian planes were bombing Finnish cities. 'Facts are facts,' he said, while blithely denying them.

The Finns made him a dramatic answer. Four-man teams used the potassium chlorate and coal-tar mixture in Molotov cocktails to destroy Russian tanks. One man jammed the tracks with a log, then two men lobbed their screw-top glass bottles on to vents at the back of the tank, where either the 'Bengal match' taped to the bottle or the vehicle's engine heat ignited the mixture and set fire to the tank's 50-gallon fuel tank. The fourth man with the Suomi sub-machine gun shot any crew who tried to escape death by burning. Most of the Molotov cocktail teams themselves died.

Wave after wave of Russian soldiers followed the tanks. A wounded Finnish soldier told the *Daily Telegraph* correspondent Herbert Beck, 'The Russians are like a herd of reindeer. They just put their heads down and advance without knowing how or why. We shoot and shoot until our ammunition is exhausted, but still more of them advance over the bodies of their predecessors.' These soldiers wore cheap wool coats, thin cotton uniforms, and had no boots, just ordinary shoes. Many had no idea where they were, and had been told they were defending Russia from invasion. Early in the war, the Finns captured a Polish woman on the Karelian front, 'one of the herds of half-starved Polish refugees and prisoners of war whom the Russians are driving forward in front of their shock troops to explode land-mines and to shield themselves', according to a *Telegraph* report. As the temperatures dropped way below zero in one of the coldest winters for a century, hundreds of Russians froze to death. An awed correspondent wrote of 'a forest full of Russian dead'. The Finnish troops had white uniforms and cloaks and flitted like ghosts on hissing skis. In the brutal hand-to-hand fighting on the white snowfields and among the black trees some Finnish soldiers volunteered to become 'human searchlights', skiing with battery lights strapped to their chests that they would suddenly switch on to dazzle and illuminate Russians huddling together for warmth, so that their Finnish comrades could kill them.

3

Just before Christmas 1939 Steer was at sea on a blacked-out ship with Esmé, who was four months pregnant. They were among the forty-one passengers on the grey-painted anonymous vessel, 'the pride of the Union Castle line', that was making a wartime run with maize and possibly gold from Cape Town to Southampton. The ship did strange manoeuvres in its deadly hide-and-seek with the German Navy, which was preying on merchant shipping. The biggest predator it avoided in the South Atlantic was the pocket battleship Steer had seen off the

Basque coast in 1937, the *Graf Spee*, which had sunk four ships before being caught by the Royal Navy off the River Plate and finally scuttled outside Montevideo. 'What a kick to have been in that fight,' the stewards afloat with Steer said wistfully. He wrote an evocative piece about the voyage for the *Daily Telegraph* of 29 December. ('The passengers sat about in little dumb groups, like islands in a very Pacific of a lounge. A gramophone, greatly daring, muttered George Formby to a brace of Scots schoolmistresses in a corner . . . And astern the lean gunner on watch stepped backwards and forwards against the stars.')

The byline 'George L. Steer, *Daily Telegraph* correspondent' appeared on 18 January 1940 over a story from Stockholm reporting the Swedish Prime Minister's statement that Sweden would stay out of the European war and not intervene in the Russo-Finnish conflict. Nor would Sweden permit transit of troops or allow bases to be established. (This would make the Finns feel very bitter.) Steer was in Stockholm on 23 January when a labour movement delegation arrived from Britain. The trio included Sir Walter Citrine, General Secretary of the TUC, and Steer's friend the Labour MP Philip Noel-Baker, whom he interviewed. Noel-Baker greatly admired the Finnish athletes he had run against in the Olympic Games, such as Paavo Nurmi, and said later, after a two-week tour of bomb-damaged Finland, that 'the Finns are splendid . . . but they need weapons'.

'British Bombers Used by Finns' was the bold headline on Steer's front-page story of Friday, 2 February 1940. The *Daily Telegraph* Special Correspondent was 'now able to divulge' that British Gloster Gladiator fighters and Bristol Blenheim bombers were in use. The British had come fully onside. 'These are the planes over which General Smuts, the South African Prime Minister, released the Union's prior rights in response to the League of Nations appeal for aid to Finland.' R. A. Butler made the official announcement that day in the House of Commons. Three weeks later it was revealed that Britain had sent Finland 120 fighters, 24 bombers, 25 howitzers, 24 anti-aircraft guns, 30 field guns, 12 six-inch guns, 4 tanks, 10 trench mortars, 100 machine guns, 150 anti-tank rifles, 10,000 anti-tank mines and 50,000 hand grenades to fight the Russians. What might even a quarter of that have done for Ethiopia, or Euzkadi?

Steer began getting the big front-page stories. His exclusive interview with the Swedish Foreign Minister made a big splash. On 3 February 'Finns Defeat Russians' Newest Weapon' was the page-one lead and on

Monday, 5 February he revealed 'Germany Sending Arms to Russia'. A week later, 'Finns Wearing Down Big Offensive', his page-one lead story next to the death of John Buchan, was filed from Helsinki.

It was a busy first week in Finland: every day from Monday, 12 February to Saturday, 17 February 1940, Steer had a front-page story, usually the main one, about the huge battles on the Mannerheim Line; but he also had three large page-six op-ed articles about Scandinavian defence, strategy and security.

It was a war of savage and relentless bombing. The Soviets, like the Japanese, had studied well the Nazis' tactic in Spain, hitting symbolic targets hard to cause psychological distress. One of Steer's pieces, published on Valentine's Day 1940, was about his visit to the small town of Porvoo, once home of the Finnish national poet, the patriotic Johann Ludwig Runeberg, who wrote the words of the Finnish national anthem, 'Maame', 'Our Land'. His works were compulsory reading in Finnish schools, where they rallied the spirit of independence, and Runeberg's words: 'Let not one devil cross the bridge', became the motto of the Finns holding the Mannerheim Line against the Russians. It was no accident that his home town was selected as a target by the Russians. Like the Nazis and Fascists in Spain, they understood that you struck at independent nations by attacking their cultural strongholds. Just as Guernica was sacred to the Basques as the place where their fueros were ratified by the medieval Spanish kings, Porvoo was revered by the Finns as the place where Tsar Alexander I had conceded Finland its constitution, religion and estate rights in 1809. Now the Russians demonstrated that this independence was fragile.

Steer witnessed the poet's pretty home town 'cruelly mutilated by Soviet bombers'. Eight two-engined aeroplanes dropped thermite bombs that started dozens of large fires among the wooden houses and demolished the main street. The population preserved 'an almost fantastic calm' as planks fell from their burning houses and only the stone chimneys remained standing. Steer was comforted by finding a lovely church with a detached bell tower that was untouched. In its graveyard lay the body of young Eugen Schauman, another Finnish national hero, who had assassinated the Russian Governor-General Bobrikoff in June 1904. 'He sleeps undisturbed by Red or White.'

> Porvoo, on its hill above the frozen river, is perhaps the prettiest of
> Finnish coastal towns. There are two good schools, and Runeberg's

house is a place of pilgrimage for literary Finns and Swedes. There is even a home for indigent authors.

Military objectives are lacking at Porvoo as much as anti-aircraft defences, whose absence enabled the Russian bombers to fly so low and circle so nonchalantly. The port lacks industrial equipment. It can, in fact, be described as a Finnish Lyme Regis.

But if to put terror into the civil population was the motive of the Russian bombers, their fires failed before they were put out.

On Monday, 26 February 1940 Steer entered Viipuri or Vyborg, Finland's second largest city, the closest to the Karelian front line, and found a once charming and historic town in ruins. 'When I visited the place yesterday,' he told his readers, 'its black shell of desolation was like the broken towns of Flanders and Northern France after 1914.

'Russian explosive and incendiary bombs and intensive artillery fire have shattered a city which once held 73,000 people and is not now inhabited by a single soul . . . The only other place where I have seen such havoc was Guernica, the ancient town of the Basques, after the German bombers had repeatedly raided it.'

Steer climbed into a house whose windows had been blown out and stood in a stranger's abandoned bedroom. There was a tin alarm clock, a rumpled bed, and open drawers rifled for warm clothes to flee in.

On Wednesday, 6 March Steer reported another air raid that he saw sixty Russian bombers make on 'a small town of 10,000 inhabitants near the lakes of Central Finland'. Three relays of bombers flew low over the town. The third was the most precise and deliberate, and the bloodiest. The Russians scored six hits on the hospital, which had a big Red Cross flag, dropped incendiary bombs on the school and air-raid shelter and 'drove a lane of destruction about 200 yards wide across the town'. The hospital burst into flames, and Steer saw terrified women with bloodied faces and torn clothes, 'their appearance dazed and wild'. He saw one fall down, crying 'Let me die,' in a street strewn with charred wreckage. As at Guernica, an air-raid shelter was hit. 'The interior of the shelter was a rubbish heap. Six victims were dragged out, bleeding and covered with yellow powder. Two women had had their legs cut off when the door was blown in.'

The war ground to an exhausted halt on 12 March 1940. A Finnish soldier told Steer he had only four bullets left. The Finns had 58,000 dead and wounded; Russian casualties were in the hundreds of thousands. In the armistice deal Finland managed to keep her independence, although she surrendered 10 per cent of her territory to Stalin's Russia. 'Finland shows what free men can do,' said an admiring Churchill.

4

Steer also had good sources in the Swedish Foreign Ministry and Scandinavian military intelligence. He returned to England with a story, headlined 'Germans Stop Narvik Iron Ore Traffic', that the *Daily Telegraph* ran in the right-hand column of the front page on Thursday, 4 April, the day after he got back. It warned that the Germans had 400,000 soldiers and many flat-bottomed boats at Bremen ready for 'a landing in full force on the southern Norwegian coast'. That day Prime Minister Neville Chamberlain crowed that Hitler had 'missed the bus'.

Denmark and Norway were duly invaded by German troops on 9 April. The iron-ore port of Narvik in Norway was recaptured by British troops on 16 April, but after a short and ineffective Norwegian campaign the surviving 12,000 British soldiers were pulled out and evacuated back to Britain. 'Premier Defends The Allies' Withdrawal. Trondheim Not a Second Gallipoli' said the *Daily Telegraph* headline on 8 May.

Steer went to Scotland to talk to the returned soldiers of Sickle force. His 8 May story was filed from 'A North British Coast Town, Tuesday' and his piece, headlined 'British Troops' Dogged Fights In Norway. Soldiers Give First Full Story of Defeat', tells how the infantry of General Paget's 15th Brigade, many of them territorials, fought a retreat from Dombaas to Aandalsnes. They did not think much of the German infantry at close quarters, but German artillery and particularly the low-flying fighters and bombers were overwhelming. 'Casualties due to bombing were small, but the shock effect was much greater. And so it was this unanswerable weapon in German hands which obliged evacuation.' The 'phoney war' was over.

On 10 May 1940 Nazi Germany launched a blitzkrieg attack on Belgium, the Netherlands and Luxembourg. On the same day, Neville Chamberlain resigned and the aristocratic adventurer Winston Churchill became British Prime Minister and Minister of Defence. Churchill was sixty-five years old, and he formed a coalition government with the Labour Party. 'You ask, what is our policy? I will say: it is to wage war . . . You ask, what is our aim? I can answer in one word: Victory.'

The day after the famous 'blood, toil, tears and sweat' speech, on 14 May 1940, Esmé gave birth to a baby son called George. She asked the Emperor Haile Selassie to be the boy's godfather, and he accepted '*avec le plus grand plaisir*' on 25 May. The christening was to be in St Paul's Cathedral, London, on 8 June.

Between little George's first cry and his chrism, the hinge of the world turned. In his masterly book *Five Days in London, May 1940*, John Lukacs claims that Winston Churchill saved Western civilization between 24 and 28 May 1940, by persuading the British Cabinet to fight on. France was falling, Dunkirk was potentially the greatest British defeat in history, and many conservative siren voices were singing for an accommodation with *der Führer*. Nearly 340,000 Allied troops were safely evacuated from the shambles of Dunkirk by early June, but the rest of Europe had fallen to the Nazis. An ordinary soldier summed it up: 'Anyhow, sir, we're in the final, and it's on the home ground.'

Churchill the reactionary Whig was born for this moment, to dig in his heels on the edge of what he called 'the abyss of a new Dark Age, made more sinister, and perhaps more protracted, by the lights of perverted science'. Lukacs writes:

> Churchill understood something that not many people understand even now. The greatest threat to Western civilization was not Communism. It was National Socialism. The greatest and most dynamic power in the world was not Soviet Russia. It was the Third Reich of Germany. The greatest revolutionary of the twentieth century was not Lenin or Stalin. It was Hitler. Hitler not only succeeded in merging nationalism and socialism into one tremendous force; he was a new kind of ruler, representing a new kind of populist nationalism . . . [I]n 1940 he represented a wave of the future.

Steer had been writing against fascism for five years, in Ethiopia, in Spain, in North Africa, in South Africa, in Scandinavia. Millions of others were now falling into step; but the freedom of the press would be limited. If he stayed on as a successful journalist and did his job honestly, sometimes exposing what his government did not want people to know, he would be helping the enemy. This world war was his generation's fight, and George Steer now wanted to take part directly.

EIGHT

Khaki

1

On Saturday, 8 June 1940, a small group of family and friends gathered by the giant marble font under the dome of St Paul's Cathedral in London for George Steer junior's christening. His father was moved to see the flag-hung monument to Sir John Moore, who had died during Wellington's campaign in Spain. Perhaps he recalled Charles Wolfe's poem about Moore's burial by his men:

Few and short were the prayers we said,
And we spoke not a word of sorrow;
But we steadfastly gazed on the face that was dead,
And we bitterly thought of the morrow.

The Battle of Britain was about to begin, followed by the London Blitz, when fire from German bombers would ring St Paul's Cathedral. (US war reporter Ernie Pyle described the fire bombs on London in December 1940: a foot long, with four fins, weighing two pounds, magnesium alloy, thermite core, they were the same as those used on Guernica.)

The baby boy was christened George Augustine Barton Steer, and the Emperor of Ethiopia (who had warned the League of Nations they would be next) placed around his neck a gold cross. Then the men retired to Canon Mozley's study in Angel Court to talk tactics and strategy. The Emperor reviewed the situation with George Steer, Sir Sidney Barton and Philip Noel-Baker, MP. France was collapsing, and it looked certain that Italy would enter the war on Nazi Germany's side. In that event, a revolt within Ethiopia, led by the Emperor, could strike a major blow against Italy, and they vowed to achieve this end.

The Emperor had written to Lord Halifax, the British Foreign Secretary, saying he was ready to act, but had had no reply. There was prejudice against the Emperor among English colonial officials in the Sudan, and against 'the Abyssinian' generally. 'His habits make them see red over their pink gins,' Steer remarked. Italian propaganda, too, always said that the Emperor was feudal, cruel and hated by his people, and asserted he had run away with lots of money; but all the old Ethiopia hands knew that only Emperor Haile Selassie could unite most Ethiopians without causing a civil war. Reassuring the Emperor that they were behind him, they recommended he write to the Foreign Secretary again.

The group met two days later at Steer's house, 7 Whiteheads Grove, Chelsea. On Monday, 10 June Steer heard on the BBC Home Service's six o'clock news that Italy would join the war against the Allies from midnight. The Emperor arrived after dinner from the Great Western Hotel, Paddington, carrying his dossier of loyal letters from Ethiopia. (In his suite he had artfully, piteously stirred up Sylvia Pankhurst to another campaign of vigorous pro-Ethiopian lobbying.) All his friends now played their parts in applying pressure to the British government. Sidney Barton was the experienced diplomat, scrutinizing everything the Emperor's aides wrote for errors. Steer, the journalist, wrote a memorandum for the Foreign Office. Philip Noel-Baker, the politician, arranged for the Emperor to meet R. A. Butler, Under-Secretary of State for Foreign Affairs, the next day, at the home of Henry 'Chips' Channon, the American-born Conservative MP for Southend-on-Sea. Channon wrote in his diary on 11 June: 'This afternoon the Emperor Haile Selassie came to [5] Belgrave Square to tea; it was a very secret meeting arranged for him to meet Rab. Philip Noel-Baker was also here. I met the Emperor at the door, and he entered gravely wearing a bowler hat and the famous cape. He has dignity, but he has aged since the night I dined at Boni de Castellane's to meet him in 1925 – or 1926.'

2

Major General Archibald Wavell, General Officer Commanding-in-Chief, Middle East, liked unconventional soldiers and leaned towards the unorthodox in war. It was in his blood. His grandfather had been a soldier of fortune in Spanish-speaking countries, his father had commanded irregulars in South Africa, and a cousin had gone to

Mecca disguised as a Zanzibari and led Arab volunteers against the Germans at Mombasa in the Great War.

As soon as he took up his appointment at GHQ in Cairo, in August 1939, Wavell began preparing to meet the threat from Axis forces in Africa. A key part of his plan was to raise a revolt in Abyssinia against the Italians.

General Wavell's Middle East Intelligence Centre started gathering people who knew about Ethiopia. A fifty-seven-year-old former soldier named Daniel Sandford was brought out to Cairo on 1 September 1939, made a colonel again, put in charge of the Ethiopian section of Middle East Intelligence and sent to Khartoum. Steer knew him of old:

> Myopic, optimistic, hairy and hale . . . he had come out to Abyssinia in the early 'twenties after a career in the gunners (DSO and bar) and in the Sudanese political service. Here . . . Dan . . . wrote for *The Times* and the *Daily Telegraph*, broke in horses . . . grew straw-berries and plums on a farm overhanging a tributary of the Blue Nile, sold jam in Addis Ababa, rode long distances ahead of the caravan and slept alone under haystacks, walked booted into the Emperor's study to shake hands and to talk . . . [H]e developed that finger in every pie which was the mark of every European in the old ramshackle Abyssinia.

Sandford brought together other old Ethiopia hands, including the sixty-one-year-old ex-Consul Major Robert Cheesman, author of the classic book *Lake Tana and the Blue Nile* (1936), who would run the intelligence bureau in Khartoum; fifty-seven-year-old Major Arthur Bentinck, who had taken the gas masks to Dessye with Steer; sixty-year-old Lieutenant Colonel Lawrence Athill, another ex-Consul, and the sixty-three-year-old Australian Senator Arnold 'Rocky' Wienholt, author of the 1939 pamphlet 'Unconquerable Ethiopia'. Wienholt, a grizzled old hunter once mauled by a lion in the Kalahari, had been a Red Cross transport officer during the Italo-Ethiopian War.

Dan Sandford, the ex-gunner, called his hand-picked crew 'Mission 101' (after the British Army percussion fuse 101 that set off bigger explosions); but Sandford understood that Haile Selassie was the missing vital ingredient for a rebellion against the Italians. The Emperor had to be got out from England to the Sudan. Sandford told Middle East Intelligence that George Steer was the man to do it.

3

In London, Steer was informed by a mysterious 'Major C' that he had been appointed to the Army Officers' Emergency Reserve (Egypt) and now had an emergency commission as a second lieutenant. His first job was to help the Emperor record, in a cavernous BBC studio, two speeches in Amharic directed to Ethiopian chiefs and to fighting men. Then Steer was to fly with Haile Selassie to the Sudan. Miraculously, permission and planning only took two weeks, thanks to an impatient Churchill. France was falling, flights becoming hazardous; it was now or never to get the Emperor out to Africa. Steer signed the Official Secrets Act on Friday, 21 June 1940.

Zero hour was Monday, 24 June. It was a sunny morning when Steer walked round to Neville Street to say goodbye to his in-laws, the Bartons. The fishmonger's in the Old Brompton Road had silver fish in its window, mirroring the fat barrage balloons tethered in the sky above. Steer thought the new brick air-raid shelters might never be used.

> Life was normal; there were still flowers for sale; the midday news-bills echoed some dull sensation. I came back to Esmé. There were some policemen in the street. I love Esmé, therefore it is odd that I cannot remember what I said to her that day, or she to me ... but we were a long time together over my 15 kilos of packing for the flying-boat. She quite frankly hated my going and said that I would never get other countries out of my head. But there it was, one day we would meet again.

The Emperor came to lunch, with Prince Makonnen his second son, who was taking leave from Wellington College, and Major Clively. The two Ethiopian secretaries, Lorenzo Taezaz and Wolde Giorghis, were late because they had been removing small parcels of luggage all day so as not to arouse suspicion in the hotel staff. They all lunched on a spread from Fortnum and Mason's – lobster, caviar, foie gras and champagne. Esmé tried not to cry. A diplomatic incident was just averted when the Steers managed to stop May the maid from using Imperial dessert plates, looted from the Little Gibbi Palace in May 1936 and given to the Steers as a wedding present in July 1939. There were gaseous toasts, then Steer 'said goodbye to a wrinkled inarticulate son shaded by a perambulator in the back yard'.

They left in two Daimlers: the Emperor, the Prince and Major C in the first; Steer and the two Ethiopian secretaries in the second. Steer's

job for the next eight hours was to keep twisting round to see if some
waiter from Soho was following them, spying for the Italians. They lost
their way twice, because Sir John Reith had had all the signposts taken
down to baffle German parachutists; but after draining another bottle
of champagne on the Wiltshire Downs while a country lad cycled
whistling by, they managed to reach Plymouth.

By 10 p.m. their Coastal Command Short Sunderland flying boat had
taken off, on its second attempt, and was heading south towards
Bordeaux and surrendered France. Below them, the Luftwaffe were
hopping over French aerodromes like halma men, but cloud and a
lightning storm concealed the little Emperor's big plane.

It was a cold, unluxurious night, with no deferential steward as on
Steer's last flying-boat trip in East Africa, and little food or drink. The
Emperor dossed down in his greatcoat on a forward bunk, his secre-
taries by the Browning machine-gun turret. Steer tried to kip in a flea
bag on the freezing metal floor under a rack of anti-submarine bombs.
His imagination gnawed horribly.

He woke to see sunlight striping the uplands of the French colony
Tunisia, where the year before he had ridden the grey to Maktar
through the mustard and marshmallow, apricots and olives. In a year
the military might of France had collapsed, and many feared that the
Vichy regime would hand over its navy to the Nazis. In just over a
week's time Churchill would order the Royal Navy to sink the French
Atlantic fleet along the North African coast in Algeria, killing over 1,200
French officers and men, in order to stop their ships joining the Axis.

By 4 p.m. on Tuesday, 25 June 1940 the Short Sunderland flying boat was settling on the water at Alexandria, in Egypt. A lighter came chuffing out and
Steer saw the sharp features of Andrew Chapman-Andrews, former British
Consul in Harar and now Oriental Secretary at the Embassy in Cairo. 'In
these early days of 1940, I recall with some shame, we eyed each other
rather foxily, wondering which was to be the new Lawrence [of Arabia].'

(There were many adventurers who wanted to don T. E. Lawrence's
robes in the Second World War, and become the romantic leaders of
native revolts, and most of them lacked Steer's wry self-knowledge.
The South African mining magnate Sammy Marks once said to Sir Abe
Bailey, 'Abe, my boy, I see the papers keep on saying that the mantle of
Cecil Rhodes has fallen on you.' 'Well, yes, they do,' replied Bailey,

smugly. 'You be careful,' said Marks, 'I've been in the second-hand clothes business myself quite a bit, and they don't always fit.')

The Emperor and his son stayed on board till after dark and then were smuggled past the Egyptian police to a boating club from which portraits of Mussolini had been hastily removed. Alexander Clifford of the *Daily Mail* later wrote: 'In the former Italian yacht club an RAF squadron gave a party for the King of Kings. He donned his gorgeous uniform as Commander-in-Chief of the Ethiopian Army, presented a gold watch to the pilot who had brought him out, invited every one to visit him in Addis Ababa, and flew off south to Khartoum.' According to Leonard Mosley, the festivities took place in the yacht club's washroom, and George Steer remarked, 'First time I've ever had a party with an Emperor in a lavatory.'

The British Ambassador in Egypt had had no advance warning that Haile Selassie was coming, and wanted nothing to do with him. The Imperial party was rushed south towards Sudan the next morning. News of their imminent airborne arrival caused consternation in Khartoum. Sir Stewart Symes, the Governor-General of the Sudan, was married to an Italian and had been cosying up to the Duke of Aosta, partly because the Sudan Defence Force had only 7,500 troops to defend 1,200 miles of frontier against 250,000 well-armed Italians. They were holding their breaths in a china shop, and now a bull had appeared.

Symes ordered the Emperor's flying boat to go no further south than Wadi Halfa on the Egyptian–Sudanese border, and asked the Governor of Kenya if he would take in the Ethiopian party. Andrew Chapman-Andrews, from the British Embassy, left the Imperial party at the Nile Hotel and flew on down to Khartoum to wrangle with Symes. Of course, Symes yielded eventually: the British were meant to be at war with the Italians, not appeasing them with polo matches.

Meanwhile, Steer and the Emperor waited in the desert.

We filled a week of mental inactivity in the dry oasis of Wadi Halfa with shandy, and Charlie Kunz on the radiogram, and with journeys in the hotel launch along the Nile to the ebony shining cataract, to the little temple where Thothmes and his brilliant sister sat among fallen pillars in the unaltered dignity of bas-relief, and to the still smaller cell of a Coptic church, the oldest in these parts, where we held lamps against the wind and in the rushing twilight to faint dreamy daubs of the Saints on horseback and of the Christian Nubian king crowned with horns. The emperor gazed in long fascination at these first traces of his people's religion. And we took tea in a remote palm garden under a Dervish fort as the river glided by. But he remembered always that the water came from Abyssinia.

On 28 June 1940, Chapman-Andrews and Dan Sandford sat down for a conference with Haile Selassie. It was a disillusioning moment for the Emperor. He had been led to believe, or wanted to believe, that a large force with tanks and guns and planes would be magically placed at his disposal to invade Ethiopia. His code name was 'Strong'; his real position was feeble. Dan Sandford said there were no tanks; no planes for a land offensive; no artillery or anti-aircraft guns. There were only four mortars with a hundred shells each. There were thousands of rifles and millions of rounds of ammunition available, but outside Ethiopia there were only 1,620 scattered Ethiopian refugees to use them. They would be confronting at least 200,000 Italian troops and 200 planes. Steer saw the Emperor strike his head several times with his delicate hand, and say: *It would have been better if I had never left England.*

By the evening, the Lion of Judah was more composed. He wished to gather the Ethiopian exiles at Khartoum, and make his headquarters there. On 1 July they travelled by train to Khartoum, in the curtained private coach of the Assistant General Manager of Sudan Railways. The Emperor's ticket was in the name of 'Mr Smith'.*

4

On 4 July 1940 the Duke of Aosta's great army invaded Anglo-Egyptian Sudan from Italian Ethiopia and noisily took Kassala on the frontier. The few Sudanese resisted and fell back in good order. All prayed that the Italians would go no further, and luckily they did not. As the Italians dug tank traps and spread barbed wire, their printing presses went into overdrive, with bombastic propaganda claiming, untruthfully, that they had defeated many English divisions. Behind sandbagged strongpoints the Italians felt safe but nervous, with the Sudanese machine-gunners and armoured cars buzzing about on the western horizon.

*

* It may be significant that in vol. II of his autobiography Haile Selassie calls Sir Stewart Symes 'Sir Stewart Smith'. After several complaints by the Emperor about Symes's obstructiveness, Churchill sacked him as Governor-General in November 1940. In his 1946 autobiography *Tour of Duty*, Symes pointedly makes no mention of Haile Selassie after his 1930 coronation.

The Emperor was settled semi-incognito in a holy man's house on the furthest boundaries of Khartoum. The journalist Alan Moorehead described it as 'a shoddy pink villa surrounded by a garden of lifeless shrubs along the Blue Nile.' Moorehead was impressed by the Emperor's dignity during a visit by press and news cameramen, but thought 'his surroundings were shabby, his hopes remote and his whole cause a tiny dagger in a world of heavy bombers and battleships'.

When Moorehead's interview for the *Daily Express* and film footage for Paramount News were both embargoed, the Emperor had difficulty in understanding, and Steer in explaining, exactly why 'security' so required it. While higher up the chain of command arguments about the Emperor's role continued, Steer as aide-de-camp was given a car and a personal weapon to protect 'the little man' against assassination, and drove him to Indian tailors and Armenian shoemakers. He lunched with Haile Selassie every day at his remote palace and found 'a strange commingling of sweetness and bitterness, of farsight and obstinacy, a sponge as it were for all the emotions of exile, a person enamelled always by his lovely manners and solidified by a patience which prepared him to wait till Doomsday for what he wanted, without showing that he was waiting for anything at all'.

The Emperor knew that George Steer was not a courtier, and was not unhappy when Acting Captain Steer transferred to the newly established Intelligence Corps. In the Second World War's vast mobilization of intelligent people into khaki, George Steer found his final *métier* in PSYOPS, or Psychological Operations. On 15 July 1940 he was put in charge of Offensive Propaganda for the Ethiopian campaign.

Steer had seen the enemy's 'falling leaves' in Ethiopia and Spain and now had a chance to produce his own. He did not enjoy the resources at Robert Byron's disposal when the travel writer drafted the first of 20 million leaflets a week to be dropped on Germany in September 1939. Steer's crew started with single-sheet handwritten leaflets reproduced on the 500-copies-per-hour 'Douglograph' of the Sudan Survey Department. The first *Awaj* or Decree (written in Amharic by the Emperor and Lorenzo Taezaz and dated 8 July 1940) bore the Imperial seal of the Lion of Judah carrying a standard, and the titles Haile Selassie the First, Elect of God, Emperor of Ethiopia, together with the coded phrase from the Psalms that Lorenzo had agreed with the chiefs as a signal for uprising: *Ethiopia Raises Her Hands To God!*

The leaflet, addressed to the 'People, Chiefs and Warriors of Ethiopia', praised their courage and said their sufferings had not been in vain because deliverance was at hand. 'From today, Great Britain grants us the aid of her incomparable might, to win back our entire independence . . . You know what you have to do. Those among you who have submitted to the enemy must redeem themselves at once by deserting the Italian ranks and uniting with the Ethiopian forces.' The leaflet also appealed to the people of the six provinces of Eritrea, saying, 'Your destiny is strictly bound with that of the rest of Ethiopia.' There was a promise that after the war: 'We will perfect our institutions, we will modernise our administration and we will develop the best possible relations with other peoples, and improve our commerce, agriculture, industry and education. In an Ethiopia that is free and prosperous we wish to see citizens who are free, equal, united and enlightened.' It added, 'The English wish to crush the power of our common enemy and to restore our complete independence. They do not covet our territory. Whether you meet British officers or British soldiers, receive them as your friends and your liberators . . . Long live Ethiopia, free and independent! Long live Great Britain!'

The boldness and idealism of this declaration, and others that Steer helped produce, had political consequences later. Some Ethiopians would claim that such wartime promises were guaranteed policy. Strictly speaking, every piece of propaganda Steer produced should have been vetted and approved by higher authority; but whether a British military censor could read Amharic or a busy superior officer could understand the full diplomatic implications of a claim to Eritrea is a moot point, and Steer was given his head.

In late July the RAF said they would drop some leaflets on Kassala. Steer gave them 15,000 decrees to accompany the 21 tons of high explosive. The Italians instituted the death penalty for anyone caught reading the propaganda, but Eritrean askaris were seen to kiss the seal, press it to their foreheads and weep. Some deserted, too.

Because Steer ran Propaganda, he also ran Desertion, which meant he debriefed all those who defected from enemy lines, and so he learned a lot about the organization and morale of the Italian colonial army.

5

Despite regular assaults by filthy *haboob* dust storms, Khartoum was a surprisingly spick and span city, smartly run by the 'Kaid', General William Platt, who was Steer's commanding officer. Alan Moorehead called Khartoum 'a well-run empire country club'. In June 1940 the authorities had all the lions and dangerous animals in 'Pongo' Barker's zoo killed, lest they run amok in the Khartoum streets after an air raid. To the tidy Sudanese official mind, the wild, chaotic Ethiopians were a similar threat. Platt was suspicious of the Emperor's shaggy-haired irregular Patriots, believing that only trained Imperial troops could defeat the Italians. In fact, both were necessary to achieve victory. On the day Italy declared war, Platt signed the tough linen war letters sent in a cleft stick by runner across the frontier to the Ethiopian chiefs: 'If you need rifles, ammunition, food or money, send to us men and pack animals to the place which the messenger will show you. Whatever you want we can help you.'

The peppery Platt was not quite yet used to opinionated junior officers like Steer. 'He stamped his foot at me!' he exclaimed years later. Steer was always stubborn: 'perverse obstinacy' was reported at school; at university he was called 'thrawn', which means 'intractable'; and in a 1943 diary entry after a quarrel with a brigadier, Steer noted his own 'morbid aversion to opposition'. Despite, or because of, their disagreements, Platt and Steer grew very fond of each other.

British Somaliland was a very hot, very dry and rather empty small protectorate on the Gulf of Aden. Before the war it had been home to about a hundred Europeans, mainly officials who administered the handsome Somali dwellers and nomads who lived there. Now it was an isolated stretch of desert, a week away from reinforcements in Kenya. On 4 August 1940 the Italian forces in Ethiopia marched east from Jijiga to invade the colony.

The small British garrison was told to inflict as much damage as it could, and then withdraw to an all-tide jetty rigged by the Royal Navy at Berbera, the capital. The little force was outnumbered, Steer wrote, 'certainly by ten to one, possibly by fifteen to one'. They made a stand across the Tug Argan gap, the low, sandy hills that the road from Hargeisa traversed on the way to Berbera. Pouring towards them on 11 August came an Italian army of 25,000 – 'five colonial brigades, three

Blackshirt battalions, three Banda groups, 100 armoured fighting vehicles including 27 tanks, and at least 20 guns'.

The British have always admired a good fight against the odds, and the African, Asian and European soldiers in the British force did the tradition proud. The first shot from the light artillery killed an Italian general on a white horse at 2,000 yards, and then they fought almost continuously for five days and nights, until the survivors were evacuated to Aden early on 16 August 1940, leaving their burning kit behind. Captain E. T. C. Wilson of the Somaliland Camel Corps won the twelfth Victoria Cross of the war. Badly wounded in both arms, he carried on for three days at his machine-gun posts until they were overrun.

Propaganda meant not just pamphlets, but stage management. As the Emperor was not doing much in Khartoum, Steer arranged a photocall at Gedaref in south-east Sudan in early September 1940. Haile Selassie had already been photographed standing by a Blenheim bomber for propaganda purposes, but this time things were on a grander scale. They flew down in a large Vickers Valentia troop carrier, escorted by two Vickers Vincents. The obsolete aircraft 'were apparently sustained by string alone and they creaked as they flew, if flying indeed is an honest description of a motion whereby for minutes on end the part of the earth immediately beneath one seemed to remain in all essentials unchanged.' On the green polo ground at Gedaref, ringed by 'anti-aircraft Bren guns standing like praying mantises in the tall vivid grass', the District Commissioner had set up a large tent and an Ethiopian flag to greet them.

Hundreds of Ethiopians from the Gojjam province of western Ethiopia paraded before the Emperor, who sat impassively happy under the canopy, among his lords and abbots, with women ululating in the background. In the war dance called *fuqera* the warriors were yelling in falsetto of their kills and wounds, their fantastic exploits and how they had longed to see their Negus again. Many had vowed not to cut their hair until Ethiopia was free.

They strutted like fighting-cocks from side to side in front of him, jutting their heads to left and right like beaks in their boasting. They threw on the carpet in front of him spurs, epaulettes, stars of the Italian officers that had fallen to them. 'We are your servants and your slaves; you are our umbrella!' they shrieked. Their hair was very long and stood in gollywog style around their heads, but their features were regular and almost feminine, even in this frenzy. Priests in white turbans had accompanied the caravan, and holding their silver crucifixes in handkerchiefs they droned away to themselves a contemplative psalm of praise, like bees at honey. It was the greatest day of their lives.

To British officers, permeated with the Italian propaganda that the Gojjam region was separatist and anti-Haile Selassie, this occasion was a revelation. They loaded the Gojjamis up with pamphlets, photos of the Emperor with the Blenheim, khaki kit, guns and ammunition. Then, driving new bulls and donkeys, the Ethiopians crossed the border to spread the word that the Emperor was back with weapons and aeroplanes.

In September 1940 the Ethiopians celebrated Maskal, the traditional Feast of the Finding of the True Cross, and news came that Dan Sandford (code-named *Fiki Mariam*, or the Love of Mary) had successfully entered Ethiopia. It had taken Dan twenty-eight days to reach Zibist, 100 miles from the frontier, where he started unifying the opposition. He radioed that what was really needed was the sight of the Emperor with his bodyguard of 3,000, and British aircraft dropping bombs on the Italians. In October the RAF began bombing Ethiopia.

6

In September 1940 George Steer was appointed General Staff Officer, grade III, with the rank of Acting Captain in the GSI(J) branch of Intelligence. He was looking fitter and leaner: the lines of his father's face show in the two Khartoum photos taken against mud-brick walls with *Thunbergia* clock vine dangling its flowers behind his khaki bush shirt and shorts. He was becoming an energetic leader, too.

He took his propaganda near to the front, scattering yellow pamphlets along the Sudanese–Ethiopian border. He found that Galla askaris fighting for the Italians had destroyed and looted property, and used this information in a fortnightly Arabic news-sheet aimed at turning the local populations against the Italian occupation. Steer settled down with Mamur Omar Effendi el Amin, a pipe-smoking old Sudanese civil servant in gold-rimmed spectacles, and together they wrote the first of several vigorously sarcastic letters to the people of the frontier between Sudan and Ethiopia.

A prime target was the Italian-led garrison in Gubba, a small town on the best road into Ethiopia; but Steer knew literature alone could not drive them out: propaganda was only 'a weapon of co-operation'. A clear message to quit had to be reinforced by constant patrols, irregular sniping and ambush on the ground, plus bombing from the air. Much of Steer's work was about co-ordinating words and actions.

Perry Fellowes, working for Steer, was in charge of producing a weekly propaganda newsletter in Amharic called *Banderachin*. The title came from the deserters' reason for deserting: they wanted to die *Negusachin Banderachin* (for our King and our Flag). So *Our Flag* – with the green, yellow and red colours of the Ethiopian flag striped across the top – became the title of the series of twenty-eight weekly two-sided newspapers. The copy was written at first by a scholarly Falasha, Professor Tamrat Emmanuel (who deplored the name *Banderachin* as half a vile Italian loanword), and then by the former Ethiopian Foreign Minister's son, Sirak Herrouy, whose brother George had been shot in the aftermath of the Graziani massacre in 1937.

The whole propaganda operation was a makeshift affair set in a long, hot, crowded room with only one fan, and all the hullabaloo and baloney of a comic American newsroom. Steer gives a snapshot of it in *Sealed and Delivered*. He himself is sitting, stripped to the waist in the heat, at a typewriter crackling with dust, trying to interrogate a queue of tired deserters with the help of an intransigent Amharic-speaking interpreter. Mamur is smoking his foul pipe over the Arabic newsletter; Perry Fellowes is working out how to scrounge some equipment from the Quartermaster; the dapper-suited Eritrean-Greek printer has brought in all his children, drinking lime juice; Mollie Harvey, the secretary, cannot find what Steer has misfiled; Lorenzo Taezaz wants a private word about a high-up Anglo-Ethiopian row; then an Air Intelligence liaison officer comes in to demand the pamphlets for tomorrow's raid.

Banderachin was dropped by the RAF on bombing raids inside Ethiopia, and carried by patrols. Although it led to many desertions from the Italians' colonial troops, propaganda was a cause of mirth and derision to many of the British. The RAF considered the leaflets bogbumf; they thought throwing paper was effete, because real men dropped incendiaries. Some 'Brylcreem boys' changed their tune when they heard what Ethiopians did to the testicles of captured Italian airmen. They became only too eager to carry a printed talisman of the Emperor's colours – a 'goolie-chit' – in case they themselves were shot

down and mistaken for Italians. Steer delivered 7 million leaflets to
Ethiopia, and argued that written propaganda added 'the right propor-
tion of moral sting to a bomb-load'.

In October 1940 Steer proposed to General Platt the development of
Field or Forward Propaganda Units. These would go in with front-line
troops and try to undermine the loyalties of the African askaris fighting
with the Italians. He wanted the Ethiopian flag to be flown on some
armoured fighting vehicles, and every infantry unit to contain a group
of four Ethiopians, also with a flag, who would megaphone the enemy
during lulls in the shooting. At night, they should take their mega-
phones in closer. Before an attack, he would leaflet the enemy's retreat,
giving indications to deserters of how 'to reach our lines'. General Platt
smiled at the flags, but approved the rest.

Steer was just too late to try out his Field Propaganda Unit in the first
British land offensive of the Second World War. On 6 November 1940
7,000 troops of the 10th Indian Infantry Brigade, under Brigadier Slim,
tried to recapture the fort of Gallabat on the Sudan–Ethiopia border, so
they could drive through a supply route to Dan Sandford in western
Ethiopia. The tanks broke down, and Italian bombers and fighters
repulsed the British on the 7th. The Indian soldiers were staunch but,
embarrassingly, the Englishmen of the 1st Essex ran away.

7

In November 1940, when George Steer met the members of the first
Ethiopian Forward Propaganda Unit, whom he had not picked, he was
unimpressed. These men were not an elite unit, but old refugees from
Kassala and Gallabat. During the early stages of the war, when 'they had
hopped around Gallabat without blankets or shoes', continuous rain
'did not extinguish their untrained enthusiasm nor wash away their
utter incompetence . . . The thirtieth of them got himself inserted at the
last moment because he was a tailor and wished to salvage his sewing
machine.'

The rag-tag squad drove in four trucks down to Gedaref, where they
all got drunk, and came back late. To discipline them, Steer gave
them nothing but a biscuit each to eat for twenty-four hours. He was
'determined to be original because this was my first experience in the
field except as a war correspondent'. At Tuklein Wells they settled quietly

into camp to clean their rifles and practise marching through the thick elephant grass and glossy green thorn beside the Atbara River. Both Steer and his troops were untrained, but his interpreter Shallaka Kassa was a good sergeant, and Steer proved his right to lead by killing a crocodile at 200 yards with his rifle.

The Atbara was the river that Robert Monnier, sick with malaria, had crossed exactly a year before. He had told people about his comrade Steer, saying he was a good shot, and looking forward to the day when they would have great sport together in the Sudan. Now the game was over for the Frenchman, and Steer's friend was buried in the bush at Aussa, not so very far away across the river and the wide sea of grass and flat-topped acacias.

From their camp in the deep shade of big old trees Steer's men went out trying to find the enemy. The practice of war was not at all like the theory. The front was enormous and they could only see for twenty yards. Steer had imagined well-plotted enemy lines, and clearly marked machine-gun posts and trenches. In fact, it took them five days of patrolling the bush before they even found an enemy position; but they learned how to move in Indian file through the thorn and boulders, putting out flanking guards on every shallow crest, ready for fire from a sudden unknown enemy.

They found some Italian scouts on the top of a hill called Jebel Dafeis, and later the advance guards of Steer's unit walked straight into an Italian camp.

> The enemy, as alarmed as ourselves, opened the usual blind innocuous hail of musketry upon us . . . There was the usual panic of untrained troops shouting that they are surrounded and beating back. Comic relief was provided by the tailor of Gallabat, who was last seen literally backfiring at the foe, for he ran off with his rifle pointing behind him over his right shoulder and ingeniously pulling the trigger with his left, the while he uttered ferocious war cries. He thus nearly killed me twice, who was following hard on his heels.

After that, Steer only went out at night with Shallaka Kassa and three or four of the less alarming members of the unit, and Kassa would talk through the megaphone up the hill while the enemy fired over their heads. Steer admitted wryly that they did not win over a single deserter.

Steer learned five points from his initial failure at Tuklein Wells, and all of them would help him to later successes. First, if propaganda was, as he had realized earlier, 'a weapon of co-operation or exploitation', it did not work at inactive periods when no one knew which side was winning. Second, field propaganda required trained, alert and disciplined officers and men. Third, others should reconnoitre the line first, before the Field Propaganda Unit went into action. Fourth, Propaganda Units should be armed for defence, but should only fight the enemy as a last resort. 'Otherwise they lose their heads and go as animal as any infantryman.' And fifth, a leader should know his men before giving them jobs. Ethiopians, if surprised, showed 'astonishing extremes of cowardice and courage'; but 'the essential quality of a Propaganda Unit is neither courage nor cowardice but collectedness and the cool performance of a programme'.

Steer now made a very surprising decision, typifying his capacity for original thought. He started reconstructing his Forward Propaganda Unit with deserters, whose psychology he had begun to understand through debriefing them for information. He chose the best available men from among those Eritreans and Ethiopians self-possessed and enterprising enough to have got out of Kassala and reached British lines. Such men not only understood the thinking of those serving under the Italians, but were powered by the convert's zeal. Persuading others to do what they had done justified their own choice and reinforced their self-esteem. A decade later, this technique of using deserters to catch and convert their ex-comrades became the standard operating procedure in successful British counter-insurgency operations in Malaya and Kenya.

Propaganda also had its artistic side: the challenge of finding effective visual and literary ways to make its points. When the first Field Propaganda Unit went into Ethiopia with the Emperor, they carried coloured inks and a small hand printing press, formerly used for large visiting cards, that could make pamphlets about four inches square for the people to read. A compositor and a proofreader were put into khaki and issued with rifles. From Cairo the Propaganda Unit ordered images of the leonine Imperial seal, nine feet high, in black, scarlet and gold, designed to impress the people of Gojjam. George Steer, in his imaginative way, knew that these bright lions, pinned up along the road of retreat, would also dishearten the enemy soldiers running away. The Ethiopian campaign was about to roar into action.

NINE Into Ethiopia

1

On 28 October 1940 a three-day conference began in Khartoum between Anthony Eden, now Secretary of State for War, General Archie Wavell, Field Marshal Smuts of South Africa, and Generals Dickinson and Cunningham from East Africa, to get the Ethiopian campaign up and running. Two staff officers were present from the Special Operations Executive, set up by Churchill on 19 July 1940 'to co-ordinate all action by way of subversion and sabotage, against the enemy overseas'. SOE was bankrolling Sandford's Mission 101 with 2 million Maria Theresa dollars a month from the mint in Bombay.

Wavell found the Emperor Haile Selassie 'an attractive personality, though not always easy to deal with'. There were procedural difficulties. His Imperial Majesty understood French and English but would only speak Amharic. Sometimes the translations had to go from Amharic to Arabic to French to English and then back again. Wavell's waspish ADC, Peter Coats, described Haile Selassie as '"quite the nicest emperor I've ever met" . . . rather pathetic, and . . . touchingly confident that the British would restore him to his throne'.

Haile Selassie, however, was complaining of crippling dependency and inadequate support, and needed placating. A battalion of Eritreans who had deserted from the Italians were being held as prisoners of war by the British, building roads in Kenya, and the Emperor naturally thought they should be allowed to rally to him. When Anthony Eden was informed of this debacle, Steer says he 'uttered a single word which is among the most expressive in the English language'. The Eritrean deserters were asked if they would like to fight for the Emperor and went mad with delight, volunteering to a man.

Anthony Eden again took up the Ethiopian cause that he had defended at Geneva in 1935, but he stopped short of negotiating any treaty of friendship and alliance with the Emperor as an independent sovereign. At the closed military meeting, the generals decided on a three-pronged attack on Ethiopia to come early in 1941. Steer said: 'The bag . . . opened, and out . . . poured rifles, ammunition, light machine-guns, heavy machine-guns, hundreds of officers and NCOs and about one million pounds Egyptian.'

'Operational centres' were set up, each commanded by a British officer and staffed by five British NCOs, to train and lead the Ethiopian guerrillas across the frontier. One operation centre commander was the South African fabulist Laurens van der Post, who later wove Haile Selassie into his novels as the embodiment of ancient African wisdom. Two new officers came down to Khartoum to liaise between the British military authorities, Dan Sandford's Mission 101 and the Emperor. One of those officers was a brilliant soldier whom Wavell had spotted in Palestine: Major Orde Wingate, DSO.

2

Orde Wingate was a ruthless idealist and a Christian Zionist, who renamed Mission 101 'Gideon Force', alluding to the biblical Gideon who selected his 300 warriors from the alert and cautious rather than the rash and thirsty. Wingate had won his Distinguished Service Order, the second-highest gallantry medal, for founding and leading the 'Special Night Squads' of Jewish soldiers against Arab terrorists in Palestine. Wingate, whose dark, fiery, eager appearance reminded Wavell of a leader of Spanish partisans in the Peninsular War, felt that courage, bluff and surprise were the best weapons of modern war. Scruffy-looking Wingate was no stranger to the Ethiopian frontier, having served in the Sudan Defence Force from 1928.

After Wingate was disappointed in his desire to raise a Jewish Brigade to fight against the Nazis, a letter he found in the files at Middle East GHQ uplifted him. It was signed by five Australian soldiers who had talked to some Ethiopians while on leave in Jerusalem, and felt for the first time that the war made sense:

We have all read about the conquest of small countries by big ones, of the brutal aggressions of Hitler and Mussolini. But in Jerusalem, from these simple Ethiopians, we learned for the first time from the lips of the victims what conquest can mean, and what liberation can mean too. We began to see that we are in the Middle East for a reason, and that we have a part to play. We hope that the part we play will be concerned with the liberation of Ethiopia. Hence this letter. It is a formal notification that the undersigned are prepared to volunteer for service, in any . . . operation planned for the liberation of Ethiopia. We should be honoured to fight with any army pledged to bring the Emperor and his exiled followers back to their capital.

Wingate sent the letter to Wavell with a memo saying he wanted these men to report to him at once as his first volunteers. Steer gives a marvellous description of this mad (and maddening) genius:

[Wingate] was a bully, but not the stupid, full-necked kind. Lank and sallow, with a stoop of the hyena in his shoulders, he had a nose of Wellingtonian bone and eyes that however narrowly set above it proclaimed his drive and brilliance. He was something of a show-man, and he loved the odd and (in the ritual biblical sense, for he had a completely pure mind by modern standards) the unclean. Over the dinner table he described with icy gusto the technique of hyena-hunting by moonlight, with pistols, in the country round Kassala. He would then describe the social habits of the hyena, and paint a scene of their dangerous eyes glowing when they were wounded and dragged their legs behind them, and of the aid offered by other hyenas. Somehow the conversation then switched to camel-dung, and how it breeds flies; hence to the behaviour of flies when you put them under tumblers and later reverse the tumbler. When after an aggressive day in the office this student of Beelzebub retired to bed he regularly massaged his backbone with a rubber hairbrush. The alarm clock that roused him in the morning he carried in his hand all day.

Wingate ascertained in advance exactly how low he should bow when he first met the Emperor, in early November 1940, and surprised Haile Selassie by pledging his support in Arabic. He then read out a statement:

I bring you most respectful greetings, Sire. In 1935 fifty-two nations let you and your country down. That act of aggression led to this war. It shall be the first to be avenged. I come as adviser to you and

the forces that will take you back to your country and your throne.
We offer you freedom and an equal place among the nations. But it
will be no sort of place if you have no share in your own liberation.
You will take the leading part in what is to come.

Wingate had chosen the Wolseley cork helmet as his preferred headgear in 1935, in emulation of the Emperor's sola topi. When Wingate
grew a beard he looked curiously like a burlier version of his hero. It was
Wingate who insisted on the term 'Patriot' being used for the Ethiopian
irregulars. He was also exactly the right kind of religious fanatic to re-
inspire Haile Selassie with energy and idealism.

Wingate also flew across the border into Ethiopia to converse with Dan
Sandford, landing riskily on an improvised airstrip on a mountain table
top at Faguta on 20 November. (His pilot, Flight Lieutenant Collis, got the
Distinguished Flying Cross for managing to land and take off safely
again.) Sandford, who had spent nearly a hundred days inside Ethiopia
being chased and machine-gunned by the Italians, had run out of money
and food, and was delighted to learn that the big push was now on.

As Wingate flew back, he saw the mountain of Belaya, a landmark by
day, and what looked deceptively like smooth, trackless bush between it
and Umm Idla on the border. He decreed that that would be the invasion
route into Ethiopia. 'Get me 20,000 camels,' he ordered. They gathered
18,000 camels from all over the Sudan to transport the guns and explosives across the Shankalla wilderness, up the escarpment to the Gojjam
and on to the highlands of Shoa. But Wingate was deluded: the 'smooth'
terrain turned out to be so punishing that only fifty-three of the valiant
beasts ever reached Addis Ababa alive, and those were so exhausted and
broken by the highland climate that they had to be shot by *Bash Shawish*
(Sergeant Major) Said of the Sudan Defence Force. William Allen, the
scholar and MI5 agent, writes about this in his fascinating *Guerrilla War
in Abyssinia* (1943). When Allen first arrived in Khartoum, in January
1941, he was awed by 'the inner circle' of the unusual military operation,
which included 'George Steer, the Emperor's confidant'.

3

At the beginning of 1941 Steer focused psychological pressure on
Gubba, the little Italian-held town inside Ethiopia, which had now been
'bombed and propaganded' seven times in two months:

Our theme, rammed home as all good propaganda must be, was always the same. We said in Amharic and Arabic, under the joint arms of the British and Ethiopian Empires, that the garrison if it did not desert was doomed to die by disease and by bombing; that it was encircled by hostile tribesmen whom we were arming; that our Sudanese patrols and armed convoys were passing Gubba freely and would compass its downfall . . . The principle of this propaganda was that it seized on data already known to the people and garrison of Gubba . . . and built them into a complex of fear entirely unjustified by the material means that we could in fact have mobilised against Gubba.

This time it worked. The Italian-led garrison grew afraid, clamoured for reinforcements that never came, and finally broke and fled, leaving the door to the Gojjam wide open.

On 8 January 1941 a Vickers Vincent landed on the rough aerodrome at Gubba, deposited two passengers and then flew away. George Steer and his Sudanese assistant Mamur Omar Effendi El Amin were left on the soil of Italian-occupied Ethiopia for the next hour and a half in a propaganda *coup de théâtre*.

The small slim white man and the black man with a big gut and bow legs were holding a large Ethiopian flag between them as they walked into the town, shouting out in Amharic and Arabic that they were friends. They were also lumping a bag of 500 silver thalers and a letter from the Emperor declaring his sovereignty over Gubba.

The garrison had just made its panicky retreat. Steer and his companion found dead men round a burning food store, empty huts, discarded mule packs, flags, and abandoned maps of excellent quality. The deserted township was a monument to the terror their bombing and messages of doom had sown.

The man who had told the world about Guernica, and stood in the ruins of Vyborg, was now himself the beneficiary of bombing. It gave Steer a curious feeling so to have disrupted the 'sunny intimacy' of African Gubba; but the two men ran up the Ethiopian flag, and pinned the Emperor's letter to the Commanding Officer's door. In the smell of wood smoke and dead bodies, Steer's propaganda team occupied one of the first Italian outposts in the East Africa campaign.

4

In January 1941, a gigantic Commonwealth pincer movement began closing on Italian East Africa. From Khartoum, General Platt led the Indian Divisions' attack on the north. From Nairobi, General Cunningham led the South African Division's attack on the south. The Patriot guerrillas and Sudanese of Wingate's Gideon Force came in with the Ethiopian Emperor from the west. Together they forged the first great Allied victory of the Second World War.

The best outline history of this event is still *The Abyssinian Campaigns: The Official Story of the Conquest of Italian East Africa* (HMSO, 1942), which was written by George Steer. With 140 photographs and 14 excellent maps, it is an energetic piece of Allied propaganda. On its sepia front cover a smiling General Platt is shaking hands with four turbaned and scarified members of the Sudan Defence Force, and the back cover shows a defaced statue of Mussolini with a line from Shelley's *Ozymandias* underneath: 'On the sand, half-sunk, a shattered visage lies'. The pictures on the contents page show the multiracial, international, Commonwealth army that first defeated Fascism – soldiers from Ethiopia, East Africa, West Africa, Sudan, Britain, South Africa, Free France and India.

The Ministry of Information, under whose name *The Abyssinian Campaigns* appeared, had started as something of a joke (satirized by Evelyn Waugh in *Put Out More Flags*). By 1941, however, it was more effective. Hilary Saunders at the Air Ministry was the first to realize how stupid the 'sealed lips' policy of official secrecy was when the public was hungry for vivid factual information about the war. In March 1941 Saunders published *The Battle of Britain*, which shifted 300,000 copies on its first day (and has sold 15 million copies to date), followed by *Bomber Command* in autumn 1941. A brilliant publicity scheme began, known as 'RAF Writer Command', whereby people like Noel Monks, H. E. Bates and Philip Guedalla were given military access in order to write books. The army was slower off the mark. Although Eric Linklater wrote *The Defence of Calais*, *The Highland Division* and *The Northern Garrisons* under his own name for the War Office, a change of personnel at the top led to a desire for a more official feel to the 'Army at War' series of pamphlets, so David Garnett was not properly credited for *The Campaigns in Greece and Crete*, nor George Steer for *The Abyssinian Campaigns*.

*

The Khartoum propaganda section split into two for the invasion of Ethiopia. One unit, under Perry Fellowes, went in with Wingate and the Emperor, who crossed the frontier at Umm Idla at 12.40 p.m. on 20 January 1941. Camels carried the portable Amharic printing press, 'shidding up', or loading, an hour before dawn, and slouching at 2½ m.p.h., a slow, dreamy rhythm, through the thorn and the bleached straw of the elephant grass and the forests of bamboo, over sand and gravel and cotton soil and clinkered lava towards Mount Belaya, unloading an hour after dusk to eat and bed down, before getting up the next day. The Emperor had a harder time, trying to follow by lorry along a rough track marked by the sight and smell of dead camels.

Steer meanwhile concentrated on the military campaign against Eritrea in the north. He organized pamphlets for the RAF to drop on the Italian troops and Eritrean askaris, telling them to desert or surrender. Kassala and the towns and villages to the east all fell to General Platt's forces by 1 February; but that was the easy part: ahead lay the mountains of Eritrea and the real Italian defensive line along the impregnable cliffs of Keren. Italian engineers had blocked the only road east to Asmara by bringing down landslides on the Dongolaas gorge, so the only way through was over the sheer mountains. British troops would have to scale cliffs and slopes up to stone ridges that were defended by the Italians' well dug-in and best-equipped battalions, who also had a 9:4 numerical superiority.

General Wavell switched the 4th and 5th Indian Divisions south from Libya to Ethiopia and Platt moved them up to Keren. The troops were from Great Britain and the Indian subcontinent: Scots of the Camerons and Highland Light Infantry, English from Worcestershire and West Yorkshire, together with Baluchis, Dogras, Garwhalis, Gurkhas, Madrasis, Mahrattas, Pathans, Punjabis and Rajputs from India and what is now Pakistan. When the 4th Indian Division first went overseas, none of its Indian soldiers had ever seen the sea. They had no modern equipment. None of the officers or men had ever handled an anti-tank gun or a mortar. They had no motor vehicles and no trained drivers. Yet they adapted to desert and mountain warfare and all the new technology that came their way, and they fought like tigers. It was harsh and dry country they found themselves in, with scrub thorn yielding only to obdurate rock. There was little water and many flies. In the fifty-three bloody days at Keren they lost nearly 3,000 men, but they won one of the great infantry victories of the Second World War.

Black-moustached Subadar Richpal Ram of the 6th Rajputana Rifles took command of his company of thirty men when his officer was wounded, seized the Italian position on Acqua Col with the bayonet, and beat off six attacks in four hours. When they ran out of ammunition and were surrounded, the Indians charged out through the enemy to get back to their own lines. Subadar Ram led another attack on the same place five days later. With his right foot blown off, and other fatal wounds, he continued to encourage his men uphill. He was awarded the Victoria Cross, posthumously. His last words had been, 'We will capture the objective.'

A month later, however, the objective was still not taken. Attacks all along the line, from Cameron Ridge in the north to Zelale in the south, had been repulsed. While General Platt gathered all his artillery and air-craft, and 1,000 trucks brought up supplies for a second massive assault of 13,000 men, Steer's propaganda teams were also doing their bit to weaken enemy resolve.

5

Print and sound assailed Eritrean askaris and Italian soldiers. *Banderachin* leaflets promised Eritreans their own country and their own flag; the night was full of music and voices. Brigadier Slim recalled in *Defeat into Victory* how the propagandists used the Ethiopian Emperor's royal drums to beat out a rallying call, summoning his subjects in the Italian regiments back to their allegiance. In the first fortnight of February, 1,500 men deserted from Keren with pamphlets in their hands.

Sometimes truth made the best propaganda. One of Steer's most effective leaflets of early March 1941 was a news summary telling the Italians of Keren plainly about their compatriots' massive defeat in North Africa in January and February 1941. The tone of this leaflet is rational and informative.

At moments in war there comes a pause in the struggle, when one side can speak to the other above the sound of the guns. Such a moment has come in the battle of Eritrea.

We are not today giving you propaganda pure and simple. We are doing something original in warfare. We are publishing in Italian a summary of our own Military Intelligence, extracted from our staff files; so that Officer can make himself understood to Officer without the exaggeration associated with the press.

Another leaflet, explaining to the Italians that they no longer had air cover because the RAF Hurricanes had destroyed or damaged 115 of their planes, soon followed. 'Ideal propaganda', Steer wrote, 'is that taken straight out of the enemy's own mind, rationalized and put back again to revolve the faster.' The function of the best pamphlet, Steer thought, 'is neither to sermonize nor to bribe, nor to give startling news, but to work back from the known to the unknown'.

The RAF dropped many thousands of small Ethiopian flags, a rich green, yellow and red, with the symbolic lion in the middle and the Amharic inscription 'The Lion of Judah has Conquered'. On the back were the Emperor's seal and the motto: 'Fight for your own King and your own Flag', in Amharic and Tigrinya. When this had been absorbed, they dropped another half a million flags that were four times bigger, with a portrait of the Negus in regalia and the inscription:

O my King Haile Selassie
I am ready to fight and die for you;
I wish to be a free man!

In his history of the campaign, *Eritrea 1941* (1966), Colonel A. J. Barker confirms that the morale of the askaris fighting for the Italians dropped lower and lower as the bombing and shelling increased. When 1,000 were killed and over 2,000 wounded in five days, many more were ready to desert. Steer's pamphlets thundered on: 'The time has come for you to say NO; to refuse further orders from the Italians to go and die for them *without victory or burial.*' A special one was aimed at the Eritrean NCOs: 'You deserve to have A FLAG! You deserve to have the right to become OFFICERS! You deserve to fight with BETTER WEAPONS than those that the Italians give you!'

On 17 February 1941 Steer arrived for a short visit to the Keren front. He went to see Major General Beresford-Pierse, commanding the 4th Indian Division. The General sat in a fly-proof chamber attached to a luxurious motor coach looted from an Italian Army Corps commander after the great victory at Sidi Barrani. Outside stood a bright thorn tree, hung with the striped and checkered *hizams*, or cummerbunds, of the different Italian battalion members who had deserted. Steer got his permission to try a new form of propaganda to bring in even more.

Stanley Baldwin's son Oliver (also known as Viscount Corvedale, after his father became Earl Baldwin) was the first to try it out, working in Steer's unit in Eritrea. Because a man with a megaphone could only be heard by a few, Steer had been experimenting with electric loud-speakers to broadcast recorded speech or music. When Richard Dimbleby, the BBC's first war correspondent, and later the most famous broadcaster in Britain, came out to the Sudan in 1941, with a grizzled wireless engineer, Steer was extremely interested in their truck-portable field recording kit. The Germans had already invented magnetic tape, but the British were still cutting 12-inch, four-and-a-half-minute, 78 r.p.m. gramophone records on the Type C recorder. In the garden of Dimbleby's Khartoum house and using his equipment, whose record-ing machine, amplifier and supply unit weighed 450 pounds, Steer made several propaganda discs with exhortations in Amharic and Tigrinya.

The final assault on Keren began on 15 March 1941. A hundred guns and scores of bombers plastered the ridge, the railway and the road. Then the 5th Indian Division moved on Fort Dologoroduc. First the Mahrattas took 'the Pinnacle', with heavy casualties, and then the Frontier Force Sikhs and Dogras took 'the Pimple'. The 2nd West Yorkshires went up Razor Ridge and finally got into the fort, which was merely a trench surrounding a one-acre hilltop under the blazing sun. They held this vital ground for ten appalling days and nights, with erratic supplies of food, water and ammunition, against snipers, machine guns, artillery bombardments and eight infantry assaults, until the Italians broke. A brigadier told Richard Dimbleby that Dologoroduc was 'the worst place I've ever been in; a terrible hole'. The BBC reporter never forgot the smell of death and infected wounds in 'Happy Valley' at Keren.

Steer's loudspeaker unit was the first used by the British Army in the Second World War. They first went into action on the night of 16 March 1941, carrying their loudspeaker forward into no man's land and set-ting it up in a native hut that was naturally christened 'Broadcasting House'. Shallaka Kassa made a fluent appeal in Tigrinya to the troops opposite. Then they played Italian records, 'Peace, Peace, My God!' and 'Your Little Hands Are Frozen', to make the Blackshirts long for home, until the British artillery behind them told them to shut up. They stopped at midnight, but before dawn they were woken by a patrol that had deserted from the enemy lines towards the sound of the loud-speaker. Sixty deserters came in that first morning; field propaganda broadcasting was a success.

In *African Trilogy: The Desert War 1940–43*, one of the most out-standing books of the Second World War, Alan Moorehead of the *Daily Express* wrote of one his visits to Ethiopia:

> Viscount Corvedale, son of Earl Baldwin, had been down there speeding up desertions from the Italian lines. He had rigged up a big loud-speaker at the front to broadcast across the valley to the enemy. The British commanders demurred at first at this new-fangled idea, on the ground that it would draw fire. Apparently it had the reverse effect. It used to stop the war. Corvedale would play selections from Italian opera and then put across a short talk full of bad news about the Italian army. The Italians, fascinated, stopped shooting to listen. Corvedale got deserters, as he richly deserved to. Everything here to do with propaganda and the fifth column was in fact being handled with dispatch and vision.

However, Steer's unusual energy and invention in this field won him no favours from a dull bureaucracy. Middle East Headquarters censured him for using an atrocity photo (taken from an Italian officer's wallet) of six Ethiopians swinging from a gibbet, over the caption 'Italian civili-sation elevates the Ethiopian'. Steer was not allowed to frighten the Italians by mentioning the revenge attacks that Ethiopians might wreak on Italian civilians, and there were other 'gentlemanly' constraints on what Steer saw as a valid weapon of war. Ruthless in his pursuit of a just end, he produced leaflets attacking the character of Colonel Lorenzini, the brave defender of Keren, saying he was a skunk and a coward and had run away from the Sahara. These falsehoods outraged a British Divisional Commander of the old school, but Steer said he was speaking to Ethiopians and Eritreans who were from a culture well used to exclamatory boasting and derision. Even Lorenzini's death in an artillery bombardment did not deter him: 'If I had thought that such a story could have passed a British censorship I would have announced that he had been shot in the back by a deserting Eritrean askari', he wrote in *Sealed and Delivered,* his autobiographical book about the Ethiopian campaign. Ultimately honest about his own ruthlessness, Steer also con-fesses in that book to having forged the Emperor's signature on a tract urging Ethiopian factions to unite against the Italians.

Steer's frankness offered hostages to fortune. Franco's journalist Luís Bolín quoted these incidents against Steer in chapter 33 of his own autobiography, *Spain: The Vital Years*, dealing with what Bolín calls 'The Guernica Myth'. 'In boasting of the lies which he circulated in the world war, Mr Steer is self-convicted as the author of mendacious propaganda.' But history has judged who lied about Guernica.

6

In mid-March 1941, Steer flew 300 miles into occupied Ethiopia to see the Emperor. At Burye in Gojjam a captured Fiat drove him up to the recently liberated Fort, where he found the Propaganda Unit's printing press clicking over by candlelight under the supervision of Perry Fellowes. (The Muslim printer Mohammed el Tom was drunk every day, but got his work done: just like Fleet Street, thought Steer.)

The next day they went by mule to the Emperor's camp, and talked about Ras Hailu, the great, rich prince who ruled the province of Gojjam in western Ethiopia by collaborating with the Italians. Steer described him as a 'dark plotting African; acquisitive aristocrat; mannered statue of black marble, tall, handsome and grim'. This treacherous old chief in his black curled toupée now held the city of Debra Markos for the Italians. He had gone on the tour of Europe with Crown Prince Ras Tafari in 1924. They were at Buckingham Palace, in London, when someone spoke to the aristocratic Ras Hailu of Gojjam through an interpreter, asking, 'Do you speak English? Do you speak French? Do you speak German?' To all of which the answer was 'No'. Then Ras Hailu said to this man, 'Do you speak Amharic? Do you speak Gurage? Do you speak Tigrinya?' and when the man shook his head three times, Ras Hailu said, 'So, we are both equally ignorant.' Then Queen Mary asked, 'Why is His Majesty laughing so much?' and King George V replied, 'Because this Abyssinian has called me ignorant.'

Chewing stalks of grass in a shady eucalyptus grove by the church at Burye, which had a mural of St George spearing the dragon, Steer and Fellowes planned their propaganda campaign against the cunning Ras Hailu. They had no idea that within weeks the old rogue would be in the Emperor's victory parade. 'Ethiopia is full of forgivenesses and collusions, pardons and policies difficult for the Englishman to understand.'

*

The Emperor had more disagreeable English visitors at Burye. One of them was Brigadier Maurice Lush, a good staff officer, well trained, painstaking and obedient, the sort of practical, unimaginative man who did thoroughly every job he was given. Lush had started his administrative career with three years at the British Legation in Ethiopia, and then spent eighteen years in the Sudan, ending up as Governor of Northern Province.

As the British started planning to administer the enemy territories they liberated from Italian occupation, Brigadier Lush became responsible for Ethiopia. Recently recovered from a bad smash on a railway bridge at night, Lush flew in to Ethiopia fretful with pain and fundamentally at odds with the Emperor. Haile Selassie insisted on his right to rule Ethiopia; Maurice Lush on his duty to run Ethiopia. Haile Selassie saw a free and independent Ethiopia; Maurice Lush saw Occupied Enemy Territory. Misunderstanding and resentment followed.

Curiously, Lush's opposite number, the chief adviser to the Emperor, was his own brother-in-law, Dan Sandford, who had got the position after Wingate took over Mission 101. Lush had served under Sandford in the First World War (Sandford got two DSOs, Lush two MCs), and introduced his older sister Christine to his commanding officer, who had married her at the end of the war. (They were married for fifty-four years.) Nevertheless, Maurice Lush and Dan Sandford disagreed profoundly over the future administration of Ethiopia.

Orde Wingate, meanwhile, had asked the Propaganda Unit to get pamphlets on the collapse of Keren, and paper Ethiopian flags, into the houses and streets of Debra Markos, deep in Ethiopia, and to pin up a hundred rag portraits of the Emperor along six miles of the enemy's southward line of retreat.

Psychological fear was the heart of Gideon Force's campaign. The truth was that a scant few hundred British and Sudanese were pitched against many thousands of Italians and their colonial troops, but fear and regular ambush made the guerrillas loom huge in the Italians' imagination. The legend of Lawrence of Arabia had convinced the Italians that the British were masters at stirring up native revolt. Steer reckoned that the tiny Gideon Force managed by bluff to hold down as many as fifty-six Italian battalions.

Wingate followed the precepts of the Old Testament Book of Judges where Gideon's 300 defeated the Midianites and Amalekites by scaring them at night. At Debra Markos, every night for nearly three weeks, between midnight and the hour of the wolf (3 a.m.), the British-led guerrillas would creep up on Italian positions, each man armed with rifle and bayonet and a couple of Mills bombs. From thirty or forty feet away they would throw the grenades, rush the position, beat off a counter-attack and then slip away.

On 3 April 1941 the Italians cracked and fled Debra Markos. Three days later the Emperor arrived in the city in a Morris truck. Twelve of these vehicles had been brought from the Sudan and manhandled, unharmed, up the 3,000-foot escarpment on a track the Sudanese had hacked out of bush and rock. Haile Selassie was in Debra Markos when the great news came: General Cunningham's soldiers had liberated Addis Ababa.

7

The Allied attack on Ethiopia from the south had been an astonishing success. General Cunningham's 11th and 12th African Divisions crossed the frontier of Italian Somaliland on 24 January 1941. Men from the Gold Coast, Nigeria, Kenya, Rhodesia and South Africa fought their way up from Jubaland through hellishly hot desert sand and scrub. From Mogadishu the Nigerians dashed more than 700 miles north to Jijiga in just over a fortnight. Now mountain fighting began. The South African Air Force shot up the main Italian airbase at Dire Dawa, and Harar fell on 27 March. Repairing or replacing damaged roads and bridges, the Springboks – the South Africans – led the race towards the capital, and made camp outside it on 5 April 1941. In just ten weeks the British Empire's African soldiers had swept up all the Italian forces for 2,000 miles.

The entry into Addis Ababa on 6 April 1941 was low key. The Italians were anxious to surrender and have their civilians protected; the Allies staged no triumphant, Fascist-style march-in. The press arrived first, in fourteen motley cars and trucks, carrying a grubby bunch of cine-matographers, broadcasters, war correspondents, escort officers and native batmen. The route was lined by armed Italian soldiers and police, hundreds of Italian civilians, and thousands of Ethiopians. Driving ostentatiously on the left, in the British manner, the hack-pack swept in through the wrought-iron gates of the Emperor's Little Gibbi,

which had become the Duke of Aosta's palace. The Military Governor
of the capital, General Mambrini, stood waiting on the steps with a
Fascist guard of honour, almost on the very spot where Graziani had
been attacked by Ethiopian grenades in 1937. The unshaven journalists
jumped out and started setting up their microphones and tripods,
while their servants unrolled bedding soaked in a downpour. Laundry
steamed on the sunny lawn as they all waited for the top brass.

A covey of black-clad Italian motorcyclists escorted in a handful of
British staff cars bearing the Divisional Commander Major General
Wetherall, Brigadier Dan Pienaar of South Africa and Brigadiers
Fowkes and Smallwood of East Africa. They had no troops with them;
their only show of force was an odd-looking Edye armoured car nicknamed 'Billie', hammered and welded out of boilerplate in Kenya, flying
a small, homemade Union Jack.

After lunch, Major General Wetherall went to the Great Gibbi and
asked the Ethiopian notables to keep order in the city. Then the standard of Haile Selassie was hoisted up the halyards of the high flagpole,
and the Ethiopians started singing and clapping, dancing and crying.
It was Palm Sunday, and when the South African Press Association
journalist Carel Birkby saw the Lion of Judah's flag break out on the
city's skyline: 'I heard rising from the crowded streets far away a hum as
of bees in swarm, a drone that swelled second by second and then rose
to echoing waves of cheering. It spread right over the city in a minute
until it sounded as though all the generators had been switched on in a
silent power station.'

The women started ululating, and smiling men fired rifles into the air
in celebration. Addis Ababa became an extraordinary place for the next
forty-eight hours, feverish and unreal. Up to 12,000 Italian soldiers
wandered around with their weapons, waiting for someone to disarm
them. Some wore all their medals, including Spanish Civil War ones;
others had thrown away their uniforms. There were 42,000 Italian civilians in Addis, too, including 14,000 women. Protecting them from the
revenge of 150,000 Ethiopians were a battalion of Natal Carbineers, a
few Nigerians and a few King's African Rifles. South Africans took over
the policing of Addis Ababa from the Italians. They disarmed thousands of Blackshirts, manned the forts and blockhouses with Patriot
irregulars, and then enlisted 1,000 Ethiopians to train as policemen.

Carel Birkby described the bar of the Imperial Hotel as the hub of
Addis Ababa: 'noisy, full of Italians in uniform and South Africans in

uniform, adventurers, spies, stranded chorus girls, war correspondents, Intelligence officers, Greeks without business and Armenians forever concerned with some mysterious business.'

Alan Moorehead stayed there in April 1941 and thought Addis Ababa was 'a complete madhouse', with brazenly impudent Italians jeering at the troops who were protecting them from the Ethiopians. Although things were outwardly quiet in the capital, in the surrounding villages, full of terrible old men with spears and knives, 'you saw all too clearly that the one ruling thought among the tribes was to get into Addis Ababa quickly and have at those Italians'. British soldiers frequently had to rescue Italian settlers from enraged Ethiopians, and Moorehead's Cockney driver asked, 'Oo the hell are we fighting anyway, the Wops or them niggers?' Moorehead confessed he simply did not know.

Brigadier Maurice Lush started administering Occupied Enemy Territory, and installed himself in Sir Sidney Barton's former Residence at the British Legation. (The Italians had stored ammunition there because they thought the British would not bomb their own property.) Lush planted two bougainvilleas and used Italian POWs to install two new bathrooms and a hot-water system. To all who asked when the Emperor would return Lush replied, 'When the military situation permits.'

At Lush's request, George Steer joined his team in April 1941 as Press Propaganda Officer. Steer flew to Addis Ababa over the reconquered land.

A Brigadier and two Colonels were in the same plane. They did not seem enormously interested as we swung over Mount Entoto and Addis Ababa lay in its sprawling long-distance beauty among the millions of eucalyptus beneath, the copper domes suggesting wealth, the green plains and darker mountains beyond assuring defence and a comfortable life. But my senior companions had no comparisons to make with the past. A young officer in gloves met them with a car at the aerodrome: I sat forgotten with my friends the Sudanese clerks, eating their cheese and olives, for a full hour, looking round and trying to assimilate the new Addis, among the wreckage of Italian aircraft, spilled, unsalvaged boxes of Italian grenades and field altars.

Steer was not impressed with what the Italians had done. Electricity had been installed, but there were no spare bulbs, and the power failed regularly, as did the water supply. The Città Industriale was unfinished and the Ethiopians lived in a segregated area, with a colour bar in all hotels, cinemas, restaurants and pubs. Bureaucratic corruption had set up monopolies in all goods and services. The five years of Empire had been a massive swindle. In the Political Affairs office, Steer found the gimcrack gewgaws that Italians had handed out to obedient Ethiopians: silvery crowns, velvet cloaks, shaky-handled swords, ribbons, big tin medals and scrolls giving titles to whoever put their names on the dotted line. He also found many files of confiscated Ethiopian property and dusty unfinished claims.

8

George Steer had not forgotten his young Ethiopian friends and was trying to find out where they were. Many were dead, others dispersed, but Elizabeth Workneh, the wife of Yilma Diressa, a Galla nobleman employed in the Foreign Ministry, remembered how Steer sent word out asking, 'Where is Yilma?' After the Emperor had fled, in May 1936, Yilma Diressa had gone back to his own region, Wollega, to help carry on the fight. In one spectacular ambush, the young Ethiopians had killed the Commander of the Italian Air Force, General Magliocco, and a group of high-ranking officers. After Yilma had surrendered in November 1936, he had been imprisoned on the Mediterranean island of Ponza, where the London School of Economics graduate translated H. G. Wells's *Outline of History* into Amharic, before returning to Ethiopia in late 1940. Elizabeth remembered the excitement of British troops entering Addis Ababa and how George Steer came back into their lives. She drove her husband, rather shakily, because she had just learned to drive, up to the radio station, where the two friends met again. Steer was in high spirits: she remembered him laughing and cracking jokes.

One of Steer's main jobs was to get public broadcasting going again in Addis Ababa. Lieutenant MacSweeney, an Irish signals officer, replaced the wires running from the radio station to the loudspeakers throughout the city, and then repaired the 1-kilowatt station itself, commandeering every valve going in Addis Ababa. Steer gathered all the Galla and Amharic announcers of the Italian regime and put them back to public service work on the other side, together with the four Italian engineers who had run the place. Scripts were written or vetted by George Steer, and Yilma Diressa, who spoke Galla, Amharic and

English fluently, would help him. Steer found 'a Jew from Milan who did not worry whether other Italians loved him or not' to start an Italian programme. When an Italian engineer did not want to broadcast anti-Italian propaganda, Steer told him that if ever he let the radio system break down, the Ethiopians might become an uncontrollable mob, and who could say what vile things might then happen to the 30,000 Italians in Addis? Or Steer would feign deep hurt at Italian ingratitude in not repaying the moral debt to Britain, which had saved them from this horrible fate. So, by bullying and cajoling, he kept the service going, but described its effect on the crowds in the streets and squares of Addis Ababa with a certain irony: 'Rhythmical clapping followed every pellucid phrase that now bubbled from the well of truth.'

In his book *It's a Long Way to Addis* (1942) Carel Birkby mentions Captain George Steer 'in charge of propaganda services' and says that the radio station used to give out 'news and announcements in English, Italian, Amharic and Tigrean each afternoon, and when a war correspondent came back from a battle he would give the people an account of it . . . Nightly the names of the next batch of Fascists to be deported to Diredawa was announced. The Italians sat in their homes and listened anxiously.'

The South African Maurice Broll visited Addis Ababa in late April 1941. In *Mud, Blood and Laughter* (1943) he writes of seeing a large crowd outside a leading hotel: 'on investigating [we] found that a loud-speaker had been set up through which were announced the names and numbers of Italians who had been killed. It was really most pathetic, as every now and then some woman would scream or faint. Till then war had been to me a kind of adventure. It now struck me what a cruel business it was.'

Steer's *Sealed and Delivered: A Book on the Abyssinian Campaign* identifies three problems the British faced after the liberation of Addis Ababa in April 1941:

> One was the colour bar. It flourished still in Addis Ababa when I arrived, and was the first thing that we had to break. I have no doubt that this part of the Italian regime was the most offensive to the proud Shoan. Hairdressers refused to cut Ethiopian hair and barmen stuck up notices, 'NO NATIVES SERVED HERE' by which they hoped to curry favour with South African troops.

There were some incidents when the Emperor's men came into Addis Ababa. Finally we got an arrangement by which three bars in the town were reserved severally for British officers, NCOs and men; all other places of public resort were open to everybody.

The second problem was occupied Ethiopian property. Five thousand Italians had to be moved from the houses they had taken over in the centre of the city out to a special security zone.

The third problem, the biggest, was the hardest to solve. Steer was crucially involved. He asked, 'Who was the ruler of Ethiopia? For whom were we speaking?' and his answers show, I think, that he had probably carried the Ethiopian flag far further than cautious British policy would have liked. In 'our printed propaganda, which for the Ethiopians was more real than statements made in the House of Commons', the British had promised, and 'had allowed the Emperor to promise, the entire independence of Ethiopia'. They had also 'stated that the Emperor Haile Selassie was the rightful ruler of Ethiopia and that we were supporting him with arms; we were also allowing him to issue Orders ("Awajes") to his people as an act of sovereignty'. The Emperor had said that he would 'seek the advice of friendly nations in the League and particularly Great Britain' in the modernized government he had promised.

Most Ethiopians understood this to mean that the Emperor was sovereign of an independent Ethiopia, able to choose his advisers and his own ministers, with British administrative officers helping to run the provinces; but the British military were unwilling to cede full power to the Emperor and the relationship soon became acrimonious. 'Propaganda during this interim before the full restoration of Abyssinian independence was bound to be delicate,' wrote Steer, with svelte understatement.

Maurice Lush's report on the Administration of Ethiopia from 1 February to 1 September 1941 points out that 'the imposition of British Military Administration' on 'the Emperor, who, in his own opinion and in that of his followers and subjects, was entering his country as a sovereign ruler' was 'a matter of no little difficulty'. The result was a dual administration in which true collaboration was impossible 'because one of the parties has refused to accept the position or authority of the other'. Unsurprisingly, Lush thought the Emperor's attitude was Amhara-centred, and that he was 'stubborn', 'discourteous' and 'impatient'.

The treaty between Ethiopia and Great Britain was not signed until 31 January 1942.

Intermediaries were needed. In Ethiopia, the Armenians had been an early and useful bridge between cultures, teaching the Ethiopian aristocracy how to use European cutlery and glassware with European food, and imparting niceties of dress and manners.

Avedis Terzian, the son of Sarkis Terzian, the man who had sold Emperor Menelik the guns to defeat the Italians at the battle of Adowa in 1896, was ninety-seven years old when I met him at his house in Addis Ababa, but his multilingual mind was clear. Sitting in a flamboyantly orchidaceous towel dressing gown, he remembered George Steer as 'very active, very pleasant, liked by everybody. He was pro-Ethiopian; he liked Africa and he liked Ethiopia. Living in Africa does create a certain affection. The *Banderachin* newspaper shows his love for Ethiopia. He was a fine gentleman who was a friend of the country.'

Terzian, once interpreter for the American Ambassador, acted as Oriental Secretary for the British Army when Brigadier Lush arrived as Deputy Chief Political Officer. He said it was important to remember that Ethiopia was not recognized by the Allies as an independent country at first. 'It was Occupied Enemy Territory and the administration was AMGOT – Acting Military Government of Occupied Territory. This made a peculiar kind of trouble because the military thought about it in their own way. For some time they didn't want to let Haile Selassie back into Addis Ababa. Eventually orders came from London that the Emperor was to go to Addis Ababa, and Brigadier Lush asked me to organize a cavalcade.' Terzian had to find a foreign car, because the Emperor could not be seen coming back into Addis Ababa in an Italian vehicle. He found a big open Ford in the Duke of Aosta's garage that would do nicely for General Wetherall and Haile Selassie.

9

Brigadier Lush had no choice but to get the Emperor back into Addis Ababa: he was under pressure from London, from Nairobi, from the Emperor via Dan Sandford (quietly) and from Wingate (loudly). Lush said he waited because he did not want some enraged Italian or dissident Ethiopian taking a pot shot at the King of Kings. 'This was a matter which depended on one's judgement and my judgement turned out to be correct,' Lush wrote in his autobiography, *A Life of Service*. 'I also remembered that 5 May was the anniversary of the Italian entry into Addis Ababa. This would be good press news.'

I think it far more likely that the professional journalist George Steer (who had personally witnessed the fall of Addis Ababa to the Italians) remembered 5 May and suggested the date as suitably symbolic and 'good press news'; but brigadiers outrank captains and take credit for their ideas. Steer also knew Ras Abeba Aragai, the police chief turned guerrilla leader, who promised Lush that his 7,000 Shoan Patriots would cause no trouble as they lined the route of the Emperor's procession.

George Steer performed a piquant act of chivalry in late April 1941 at Ras Abeba Aragai's former home in Addis Ababa, which had been commandeered by the Italians. The incident was witnessed by a twelve-year-old Italian girl, Paula di Montezemolo, who was sheltering there with twenty other Italian women and children. One day they were terrified to see dozens of shaggy Ethiopian heads peering over the garden wall (the Patriots had vowed not to cut their hair until Ethiopia was freed); they were afraid the men were *shifta* come to rape and murder them. Then through the front gate came Ras Abeba Aragai himself, accompanied by a small, thin European in British uniform. This officer ('he was very English') introduced himself as Captain George Steer and said he was 'in Intelligence'. Paula di Montezemolo's mother asked what that meant and he replied that it meant he knew everything about her.

'Your husband is Generale Alberto Cordero di Montezemolo, who is chief of staff to the Duke of Aosta, and they are both now at Amba Alagi. Your maiden name was Alessandra Muzi Falconi. Your younger brother Filippo married Sir Sidney Barton's daughter Marion. I married his other daughter Esmé, so we are related by marriage. How are you? May I introduce Ras Abeba Aragai?'

'Good morning, *marcchesa*.'

'I know that we are occupying your house.'

'You have kept it very well.'

'The women and girls are very afraid of those men looking over the walls.'

'Do not be afraid. My soldiers are here to protect you.'

10

The day of the Emperor's triumphant return to Addis Ababa, 5 May 1941
– 27 Miazya 1933 in the Ethiopian calendar – dawned clear and bright.
Fifteen thousand shaggy-haired Patriots marched into the city early, led
by Ras Abeba Aragai's twelve-year-old son Daniel, dancing on a fine
white pony, wearing crossed bandoliers of ammunition, a belted pistol
and a modern rifle.

The Italians skulked indoors. The Ethiopian national anthem came
over the radio, played on the only surviving gramophone record, which
had been saved by an Armenian jeweller. People were putting up eucalyptus poles painted green, yellow and red along the route to the Great
Gibbi, Menelik's old palace, preparing makeshift Ethiopian flags and
garlands of flowers, putting on clean *shammas*.

> Slobbering droves of oxen went in dust up the winding highway in
> the eucalyptus to Entoto, where they would feast the Rases' men in
> the evening. Women passed, in men's clothes and bearing arms; and
> old Ethiopian warriors rode by on horseback with bandages round
> their heads and tilting lances in their hands and chanting; and
> priests passed in a daze under their silk umbrellas, holding high
> their flat, ornate silver crosses; and there were a few Italian prisoners
> in chains who, one had to explain to fellow South Africans, would
> not be eaten alive or even mutilated at the end of the day, but if they
> liked raw meat would get their fair slice of the banquet.

The Emperor arrived at the summit of Mount Entoto around midday, in an open car, with the loyal chief Ras Kassa at his side. The king
with the Christly face walked bareheaded into the octagonal Church of
the Virgin Mary to pray, and tears started from his eyes as he prostrated
himself on the carpet before the altar.

The procession formed up among the rocks. It was Captain George
Steer, in his loudspeaker van flying the Ethiopian flag, who led it off, preceded only by a single South African motorcyclist. Steer was followed by
six South African motorcyclists abreast; three South African armoured
cars; two red Italian fire engines carrying 'a scramble of the Press'. Orde
Wingate, close-shaven like all his officers, whose beards he had ordered
removed, was carrying a long leather whip, and riding a white horse in
shorts, which chafed his legs badly. The Patriots of the 2nd Ethiopian
Battalion, marching with their flag, followed Wingate. Then at last came

the little man who was so eagerly awaited, the Emperor, driven in the
borrowed Ford, surrounded by Ethiopian police riding on white horses
and carrying carbines. Then came other cars with the young Princes, the
Ethiopian chiefs, Dan Sandford and Lorenzo Taezaz. Then the Sudan
Frontier Battalion, as Steer said, 'in clean turbans and grins, with a rich
green flag of silk sporting their badge, a golden lion', then lorries of
Ethiopian exiles and armoured cars. They moved slowly down the steep
slope into Addis Ababa, whose streets were crowded with thousands of
waving flags and bowing people.

Carel Birkby remembered the route through the sighing eucalyptus
trees, bright with green, gold and red banners. There were Hellenic flags
flying, too, and groups of Greek merchants doffed their hats; they were
the only whites in the milling, chanting, clapping crowd. There was a
cacophony of Ethiopian music on strings, flutes and drums, women
ululating 'li-li-li', and children with their heads decorated with the seal
of the Lion of Judah singing songs of welcome. Flowers rained on the
Emperor.*

As they came down into Addis Ababa, George Steer was at the head
of the column in his loudspeaker van, with his Ethiopian friend Yilma
Diressa at his side, calling into the microphone, 'Today, five years ago,
the Italians entered our city to murder and pillage; today, five years
after, our king returns, with the aid of a just God and of the English!'
It was one of the greatest moments of Steer's life, 'the restoration in
prototype of the liberties of the globe'.

Looking through the sides of the van, Steer watched the expressions
of the crowd: shock, recognition, sorrow, release from sorrow, tears,
ecstasy, people lifting their arms to the sky or falling flat to kiss the
ground, women humming like bees, men giving the short, sharp clap,
people running, throwing flowers. Steer saw faces in the crowd he had
not expected to see again; remembered those he would never see again.

At the gates of the Great Gibbi an artist, encouraged by the Propaganda
Section, had painted a horrible representation of the Ethiopian lion
disembowelling the Italian wolf. General Cunningham waited with an
honour guard of the King's African Rifles and a battery of captured

---

* Birkby's description of the procession is in the London edition of his book *It's a Long
Way to Addis*, but the entire chapter 'Haile Selassie Comes Home' is missing from the
Johannesburg edition, *Springbok Victory*. The restoration of a black king by white troops
was not good copy in South Africa in 1941.

artillery. They fired Italian ammunition in a twenty-one-gun Imperial salute as the Lion of Judah's standard rode up the halyards.

The Emperor, in uniform with a khaki pith helmet, climbed up the steps where Steer had seen the war drum beaten in October 1935, to a microphone stand fringed with flowers and palm fronds. The electric power, worked by Italians, chose this moment to fail Steer's loudspeaker system; but MacSweeney, his Irish signals officer, was up to the challenge, switching on the back-up generator.

Avedis Terzian remembered well Haile Selassie's 'very conciliatory' speech that day. Terzian explained that the country was divided into three groups. The Patriots had fought on their own and did not want Haile Selassie, because he had gone away into exile. Many of the cheering crowds in Addis Ababa that day supported the Patriots in the procession, not the Emperor. Then there were the Émigrés who had come back from the Sudan, and who supported Haile Selassie. Thirdly there were those who had collaborated with Italy. Haile Selassie found that the Patriots were not with him, so he approached the Collaborators (who were also afraid that the Patriots would plunder them) and they joined the Émigrés in supporting him. Terzian said he had to explain this to the British, who did not understand Ethiopian politics.

George Steer may have had a hand in the Emperor's speech in Amharic on 5 May 1941; Elizabeth Workneh told me that Yilma Diressa certainly helped to draft it. There is no mean-spiritedness or gloating in the address, which says that 5 May will for ever after become an Ethiopian national holiday: the day of liberation, of reuniting in love and of remembering those who died in the struggle. The speech pledges, 'In the new Ethiopia we want you to be an indivisible people, equal before the law, free men all,' and the Emperor repeats the promises of his first *Awaj* or Decree from Khartoum about developing the country. Haile Selassie ends with a Christian admonition:

> Do not reward evil for evil. Do not commit any act of cruelty like those which the enemy committed against us up to this present time. Do not allow the enemy any occasion to foul the good name of Ethiopia. We shall take his weapons from the enemy and make him return by the way that he came. St George who slew the dragon is the patron both of us and of our allies. We should therefore fasten our friendship for ever in an indissoluble bond, to defeat this

ungodly and newly spawned dragon that vexes mankind. Our allies
are our friends and our own blood. Take them to your hearts!

The rain came down and washed Addis Ababa into grey. Steer pressed
his nose against the window of Menelik's audience hall and saw the
Emperor and British staff officers inside drinking champagne. Later the
Ethiopian chiefs came in and kissed the dais and each other, with tears
coursing down their cheeks.

The dripping white horses cantered by and slipped on the tarmac.
The armoured cars slithered into place. Our driver swallowed the
end of his sandwich. We shoved up the cover of the Emperor's car
and rescued his camel-hair coat from the slush.

The rain cooled hot heads and there was little over-excitement that
night; but the young Ethiopians who survived invited George Steer to a
dance, the first they had held since the Italian occupation. Elizabeth
Workneh's sister Sarah had been collecting the best American jazz
records since her return from prison in 1938, and someone else raked up
others from before 1935, the dance tunes that Steer had known with
Margarita in the old days of Addis Ababa at Mon Ciné and the Perroquet.

Everybody there except me, the only Englishman, had lost a brother,
or father, or cousin under the Italians. But something made them
forget it. They were dancing.

TEN Special Operations

1

When Orde Wingate arrived in Cairo in early June 1941, the highly strung soldier was already overwrought. He had left Ethiopia under a cloud, having been told that Gideon Force was disbanded, that he no longer had a command, and that he must report to GHQ Cairo forthwith. Although Wilfred Thesiger and others thought that Wingate should have been knighted for all he had achieved in the Ethiopian campaign, a senior officer had accused him of disloyally encouraging Emperor Haile Selassie to appoint his own Ethiopian government ministers without British approval.

In Cairo, Wingate wrote an appreciation of the Ethiopian situation for his superiors that was typically concise and insulting ('military apes' was a characteristic phrase). General Wavell, the chief who had picked him in the first place, sent for Wingate and, as he said, 'had out with him as man to man the grievances he had voiced'; but Wavell was sacked and replaced as Commander-in-Chief by Claude Auchinleck on 21 June, and Wingate became locked in a battle with bureaucracy, as he tried and failed to win hardship allowances for his men's sufferings in the guerrilla war they had won.

Cairo in summer is swelteringly hot. In this disagreeable climate, Orde Wingate was not only festering with resentments but also suffering from acute malaria, which he was unwisely trying to cure with overlarge doses of the drug atabrin. He felt he was being persecuted for supporting Ethiopian independence against the British Establishment, and became obsessed with the idea that he had unwittingly been a pawn in an imperialist plot, another T. E. Lawrence used to betray the people he loved so that their lands could be annexed as British

colonies. 'I thought our . . . talk of liberation miserable cant,' Wingate
wrote later.

(Many historians, including Richard Pankhurst and Harold Marcus,
have agreed in whole or in part with Wingate's analysis. Sidney Barton,
in the introduction that he wrote to Steer's *Sealed and Delivered* in
January 1942, as the treaty between Ethiopia and the UK was being final-
ized, spoke critically of those 'remnants of the Colonial and Colour-bar
minds capable of delaying the recognition of racial equality as an essential
concomitant of freedom', and he hoped they would receive no encour-
agement from Winston Churchill. The five great friends of Ethiopia who
worked so hard to swing British policy towards restoring genuine sovereignty and independence to the country were Sidney Barton, Sylvia
Pankhurst, Daniel Sandford, George Steer and Orde Wingate.)

However, at three o'clock in the afternoon of 4 July 1941 Wingate was
running a temperature of 104°. He tried to get more atabrin but could
not remember where the doctor's house was. This is not unusual with
high fever and stress, but Wingate thought he was losing his mind. Back
in his room at the Continental Hotel, he found his pistol; there was no
ammunition, so he picked up an American hunting knife in his right
hand and went to the mirror over the washbasin. Wingate drove the
point into the left side of his neck, and tried to cut. Then he remembered the door, and with the knife still sticking out of his neck, crossed
the room, locked it, and went back to the mirror. Watching himself, he
pulled the knife out and then, with his left hand, pushed the blade
forcefully against his jugular vein, before fainting on the floor.

Colonel Cudbert Thornhill was 'doing Egyptian PT' (taking a siesta)
in the room next door. 'When I hear a feller lock a door, I don't think
anything about it, and if I hear a feller fall down that's his affair, but
when I hear a feller lock his door and then fall down – it's time for
action,' he said laconically later. Thornhill and the Swiss manager broke
in and got Wingate, soaked in blood, to hospital.

George Steer and the diplomat Andrew Chapman-Andrews visited
him in the Cairo hospital a few days later, in early July 1941. Wingate was
sitting up in bed with a large bandage round his throat. He would not
say why he had done it, but he did tell them how his suicide attempt had
gone wrong. He had simply not studied the problem properly. He
should have relaxed his neck muscles in a hot bath before using the
blade. Christopher Sykes describes the scene in his 1959 biography *Orde
Wingate*.

His visitors listened in some disquiet as he illustrated his meaning with graphic gestures. Chapman-Andrews said something about being glad he had failed, to which Wingate answered, 'That shows I am destined for great things.'

As they went away from the hospital, George Steer remarked that Wingate had lost a certain dangerous look in his eye.

2

Wartime Cairo, according to the head of SOE, was 'a sink of iniquity with an evil atmosphere that poisoned every service there'. Fighting soldiers, known as 'desert rats', referred to the staff officers of Cairo as 'gabardine swine'. An alphabet soup of secret and semi-secret units bubbled and brewed around Middle East Headquarters.

Esmé had used her experience working with Sir Vernon Kell at MI5 in London to wangle herself a job at SIME, Security Intelligence Middle East, which did the same kind of counter-espionage work out of Cairo. At least George Steer could sleep with his wife again. He himself had been on the payroll of SOE, the Special Operations Executive, from 1 April 1941. He had initially been selected to join SO1, the Propaganda Branch of SOE, but it is clear from his personal file that others wanted him too. In August 1941, after Steer had left Ethiopia and Khartoum, the Middle East Intelligence Centre at Cairo wrote that it was 'very anxious to get hold of him for Dudley CLARKE's section', adding that the Commander-in-Chief 'lends us his support as he takes a keen personal interest in this particular work'.

Dudley Clarke's section was the top secret 'A' Force, started by Wavell in December 1940 to practise strategic deception. As Sun Tzu observed 2,400 years ago, 'All warfare is based on deception . . . When capable, feign incapacity; when active, inactivity . . . Offer the enemy a bait to lure him; feign disorder and strike him.'

To this end, Dudley Clarke invented imaginary units (the now famous 'Special Air Service', or SAS, began as a Clarke fiction, but the name appealed to Colonel David Stirling, who founded the real regiment), with bogus wireless traffic and fake manoeuvres; he employed double agents to send false information, and generally used every trick in the book to disguise Allied weakness or strength, decoy enemy attention and tie down troops that might do real damage elsewhere. Dudley Clarke used the illusionist and stage magician Jasper Maskelyne to run a camouflage unit that faked up vehicles, buildings and even entire ports to deceive enemy spotter planes. (They did not always pass muster: the Italians, rather wittily, once dropped a dummy bomb on to a dummy airfield.)

However, the tricks and games and toys and models and fake signals that 'A' Force used had a deadly serious purpose, and they worked. Documents captured after El Alamein in 1942 showed that the Germans had overestimated British armoured strength in North Africa by 40 per cent, their infantry strength by 45 per cent.

George Steer was posted to General Headquarters, Middle East Force on 24 September 1941. Whether he did in the end work for Clarke is obscure, and the documentary evidence for this part of his life is scant; but it is quite possible that Steer took part in 'A' Force's first attempt at 'Sonic Deception' at Helfaya Pass on Christmas Eve 1941. An Egyptian film company's sound-track recordings of massed tank movements and engine revvings 'were broadcast across the German wire through the amplifiers of a propaganda unit, and were thought to have had a useful effect'. A much later diary entry of Steer's mentions his Mauser rifle being fired by a Polish officer in 'the retreat from Benghazi' of January 1942. Family legend also has it that Steer escaped from the fortress of Tobruk, which fell to Rommel's Afrika Korps on 20 June 1942, 'by driving the wrong way'. Presumably this means Steer drove west through German lines before looping round to head back east to Cairo.

Steer kept busy. He was writing *The Abyssinian Campaigns* and *Sealed and Delivered* in the second half of 1941, and also carrying on front-line propaganda against the Germans in the Western Desert. The historian M. R. D. Foot once met a man who worked under Steer at the time, shouting slogans Steer had composed, in German, through a megaphone at German soldiers entrenched near by.

3

Early on Sunday, 7 December 1941, Imperial Japan entered the Second World War with a massive air attack on Pearl Harbor. The pre-emptive strike on the US Pacific fleet anchored at Hawaii was the old samurai tactic of getting in a crippling first blow; Japanese wars against Russia in 1905 and China in 1931 had also begun with a sudden attack.

The Japanese military had learned all the lessons of air power that the West had to give, and adapted them to use against their teachers. Waves of high-level bombers, dive-bombers, torpedo planes and fighters struck the harbours and air fields of Oahu. They sank or damaged eighteen US vessels, including eight battleships, destroyed nearly 150 planes and damaged scores more, killing and wounding 3,600 people. What President F. D. Roosevelt called 'a day that will live in infamy' goaded the United States of America into the war.

Simultaneously, the Japanese Imperial Army attacked the British Empire in the Far East, in Burma and Malaya, threatening Singapore and Hong Kong, even India. On 10 December the shocking news came that Japanese aircraft had destroyed two of the Royal Navy's largest vessels, the battleship *Prince of Wales* and the battlecruiser *Repulse*, on the high seas. Unprotected from air attack, these capital ships with their giant guns sank with the loss of 840 lives.

Britain's top soldier, General Sir Alan Brooke (later Field Marshal Lord Alanbrooke) saw that this loss, together with Pearl Harbor, 'puts us in a very serious position': 'It means that for Africa eastwards to America through the Indian Ocean and the Pacific, we have lost command of the sea. This affects reinforcements to Middle East, India, Burma, Far East, Australia and New Zealand!'

As Japanese troops took over Malaya and the Dutch East Indies with their tin, rubber and oil, and raced towards India through Burma, they claimed that they were liberating the black, brown and yellow peoples of Asia from the yoke of white imperialism and colonialism. The Empire of Japan seemed to have an invincible psychological advantage. It was a formidable new challenge to those like George Steer who worked in propaganda.

Now Steer was even more in demand. In the first half of 1942 he wrote a memorandum on propaganda that reached the Secretary of State for India, Leo Amery, who considered it very good. Amery telegraphed the Viceroy of India, Lord Linlithgow, recommending that Steer be employed by SOE India to organize their forward subversive propaganda; but just as Steer was being head-hunted for India, he was poached for Madagascar by Sir William Platt, formerly his general in Khartoum.

The huge red island of Madagascar was strategically vital, straddling the Indian Ocean sea routes to and from the Gulf. Madagascar had an enormous natural harbour at Diego Suarez in the north that could become a dangerous base for Japanese submarine raiders. The pro-Axis Vichy French government controlled the island, and was known to be negotiating with the Japanese. The German Nazis also had their eye on Madagascar as a tropical camp for European Jews.

On 18 December 1941 the Chiefs of Staff in London had their first long meeting 'to consider the desirability of seizing north Madagascar to stop the Japs getting it'. Singapore fell to the Japanese on 15 February 1942, and two days later three Japanese warships were reported to be already in Madagascar's Diego Suarez harbour. Code-named Force 121, the Madagascar expedition sailed from England on 23 March 1942. They passed the Cape of Good Hope in April, uneasily aware that earlier that month the Nagumo Fast Strike Force, the Japanese naval fleet that had attacked Pearl Harbor, had been reported in the Indian Ocean.

Operation Ironclad, the first large-scale opposed landing on enemy territory since the Dardanelles in 1915, was launched on 5 May 1942. Allied troops landed successfully at Courrier Bay and Diego Suarez itself was taken in a daring raid when fifty Commandos seized the main barracks; but then the operation bogged down. The Vichy French refused to surrender the rest of the island. A Japanese midget submarine managed to put two torpedoes into one of the British battleships, *Ramillies*, in late May, and in the next two months Japanese submarines sank thirty-four ships in the Mozambique Channel. Another push was needed to finish the job and clear the island.

General Platt had summoned Steer to help with the second phase of the Madagascar operation. On 13 July 1942 he was appointed General Staff Officer II (Intelligence Officer) and four days later proceeded to East Africa to join Platt's new East Africa Headquarters in Nairobi. Platt promoted Steer to Captain and then Temporary Major.

A list of US and UK naval code words from the Second World War includes two interesting items: ESME A and ESME B. 'Esmé A' was a military diversion during the successful amphibious landing to capture Majunga, Madagascar on 10 September 1942, and 'Esmé B' was the capture of the big island of Nosy Bé, off north-west Madagascar, on 11 September 1942.

These operation code names bear the mark of George Steer, whose pregnant wife Esmé was in Pietermaritzburg in South Africa at this time, shortly to give birth to their daughter Caroline in October. Soon afterwards, the Allies were in control of all Madagascar, and the armistice with the Vichy forces was signed on 6 November 1942.

4

Platt finally let Steer go in late 1942. Steer got leave for Christmas and went to South Africa to see his parents and spend time with his wife and children. His son George Augustine – 'Augustus was a chubby lad' – was two and a half years old, and Caroline a two-month-old baby. All too soon he had to leave, flying via Nairobi and Cairo to an unknown job in India. He kissed the family he would never see again.

Steer spent New Year's Eve 1942 stuffed full of aspirin, rum and lemon, sweating out 'a foul cold' under blankets in the Savoy Hotel, Beira, Mozambique, reading Gibbon's *Decline and Fall of the Roman Empire*. On Friday, 1 January 1943 he wrote to his wife:

Darling, sweetest Ezzie

It was horrible having to say goodbye to you and I shall always have it stamped on my mind: I don't know why, but every time we've parted I find I love you more than ever before, and somehow or other I got the idea that *you* loved me more this time: and at the back of it one felt that this was going to be a longer separation than the other, both in space and in time: and too we are family now, which makes each so much more part of the other. Do you remember that wire you sent me when I left for South Africa in 1937 – *mon coeur vole attrapele* – is that right? Right or not, after five years I feel the same, and long for the end of this disgusting business when we can get our house, and you can teach me really how to dance and I teach you how to play bad squash & Augustus how to win scholarships. But that's two years ahead at least, and you'll probably be in love with somebody else by then. Please don't. Please stay mine, promise. As for me, I'll observe the rules that we laid down in tearful conference: but even if I didn't in the past, it wasn't because I ceased to love you *far* more than anything else, for that could never happen, even if *you* loved another. I just am tied to you, heart, wrists and ankles, and I don't want to and don't know how to wriggle free.

In Cairo in the New Year, Steer bought the sand-coloured Scribe Diary for 1943, which gives a page to a day. The writing in blue and green ink starts on Sunday, 17 January and runs till the last week of March. Six days in April are recorded, and the first two weeks of May, in faded purple and pencil. There are wild flowers pressed in some later, empty pages of G. L. Steer's only surviving diary.

5

Steer slept through the early-morning flight east from Karachi, though he was wide-awake when the flying boat landed on an Indian lake. He found it 'very beautiful . . . clear morning air, great white palaces towering from the bushy hills . . . in the middle of hard brown land'. The flight ended at Gwalior.

In the town that Sunday, Steer noted the shop fronts like the tops of wedding cakes, and 'colossal competition in expenditure on cheapness'. There were long-haired beggars and wandering cows, 'overfed Townees going back to lunch and weighing down the back of *tongas*'. Steer fell in with an Australian lieutenant colonel, a man of 'uncultured but vigorous taste', who dragged him off to the zoo, where the Australian was disappointed to find the tigers had already been fed. 'Full of aggressive complaint, vulgarity & good spirit, this appalling man was most likeable.' Over lunch, the 'Aussie expressed lewd desire for lone woman at neighbouring table, not having had one for six weeks.' A joggly, dusty train then took Steer to Old Delhi.

The next morning, Monday, 18 January 1943, an Indian officer gave him a lift up to GHQ in his car. The weather was cold and sparkling with intervals of mist, and Steer found New Delhi (described by Robert Byron in 1931 as 'the Rome of Hindostan') 'amazing'. Its architects, Sir Edward Lutyens and Sir Herbert Baker, had planned the city as the crowning glory of the British Raj, so lions mixed with elephants, classical columns with bells and lotuses. It had cost £15 million, taken twenty years and over 30,000 masons and labourers to achieve the symbolic city; but in two more decades, the British Empire itself would be history.

As the Indian officer's car took Steer up the ceremonial mall known today as Rajpath, he watched rise into view 'beyond a vast expanse of green and mist up the centre of which everybody except Americans and us plodded or bicycled, the mystic domes of GHQ, the Secretariat & the Viceroy's House'.

Major George Steer was not dressed conventionally for the Indian winter as he entered GHQ. 'My shorts surprised many; my presence surprised . . . P. Fleming.' This was the writer Peter Fleming, older brother of Ian Fleming of Naval Intelligence, who later created the fictional spy James Bond. After having written some amusing travel books, composed fourth leaders for *The Times*, married the actress Celia Johnson and joined the Grenadier Guards, Peter Fleming had become an early recruit to SOE. W. H. Auden and Christopher Isherwood had noticed 'the flattering brutality of a born leader' in Fleming when they had met him in China in 1938. In *Journey to a War* they wrote: 'Fleming with his drawl, his tan, his sleek, perfectly brushed hair, and lean good looks, is a subtly comic figure – the conscious, living parody of the pukka sahib. He is too good to be true and he knows it.' Fleming was now running GSI(D) Deception in India. 'We never asked for you,' he said to Steer. 'Where have you come from?'

Steer had no idea who had sent for him but in forty-five minutes (rather fast, thought Peter Fleming) they had traced the origin of the signal: from Special Operations Executive. Steer then had lunch with the head of SOE's India Mission, Colin Mackenzie, whom he described as 'lame, pale, rather clerical, soft eyes & voice, wearing a Guards tie. Just a little, a Buchan figure of conspiracy.' Mackenzie, an Old Etonian, and a personal friend of both the Viceroy of India and the head of SOE, explained that Steer's new job was to pull together offensive propaganda. The Director of Military Intelligence, India had asked SOE to form an Indian Field Broadcasting Unit (IFBU) to carry out combat propaganda in the field, and Steer was to create and lead this unit, which would eventually have thirty officers. Instead of getting a Japanese or Eastern expert for the job, they had co-opted, as Steer wryly said, 'a journalist who was neither'. His new code number was B/B 209 and his pay was 1,600 rupees a month. He asked if Esmé and the children could join him in India. 'Nobody knows. Nobody knows very much in India.' They never came.

6

By May 1942 the Japanese Imperial Army, invading from Siam (now Thailand), had ruthlessly driven the British and Indian armies, the Americans and the Chinese right out of Burma. The retreat had been appalling, chaotic, demoralizing. Many Burmese turned against their British overlords and started killing both them and the Indians the British had employed. The frontier between Burma and the north-eastern province of India, Assam, was now the bristling front line. Steer arrived in January 1943 just as the first military offensives against the Japanese were under way. Time was pressing, because from April to October the monsoon made movements in Burma impossible. Steer was to be sent to 'Lloyd's Division', the 14th Division of XV Corps of

the Indian Army under Major General W. L. Lloyd. His current operation, CANNIBAL, was intended to sweep down the Mayu peninsula
and take the island of Akyab on the Bay of Bengal, whose airfield could
then be used to bomb Rangoon, some 300 miles away. The 3,000
Japanese who were 'determined to fight it out at Akyab' were thought
to be an ideal target on which the first experimental Indian Field
Broadcasting Unit could try out front-line psychological warfare.
Because this area is in the Arakan province of Burma, the operation is
now known as the First Arakan Campaign. Steer was now launched
into something which the historian Ronald Lewin has described as
ending in 'unmitigated and unpardonable disaster'. Although more
than 5,000 Allied soldiers were killed or wounded or went missing, the
front line did not move an inch.

Steer set off on Wednesday, 20 January to travel from Delhi to
Calcutta in 'the filthiest and most spacious railway carriage of my
experience . . . When the train stops all the classes of India make a
beeline for the 1st class carriages. Waiters in lofty turbans come rushing with food or luncheon orders, each desiring the defeat of the
other. Shoeshiners burst in to shine shoes, sweepers more humbly to
sweep.' As the long day went on, Steer found himself 'getting insensi-
bly dirtier and dirtier'.

They breakfasted next morning in Allahabad on the Ganges. Gandhi
was at the time leading a campaign against the British; when his slogan,
'Quit India', appeared on walls, squaddies added below, 'I wish I bloody
could.' Sabotage and hostility were growing, and Steer noted that the
Indians 'will NOT smile except when they are little, this strikes one
again and again; as does a fat, unwarlike middle class with spectacles
and umbrellas, probably suffering from indigestion'.

In Calcutta, Steer set about the job in hand. He had done this kind of
thing in Africa, but no one had ever taken propaganda to the Japanese
before. The idea was to get as close as possible to their front-line troops
and assail them by loudspeaker and with pamphlets to undermine their
morale.

He needed people: Burmese porters, Indian technicians, competent
intelligence officers to write and edit scripts, fluent Japanese-speaking
translators and broadcasters, and soldiers to protect them. The second
requirement was kit: battery-run wirelesses to receive the BBC from
London and broadcasts from Tokyo; microphones, long cables,

amplifiers and large loudspeakers on tripods to transmit speech and music.

The 'apparatus' they would develop was a further advance on what Steer had pioneered at Keren in Africa to demoralize the Italians and Eritreans. A public-address system or 'ampradiogram', it had two loud-speakers, or 'horns', which they would test together or separately, above, below and behind banks, open and covered, by day and at night, with the microphone close, or at the end of a long cable, aiming for audibility 400 and 500 yards away. Raising the horns in pairs improved audibility, but made them more prominent for the enemy to spot. They would learn to hide the horns' shape, shine and shadow, and conceal the wires, in exercises where one group tried to set up and use the loudspeakers for a fifteen-minute broadcast while the others tried to hunt them down. Then he needed transport: porters, mules, trucks, small boats and so on.

Steer constantly turned over new questions in his head. Would it be possible to print in the field, and where could one get Japanese type and typesetters? If one could only duplicate leaflets, how best to deliver them to the enemy lines in the jungle? If aeroplane drops were impos-sible, what about kites? The Arakanese had eight-foot-wide coloured paper kites for festivals that could hold leaflets, which you could then drop on their heads. Steer imagined making 'flying elephants and winged pigs'; but how would you release them? What about another kite with ground glass stuck on its string that could cut the other one open? How about luminous paint to exploit people's fears of ghosties? Steer never stopped thinking up ideas. In the field he noticed that the bully-beef tin was almost the same calibre as the 2-inch mortar and he wondered if the tin could not be adapted to hold a roll of leaflets, which could then be fired over the enemy.

And what was to be in the leaflets? What was the best tone to use? Would abuse be helpful? Or playing on Japanese fears? Or evoking nos-talgia? What was the appropriate language or the right music? Could you appeal to their hopes for an anti-militarist, anti-capitalist and peaceful Japan? Most of all, how could you turn them against the tenor of their training?

Steer's task was all but impossible. The twentieth-century Japanese military had managed to inculcate into their soldiers an absolute shame and horror of surrender. They had been trained, often brutally, to serve a living god, the Emperor Hirohito. If they died in action they

believed they would go to heaven and the Emperor himself would pray
for them. To surrender was to disgrace self, family, regiment, nation and
Emperor. This rigid belief system is part of the reason why the Japanese
in the Second World War treated their 140,000 prisoners of war so badly
(over a quarter of them died), and have never made any serious reparations. The Japanese sincerely believed that by allowing themselves to be
captured Allied soldiers had become less than human. In turn, many
Japanese believed that if they were captured, they too would be mistreated and tortured. Better to kill yourself or die in a banzai charge. By
early 1943 there were therefore remarkably few Japanese prisoners.
Indeed, the British Jungle Warfare Training Centre warned, 'Be on the
lookout for false surrender; any offer of surrender must be suspected as
an enemy ruse.' Faced with a system that produced suicide bombers and
kamikaze pilots, it is little wonder that some Allied soldiers thought
Steer's propaganda work was mad. Moreover, when Steer arrived, the
Japanese land forces seemed to be still winning. Psychologically they
were not ready to desert.

7

Steer's experimental unit went out into the Bengali countryside for six
days' field training. He liked their camp, overlooking a placid sweep of
the river where rowing boats with sharply tip-tilted bows were fishing,
though the view downstream was ghoulish: 'a burning ghat, big vultures squatting, crows, dogs better fed, tougher and less mangy than
usual, one with a human limb in its mouth, & skulls rolling in the
mud.' Small Arakanese soldiers ran around in shorts too long for them.
A Chittagonian carpenter with a grey beard 'rapidly made cradles for
our apparatus, two sets, with bamboo poles, and we ran it down to the
river and experimented'.

Steer was getting fitter for the field. The mornings began with PT at
seven-thirty, which made him feel faintly sick, but in a few days his pot
belly shrank, as it had in Tunisia. One of the last photographs of him,
(see plate 19) sitting cross-legged with a group of IFBU officers outside
an Indian bungalow, shows him looking slim and fit.

His team assembled for training and exercises: Bengalis, British,
Burmese, Indian. A tea planter called Hardwick turned up on a bicycle
with six Naga hillmen and all their kit in bullock carts. In one village,
'when we put camouflage hay on our hats and crept serpentlike along,

children wanted to know whether we were stealing chickens'; if so, they
wanted to help. When the men practised silent landings from a sailing
sampan on the Hooghly River and then climbing up the riverbank, 'one
or two could not help coughing, one sneezed and another farted. Titters
for most, especially the last.'

Steer enjoyed the riverside life, the sharp brown boats 'with nets like
sails dipping in great sweeps over water', the water buffalo being washed
twice daily in the river for ticks, 'others swimming nose uppermost
across with boys on their backs . . . Women with blazing bronze jars
bathed, exposing the profile of their breasts and wearing the sari.' Steer
must sometimes have missed Esmé badly. On their last Friday in camp
he played music on the gramophone, especially 'Yours', which reminded him of a banjo on a South African train taking him back to his wife.
Two large rums and a long hot bath put him in a coma, 'enjoying the
feeling that I was not doing the things I ought to be doing, including
letters home, I fear – but what can one write about?'

The next night Steer and his men took a train from Calcutta to Golando
at the mouth of the Ganges. When the head of the porters tried to over-
charge them, 'the Road Transport Officer, a big Sikh captain who could
have rolled on him and flattened him out, told him with the gentlest
disdain to fuck off. No more said.' Their rusty steamer, the *Ostrich*, took
them down the Ganges and over to Chandpur, from where they boarded
another train to the melancholy and neglected port of Chittagong,
arriving on Monday morning, 1 February 1943. Anti-aircraft guns were
banging away at Japanese bombers overhead, and the mood in the mess
was sombre.

The sense of defeatism seemed to thicken when they got to Cox's
Bazaar, the most southerly city of modern-day Bangladesh. Down the
coast beyond the Bazaar a series of beaches and hilly peninsulas
stretched for 120 miles to the island and town of Akyab, whose airfields
the British wanted because they could supply air cover for an attack on
Burma's Japanese-held capital, Rangoon. 'Take Akyab,' Wavell had
directed in September 1942; but the Japanese, moving up from the
south, had dug in across the Mayu peninsula north of Akyab, using
well-engineered bunkers to hold the British tanks and infantry at bay.
Steer was to be at both places where the British tried and failed to break
through: at Donbaik beach on the west side of the Mayu peninsula, and
Rathedaung on the east bank of the Mayu River. Not until 1944 did the

British learn from Australians and Americans how to destroy such bunkers: with tanks or artillery at point-blank range, before using flamethrowers, grenades, bullets and bayonets.

Meanwhile, the British infantry's frontal attacks at Donbaik were failing, bloodily. Steer met a bearded newsreel man called Maurice Ford, who was full of gruesome stories about Inniskilling Fusiliers' corpses floating out to sea at Donbaik and being eaten by sharks in the Bay of Bengal.

ELEVEN Forgotten Army

1

On Friday, 5 February 1943, Steer's unit sailed south down the river that forms the border between present-day Bangladesh and Burma. The Bengal shore on their right had paddy fields in front of a teak-covered range of hills about 900 feet high, with bald patches of precipice showing. On the other side of the river was ominous Burma, 'to which Shwe Bu proudly told me all islands in the river belonged', with higher jungled hills whose steep slopes were intercut by *chaungs*, or small rivers. They unloaded in a cloud of flies at Maungdaw, and drove to a camp five miles away in semi-tropical jungle. Steer thought the birds were 'wonderful'. There were jays, crows, magpies and game birds, but also babblers, bulbuls and laughing thrushes, bee-eaters, fly-catchers, flowerpeckers, kingfishers, spider-hunters, weaver birds and woodpeckers.

After dinner, rather astonishingly, Lieutenant Colonel Peter Fleming, head of D Division in India, came round to 'put them in the picture'. Fleming told Steer that his Propaganda Unit could operate easily any-where: British troops were at some points only thirty yards from the enemy; but he also thought that, for the Japanese, the idea of 'No Surrender' was 'engrained, like not wearing brown boots with a bowler'. Fleming regarded the Japanese as 'queer little creatures. You must divert their attention . . . They were somnolent by day, come out yowling at night.' Steer recorded that his lieutenants H. J. Hardwick and 'N. Roy Esq' 'didn't seem impressed' by this Old Etonian lecture.

An army lorry drove Steer and his men south down the coastal road to the front line above Donbaik. The Headquarters of the 55th Indian

Brigade was concealed in jungle; green parakeets with pink heads flew about, and wild-elephant droppings steamed beside a nearby *chaung*. The Brigade Major told Steer the difficulties his battalion, 2/1 Punjab Regiment, were facing; only a week before, a concerted attack by eight British tanks supported by artillery and infantry had ignominiously failed to break the cunningly dug-in Japanese line. After lunch Steer joined C Company of the Punjabis at an observation post a few hundred yards away from a creek with a ditched British tank 'where dead Rajputs lay, eaten by vultures'. Then they scrambled along the jungle edge to a point only fifty yards from the Japanese. 'Men in trees, an evacuated hole with blood in it.' Half C Company had been wounded by sniper or mortar fire.

Higher up there was a good view of the river and the village: 'high-treed Donbaik, dead Rajputs, tangle of jungle in loop of chaung below, where Dogras stood'. British artillery was shelling with shrapnel two hills where the enemy had been seen digging in. The Japanese had cut a British telephone wire in the creek below, then set snipers to kill the linemen who came to repair it. On the Twin Knobs Steer met Major Gillespie, a red-faced man with a fair moustache, who was cheerfully guarding a razor-edge hilltop with two companies of 8/6 Rajputana Rifles. The hillsides were so steep that the trenches were like theatrical boxes. Steer took tea with them ('best chaps I had met yet') and from the South Knob saw a Japanese position thirty yards off; a little occupant had just scooted from the hole made in it by a British anti-tank rifle. Back at Brigade HQ, a new blackout order forced them to eat their meal in the dark, lit only by the glow of cigarettes. The wireless was also forbidden. Steer found it difficult to fork the food and find his mouth in utter darkness. He went to bed at eight-thirty, in open air rich with noisy and biting insects. He felt a long way from home.

From Monday, 8 February 1943, Steer began trying to persuade senior officers to use his experimental unit, broadcasting in Japanese through loudspeakers. Brigadier Hunt at Donbaik thought Steer was a new padre at first, and then sent him to see Major General Lloyd at Divisional Headquarters at Maungdaw. Lloyd had been with the Indians at Keren and remembered what Steer's Propaganda Unit had done, but he wanted Steer's unit to go further east and find a berth with Brigadier Hammond of 123 Brigade, on the other front line against the Japanese, at Rathedaung.

Steer worked till midnight in the Divisional Intelligence office. He discovered from recently captured Japanese prisoners of war that Japanese troops were receiving absolutely no news from home at all. He thought that news bulletins would be a good way to get enemy troops to listen to his broadcasts. Steer began mining all the reports from the Interrogation Centre in Delhi for further useful points.

On 10 February 1943 Steer drove east along the tangled jungle valley to the riverside port of Buthidaung, lunched on bully beef under a tree and then took a motor launch southwards on the afternoon high tide down the Mayu River to find his new brigadier. On the three-hour journey he saw white egrets, pagodas, and old people fishing with circular nets. They arrived at Htizwe at 6 p.m.

At last Steer found someone receptive to his propaganda ideas; Brigadier Hammond gave him carte blanche. Though British attacks since the end of 1942 had gained no ground, Hammond was sure the enemy was now becoming very tired. Steer hung his mosquito net in a murky carved-wood Burmese house and slept on smoked-bamboo poles. The next day, having walked two and a half hours south to 123 Brigade HQ and ridden back on a borrowed tough horse 'with reins of iron & irritating saddle-bags & in my galling shorts', Steer was back in Htizwe to collect the others, including Hardwick and his Naga hillmen. Eight mules brought their stores and machinery along the dusty track. They stored their kit in the Buddhist pagoda on Temple Hill, which the Japanese sometimes attacked at night, and managed to get some meat after the Rajputana Rifles agreed, against their Hindu beliefs, to allow cattle to be butchered. The little group settled in among the banana trees and bamboo, and prepared to broadcast a propaganda programme.

The Bengali communist N. Roy twiddled the dial on the radio. Singapore was loud and clear, Chungking better than Peshawar. They found Tokyo and then four more Japanese stations. Steer thought the Japanese propaganda in English was 'very feeble, nothing of the early character of Haw-Haw, dreary voice, undistinguished sarcasm and heavy illogicality'.

There was a dogfight of Hurricanes and Zeroes overhead; ignoring it, Steer caught a black-and-white butterfly. He sent the sketch that Roy made of another Acracinae swallowtail, caught on a shrub like the *kaffirboom* of home, to his father in South Africa. Bernard Steer tenderly stowed it in the moth and butterfly folder he had made for his schoolboy son in 1921.

2

The first hour-long programme by the first Indian Field Broadcasting Unit went out on the Sunday afternoon of St Valentine's Day 1943, just north of Rathedaung. The loudspeaker horns were pointed towards the Shaving Brush hill 350 yards away; from a cramped dugout Jack Tarr, Steer's Japanese-speaking interrogator, spoke 'not too precisely', three of Mr Woo's five-minute records were broadcast, and some Western music. There were several hitches, and straight afterwards the radio broke down. Steer cursed the flimsiness of the apparatus. The records soon became useless because the gramophone and pick-up were no good. They also needed better 'talent' behind the microphone.

Jack Tarr was a slow translator (his dictionaries could not help him with even a phrase like 'Goebbels admits'), and temperamental in the field. His best broadcast, booming from the front verandah of the Buddhist pagoda on Temple Hill, was also his last, because he was scared by the Japanese gunfire that it produced. His Korean replacement, Mr Woo, was far better. 'Woo disregarded mortar fire and the pops of our own snipers. He could not be stopped, he fired off at them impromptu until darkness threatened. While British Officers were cowering in their holes . . . Woo went on.'

Slowly the Broadcasting Unit settled to the pattern of their work in Arakan. They broadcast morning and afternoon, and adapted to their new quarters, on a stony ridge, 'in snug rustling bamboo in which the fascinating Nagas are building gravely a new earth closet'. It was much like any other radio show, except that the audience sent over the odd mortar round to show they were listening. To their east, Blenheim bombers bombed other potential listeners, and at night they heard the dull thud of the guns in the west over the river as yet another British attack failed to take Donbaik.

Steer lay in bed in the early morning, writing talks in his head, listing Allied superiorities and Japanese difficulties. He would boast of massive reinforcement from India, and the subcontinent's determination to fight. If India was in revolt, as Japanese propaganda claimed, why would 2 million men, 50,000 recruits a month, be joining the Allies to defend India and reconquer Burma?

Steer plucked ideas from Intelligence summaries. When he found that one regiment, now reinforcing Akyab, had once been smashed in

New Guinea, he made it the subject of a scornful talk. He niggled at grievances: why did the Japanese Navy not come to help the Japanese Army? *No one will assist you here. You are on your own. Surrounded.*

A lot of this was whistling in the dark. In fact the British were afraid that the Japanese were more cunning and more ruthless than they were at jungle warfare. The claims about the pro-British sympathies of Indian soldiers were dubious, too. When a Punjabi patrol went missing without shots being heard, you could never be quite sure whether they had deserted. Gandhi was fasting himself to death in the 'Quit India' campaign, and senior British officers were afraid of the reaction of Indian troops if he died. The Indians were already jittery, firing off too much ammunition into the darkness.

The Japanese started yelling 'Singapore, Singapore' across the lines to the Indians at night, to remind them of what had happened exactly a year before on 15 February 1942, when 'Fortress Singapore' had suddenly fallen to the Japanese and with it the prestige of the British Empire and the myth of white invincibility. Of the Indian Army prisoners captured by the Japanese at Singapore, between a third and a half had switched allegiance and joined the Indian National Army, Azad Hind Fauj, to fight for Indian independence and against the British.

Some of Steer's subsequent propaganda in Burma would be directed at these ex-Indian Army men, trying to woo them back to their old allegiance to Britain. Many did recross the lines from the INA, including, once, 250 members of the Nehru Brigade in a body. A captured IFBU man once talked his captors into rejoining the British; but others resisted the blandishments of the loudspeakers and fought on against their ex-comrades because they believed this was best for Indian freedom. This passionate conflict of loyalties led to some dramatic ironies.

Steer himself was leading an IFBU patrol, containing many Indian soldiers, on 23 March 1944 at Lamyang in the Upper Kabaw valley on the Burmese front when they ran into an Indian National Army unit and had to fight their way back. Steer's Indian soldiers took up a defensive position and in a six-hour fire fight killed eight Indian National Army soldiers and captured a light machine gun. Then, as Steer's unit withdrew, a third Indian force arrived: the IFBU came under so-called 'friendly fire' from Madrasi Indians supposed to be on the British side, but possibly better disposed towards the Indian National Army.

Steer's first propaganda initiative against the INA in Arakan was sarcasm directed at Captain Mohan Singh, the founder of the INA.

An Indian voice boomed out from his loudspeaker over the jungle, leaving pauses for birdsong between rhetorical questions. 'We fight for our country, but we believe Mohan Singh gets more than twenty-two rupees – and from what? – from what the Japanese looted from China. And finally, Mohan Singh, where are you? Where are you? Where?' And when no answer came: 'You see, Mohan Singh isn't here. He is in *Tokyo*.'

3

Japanese and Indians were not Steer's only target. From the beginning Brigadier Hammond liked Steer's idea of distributing subversive anti-Japanese pamphlets among the local Arakanese of this area of Burma. Steer's unit began doing written propaganda aimed at one particular ethnic group, the Mhugs, a Burmese tribe who had a horrible reputation for ambushing soldiers and terrorizing civilians on behalf of the Japanese. Steer's unit also published an Arakan news-sheet for villagers and refugees, and he actively searched for Burmese agents.

Steer's entry into the Burmese 'hearts and minds' campaign began one morning at Htizwe. His new Arakanese helpers were sitting disconsolately in dirty quarters, having eaten all the rice they had been given; Steer managed to fix them more rations. Then a ferry, manned by bearded and turbaned Sikhs, took them towards what Steer called insouciantly 'British Mugland'. On the way to Myoksogyangywa through half-sacked and half-burned villages, he saw the first of the feared Mhugs, 'four in a field, coppery, pink lungis like bloomers, blue tattooing on legs, back and stomach, like pagodas & twists & twirls, plucking beans in narrow-necked baskets'. Steer raised his hand to his forehead, and 'bowed slightly in token of respect'.

He tried to win support and gather intelligence from the local people by setting up much-needed village markets through a stout, pipe-smoking Burmese headman called U Baw. Because undisciplined Indian troops, Burmese bandits and Japanese soldiers had all been looting them, the Kamwe villagers were desperate for kerosene, matches, cooking oil, salt, tea, sugar, garlic, chillies, blankets, vests and cloth for wraparound *lungyis*. They were also keen to get hold of the strong-smelling dried fish they liked and, if possible, pigs. So Steer began wheeling and dealing, obtaining some army rations to sell on (a court-martial offence) and transporting goods to village bazaars. Steer's diary records the Arakanese calmly puffing on cheroots as they loaded a combustible mixture of 900 boxes of matches, tin after tin of kerosene and bolts of bright cloth into the back of an army truck.

General Lloyd did not like Steer's idea of 'economic propaganda' and questioned him closely about both the goods and the money. Lloyd was not a man you could discuss things with; he thought any discussion was 'arguing'. He refused to allot any extra transport to Steer and said he did not want small shows getting in the way of his big one. Steer's armed patrols and placing of agents in villages was seen to be going beyond his responsibilities. Nor did other senior officers agree with Steer's idea that Burmese people should be encouraged to bring their families back to the shelter of the British area, or that Buddhist priests should circulate propaganda pamphlets. This frustrated Steer, who saw the importance of building more of these connections among the local hill tribes.

Violence could erupt anywhere in Burma. Drifting down the Mayu River in a Burmese sampan, potshotting at *padi* birds with his tommy gun, Steer suddenly saw three bombers and eight fighters flying overhead. As they turned across the sun, he confirmed they were Japanese. They dropped their bombs south of Htizwe; the concussion rumbled over the water, and a tree of smoke grew up into the air.

4

When George Steer reached Divisional HQ at Maungdaw at one o'clock on Wednesday, 10 March 1943, he found an unexpected visitor in the mess for lunch, General Bill Slim, the Corps Commander. Slim remembered Steer from the Ethiopian frontier at Gallabat and they reminisced about the Lion of Judah. Slim had been sent down to check on what was going wrong with Lloyd's command. He saw at once that morale was very low, and that the plan for taking Donbaik was wrong-headed. The Indian Division seemed scared of the jungle and unwilling to tackle the Mayu peninsula ridge. Soon things were going to get worse.

The next day Steer had lunch with Brigadier R. V. C. Cavendish, who suggested that the Indian Field Broadcasting Unit should go down to Donbaik and find a position to broadcast to the Japanese at a strong-point known as Sugar 5. Cavendish would be killed three weeks later, when the Japanese overran his brigade's new HQ at Indin, in the final collapse of the First Arakan Campaign. When the Brigadier knew he was surrounded he self-sacrificingly ordered the British artillery to shell the village where he himself was, as soon as the enemy entered it. The

Japanese officer leading the attack, Colonel Tanahashi, later told his son
that Brigadier Cavendish was the bravest man he had ever known.

Donbaik was the sort of dusty, malarial, snipers' haunt that the soldiers
of the 1914–18 war had known in places like Gallipoli or Salonika. After
a stealthy night when Royal Engineers pushed out an elaborate cart
with hundreds of pounds of guncotton or ammonal to try to blow up
the enemy's entrenched positions, the morning brought barrages of
shelling and low-level Japanese fighters swooping over to strafe the
British lines. Steer called this 'the morning hate', using the old term
from the Great War.

Lines of loaded mules in fringed headstalls, hauled by effing and
blinding men, plodded the tracks to elaborate dugouts in ditches
among the bamboo. The enemy was on the other side of no man's land,
where the dead bodies lay under long-billed vultures that were tugging
out their guts through bulging battledress. The sound of machine-gun
fire seemed to follow Steer's men over the top of the trees as they headed
for the beach after a night of loudspeakering the dark. On the bright
strand as the tide receded, the scarlet crabs dodged into holes, missed by
erratic revolver shots. Army trucks raced along the sand in front of the
pink convolvulus with its pulpy leaves, and puffs of smoke hung over a
distant creek. South-west over the blue Bay of Bengal Steer imagined a
line curving around Ceylon and over the Indian Ocean, all the way back
home to East London and South Africa, where Esmé and his family
waited.

When Steer noticed the graves freshly dug outside the Advanced
Dressing Station at Brigade HQ, he knew there was a big fight coming.
The Welsh soldiers joked about it: 'Donbaik the news to Mother,' they
called out to the broadcasters. The men liked the IFBU because it
brought them news from home and the outside world. The brigade's
own radios were all tuned to signals work, so Steer copied down the
BBC and All India Radio news in shorthand and put together his own
bulletins for the troops.

The 1st Battalion Royal Welch Fusiliers' Commanding Officer,
Lieutenant Colonel Humphrey Williams, referred in his diary to
'George Steer and his Burmese band'. Colonel Williams was very Welsh.
He had been a schoolmaster before the war and worked for the BBC in
Wales after it, and Steer was very surprised to find he had read both
Caesar in Abyssinia and *The Tree of Gernika*.

5

The 'big push' came early on Thursday, 18 March and, as in the First World War, the British heralded its coming with a massive artillery bombardment just before dawn. Williams and other senior officers did not want this to give away the attack, but higher authority overruled them. The Royal Welch Fusiliers' objectives were to capture Sugar 4 and Sugar 5 with A Company, Sugar 10 with C Company and a strong-point to the south called Monkey 16 with D Company. B Company were in reserve to support them. From an observation post, Steer watched the initial Fusiliers' assault with their Commanding Officer, Colonel Williams.

> Flashes and smoke continuous on S4 and S5, as Japs registered mortars and rolled grenades from own positions. Could see nothing, only smoke, flashes, & upward slanting morse of tracer. Little human noise. Mortar burst just behind us, wounding CO's orderly. In smoke, Wilson, D Company's commander, appeared, led in, crouching, 'take me to the CO, I can't see', blinded by grenade, blood all over him.

Two platoons from A Company reached Sugar 4 and Sugar 5 but were met by showers of grenades, crossfire from machine guns, and accurate rifle sniping. A number of the Royal Welch were killed on top of the enemy bunker because the Japanese brought down mortar and artillery fire precisely on their own deep fortifications. One NCO managed to get into the concrete pillbox through a heavy steel door but crawled out instantly, wounded. Others entered and found empty rooms, baffles, traps.

The leading platoon of D Company was cut to ribbons by machine guns camouflaged low down in gullies and below banks, set up with interlocking fields of fire. The Japanese foxholes and trenches were linked, so that when one position was assailed, the enemy could dive down tunnels and pop up elsewhere to attack the attackers. Two of the wrecked British Valentine tanks had been turned into Japanese strongholds. However, a Royal Welch sergeant and eleven men managed to reach their objective, Monkey 16, where they held their ground all day against snipers and grenades.

From his observation post Steer watched the dead and the dying. One of the Royal Welch, creeping back wounded, was machine-gunned to death ten yards away from him. The Royal Welch Fusiliers were incredibly brave. Steer recounted the heroism of a little man called Fields – not strong, but a mad Welshman – who had gone down the gully 'singing and fucking', with two grenades in each hand with the pins out to throw with himself on to a Japanese machine-gun post. Of course, he had died. Then there was David Graves, the son of Robert Graves, author of *Goodbye to All That*, one of the Royal Welch Fusiliers' famous writers of the First World War. When his B Company was pinned down by machine-gun fire, Lieutenant J. D. N. Graves pressed forward together with a sergeant and a fusilier (both called Jones). With the sergeant covering them, and the fusilier firing his Bren gun from the hip, David Graves bombed his way into an enemy machine-gun post at Sugar 10. Both Joneses were wounded, but Graves ran back for a further supply of hand grenades and then advanced again, ducking, diving, throwing, into two more enemy trenches. He was last seen falling backwards as he was shot. His body was never recovered. Colonel Williams recommended David Graves for a posthumous Victoria Cross, but he ended up with only a Mention in Dispatches to reward his extraordinary bravery.

The ambulances went up and down the beach, and Colonel Williams told Steer his battalion had 'taken a packet': 13 officers and 162 men were killed, wounded or missing. At midnight the Royal Scots soldiers started coming through, moving forward to relieve the Royal Welch. At 00.30 Steer heard the crack of grenades and Scottish voices shouting, 'Come on, you fuckers, get up!' But no success signal went up, and the fighting never reached far beyond the line the Royal Welch Fusiliers had established. Mortars, machine guns and tracer split the night.

The Royal Scots were now taking 50 per cent casualties. Wounded men began to come in and were laid by Steer's bed through the night. Every now and then stretcher bearers peered at him in the moonlight to see if he was wounded. Steer overheard Lieutenant Colonel Jackson of the Royal Scots telephoning Brigade HQ to say in a low voice that he was sorry, but he was calling off the attack because to go on would be murder. This meant there would now be no relief for the Welshmen stuck out among the Japanese positions. 'Bugger!' said Colonel Williams, and turned to Steer's IFBU again. Humphrey Williams's After Action Report praises 'the valuable services rendered . . . by Major G. L. Steer who changed the position of his loudspeaker apparatus several times in order to get my messages across to the troops who were isolated'. Williams spoke in Welsh so that the Japanese could not understand him and instructed his men to signal their numbers and positions by specific rifle shots in reply to his questions.

When the moon was down, Williams called out to his men through the loudspeaker for the last time, telling them in Welsh to 'come back before dawn'. Thanks to the loudspeakers, all who remained alive made their way back safely.

6

This new use of the loudspeaker, 'to control and extricate our own troops embedded in enemy positions', featured in Steer's report on the experimental Forward Propaganda Unit that he submitted on 7 May to SOE HQ. He was clear-eyed about its successes and failures and adamant about the need for training officers and men to work in small, self-contained, highly mobile units. He considered the setting up of markets for villagers as 'our finest instrument of propaganda penetration'. He now wanted to get Urdu- and Burmese-speaking officers, trained in jungle fighting, men who understood Burmese ethnology and Japanese tactics, to lead Naga and Karen troops with plain-clothes local agents into villages ahead of the Allied advance. It is a prescription for classic counter-insurgency work as practised in later wars of the twentieth century.

SOE approved, and Steer was told to develop four more Forward Propaganda Units. In May 1943 he went to look for a training ground in the foothills of the Himalayas in North Bengal, which had Alpine-type jungle called *Sirok*, with tall, straight sal trees, rather than thick bamboo forest. The IFBU camp was eventually established north-west of Siliguri in Darjeeling District, in an area known as the Western Dooars, a word derived from 'doors', because it is the threshold between the Bengal plains and the mountains of Bhutan. This was forested tiger and elephant country, where for a century Scottish tea planters had been carving out green estates known as 'tea-gardens'.

The IFBU camp was a flat army training area at Fagu, lying on a low bluff between the Chel River and a small creek. To the north lay a tea-garden and steep hills. The camp entrance was just across the Chel from where the village of Gurubathan now stands. The IFBU dry-season sports ground, below the camp in the river valley, is now called

Happy Village, thick with betel nut and banana trees. All the buildings have long disappeared from Fagu camp, but the Indian Army, out on exercises, sometimes tents there among the brown grass and black boulders. The holes for their goalposts on a flat, dusty pitch were probably inherited from the IFBUs, who played soccer when they got a chance. Steer managed to select and train five IFBUs of sixty men each to go into the field in Burma in January 1944. Three units were at Imphal, and two in Assam and Arakan. The men were of many cultures and spoke seventeen languages; there were Madrasis, Nagas, Mahrattas, Punjabi Muslims and Gurkhas. The IFBUs mostly did loudspeaker work, often using Korean National Army Liaison Unit officers who spoke fluent Japanese as the broadcasters. Because some of the Koreans spoke no English, Steer found Captain Roland Bacon, a former Canadian missionary to Korea, who was fluent in Korean, to work with them. Steer thought the Koreans were 'a handful, and then some', but Bacon had the boisterous energy to match theirs.

Steer wanted to use Japanese prisoners of war to speak to their comrades. They would be living proof that people who surrendered would not be mistreated. Steer came to realize that propaganda references to Germany and world events were futile because most of the Japanese soldiers were peasants and fishermen and small tradesmen, only interested in food and going home. Now the units played sentimental Japanese music and used poems in the leaflets to induce homesickness. Sometimes it worked: in April and May 1944, the Indian Field Broadcasting Units managed to convince the Japanese to surrender on four separate occasions.

General Slim, Commander-in-Chief of the 14th ('Forgotten') Army, approved of what Steer was doing. In a memo dated 22 May 1944 Slim wrote, 'Experience has shown that the IFB Units are of considerable operational and Intelligence value . . . more units of this type should be raised.' He recommended that 600 more soldiers be drafted in from the Assam Regiment; but army bureaucracy clogged this request.

Death was never far away. Steer and his men were doing work of extreme danger, operating only feet away from an enemy willing to kill everyone, including themselves. Captain Roland Bacon died of machine-gun wounds in Burma on 13 March 1945: the brave bespectacled missionary was shot at close quarters while trying to persuade some Japanese to surrender.

Documentary evidence exists of another death in the jungle. Stanley Charles was a combat cameraman with the South-East Asian Command Film Unit, who were roving film reporters. In Burma in March 1945, Charles met a 'very pleasant' captain who invited him to film the IFBU at work. Charles filmed them putting up their apparatus, which included a loudspeaker on a tripod, then broadcasting surrender terms in Japanese to an enemy unit in a tunnel on a hill, with the captain lying prone. He was still filming from about seventy-five yards away when a Japanese mortar fired on the Indian Field Broadcasting Unit and killed the captain.

A few days later the cameraman learned that the pleasant man whose death he had inadvertently filmed was Basil Hamilton-Temple-Blackwood, the 4th Marquess of Dufferin and Ava, grandson of Lord Dufferin, Viceroy of India. It was curious he should die in Burma; his grandfather had taken his title from the Burmese kingdom of Ava, which he had annexed in the Pagoda War of 1885–6. It was not a lucky title: the second Marquess had died young of pneumonia in 1918, the third in a plane crash in 1930.

7

George Steer's ideas about propaganda have proved influential.

Stephen Jolly's article in the March 2001 issue of the propaganda buff's magazine *Falling Leaf: The Journal of the Psywar Society* is called 'Wearing the Stag's Head Badge: British Combat Propaganda since 1945'. He begins his story with George Steer's unit, 'the first experimen-tal IFBU', and the five IFBUs later deployed on the 14th Army front, 'successful in helping make the Japanese show the white flag'. Jolly goes on to trace the subsequent history of 'Psychological Operations' units in the British Army, which were used on an improvised basis in most military operations from 1945 to 1990. After the Gulf War of 1991, the Chiefs of Staff agreed to set up a unit to be called '15 (UK) PSYOPS group (Shadow)'. According to Jolly, their badge of a yellow stag's head on a blue background was adopted in direct tribute to the badge that Steer chose for his unit, a *sambur*, or gold-antlered Burmese deer, on a black background.

In 1999, under the New Labour government, the unit's name was changed to '15 (UK) Information Support Group', in order to distance it from the term 'psychological operations', which was thought to smack

of 'black' propaganda. When I went to talk to 15 (UK) Information
Support Group in Bedfordshire in 2002, I found the unit proud to
claim descent from Steer's Indian Field Broadcasting Units. On the
wall outside the CO's office, among the notable propagandists of the
Political Warfare Executive, was the picture (see plate 17) of George
Steer talking to the Emperor Haile Selassie.

TWELVE Home

1

On 10 December 1944 Steer wrote his last letter home from India to 'my dearest Ezzie', then living in a cottage in Dorset. The air mail Christmas letterform had holly and ivy on the back. This moving and beautifully written letter is evidence of a deathly tiredness. The journalist Alan Moorehead, at the end of the same war, had become 'more sickened by ruins than stimulated by danger', but he was luckier as a civilian, with some freedom to travel and pick his assignments. George Steer had made the hard choice: to put on khaki for the duration and submit to a drabber kind of duty. It abraded his intelligence and imagination. War, as he memorably said, is 'the highest form of inefficiency known to man'.

> Anyway here I am still waiting for troops, with everybody in the highest places issuing orders that I am to have them and nobody in the lower quarters taking the slightest step to obey. The result is that we are months and months back on our programme and god knows when we will begin to do anything. One's patience gets frayed to tatters, and the loathing that one engenders for this country and its unbelievable military system reaches a stage impossible to describe. I am due for repatriation and often feel like applying. The only things that hold me back, and will (I know) keep me here in spite of everything are the feeling that one hates to go home a failure; and secondly, the knowledge that if I got back home I would not be able to contribute one iota to the defeat of the enemy whereas here I do know him, & given the tools I can do something to finish him off. It often is so difficult, though, to fight (very metaphorically speaking) with one's bare

hands, and physically one gets very exhausted. And one feels that one will never forgive or forget the stupid people who stood in the way – all the time wondering how one can be so petty, for they are certainly not worth remembering for their own sakes and not to forgive them is to take them far too seriously. I suppose really that war, especially when it is waged out here far from public criticism and almost out of the public mind, is the highest form of inefficiency known to man. Hundreds, more, thousands of gentlemen, in fact, who would be failures in any normal business and in peacetime would be kept in their place as commercial travellers, etc., are now in positions of responsibility and yet sabotage anybody who has energy and ideas, and in spite of it all, I think that I still have a bit of both and that no number of years in India will knock or dry them out of me. But this must be very boring to you & unintelligible, for I believe you live in an efficient country where there is some spirit of urgency.

Soon it will be your birthday & I will be thinking of you and wishing that I were there. The children must be completely different from two years ago when we were last together. And I shall think again of it when Christmas comes round. Do you remember the party for the children at Glenarum when Augustus, presented with a trifling amount of sherry in his fruit drink, screwed up his face and said 'I don't *like* it'. Also I remember Joan ticking you off for putting colour round your eyes, and saying that it made you look like a woman of ill repute . . . Privately I was a bit annoyed by her at the time, as *I* like it but could not say it, or Joan would have suspected me of liking the type as well. If only I could have you here, with colour round your eyes – or without, now.

Your ever loving husband
George

2

That Christmas, Steer was at the training camp at Fagu. It is a particularly hard time for men in war, far from loved ones. Steer kept himself busy: he always worked fiendishly hard, as if he knew that time was short. Andrew Chapman-Andrews said he never saw Steer take an afternoon siesta in Africa when it was *de rigueur* for officers; Steer was always writing. In 1944 he was working on a book called *Into Another Mould*, believed to be about the war in Burma and the way British operations were run. The typescript has vanished; possibly suppressed, or just lost.

Steer had somehow managed to write eight books (two of which were lost in manuscript) during an extraordinary ten years. In that decade he had married twice, been widowed, had two children and lost another, foreseen and alerted others to the Fascist game-plan in Africa and Europe, initiated a new kind of psychological warfare, and seen military action in Ethiopia, Spain, Finland, Libya, Egypt, Madagascar and Burma. It was still only a month after his thirty-fifth birthday.

The men at Fagu were Hindus and Buddhists, Muslims and animists, but there were quite a few Christians, too. There had been missionaries in the Dooars for over sixty years, and today, although only 2 per cent of India is Christian, a dozen Christian denominations have churches around the Fagu area. On Monday, 25 December 1944, the Christians at the Indian Field Broadcasting Unit camp had organized a sports day after lunch. Everyone was invited.

The sixth and final Christmas of the Second World War was Steer's second consecutive Christmas away from his own wife and children. As Officer Commanding IFBUs, Lieutenant Colonel Steer had to be father to his men. On Christmas morning, Major John Cannon recalled, 'George was his usual jovial self. He had paid visits to various Company messes as well as the local villagers. He came to my Mess at about 1 p.m. and was full of good cheer. After a drink he went off by jeep to his own Mess which was another 1,500 feet up into the hills over a distance of about 3 miles.'

Steer's mess that day was the tea planter's bungalow at Upper Fagu, which had a magnificent view south out over the Chel river valley, and east and west over the jungled spines of the mountains climbing northwards to Bhutan. The house, which no longer exists, was backed by a small hill with a great fig tree shading the water tanks. Across the road and in a small saddle to the south-west, some IFBU soldiers camped in tents, guarding a small wire enclosure holding three Japanese prisoners of war.

The current village of wooden huts at Upper Fagu is still called *Kothi Lines* ('Bungalow Dwellings'). Lok Nat Pokrail, an old villager who has lived there all his life, remembers the big party, or *tamasha*, held at the bungalow on Christmas Eve 1944, which went on long into the night.

The Christian sports were meant to start at 2 p.m. on Christmas Day, and Lieutenant Colonel Steer (who was the guest of honour) was anxious that three Indian Christians at Upper Fagu should also have a chance to take part. They were his own orderly, Rifleman Long Sing Song Kuki, another orderly, and the signaller Joseph Newton. They were already late when they went out to the jeep. Steer had a Gurkha civilian driver, Lal Bahadur Gurung. Steer liked and admired the Gurkhas and had taken to carrying a *kukri*, the Gurkhas' heavy, curved machete, though the man who once looked after the IFBU packhorses, Nar Bahadur Newar, told me 'the Colonel Sahib's *kukri* was not sharpened properly, he just wore it to frighten people'.

When the group reached the jeep, the driver was not there. Making a quick decision, Steer got behind the steering wheel on the left-hand side, Captain Halley took the front right passenger seat and the others piled into the back. Then the driver showed up. This was a crucial moment. Steer was not the most patient of men, and they were already late: if he got out to make way for the driver, more time would be wasted. It was against Steer's own camp regulations for officers to drive without written authority from a superior officer, but Steer had no superior officer there. He told the driver to climb into the back of the Willy's, and gunned the motor himself.

The jeep set off, switchbacking down the dirt road through the tall trees from Upper Camp Fagu to Lower Camp Fagu. On the way down they passed two more soldiers making their way on foot to the sports, and although the vehicle was already carrying six, Steer charitably stopped to let them get on board as well. With eight people on board, the jeep was now definitely overloaded.

It should have taken about twenty minutes to drive to the sports. For Steer, it was routine, changing gears on the corners, slowly going downhill. The war was running towards its end, too, as the industrial might of America poured out more ships, planes, tanks, vehicles, weapons, ammunition, tools, boots and food. In five months Hitler would be dead in his Berlin bunker; in eight months Japan would surrender after the atomic bomb explosions on Hiroshima and Nagasaki. Men would start going home again, to pick up their lives in a changed world. Steer would have returned to his family.

The road ran through tea-gardens south to the tea factory and the lower camp, passing between low, sharply pruned tea bushes under the shade of lines of acacia trees. It was mostly level and fairly straight, with only one curve round the end of a hill, just beyond the bridge over the dry creek, where a big *tuni* tree stood. The surface was a loose khaki-coloured gravel, but it was not made up – more like a cart track. Steer had crossed the bridge and turned the curve; he was motoring down the straight between the tea bushes. Two survivors testified the vehicle was going about 30 m.p.h., but a local who was alive at the time says he was told the jeep was going so fast 'it flew through the air'.

Signaller Joseph Newton and Rifleman Long Sing Song Kuki both remembered, 'the Jeep began to swerve to the left.' The rifleman said it 'appeared to go out of control, and one wheel went off the road'. The signaller said, 'Lieutenant Colonel Steer attempted to bring the jeep out of the swerve and in doing so caused it to swerve to the right. On swerving to the right the jeep appeared to go out of control and I remembered no more till I found myself sitting on the roadside beside Colonel Steer.'

George Steer was lying facing back towards the Himalayas, with his skull shattered. He had died instantly.

They found one of his most precious possessions, his artilleryman's gold wristwatch, away from his body. Given him personally by José Antonio de Aguirre, the President of Euzkadi, in memory of his courageous reporting of the bombing of Guernica and the siege of Bilbao, it was inscribed: *To Steer from the Basque Republic.*

Signaller Joseph Newton was the only one to regain consciousness at the scene. He was hurting down his left side and found himself sitting on the left of the road with the dead body of Colonel Steer lying near by. He heard the sound of a jeep coming up the road from the lower camp and staggered out to stop Major John Cannon, who was driving to the upper camp with a cadet. The Major saw seven unconscious bodies stretched along thirty yards of road and a wrecked jeep by some black boulders among the bushes. George Steer 'had a very severe injury to his head and he had obviously been killed instantaneously'. Major Cannon found no pulse or heartbeat. He sent the cadet on with his jeep to fetch the doctor.

Dr Lam arrived at 2.30 p.m. to find seven unconscious bodies with head injuries. Only Colonel Steer was dead. The injured were taken from the camp hospital by lorry on a three-hour journey to Siliguri, and were loaded on to the train that evening. Captain Halley died before the train left the railway station. Two more men died during the night journey. Four survivors reached hospital.

Why did the vehicle swerve? The transport sergeant later testified that the tyres, brakes and steering of the jeep were in working order, but the nearside rear wheel was badly buckled, with two securing studs torn completely through the wheel, the nearside rear spring bent at right angles in an upward direction about 2½ inches from the front securing bolt, and the rear axle 6 inches out of alignment. Some failure around the back left wheel could have caused the crash.

The man who now lives in the former bungalow's kitchen at Upper Fagu is seventy-seven-year-old Chandra Lal. His blue verandah sports a poster of Kali with a necklace of skulls. 'The Colonel was drunk,' Chandra Lal says others told him at the time. 'He did not let the driver drive.' Nar Gahadur Newar, who showed us the crash-site and where he had seen the bodies, did not mention drink. Nor did the subject emerge at the two subsequent inquiries. However, it was Christmas Day, and Steer had had at least one drink.

The jeep had hit a tree and some boulders on the right side of the road, then turned two complete forward somersaults that threw out the occupants on to their heads. The jeep spun as well as flipped, ending right way up, off the road to the right, among the tea bushes, with the bonnet and radiator bashed and the windscreen superstructure torn away, facing back the way it had come.

Driving an overloaded vehicle, George Steer had managed to kill himself and three of the men under his command. It was a bitter ending. The shock in the IFBU camp on Christmas Day was terrible. When they learned the Colonel Sahib was dead, the soldiers wept.

3

Soldiers and civilians buried George Lowther Steer on Boxing Day 1944, in the tea planters' cemetery a few miles south of Fagu. There were eighty-five graves already on James Finlay's Rungamuttee Tea Estate, a melancholy record of young Scots and their wives who had died of fever, drowning or accidents, far from home. A hundred and fifty people filed under the thatched lychgate into the whitewashed enclosure of the graveyard under palms and bougainvillea.

The padre read from chapter 11 of St John's Gospel: 'And whosoever liveth and believeth in me shall never die.' After the 23rd Psalm they lowered the coffin of reddish wood into the ground, head to the west, feet to the sunrise. 'Man that is born of a woman hath but a short time to live and is full of misery. He cometh up and is cut down, like a flower; he fleeth as it were a shadow, and never continueth in one stay.'

Over the white wall stood the green tea-garden and the ghostly boles of acacias.

'In the midst of life we are in death: of whom may we seek for succour, but of thee, O Lord? . . . O holy and merciful Saviour, thou most worthy Judge eternal, suffer us not, at our last hour, for any pains of death, to fall from thee.' They threw handfuls of Rungamuttee's red dirt into the grave. Three volleys from ten rifles echoed through the shade-trees.

The IFBU officers planned to erect a memorial tombstone with a life-size head of the gold deer that was on the IFBU cap badge modelled out of stone, but the oldest extant photograph shows only a concrete slab and a granite cross whose base is inscribed in black letters: 'In memory of Lt-Col George Lowther Steer, who died at Fagu on December 25, 1944.' Wild elephants later pushed the wall over and casually broke off the cross.

Esmé was told the news by telephone in Dorset and then got the Post Office telegram.

DEEPLY REGRET TO INFORM YOU OF REPORT RECEIVED THAT
LT/COL GL STEER INTELLIGENCE CORPS WAS KILLED ON 23RD
DECEMBER 1944 RESULT OF MOTOR ACCIDENT. THE ARMY COUNCIL
DESIRE TO OFFER YOU THEIR SINCERE SYMPATHY = UNDER
SECRETARY OF STATE FOR WAR

Her way of dealing with the shock was to go away completely on her own for a few days before returning to her life and her young children.

She was a widow now, and four-year-old George and one-year-old Caroline were fatherless. Esmé was unable to get the pension due to a lieutenant colonel's widow because the proceedings of the first court of inquiry into the accident were deemed by the authorities 'inconclusive and incomplete'. Was there culpable negligence? The conclusions of a second court of inquiry, held in April 1945, were that 'Lt-Col Steer be given the benefit of the doubt'; but the papers, sent by air mail, were then lost in a plane crash in India, so Esmé's pension was further delayed till late June 1945. She went back to work for MI5.

The bureaucracy of death followed its depressing grind. Burial returns, battle casualty forms, accident reports, cessation of special employment forms, disposal of property with intrinsic and/or sentimental value, correspondence with the Standing Committee of Adjustment, etc.

A small suitcase of Steer's letters and personal effects (including his watch and Gurkha *kukri*) was sent by air to his widow at the end of January, and Steer's remaining kit was sold by auction in Alipore on 24 February 1945: his shooting stick, his medals from Abyssinia and the oak-leaf clasp he had received for one of his Mentions in Dispatches, a roll of Africa Star ribbon, his butterfly-setting boards and three pairs of silk pyjamas. The sale made 293 rupees for Esmé.

4

The *Yorkshire Post* compared G. L. Steer to T. E. Lawrence and *The Times* called him 'one of the adventurers of this generation ... Combining the research of the scholar with the experience of the fighter and the faith of the idealist, he was as frank and accurate in his writings as he was vivid.' The *Birmingham Post* said he had died a soldier, but would be remembered as a journalist's journalist: 'He was one of the most brilliant, and at the same time one of the most sober and reliable, of that younger corps of special correspondents whom the years before the war produced.' *African World* said: 'Few men have lived a fuller or more exciting life.' *South Africa* magazine described him as: 'an elusive mortal, as restless as he was brilliant ... a man of strong opinions and a liberal mind'.

Kingsley Martin wrote in the *New Statesman* on 6 January 1945:

> I hate to know that George Steer will never again breeze into this office from foreign parts, full of racy stories of his adventures, cynical criticism of the authorities and sincere hatred of cruelty and tyranny. He was one of the best of that adventurous school of journalists who have by and large fought on the side of decency in all the wars since the Japanese began the series in Manchuria. Steer ... wrote brilliantly for *The Times* from Abyssinia and Spain. He was also in Africa for the *Daily Telegraph*; he was in Finland when the war broke out there, and later, as a soldier under Wingate, again in Ethiopia and finally in Burma, where ironically enough, he was killed in a motor smash. I think perhaps the best job of work he ever did was his account of the German destruction of Guernica. In his book *The Tree of Gernika* he finally disposed of the myth (put about by Conservative papers, which have somehow since changed

their minds about the Nazis) that Guernica was destroyed by the people who died there.

Many people sent their condolences, including the Emperor of Ethiopia from his palace in Addis Ababa:

> The news of the death of Colonel George Steer came as a shock to us. We were much aggrieved to lose such a friend. He was very helpful to us in every respect during our sojourn in the Sudan and during the course of the Ethiopian campaign. His abilities combined with the love to see Ethiopia's freedom were remarkable, and we had hoped to see him in our midst once again as soon as hostilities ceased, but alas the irony of fate willed it otherwise. He was but a loyal friend to us and to Ethiopia.

The head of the Basque Delegation in London wrote that Steer's 'unfailing devotion to our cause . . . has earned him the abiding affection and admiration of every Basque. We shall never forget him, nor his inspiring defence of our people in his book *The Tree of Gernika* and shall always cherish his memory in our hearts.' Steer is still remembered and honoured in Guernica. The Basque exile Alberto Elosegi translated *The Tree of Gernika* into *El Arból de Guernica* and clandestinely circulated 10,000 copies of the illustrated edition. It helped keep Steer's name alive among the Basques, and in 2001 a three-day historical conference in Bizkaia was held in his honour.

Esmé received many tributes from her husband's colleagues. Lieutenant Colonel A. D. C. Peterson wanted 'to put on record the great service which he has done for SOE', and said that 'without Steer I do not think there would have been any British forward propaganda units in this area . . . His great personal qualities of courage and sympathy made him an ideal leader not only of British officers, but also of the many Orientals, Korean, Indian and Assamese who served under him.' The head of SOE's India Mission, Colin Mackenzie, remembered '[George's] inexhaustible energy and ever freshly springing enthusiasm . . . It seems doubly hard that the machine he designed and improved over such a long period was just becoming ready for action this year on an enlarged scale when the accident happened. He is literally irreplaceable.' Sidney Saloman wrote from the *Yorkshire Post* that he admired George Steer, 'not only for his abilities but for that joyous character which made life with him so amusing'.

Steer's oldest friends were hardest hit. Tom Cadett said bitterly, 'What a fucking stupid way to die.' Philip Noel-Baker wrote to Sidney Barton:

> I cannot tell you how dismayed and broken I felt when I read the news of his death. It really seemed impossible that it should have happened after he had, for so many years, passed through such appalling risks and come through unscathed. Everyone had come to think of him as a man with a charmed life, to whom nothing could happen . . . that he should go by such a stupid accident seems almost too much to be borne.

Andrew Chapman-Andrews told Esmé: 'George was a great adventurer, a magnificent brain, full of guts and energy and ideas and utterly resilient. Nothing ever got George down for long and everything, every occasion, everybody brought that little onesided twisted smile of humour and real deep human understanding to his face . . . I know I shall never forget him as long as I live.'

At Winchester College, IFBU officers put up a stone engraved *scriptor et miles* in Steer's old chamber, and gave books with a deer's-head bookplate to the library. At Christ Church, Oxford, his name was carved on the bluish slate war memorial on the right-hand wall going into the Cathedral. He has a stained-glass window in St Saviour's Church, East London, South Africa. Steer is also remembered on the Rangoon Memorial in Burma, among 'the names of twenty-seven thousand soldiers united in service to the British Crown who gave their lives in Burma and Assam . . . THEY DIED FOR ALL FREE MEN.'

5

George Steer was only thirty-five when he died. Philip Noel-Baker wrote sadly to Sir Sidney Barton in January 1945, 'There is nothing he could not have done when he got back.' Steer would surely have written more books, as Alan Moorehead and Peter Fleming did, extending their range over Africa, Asia, Australia and the Pacific. He would have been in his element reporting the end of empire and the movements towards independence. Perhaps he would have gone into broadcasting, to join Richard Dimbleby and his friend Tom Cadett at the BBC. Perhaps he would have begun to write fiction. His prose had the style and dash of a novelist's, but the war years pressed him towards fact. *South Africa*

magazine said George Steer promised to be the greatest editor South
Africa had known since Edmund Garrett of the *Cape Times*. Steer
missed South Africa's turbulent modern history. He died two years
before the Eastern Cape's black activist Steve Biko was born, and four
years before the Afrikaaner Nationalist election victory of 1948
enshrined Nazi race-thinking in the Apartheid laws of Republiek van
Suid-Afrika.

But his real loss lay elsewhere. If George Steer had not died pointlessly
in a car crash, after surviving nine years of danger, he would have lived
an ordinary peacetime human life, as a man, a husband and a father. It
was the quiet life that this adventurer longed for at four o'clock on the
wet Addis Ababa afternoon of 5 May 1941, after all the exhausting years
of effort had paid off, and the Emperor Haile Selassie was at last
restored to his throne:

> How vain are the hopes of men, how fragile the buildings of the
> great, how much better it is to live peaceably, and humbly, and read
> a book and go for a walk with one's wife and drink with the friends
> of one's youth, and let sleeping dogs lie.

Epilogue

The green Ambassador car parks outside the whitewashed enclosure. A white man in his sixties, George Barton Steer, dapper in corduroy and tweed, climbs up the steps over the wall and down into the lychgate of the cemetery on the western side of Rungamuttee Tea Estate.

It feels the right place for a child of the British Empire like G. L. Steer to rest. The woodsmoke and voices of the workers' village are not far away. As the seasons change here, the wind rattles in the palm tree, the rain pounds down, the sun raises a mist from the earth and then brightens the poinsettia and crotons. At night, leopards pass by in the moonlight. A familiar corner of a foreign field.

In the morning light, the tranquil fields of tea plants level away under the pale verticals of the shade-trees. The thousands of brightly dressed women and men who prune the bushes and pluck the leaves earn a dollar a day, but they have schools and a hospital. The paternalism of an estate like this, for good or bad, owes much to older British traditions.

This book closed in the Indian tea-garden at 9 a.m. on 1 February 2002, as I watched George Steer's son, Haile Selassie's godson, kneeling at the grave of the father he never knew.

Acknowledgements and Sources

I want to thank all my friends in the BBC World Service, especially the Arts Unit, because a Meridian Feature, 'Gernika/Guernica', made for the 60th anniversary, started this hare in 1997. I particularly want to pay tribute to the remarkable George Steer *fils* who got in touch after that radio programme and then steadily helped for years with memories, papers and contacts, as well as with hospitality in Africa and travels in India, so making possible *Telegram from Guernica*, which is quite rightly (and quite against his wishes) dedicated to him. I would also like to thank the trustees of the BBC Alexander Onassis Trust and their secretary Maureen Bebb, for a bursary that enabled me to travel to Ethiopia and South Africa; the Society of Authors for a grant; and the anonymous benefactor who gave me some money to buy time.

Thank you to Abebooks, Nicky Barranger, Tom Buchanan, Angus Cargill, Caroline Charlesworth, Graham Coster, Michael Demetriadi, Elsa Dickson, Douglas Dodds-Parker, Moris and Nina Farhi, Roger Fenby, Professor M. R. D. Foot, Belinda Fraser, the late Richard Fry, Colin Grant, Jenny Hargreaves, Jackie Henley, Anthea Holme, Alan Judd, Douglas Kerr, Julian Loose, Eric and Shen Litznaisky, Motor Books, Alessandro Muzi Falconi, Bob O'Hara, Anna Pallai, Simon Pitts, Mike Popham, Nick Robinson, Dan Shepherd, Isabella Steer, Will Sulkin, Kate Ward, David Woodhouse. At my old Oxford college, Christ Church, thanks to Doreen Belcher, the Manciple, Richard Hamer, the Librarian, and Judith Curthoys, the Archivist. Dr Richard Thompson, writing a study of Steer's Christ Church contemporary Peter Burra, was most generous with his time, knowledge and enthusiasm, putting me in touch amongst others with Erica Schumacher, née Wright, and Iverach McDonald, formerly of *The Times*, to whom I am also grateful. In the outstanding archive of *The Times*, Nick Mays was my ever helpful

Virgil; thank you too to the patient staff of the Newspaper Library at Colindale and the Imperial War Museum.

In and around Ethiopia many thanks to W. F. Deedes, Patrick Gilkes, Sally Higgin, the Institute of Ethiopian Studies, V. Karibian, Julian Kay, Deutron Kebebew, Paulo Kibet Koros, Harold Marcus, Alice Martin, General Yassu Mengasha, Ellene Mocria, Paula di Montezemolo, Richard and Rita Pankhurst, my old friend John Ryle, Charles and Sarah Sherlock, David Stead, the late Avedis Terzian, Sir Wilfred Thesiger, Professor Edward Ullendorff, Teferi Wossen, the late Elizabeth Workneh; at the British Embassy in Addis Ababa, H. M. Ambassador Gordon Wetherell, First Secretary Frances Guy, British Military Liaison Officer Lt Col Richard Illingworth, and Assistant Cultural Attaché (British Council) Simon Ingram-Hill.

In India, thank you to Cox's and King's (New Delhi), the Nawab and Begum of Pataudi, Mr H. Khusrokhan, Managing Director of Tata Tea Limited, and Vice-President S. Dogra, and all the staff at Rungamuttee Estate, especially General Manager Mr Anil Malhotra, Prasanta and Srabana Bhattarcharyya, Suresh Roy, A. K. Sinha, Dilip Kumar Dutta, also Father Rocky d'Souza, Dan Man Lama, Manbir Dorjee, Nar Bahadur Newar, N. P. Rai, and the driver of our green Ambassador car, Babun Das.

In Spain, I am grateful to Ricardo Abaunza Martinez, Joseba Aizpurua, Father Felix Aretzaga, Sam Bull, María Jesús Cava Mesa, Lynne Cooper Celaya, Alberto Elosegi, Juan Gutierrez, José Ignacio Ibaibarriaga, Jon Irazabal, Iratxe Momoitio Astorkia, John and Alison Waite, Vincent West, Joseba Zulaika, and all the participants at the *Homenaje a George Steer* conference in Gernika in December 2001.

In South Africa, which hardly figures in the finished book but did in the first drafts, thanks are due to Akwe Amosu and David Coetzee, Kathy Drake of the National Library of South Africa in Cape Town, Henrietta Dax of Clark's Bookshop, Khama Nyama, Renata Shilubana of the Library of Parliament, and from the journalistic world Ted Hart, Maxwell Lee, Pam Small, Andrea Weiss and Chris Whitfield; in the farming country of the Eastern Cape near Komga, Gloria and Douglas Bowles, Cherry and Kevin Norton, Charles de Haes, and Nancy Euvrard; in Grahamstown, Guy and Jeanne Berger, Lorraine Mullins, and Sandy Rowoldt at the Cory Library of Rhodes University; in East London, Helen Boston-Smith, Glenn Hartwig and staff at the Public Library, Val Lord and Arthur Hulbert, Karl Krull, Cedric Reddy,

Albert Siqangwe, Mary Stidworthy, June Tapson, Dorothea Vaughan, Gill Vernon and staff at the East London Museum; at the *Daily Dispatch*, Denise Burger, Matt Ramsden, Len Martin, editor Gavin Stewart, and Glyn Williams. The late Donald Woods entertainingly described to me the history of the newspaper where he began his career and which he notably edited, and the important role of its proprietor Sir Charles Crewe in formulating its liberal 'line'. (*The Life of Sir Charles Crewe* is G. L. Steer's other missing manuscript.)

Finally, big thanks to my family. My brothers and sisters, Charles, John, Sarah and Trina gave me a great party to start the process. My beloved centenarian great-aunt Gwynneth Stallard hosted it, read early drafts of this book and always encouraged me. My beautiful, lively daughter Rosa Rankin-Gee endured the invasion of her room for many months so I could usurp the computer and clutter her desk and bed with arcane books and papers. My darling wife, the novelist Maggie Gee, has been behind me all the way, and not just on the household front, cooking and cleaning and washing and remembering and coping and soothing. She also read every line many times; she believed, encouraged, and edited.

The author and publishers are grateful to the following for freedom to quote work. While every effort has been made to trace copyright holders, in some cases this has not been successful and should anyone get in touch about permissions we will be happy to amend further editions. G. L. Steer's articles © *The Spectator*. Material from *The Daily Telegraph* © Telegraph Group Ltd. Steer's articles for *The Times* and other documents in the *Times* archive © (Copyright) *Times* Newspapers Limited, 1935, 1936, 1937, 1939, 1945. The Evelyn Waugh Trust and the Estate of Laura Waugh for permission to quote from Evelyn Waugh's writings. Dr Alexander Matthews for permission to quote from Martha Gellhorn. Christopher Sinclair-Stevenson for permission to quote from Peter Kemp. Lois Godfrey for permission to quote from Naomi Mitchison.

SOURCES

ONE: **In Abyssinia**

The principal source for Steer's Ethiopian experience is his own book *Caesar in Abyssinia* (Hodder & Stoughton, 1936) supplemented by the Deakin papers and Steer's file from the *Times* archive. Among many books on the Italo-Abyssinian war, I found Anthony Mockler's *Haile Selassie's War* (Grafton Books, 1987) invaluable. **2.** In *Africa: A Biography of the Continent* (Hamish Hamilton, 1997) John Reader points out that the Italians accidentally introduced rinderpest (cattle plague) via Massana, Eritrea, in 1889. In eight years this calamity devastated the cattle kingdoms of the entire continent and returned many pastoral ecologies to tsetse-fly-ridden bush. The story of Harrington's phonograph is in Paul Tritton's *The Lost Voice of Queen Victoria: The Search for the First Royal Recording* (Academy Books, 1991), supplemented by Dr Abraham Demoz's article on Menelik's reply in *BSOAS*, xxxii, 2, 1969. The Arthur Rimbaud references are from Graham Robb's excellent biography published by Picador in 2000. Flying details come from Harold Marcus's *Haile Sellassie I, The Formative Years 1892–1936* (Red Sea Press, 1996). The severed head story is told in the obituary of Sir Edwin Andrew Chapman-Andrews in the Royal Asia Society Journal. The Walwal Incident features in Arnold Toynbee's *Survey of International Affairs, 1935*, Vol II. The Vansittart quote is from *The Abyssinian Crisis* (1974) by Frank Hardie. **3.** Claud Cockburn's revised autobiography *I, Claud* was published by Penguin in 1967. There is a useful summary of British 'air control' in chapter 2 of *Human Rights and the End of Empire* by A. W. Brian Simpson (Oxford University Press, 2001). For more on the Spanish use of gas in North Africa, see *Deadly Embrace: Morocco and the Road to the Spanish Civil War* by Sebastian Balfour (Oxford, 2002). **5.** Sir Sidney Barton features in *The China Consuls* by P. D. Coates (Oxford, 1988). The former Marion Barton wrote a private memoir for her children which I have consulted, along with the history of the Barton family compiled by Esmé Barton's second husband, Kenyon Jones. (Sir Sidney was a cousin of Erskine Childers, the Irish nationalist court-martialled and shot by the British in 1922). Faber and Faber published *John Melly of Ethiopia*, edited by Kathleen Nelson and Alan Sullivan, in 1937. **6.** Steer's Ethiopian photographs are in the *Times* photographic archive in Wapping, London. **7.** Colonel Hubert Julian told the story of his life, *Black Eagle*, to John Bulloch in 1964. See also *African –American Reactions to War in Ethiopia 1935–41* by Joseph E . Harris (Louisiana State University Press, 1994) and the 1999 paper *Dislocating Diaspora: Caribbean Blacks and the Italo-Ethiopian War, 1935–1941* by Kevin A. Yelvington of the University of South Florida. **11.** The Emilio de Bono statistics are from his book *Anno XIIII, the Conquest of an Empire* (1937). George G. Harrap published Knud Holmboe's *Desert Encounter, An Adventurous Journey Through Italian Africa* in 1936.

TWO: **Death from the Air**

1. Angelo del Boca's *I gas di Mussolini: Il fascismo e la guerra d'Etiopia* (Riuniti, 1996), Giorgio Rochat's *The impact of gas in the Ethiopian War, 1935–6*, and the Documents on Italian War Crimes presented to the United Nations in 1948 (*La Civilisation de l'Italie Fasciste en Ethiopie*) tell the main story of the use of mustard gas in Ethiopia, as well as what happened at Yekatit 12 in the next chapter. See also Alberto Sbacchi, *Legacy of Bitterness: Ethiopia and Fascist Italy, 1935–1941* (Red Sea Press, 1997) for a clear overview. **2.** The election poster is an illustration in *British Public Opinion and the Abyssinian War 1935–6* by Daniel Waley. **3.** An interesting critique by Rainer Baudendistel of the failure of the ICRC to deal with chemical warfare is to be found in the *International Review of the Red Cross* no 322, pages 81–104, 31 March 1998. Gerald Burgoyne's account of the war and his widow's quest to discover what happened to him was published in three parts in the *Ethiopia Observer*, Vol XI, No 4. **5.** *An Ethiopian Diary: A Record of the British Ambulance Service in Ethiopia* by J. W. S. Macfie was published by Hodder and Stoughton and the University Press of Liverpool in 1936. **10.** L. J. Bunner wrote about John Melly in a letter to G. L. Steer's parents, expressing gratitude that Steer had helped get him out of Italian custody. John H. Spencer adds in *Ethiopia at Bay: A Personal Account of the Haile Sellassie Years* (Reference Publications, 1984) that the alarm call from the American Legation went via the Philippines and so circled the globe in four hours in order to travel seven miles. **14.** The Emperor's speech at Geneva is from *My Life and Ethiopia's Progress, 1892–1937: The Autobiography of Emperor Haile Sellassie I, vol 1*, translated and annotated by Edward Ullendorff (Research Associates, 1997). There is a good photo of Lorenzo Taezaz and Haile Selassie at Geneva, plate 12 in Bahru Zewde's *Pioneers of Change in Ethiopia* (James Currey/Ohio University Press/Addis Ababa University, 2002).

THREE and FOUR: **Torn Apart** and **Men at War**

1. The principal source for Steer in Spain is his book *The Tree of Gernika*, and papers in the *Times* archive. Luís Bolín's autobiography, *Spain: The Vital Years* was published in English by Cassell (with an introduction by Sir Arthur Bryant) in 1967. Paul Preston's *Franco* (Harper Collins, 1993) lays out the Nazi connection. Tom Buchanan's *Britain and the Spanish Civil War* (Cambridge, 1997) fills in the domestic scene. **3.** The Countess of Vallellano quote is from Marcel Junod's *Warriors Without Arms* (Jonathan Cape, 1951) translated from *Le Troisième Combattant*. The Miguel de Unamuno intervention at Salamanca is drawn from Paul Preston's *¡Comrades! Portraits from the Spanish Civil War* (Harper Collins, 1999) and Mark Kurlansky's *A Basque History of the World* (Jonathan Cape, 1999). **4.** William Stirling, who also reported Unamuno's outburst, has a file in the *Times* archive. Peter Kemp's first book was *Mine Were of Trouble*. **5.** The Jan Morris quote is from *Spain* (Penguin, 1982). **6.** Chapter 3 of Stanley G. Payne's *Basque Nationalism* (Nevada, 1975) is about Sabino de Arana y Goiri. **7.** The lost olive oil is from Dorothy Legarreta, *The Guernica*

Generation: Basque Refugee Children of the Spanish Civil War (Nevada, 1984).
4/4. I obtained the Lauaxeta video from the Basque Studies department at the
University of Nevada at Reno.

FIVE: **Gernika**
1. Lord Vansittart's *Black Record: Germans Past and Present,* broadcast on the
BBC and published by Hamish Hamilton in 1941, provided the *aperçus* of
Tacitus and Heine. Wavell's view was expressed in *The Good Soldier* (1948).
Roger James Bender's *Legion Condor: Uniforms, Organization and History* (San
Jose, CA 1992) is most informative. **2.** Frederick Muller published Noel Monks's
autobiography, *Eyewitness,* in 1955. On page 126 of *The Tree of Gernika,* the text
reads 'Christopher Corman and I thought . . .' This is odd, because Corman's
name was Mathieu and Holme's name was Christopher. But a missing comma,
silently reinstated between Christopher and Corman, restores three journalists
to the bomb-crater where once there were one and two halves. **3.** Virginia
Cowles described her adventures in Spain in *Looking for Trouble* (Hamish
Hamilton, 1941). When Steer read her un-bylined account in the *Sunday Times,*
he assumed this correspondent was a man. **4.** H. Christopher Holme's poem is
from the 1992 posthumous collection *Portrait* that his widow Anthea sent me.
5. Adolf Galland's account of the German fighter force in World War II was
published in English in 1955 as *The First and the Last* (with an introduction by
Douglas Bader). **6.** Lewis Mumford's thoughts on bombing are in *Programme
for Survival* (Abbey Books, 1946). For a brilliantly unconventional cultural history of bombing see *Higher than Heaven: Japan, War & Everything* by Tony
Barrell and Rick Tanaka (PGI, 1995). **7.** R. C. Stevenson's letter to Sir Henry
Chilton was published in Appendix Eight of Hugh Thomas's *The Spanish Civil
War* (1977). Basil Liddell Hart's Military Archive is kept at King's College,
London, across the Strand from Bush House. **8.** The copy of Steer's telegram to
Philip Noel-Baker, and Noel-Baker's letter to Pierre Cot, are in the archive of
the Peace Museum in Gernika-Lumo, Spain. The photo of Steer at Radio
Bilbaina is in the *Times* archive and is also reproduced on page 114 of *Gernika y
la guerra civil: Symposium 60 aniversario del bombardeo de Gernika* (1997).
Pembroke Stephens's report to Sir Henry Chilton is in the PRO at Kew
(FO371/21290 W8572). Following his note of this on page 162 of his book *La
perfidia de Albión: el Gobierno británico y la guerra civil española* (Siglo
Veintiuno, 1996), Enrique Moradiellos points out that the minutes of the discussion of Guernica held in the British Cabinet on 26 May 1937 (CAB 23/88) are
still not available to the public. The *Schwerpunkt* or 'thrust-point' attack that
Steer experienced that day at Gastelumendi is cited as a text-book example in
chapter 2, 'The Spanish Laboratory', of F. O. Miksche's *Blitzkrieg* (Faber, 1941)
12. Tom Cadett's memorial of Steer was in a letter to the *New Statesman* in
January 1945, in the week following Kingsley Martin's appreciation, cited on
page 248. **14.** For a cultural history of the painting see Russell Martin's *Picasso's
War: The Destruction of Guernica, and The Masterpiece That Changed The*

World (Dutton, 2002). **16.** Geoffrey Dawson's letter features in Appendix B, 'Suppression of News' in *The History of* The Times, *1929–1966.*

SIX: **Axis in Africa**
The principal sources for this chapter are Steer's books *Judgment on German Africa* (1939) and *A Date in the Desert* (1939), with the Monnier reappearance drawn from *Sealed and Delivered* (1942). **1.** The stealing of the Nazi party membership cards by a South African undercover agent is in *For Volk and Führer* by Hans Strydom (Jonathan Ball, 1984). **2.** Steer gave Basil Liddell Hart the name of Troquard when they met and talked in London on 12 January 1939. The former Conservative MP Douglas Dodds-Parker was at Winchester with young George Steer and remembers him 'looking witty as he walked about'. Dodds-Parker's remarkable war-time memoir of SOE is called *Setting Europe Ablaze* (Springwood Books, 1984). 'Recent Impressions of Italian East Africa', with circulation list, is in the library of the British Ambassador's residence, Addis Ababa.

SEVEN: **Winter War**
1. The Martha Gellhorn quote is from *The Face of War* (Hart Davis, 1959). She left a few days later, but her compatriot Virginia Cowles was in Finland much longer and gives a vivid impression of the war in *Looking For Trouble*. The cap-badge detail comes from *The Volunteers: The Full Story of the British Volunteers in Finland 1939–41* by Justin Brooke (1990). **2.** I am grateful to the Australian-born journalist and writer James Aldridge (who covered the Finnish War and wrote memorable Isaac Babel-like short stories about it) for pointing out that bottles of petrol with a burning rag in the neck had been thrown in the Spanish Civil War (and probably much earlier). The *Oxford English Dictionary* confirms that the first usage of 'Molotov Cocktail' was from Finland in January 1940. **3.** Penguin published Sir Walter Citrine's *My Finnish Diary* in 1940. **4.** An excellent book on the Norwegian campaign is *Norway, 1940* by François Kersaudy (Collins, 1990). *Seven Assignments* (Jonathan Cape, 1948) by Dudley Clarke, who went on to found the Commandos, gives a privileged insight into the chaos of the campaign. The ordinary soldier's soccer metaphor about being 'in the final now' after Dunkirk was told me by my father, but the form of words follows those of the club commissionaire quoted in chapter 10 of the abridged edition of Winston Churchill's *The Second World War* (Cassell, 1959). I was moved by reading John Lukacs's *Five Days in London, May 23–28 1940* (Yale, 1999) exactly sixty years after the events described.

EIGHT: **Khaki**
The principal source for this and for Chapter Nine is Steer's *Sealed and Delivered: A Book on the Abyssinian Campaign* (Hodder & Stoughton, 1942). **1.** Ernie Pyle's dispatch from London is in *Ernie's War: The Best of Ernie Pyle's WW2 Dispatches*, edited by David Nichols (Touchstone, 1987). **2.** The Wavell family details are from the prefatory note to *Two Unorthodox Soldiers*, his essays

on T. E. Lawrence and Orde Wingate in *The Good Soldier* (Macmillan, 1948).
3. Chapter 13 of *Front Line Diplomat* (Hutchinson, 1959), the memoirs of Sir
Geoffrey 'Tommy' Thompson, describes his official Foreign Office role is getting
Haile Selassie out of England. The Sammy Marks 'mantle' story is told in Sir
Stewart Symes's *Tour of Duty* (Collins, 1946). Alexander Clifford's account of
the flying Imperial visit to Cairo, in *Three Against Rommel* (Harrap, 1943), is also
cited in Artemis Cooper's *Cairo in the War* (Hamish Hamilton, 1989). **4.** Alan
Moorehead (Clifford's best friend) originally wrote three volumes on the North
African Campaign 1940–43 (*Mediterranean Front, A Year of Battle, The End in
Africa*) and the Cassell paperback edition, published in 2000, combines them
(with an index) as *Alan Moorehead's African Trilogy*. Robert Byron has a walk-
on part in *The Secret History of PWE: the Political Warfare Executive 1939–45* by
David Garnett, with introduction and notes by Andrew Roberts (St Ermin's
Press, 2002). **6.** William Slim wrote about Gallabat in *Unofficial History* (Cassell,
1959). One of his maps shows the hill, Jebel Dafeis, where Steer's first Forward
Propaganda Unit ran away.

NINE: **Into Ethiopia**
1. *Wavell: Scholar and Soldier* (Collins, 1964) by John Connell, and Peter Coats's
autobiography *Of Generals and Gardens* (Weidenfeld and Nicholson, 1976) are
the source for the quotes about the Emperor. **2.** The Australian soldiers' letter is
in Leonard Mosley's *Gideon Goes To War* (Arthur Barker, 1955). *The Wind in the
Morning* by Hugh Boustead, *Never a Dull Moment* by John Millard, *Bare Feet
and Bandoliers* by David Shirreff, *The Life of My Choice* by Wilfred Thesiger all
supplement W. E. D. Allen's *Guerrilla War in Abyssinia* in telling the story of a
heroic and largely forgotten campaign. **4.** *Informing The People* (HMSO, 1996)
by Anthony James is the best guide to the WW2 HMSO paperbacks. It mentions
the three books on Indian soldiers in World War Two, which recount the sacri-
fice and bravery of five million Empire and Commonwealth troops in defeating
the Axis: *The Tiger Strikes* (1940–1, in Somaliland, Sudan, Egypt, Libya, Ethiopia,
Eritrea, Syria), *The Tiger Kills* (1941–3, across North Africa and the Western
Desert) and *The Tiger Triumphs* (1943–5, through Italy). **5.** Richard Dimbleby's
African travels with Donovan, his BBC engineer, feature in *The Frontiers Are
Green* (Hodder & Stoughton, 1943). Details of the Type C recorder come from
BBC Engineering 1922–72 by Edward Pawley. **6.** Maurice Lush's memoirs *A Life
of Service* were published by his family in 1992. **7.** Re Carel Birkby's flag story,
George Orwell's diary notes that he was not happy to see a newsreel on 31 May
1941 showing the British flag being hauled up before the Ethiopian one in Addis
Ababa. **8.** Yilma Diressa became an important member of the regime after the
war: see Christopher Clapham's *Haile Selassie's Government* (Longman's, 1969).
He was murdered in the Dergue in November 1974. I found Maurice Lush's
report, Appendix E to the 1941 long dispatch from the Chief Political Officer,
Philip Mitchell, to Commander-in-Chief, Middle East, Claude Auchinleck, in
the British Ambassador's library in Addis Ababa. **9.** Paula di Montezemolo's

anecdote, and comments from the late Elizabeth Workneh and the late Avedis Terzian, were personal communications.

TEN: **Special Operations**
1. I largely follow Christopher Sykes's account of Wingate's suicide attempt. Sykes, who was in SOE and was a friend of Robert Byron and Evelyn Waugh, also wrote two books, *High-Minded Murder* (Home and Van Thal, 1944) and *A Song of a Shirt* (Derek Verschoyle, 1953) which depict war-time Cairo as vicious with intrigue. **2.** The phrase 'gabardine swine' is from Dimbleby's *The Frontiers Are Green*. George Steer's Personal File from the Special Operations Executive is now at the Public Record Office, Kew. I am grateful to the SOE Adviser to the Foreign Office, Duncan Stuart, CMG, for letting me have a copy before release. Dudley Clarke is an important figure in *Strategic Deception in the Second World War* by Sir Michael Howard (Pimlico, 1992), originally published as Volume 5 of the *Official History of British Intelligence in the Second World War*. Jasper Maskelyne wrote *Magic: Top Secret* about his colourful wartime exploits. The Sonic Deception details come from the 'A' Force war-diary at Kew. The M. R. D Foot story was a personal communication. Foot was still a Scholar at Winchester in the summer of 1936 when he heard George Steer give a talk suggesting that the higher journalism should not be despised by the classically educated. **3.** Field Marshal Lord Alanbrooke's uncensored *War Diaries, 1939–1945*, edited by Alex Danchev and Daniel Todman, were published by Weidenfeld and Nicolson in 2001. The excellent HMSO Short Military History *Five Ventures* by Christopher Buckley (the war correspondent who was killed in Korea in 1950) and *Combined Operations, 1940–42* (HMSO, 1943) both cover Operation Ironclad, the invasion of Madagascar. G. L. Steer's only surviving diary from 1943 is in the possession of his son. **6.** An excellent novel on the collapse of British Burma is *The Glass Palace* by Amitav Ghosh (Harper Collins, 2000). On Japanese military training and their indifference to prisoners see Lawrence Rees *Horror in the East* (BBC, 2001) and Gavan Daws's superb history *Prisoners of the Japanese: POWs of World War II in the Pacific* (Morrow, 1994).

ELEVEN: **Forgotten Army**
The main source is Steer's 1943 diary. **1.** On the Indian National Army see *Story of the I. N. A.* by S. A. Ayer (National Book Trust, India, 1997) and for another view see Philip Mason *A Matter of Honour: An Account of the Indian Army, Its Officers and Men* (Jonathan Cape, 1974). **4.** The Brigadier Cavendish story is told in Louis Allen's exemplary history *Burma: The Longest War, 1941–45* (J. M. Dent, 1986). **5.** I was kindly sent a copy of Lieutenant Colonel Humphrey Williams's After Action Report and other useful information on the Royal Welch Fusiliers in Arakan by his former Intelligence Officer there, Lieutenant Colonel Michael Demetriadi, OBE, TD. **6.** Captain Roland Bacon's daughter, Elsa Dickson, of Vancouver, British Columbia, generously shared with me her quest for information about her father's war-service and death with the IFBU, in response to

my appeal in the Burma Star Association magazine DEKHO. 7. On basic principles of propaganda, what Wickham Steed in *The Fifth Arm* (1940) called 'the weapon of the mind for the battle of wits', see *SOE Syllabus: Lessons in Ungentlemanly Warfare, World War II* (Public Record Office, 2001).

TWELVE: **Home**
The main sources for this chapter are Steer's SOE personal file, and the letters and newspaper clippings preserved by Steer's widow, now held by their son. We visited the Fagu area in late January 2001 and spoke to several people who were alive at Christmas 1944 and were still living locally. Our interpreter was the Catholic priest Father Rocky d'Souza of St Francis of Assisi Church, Lower Fagu, who speaks seven languages. One witness, Nar Prasad Rai, 74, had actually been at Steer's funeral.

Index

'GS' indicates George Lowther Steer.

'A' Force (Deception, Middle East) 215–16
Aandalsnes, Norway 170
Abbi Addi, Ethiopia 42
ABC (Madrid monarchist daily) 78
Abyssinian Association 75, 76, 149
Acqua Col, Keren 194
Adams, Vyvyan MP 75
Addis Ababa, Ethiopia 5, 17, 22, 70, 159
    described 7, 14–15, 33, 99–103
    GS arrives in 14, 15
    GS meets Barton 15
    fall of 58, 208
    Italian propaganda 58–9
    undefended 60
    looting 64–5, 82
    fires spread in 68, 69
    Italians enter 72
    GS expelled by Italians 14, 74
    Fascist HQ 98
    liberated 201
    Italians after liberation 202, 209
    Lush installed in 203
    changes by the Italians 203–4
    problems after the liberation 205–6
    Emperor returns 207–12, 251
Aden, Yemen 9, 10, 23, 150
Adi Quala, Ethiopia 45
Adigrat, Ethiopia 34
Admiral Graf Spee (pocket battleship) 105,
    166–7
Ado, Ethiopia 11
Adowa, Tigre 9, 13, 15, 34
aerial bombing xii, 1–5, 10, 11 13, 17, 34, 36, 37, 41,
    42, 45, 46, 48–55, 59, 77, 79, 81, 82, 93, 96, 101,
    108–24, 126–34, 141–4, 149, 150, 155, 162,
    164–5, 167–70, 172, 183, 184–5, 191–2, 197,
    216–17, 222, 225, 233, 244, 248–9

Afewerk, Gerazmatch 25–9, 36–7, 41, 102
Afghanistan, British use of mustard gas in 13
African Divisions, 11th and 12th 201
African World 248
Afrika Korps 216
Afrikaaner Nationalists 162, 251
Agirre, Jon Irazabal: *1937 martxoak 31 Durango
    31 de marzo 1937* 109
Aguirre y Lekube, José Antonio de 88, 89, 90,
    92–3, 129, 132, 135, 138, 245
Air Ministry, UK 193
Akaki, Ethiopia 64
Akaki aerodrome, Ethiopia 43, 102
Akyab, Bay of Bengal 222, 225, 230
Alba and Berwick, Duke of 142
Alcázar fort, Toledo 84
Alexander I, Tsar of Russia 168
Alexandria, Egypt 176
Algeria 157, 176
All India Radio 234
Allahabad, India 222
Allen, Mr (British Vice-Consul in Helsinki) 165
Allen, William: *Guerrilla War in Abyssinia* 191
Almirante Cervera (cruiser) 105
Alomata, Ethiopia 55
Amba Aradam, Ethiopia 49, 50, 51
Ambo, Ethiopia 22
American Legation, Addis Ababa 102
Amery, Leo 217
AMGOT (Acting Military Government of
    Occupied Territory) 207
Amhara upland, Ethiopia 43
Amharic language xiii, 12, 20, 43, 58, 77, 175, 179,
    188, 211
Anale, Ethiopia 26, 37
Anarchists 81, 135
Angelopoulos, Akeos 14, 20
Anglo-Ethiopian Boundary Commission 11, 22,
    27

Anti-Gas Treaty (1925) 13
anti-Semitism 154–5
Anzac Day 116
Aosta, Duke of 150, 177, 178, 202, 207, 208
appeasement 11–12, 46, 54, 58, 76, 105–6, 125, 130,
      146–7, 152, 177
Arada Post Office, Addis Ababa 68
Aragai, Balambaras Abeba 64, 99, 149, 208, 209
Aragai, Daniel 209
Arakan, Arakanese 223, 224, 230, 232–3
Arana y Goiri, Sabino de 89, 90
Arbacegui-Gerrikaiz, Basque country 116, 117,
      127, 144
Arbex (press attaché) 119, 132
Armacheho, Ethiopia 162
Army of the Centre (Ethiopia) 50
Army Officers' Emergency Reserve (Egypt) 175
Arnold, Lieutenant Colonel of MI3 97
Arronategui, Father Eusebio 128
Arxanda Casino, Bilbao 135
Arxandasarri, Bilbao 135
Asfa-Wossen, Prince 57, 161
Asmara, Eritrea 194
Assab, Eritrea 9
Assam, India 221, 250
Assam Regiment 238
Association de la Presse Etrangère, L' 22
Astra gun factory, in Guernica 117, 119, 126
Asturians 130, 133, 134, 143
Asturias, Spain 93
Atbara River 162, 186
Athill, Lieutenant Colonel Lawrence 17, 161, 174
Atletico Bilbao 92
Attlee, Clement 106
Auchinleck, Claude 213
Auden, W. H. 161–2, 221
Auden, W. H. and Isherwood, Christopher:
      Journey to a War 221
Augustine Convent, Bermeo road, Guernica 120
Aussa, Ethiopia 163
Australia 162, 217
Austria 9, 148
Awash river valley 14
Axis 149, 155, 174, 176, 218
      in Africa (map) xii, 155
Azaña, Manuel 88

Babitcheff, Mischa 63
Bacon, Captain Roland 238
Badajoz, Spain 80, 86
Badoglio, General Pietro 35–6, 45, 100
Bailey, Sir Abe 176–7
Bakea Hotel, Biriatou 80
Baker, Sir Herbert 220

Balbo, Marshal Italo 158
Baldwin, Oliver (Viscount Corvedale) 197, 198
Baldwin, Stanley, Earl 46, 53, 105, 122, 130, 197
Balfour, Patrick 34, 35, 153
      Lords of the Equator: An African Journey 153,
      154
Baluchis 194
Banderachin newsletter 184, 195, 207
Bangladesh 225, 227
Bank of Abyssinia/Ethiopia 33, 63
Baratieri, General 9, 35, 100
Barber, Will 14
Barker, A. E. 103
Barker, Colonel A. J.: Eritrea 1941 196
Barker, 'Pongo' 181
'Barnack', East London, South Africa 162
Barrington-Ward, Robin 146
Barton, Lady 55, 70, 71, 103
Barton, Sir Sidney 66, 67, 69, 73, 172, 208, 214,
      250
      GS meets 15
      diplomatic career 15
      personality 15
      and Marion's marriage 16
      and European court etiquette 18
      and Haile Selassie 60, 173
      cheered by British community 72
      at Margarita's funeral 103
Basque country
      GS reports from 5
      Margarita and 39
      history of 86–7
      nationalism 87, 88, 89, 94, 117
      war aims 88
      flag 88–9
      government 89–90, 95, 129, 135, 138
      described 91
      GS leaves 96
      GS returns 103
      Mola's campaign 104, 108, 110, 111, 112, 123
      GS runs risks 113
      Basques evacuated 124–5
      Cabinet decision over Bilbao 132
      behaviour of Basques 135–6
Basque Delegation, London 249
Basque Department of Defence 110
Basque Foreign Affairs and Propaganda
      Department 128
Basque Nationalist Centre 90
Basra's store, Addis Ababa 68
Bates, H. E. 193
Battle of Britain 172
Baw, U 232
Bayenna (interpreter) 64, 66, 74

Bayonne, France 96
Bayreuth, Bavaria 79
BBC 160, 175, 173, 197, 222, 234, 250
Beagle, HMS 105
Bedouin 36
Begoña hill, Bilbao 109
Belahu 72–3
Belaya, Ethiopia 191
Beldarrain (of Marteartu battalion) 110, 111, 135
Belgian Legation, Addis Ababa 71
Belgian Military Mission 57
Belgium 19, 170
Belgrade 123
Bell, Sir Hesketh 53
Bellini, Captain 158
Bengal, India 224
Benghazi, Libya 36
Bentinck, Major Arthur 17, 55, 57, 174
Berbera, British Somaliland 9, 181
Berbers 157
Beresford-Pierse, Major General 196
Berlin 244
Berlin Radio 126
Bernstein, Henry Lawrence ('Colonel Pedro Lopez') 48n
Berriz, Basque country 112, 135
Besteiro, Julian 88
Bhutan 237, 243
Biarritz, France 103, 138
Biko, Steve 12, 251
Bilbao
  Basque refugees in 1, 105, 123
  GS arrives in (1937) 88, 90–91
    described 91–2
    incidents after an air raid 93–6
    blockade 105–7, 108
    bomber shot down in air raid 109–10
    the day of the Guernica raid 115–16
    fall of 132–7, 147, 160, 245
    evacuation 132, 133
    Junta de Defensa 133, 135
Bilbao Radio 128
Birkby, Carel 202–3, 210
  It's a Long Way to Addis 205, 210n
Birmingham Post 248
Birru, Ayenna 63
Bishop, Billy, VC 21
Black Arrows division (Italian) 139
Black Consciousness 12
Black Man journal 61
Blackshirts 75, 98–9, 102, 182, 197, 202
blitzkrieg 4, 170
Blomberg, Werner von 79
Blood and Fire paper 111

Blue Nile 174, 179
Blum, Léon 70
Bobie (tramp ship) 138, 139, 140
Bobrikoff, Governor-General 168
Bolibar, Basque country 116
Bolín, Luís 78–9, 84, 86, 104, 105, 126, 142–3
  Spain: The Vital Years 142, 143, 199
bombing *see* aerial bombing
Bon Voisinage Accord 161
Bono, Emilio de 35
Borah, Senator William 4
Bourguiba, Habib 157
Bowra, Maurice 49
Boxer Rebellion (1900) 15
Brauchitsch, Colonel General Walter von 158
Bremen, Germany 170
Bristol Blenheim bomber 167, 182, 230
Britain
  reaction to Guernica 3–4
  arms embargo on Ethiopia 19
  Hoare-Laval pact 35, 46
  General Election (1935) 46
  ruling class 125
  appeasement of Germany and Italy 130
  GS urges to reinforce the Sudan 150
  and arms to Finland 165, 167
  declares war on Germany 162
  Dunkirk 171
  treaty with Ethiopia (1942) 207
British Ambulance Service in Ethiopia
    British (Red Cross) 17–18, 47, 51–2, 54–5, 67–9, 72–3, 76
British Empire 126, 160, 201, 217, 220, 231
British Jungle Warfare Training Centre 224
British Legation, Addis Ababa 15, 18, 61, 66–7, 69–74, 97, 100, 200, 203
British Raj 220
British Red Cross 17, 51, 52, 54, 67, 69
British Somaliland 9, 11, 19, 181
Broll, Maurice: *Mud, Blood and Laughter* 205
Brooke, General Sir Alan (later Field Marshal Lord Alanbrooke) 217
Brophil, Captain Marius 48, 49
Brown, Curtis 76
Brown, Sidney Hamlet 47
Bryant, Arthur 143
Bu, Shwe 227
Buchan, John 168, 221
Buckingham Palace, London 199
Buie River 50
Bunner, L. J. 69
Burgos, Spain 82, 121
Burgoyne, Major Gerald Achilles 47, 48, 50, 66
Burma 5, 160, 217, 221–2, 225, 227–39, 241–7, 250

Burn, Michael 146
Burye, Gojjam 199, 200
Buthidaung, Burma 229
Butler, Father Bernard, S. J. 103
Butler, Elizabeth: *The Remnants of an Army* 159n
Butler, R. A. 167, 173
Buxton, Alfred 73, 161
Buxton, Mrs 161
Byron, Robert 179, 220

Cable and Wireless 137
    Addis Ababa office 42
Cabo Mayor, Santander 138
Cadett, Thomas Tucker-Edwardes 137–8, 140, 160, 161, 250
Cairo, Egypt 187, 213, 215, 219
    GHQ 174, 213
Calcutta, India 222, 225
Calder, Alexander: *Mercury Fountain* sculpture 141
Calvo Sotelo, José 79
Cameron Ridge, Keren 195
Camerons and Highland Light Infantry 194
Cameroons 153, 155
Cannon, Major John 243, 245
Cantabria, Spain 133
Canterbury, Archbishop of (Cosmo Lang) 17, 53
Cape Argus 8, 12, 58
Cape of Good Hope 218
Cape Times 251
Cape Town, South Africa 12, 152, 166
Capetown, HMS 75
Carlists 84 (see also Requetés)
Carlton Hotel, Bilbao 92, 111, 112, 116, 131, 132
Carmelo Monastery, Bilbao 95
Castellane, Boni de 173
Catalans 83
Catholic Church 88, 129
Cavendish, Brigadier R. V. C. 233
Cavotti, Lieutenant Giulio 36
Ce Soir 119
Cecil, Viscount 53
Central Hall, Westminster, London 149
Cervantes Saavedra, Miguel de 83, 84
Chamberlain, Neville 130, 150, 152, 170
Chandpur 225
Channon, Henry 'Chips' 173
Chapman-Andrews, Andrew (Sir Edwin) 176, 177, 178, 214, 215, 242, 250
Charlemagne, Emperor 87
Charles, Stanley 239
Charter, Major 71

Cheesman, Major Robert 174
    Lake Tana and the Blue Nile 174
Chel River 237, 243
Chelsea, London 78, 103
Chiang Kai-shek 15
Chiang Mei Ling 15
Chicago Tribune 86
Chilton, Sir Henry 123, 128
China 122, 148, 165, 216
Chittagong 225
Christ Church, Oxford 7, 31, 96, 250
Christianity 3–4, 6, 9, 10, 16, 17, 30, 32, 53, 57, 61–2, 67, 73, 80, 83, 88–9, 103, 108–9, 115–6, 128–9, 136–7, 143–4, 161, 171, 172, 177–8, 189, 209, 211, 242–4, 246–7, 250
Chungking 229
Churchill, Sir Winston 13, 106, 170–71, 175, 176, 178n, 214
Ciano, Count 101
Cillium, Tunisia 159
Ciscar (warship) 133
Citrine, Sir Walter 167
civilians as casualties of war 1–5, 17, 36, 37, 40–2, 48–9, 52–5, 58–9, 68–70, 72, 77, 80, 82, 85, 86, 94–6, 98–103, 108–10, 116–25, 140, 164, 168–9, 198, 217, 221
Clarke, Dudley 215, 216
Clifford, Alexander 177
Coats, Peter 188
Clively, Major 175
Cockburn, Claud 12
Cohen, Yakob bin 156
Collaborators in Ethiopia 211
Collins, Bill (of Reuters) 22, 38, 65
Collis, Flight Lieutenant 191
Columbus, Christopher 82
Communism 80, 171
Condor Legion 80, 108, 113–15, 117, 121, 123
Continental Hotel, Cairo 214
Convent of Custodian Angels, Bilbao 94–5
Convention of Geneva 47
Cooper, Diana 33, 35
Coptic Church 32, 61
Corazón de Jesús Jesuit church, Bilbao 109
Corman, Mathieu 111, 116, 119
Cortese, Guido 98
Cot, Pierre 129
Coward, Noel 4
Cowles, Virginia 38, 118
Cox's Bazaar 225
Crete 123
Croydon airport 75, 78
Cuba 83
Culross, C. H. 145

Culross & Co. 145
Cunningham, General 188, 193, 201, 210
Czechoslovakia 19, 151, 152

D Division (Deception in India) 227
Daggahbur, Ethiopia 26, 29, 36–7, 38, 48
Daily Dispatch 82
Daily Express 19n, 20, 179
Daily Mail 30, 143, 177
Daily Telegraph 17, 39, 74, 152, 157, 161, 164, 166,
    167, 170, 174, 248
Danakil plains 24, 43, 56
Daniels, H. G. 146
D'Annunzio, Gabriele 36
Dar es Salaam, Tanganyika 152
Darjeeling District, India 237
Davila, General 138
Dawson, Geoffrey 105, 144–7
De Caux, Ernest 142, 143
De Halpert, Frank 67–8
Deakin, Ralph 24, 51, 59, 73, 104, 146
    hires GS 12–13
    praises GS's work 30
    hires Stirling 84
    and fair coverage 105
    and Bolín 142–3
Debra Brehan sector, Ethiopia 99
Debra Libanos monastery, Ethiopia 99
Debra Marcos, Ethiopia 16, 199, 200, 201
Deedes, William F., Lord 39–41
del Rio, Felipe 93
Delhi, India 222
    Interrogation Centre 229
Denmark 170
Derio, Basque country 113
Desert Campaigns (1940-43) 160
Dessye, Ethiopia 41–2, 43, 45, 48, 49, 51, 56, 57,
    60, 63, 72, 174
Deusto, Bilbao 133
Día de la Raza (Day of the (Spanish) Race) (12
    October 1936) 82–3
Dickinson, General 188
Diego Suarez, Madagascar 217–18
Dimbleby, Richard 197, 250
Diredawa, Ethiopia 14, 23, 38, 201, 205
Diressa, Yilma 204–5, 210, 211
Djerba, Tunisia 156
Djibouti 9, 13, 14, 22, 61, 62, 64, 73, 149
Docker, Mrs B. M. 106, 107
Dodds-Parker, Douglas 150
Dogras 194, 197, 228
Dolo, Ethiopia 48
Dombaas, Norway 170
Donbaik, India 225–8, 230, 233, 234

Dongolaas gorge, Keren 194
Dooars, India 243
Dornier 17 bomber plane 109, 114, 115
Dorset 241, 247
Dougga, Tunisia 157
Douhet, Colonel Giulio 115, 123
    Il dominio dell'aria (The Command of the Air)
    45
Dufferin, Lord 239
Dufferin and Ava, Marquess of 239
Dufy, Raoul 141
dum-dum bullets 47–8
Dunkirk, France 171
Durango, Basque country 108, 109, 113, 121, 122,
    127
Durban, South Africa 151, 152
Dutch East Indies 217
Dutch Red Cross 54, 57

East Africa 8, 13, 176, 218
    Italian 193
East Africa Headquarters, Nairobi 218
East London, South Africa 152, 162, 234, 250
East London *Daily Dispatch* 12, 82, 152
Eastern Cape, South Africa 6, 7, 12, 148, 251
Eden, Sir Anthony, 1st Earl of Avon 46, 48n, 58,
    72, 74, 75, 103, 127, 188, 189
Edward VII, King of England 10
Edward VIII, King of England 103
Eguía, Joaquim 88, 106
Egypt 156, 176–7
Eibar, Basque country 112, 126
El Alamein 216
El Amin, Mamur Omar Effendi 183, 184, 192
El Greco 84
11 September 2001 4, 122
Elgeta, Basque country 110, 111
Eliot, T. S. 96
Elkano, Juan Sebastian de 87
Elosegi, Alberto 249
Elosegi, Joseba: *Quiero Morir por Algo (I Want to
    Die for Something)* 120
Émigrés in Ethiopia 211
Emmanuel, Professor Tamrat 184
Empey, Dr 67
Enecuri, Bilbao 94
England *see* Britain
English Review 78
Eritrea, Eritreans 9, 34, 35, 57, 150, 180, 188, 194,
    195, 197
Eritrean Askaris 99
Ertzana (People's Guard) 90
Escaping Club, Bilbao 93
'Escuadrilla Espana' 120

ESMÉ A 218
ESMÉ B 218
Essex Regiment, 1st Battalion 185
Estonia 164
Ethiopia
  access to the sea blocked 9
  Menelik II's victory at Adowa 9
  independence 9, 30
  Iyasu's aim 9–10
  Haile Selassie becomes Emperor 10
  Walwal dispute 11–12, 24, 25
  Italy bombs 17
  need for a seaport on the Red Sea 19
  arms embargo 19, 26
  Italian spies in 22
  Yekatit 12 98–9
  GS refused entry to 149
  patriotic resistance to Italian occupation 160
  planned revolt in 172–3
  Emperor's declaration 179–80
  RAF begins to bomb (1940) 183
  national flag 184, 185, 192, 196, 200, 209
  Emperor's return 207–12, 251
  treaty with Britain (1942) 207
Ethiopia (hydroplane) 21
Ethiopian Battalion, 2nd 209
Ethiopian Consulate, Djibouti 149
Ethiopian Empire 8, 43, 149
Ethiopian Legation, London 75
Ethiopian Orthodox Church 10
Ethiopian Red Cross 47, 48, 52, 56–7, 66
Ethiopian Women's Work Association 55, 59
Euskera (Basque language) 86, 89
Euzkadi (Euskadi) 120, 134
  Sabino names 89
  ends in betrayal 140
  last days of freedom 147
Evans, Madge 65
Evening News 1
Evening Standard 34
Eyre and Spottiswoode 78

Faber and Faber 96
Fagu, India 237, 242, 243, 244, 246, 247
Faguta, Ethiopia 191
'Fairfield', Bath 76
Falangists 84, 85
Falling Leaf: The Journal of the Psywar Society 239
Farm Street Church, Mayfair, London 103
Fascism, Fascists 3, 4, 19, 30, 36, 75, 79, 80, 83, 88,
     89, 98, 125, 147, 149, 168, 171, 193, 202, 205,
     243
Faupel, General 104
Fellowes, Perry 184, 194, 199

Fiat fighter aircraft 127
field propaganda 5
field propaganda units *see* forward propaganda
  units
Fields (of Royal Welch Fusiliers) 236
Fieseler Storch monoplane 158
15 (UK) Information Support Group 239–40
Fika, Basque country 130
Finland
  Russian aggression 122, 164, 165
  GS reports from 5, 167, 168–9
  Finnish response to the Russians 165–6
  independence 168, 170
  Finnish and Russian casualties 169–70
  armistice deal 170
Finlay, James 246
Finnish Army 165
Finnish Liquor Board factory, Rajamäki 165
First Arakan Campaign 222, 233
First World War (1914–18) 4, 10, 86, 115, 122, 151,
     152, 154, 234, 235
Fitche, Ethiopia 60
Fleming, Ian 220
Fleming, Peter 220–21, 227, 250
Foch, Maréchal 111
Foot, M. R. D. 216
Force 121, Madagascar 218
Ford, Maurice 226
Foreign Enlistment Act (1870) 165
Foreign Office 16, 69, 73, 74, 130, 142, 150, 173
Fort Dologoroduc, Keren 197
forward propaganda units 185, 187, 199, 200, 210,
     227, 228, 237, 249
Foum Tathouine, Tunisia 157
Fowkes, Brigadier 202
France
  arms embargo on Ethiopia 19
  Hoare-Laval pact 35, 46
  Popular Front electoral victory 70
  declares war on Germany 162
  surrenders 160, 171, 176
  Vichy regime 176, 218
Franco, Doña Carmen 83, 84
Franco, General Francisco
  and Nazi Germany 1, 4
  Picasso loathes 3
  and Bolín 79, 142
  Italy assists 79, 94
  bombing of Republican towns 81
  Badajoz massacre 80, 86
  and the *Día de la Raza* 82–3
  Aguirre and 92
  and Richthofen 114
  Elosegi's protest 120

Guernica a public relations disaster 121
decision to bomb Guernica 123
and Bilbao 133, 137, 140
Picasso's strip cartoon 141
a corporate fascist state 147
and Philby 147
death 142
French Legation, Addis Ababa 60, 102
French Somaliland 9, 13, 149
Friends of National Spain, The 143
Fruniz, Basque country 113
Fuerte Banderas, Bilbao 134

Gabridihari fort, Ethiopia 26
Galdakano, Basque country 109
Galla (Oromo) people 43, 50, 51, 57, 183, 204
Gallabat fort, Sudan-Ethiopia border 185, 233
Gallagher, O'Dowd 19n, 20
Gallipoli, Turkey (1915) 116
Gandhi, Mahatma 222, 231
Ganges River 225
Garnett, David: *The Campaigns in Greece and
Crete* 193
Garrett, Edmund 251
Garvey, Marcus 21, 61–2
Garwhalis 194
Gas Experimental School, Porton Down 54
Gasca, David 159
Gastelumendi ridge, Basque country 130, 131
Gedaref, Sudan 162, 182, 185
Gellhorn, Martha 38, 164
General Headquarters, Middle East Force 216
'Generation of '98' 83
Geneva 46
Convention of 47
Pact of 47
British memorandum on poison gas 58
conciliation fails 60
and sanctions against Italy 60
GS in 129–30
Geneva Protocol against the use of poison gas
(1925) 53, 58
George V, King of England 199
George VI, King of England 124
Gerahty, Cecil 143
The Road to Madrid 143
The Spanish Arena 143
Gerlogubi, Ethiopia 29
German Navy 166
German South-West Africa 154
Germany
bombing of Guernica 1, 4
and the Saar 8
Rhineland occupied 52

formal recognition of Nationalist Spain 104
British appeasement of 130
Anschluss 148
Axis formed 149
lost colonies 151–5
invades Poland 161
blitzkrieg attack on the Low Countries 170
Gernika, Basque country
bombing of (26 April 1937) 1, 2, 3, 115, 116–22,
169, 245
as the cradle of the Basque race 2, 168
civilians machine-gunned 2
reasons for bombardment 2, 117, 121, 123
Casa de Juntas (Basque Parliament) 2, 90, 119,
120
oak of Guernica 2, 90, 120, 140
Juntas de Gernika 89–90
nationalist anthem ('Gernikako Arbola') 90
legacy of 122, 124–5
international reaction 126
'blame the victim' strategy 126
Nationalists enter 128, 143, 144
propaganda battle 128, 142–4
GS reports on: *see under* Steer, George
Lowther: *writings*
'Geschwader 88' (German air units) 115
Gestapo 158
Special Wanted List 4–5
Ghanotakis shop, Addis Ababa 64, 100
Gibraltar 156
'Gideon Force' (previously 'Mission 101') 189,
193, 200, 213
Gillespie, Major 228
Gioghis, Wolde 66, 175
Glenarum 242
Gloster Gladiator fighter 167
Goebbels, Dr Joseph 151, 230
Gojjam province, Ethiopia 162, 182, 183, 187, 191,
199
Golando, India 225
Gondar, Ethiopia 41
Gorahai, Ethiopia 27, 29, 36, 37, 38, 102
Goré, Ethiopia 61, 62
Göring, Hermann 79, 80, 114, 151, 158
Goya, Francisco de: *Disasters of War* 3
Grand Hôtel des Arcades, Djibouti, Le 149
Graves, David (Lieutenant J. D. N.) 236
Graves, Robert 236
Graziani, Marshal Rodolfo 30, 35–6, 38, 40, 46,
98, 102, 150, 158, 184, 202
Great Gibbi Palace, Addis Ababa 18, 33, 62, 100,
101, 202, 210
Great Western Hotel, Paddington 173
Greeks 156–7

Greiser, Captain 101
Grenet, Filippo de 16
GSI(D) Deception, India 221
Guardia Civil 82
Gubba, Ethiopia 184, 191–2
Guedalla, Philip 193
Guernica see Gernika
Guernica (Picasso painting) xi, xiii, 3, 140–2
guerrilla warfare 34, 138, 149, 173–4, 189, 191,
    200–1, 204, 208, 213, 237
Guggenheim Museum, Bilbao 134, 142
Gugsa, Ras 10
Gulf of Aden 9, 10, 69, 181
Gulf War (1991) 239
Gurieff, General Vladimir 132
Gurkhas 194, 238, 244
Gurubathan, India 237
Gwalior, India 220

Habtewold, Ato Makonnen 43
Hague Convention (1907) 53
Haile Selassie I, Emperor of Ethiopia (originally
    Ras Tafari Makonnen) 101, 160, 240
  as regent 10
  as moderniser 10, 15
  European tour (1924) 18
  coronation (1930) 8, 10, 31, 178n
  strategy of 10–11, 15
  GS interviews (1935) 18–19
  appearance 18
  personality 18, 76, 188
  and Julian 21
  relationship with GS 24
  King's Maskal 32
  Mobilization Decree 33, 34
  advises a guerrilla war 34
  in the Italo-Ethiopian War 41, 52, 55, 60–63
  Galla revenge on 43
  constitutional crisis 60
  Council of Ministers 60, 62
  Garvey on 61–2
  decision to go west 62
  goes into exile 64, 211
  in London 75, 76, 103
  addresses the League of Nations 76
  at GS's wedding (1939) 161
  George Barton Steer's godfather 171, 253
  prejudice against 173
  records speeches in Amharic 175
  taken to the Sudan 175–9
  Decrees to his people (Awajes) 179–80, 206,
    211–12
  propaganda in Gedaref 182–3
  Wingate pledges his support 190–91

invasion of Ethiopia 194, 199
  GS forges his signature 198
  standard of 202
  returns to Addis Ababa 5, 207–12, 251
Hailu, Ras Kassa 62, 63, 199
Halifax, Lord (Edward Wood) 53, 54, 150, 173
Halley, Captain 244, 245
Hamilton-Temple-Blackwood, Basil, 4th
    Marquess of Dufferin and Ava 239
Hammond, Brigadier 228, 229, 232
Hamsterley (ship) 107
Hanner, Dr 67
Harar, Ethiopia 10, 14, 22, 23, 24, 29, 38, 40, 53,
    102, 201
Hardwick (tea planter) 224, 227, 229
Harlem, New York City 22
Harrington, Lieutenant Colonel John Lane 9
Harrison (of Reuters) 64, 65
Harvey, Mollie 184
Harvey, O. C. 75
Hassett, Hope 97
Havig, Mademoiselle 42
Haw-Haw, Lord (William Joyce) 229
Hawaii, USA 216
Hawaryat, Blatta Takkala Walda 62
Hearst newspapers 14
Heine, Heinrich 114
Heinkel He-151 fighter plane 93, 115, 116–17, 118,
    127, 134
Heinkel 111-G bomber plane 115, 117, 118, 127
Helfaya Pass, Libya 216
Hell Below (film) 65
Helsinki, Finland 164, 165, 168
Hemingway, Ernest 38
  For Whom the Bell Tolls 130
Hendaye, France 104
Henderson, Sir Neville 146
  Failure of a Mission 146
Herbert, George 130
Herbert, Laura 32
Herero people 154
Hermann, Lieutenant 94
Herrero, Gustave de 103
Herrero-Steer, Margarita Trinidad (GS's first
    wife) 40, 61, 65, 82, 99, 159, 212
  meets GS 38
  journalist 38, 97
  personality 38, 97
  appearance 38
  background 39, 78
  marries GS 70–71, 97
  prepares to leave Ethiopia 74
  dies in childbirth 96–7
  funeral 103

Herrouy, George 62–3, 184
Herrouy, Sirak 62–3, 184
Hertford College, Oxford 31
Hirohito, Emperor of Japan 10, 60, 223–4
Hiroshima, Japan 4, 244
Hitler, Adolf 151, 170, 189
    vows not to bomb open towns 4
    cancels interview with *The Times* 4
    Olympic Games 78
    supports Franco 79–80, 104
    visits Mussolini 148
    and Chamberlain 150, 152
    anti-Semitism 154
    the threat of 171
    death 244
    Mein Kampf 155
Hitler Youth 154
Hoare, Sir Samuel 35, 46, 105
Hodder and Stoughton 76, 152
Holburn, James 104, 105, 126, 128, 137, 147
Holmboe, Knud 36
Holme, Christopher 116, 119, 123, 148
    'Gernika, April 26 1937' 119
Holmes, Walter 49, 51, 54, 55
Hong Kong 217
Hood, HMS 107
Hooghly River 225
Hope-Gill (British Consul) 68, 70
Horn of Africa 8, 58
House of Commons 3, 58, 72, 74, 75, 76, 106, 127,
    146, 167, 206
House of Lords 53, 55
Household, Geoffrey: *Rogue Male* vii
Htizwe, Burma 229, 232, 233
Huber, Max 47, 54, 58
Hunt, Brigadier 228

Ibarra (a Basque) 108
Idot, Madame 39, 63
Idot's, Addis Ababa 39, 65
Igezu, Dedjaz 62, 74
Imperial Airways 151, 152
Imperial Band, Ethiopia 73
Imperial Guard, Ethiopia 19
Imperial Hotel, Addis Ababa 4, 22, 34, 39, 65, 68,
    202–3
Imru, Ras 45, 46
Inchorta hills, Basque country 110
India 194, 217, 220–21, 222
Indian Divisions 4th and 5th 194, 196, 197
Indian Field Broadcasting Units (IFBU) 221, 222,
    224, 230, 231, 233, 234, 236–40, 243, 244, 247,
    250
Indian National Army (INA) 231

Indin HQ, Burma 233
Inniskilling Fusiliers 226
Intelligence Corps 179
International African Friends of Abyssinia 22
International Board for Non-Intervention in
    Spain 165
International Brigades 80
International Catholic Truth Society: 'Why The
    Press Failed On Spain!' 137
International Committee of the Red Cross
    (ICRC) 17, 47, 54, 58
Irala, Antonio 118
Iraq, British use of mustard gas in 13
Irun, Spain 81, 139
Isherwood, Christopher 221
Italian Air Force 204
Italian Army Corps 196
Italian Embassy, London 48n
Italian Empire 158
Italian Legation, Addis Ababa 34, 35
Italian Military Intelligence 86
Italian Second Army Corps 45
Italian Somaliland 9, 11, 30, 35, 99, 201
Italo-Ethiopian War 99
    the Emperor's pre-war position 19
    Waugh and GS's books on 30–31
    breaks out 33–5
    Italian propaganda 35
    Hoare-Laval peace plan 35
    Gorahai bombed 36
    death of Afewerk 36–7
    mustard gas attack at Harar 40–41
    Gondar and Dessye bombed 41–2
    yperite bombs at Adi Quala 45–6
    nature of the war 47–9
    Ethiopian retreat south 50
    heavy use of gas in the north 52–3
    bombing statistics 53
    Melly on 54
    fall of Addis Ababa 58
    Ethiopia annexed by Italy 58
Italy
    takes and names Eritrea 9
    defeat at Adowa 9, 11
    Walwal dispute 11–12
    bombs Senussi Arabs in Libya 13
    bombs Ethiopia 17
    seizes and bombs Libya 36
    annexes Ethiopia 58
    assistance to Franco 79, 94
    British appeasement of 130
    Axis formed 149
    joins the war (1940) 173
Itxarkundia battalion 134

Itxas Alde battalion 134
Iyasu, Lij 9–10

J-88 fighter force (*Jagdgruppe-88*) 115
Jackson, Lieutenant Colonel 236
James, C. L. R. 22
Japan
    in China 122, 148, 165, 216
    in Second World War 5, 216–17, 218, 225,
        229–37
    war against Russia 216
    rigid belief system 223–4, 227
    war in Manchuria 248
Japanese Imperial Army 217, 221, 231
Japanese Navy 231
Jebel Dafeis, Sudan 186
Jerrold, Douglas 78–9, 143, 144
Jersey City, USA 22
Jerusalem 61, 75, 189–90
Jijiga, Ethiopia 24, 25, 29, 38, 41, 51, 53, 181, 201
Jimma, Ethiopia 73
Johnson, Celia 220
Johnson, Hewlett, 'Red' Dean of Canterbury 109
Johnson, Dr Samuel: *The History of Rasselas,
        Prince of Abyssinia* 44
Jolly, Stephen: 'Wearing the Stag's Head Badge:
        British Combat Propaganda since 1945' 239
Jones, Captain 'Potato' 106
José Luis Diez (warship) 133
Joseph (GS's interpreter) 33–4
Journal, Le 38, 39, 97
Jubaland 201
Julian, 'Colonel' Hubert Fauntleroy 20–22
Junkers Ju 52/3m bomber plane 2, 80, 93, 94, 118,
        127
Junkers Ju 87 (Stuka) dive-bomber 114, 118
Junod, Marcel 47, 65, 92
Junta de Defensa Nacional (Directorate of
        National Defence) 82

K-88 bomber force (*Kampfgruppe-88*) 115
Kairouan, Tunisia 157
Kamwe villagers 232
Karachi 220
Karen hillmen 237
Karramarra Pass, Ethiopia 29
Kassa, Ras 49, 209
Kassa, Shallaka 186, 197
Kassala, Sudan 178, 180, 190, 194
Kasserine, Tunisia 159
Kell, Colonel Sir Vernon 161, 215
Kemp, Peter 84, 136
    The Thorns of Memory 85–6
Kenya 43, 153, 181, 187, 188

Kenyatta, Jomo 22
Keren 194–8, 200, 228
KGB 147
Khartoum, Sudan 150, 162, 174, 177, 178, 179, 181,
        182, 191, 193, 211, 217
    conference (1940) 188–9
Khelifah, Salah ben 159
King's African Rifles 11, 202, 210
King's Chapel of St John Baptist, Savoy, London
        161
King's Maskal (Dance of the Priests) 32
Kipling, Rudyard 104
Kirikiño battalion 134
Knightley, Philip: *The First Casualty* 19n, 124
Kobbo, Ethiopia 55
Königsberg (light cruiser) 152
Korean National Army Liaison Unit 238
Koreans 228
Kothi Lines ('Bungalow Dwellings') Fagu, India
        243
Kristallnacht 154
Kuittinen, Captain Eero 165
Kuki, Rifleman Long Sing Song 244, 245
Kurlansky, Mark: *The Basque History of the
        World* 87
Kworam, Ethiopia 50, 53, 55

Labauría Porturas, Jose 128
Labour Party 3, 170
Labrely, Jean Gustave 103
Lake Ashangi, Ethiopia 50, 55
Lake Hayk, Wollo region, Ethiopia 49
Lal, Chandra 246
Lalibela, Ethiopia 60
Lam, Dr 245
Lamyang, Upper Kabaw valley 231
Lancing College, West Sussex 31
Larrañaga (communist political commissar) 131
Larrínaga prison 94
Latvia 164
Laval, Pierre 35, 46
Lawrence, T. E. 176, 200, 213, 248
League of Nations 19, 20, 26, 35, 46, 62, 160, 172
    Ethiopia joins 10
    and the Walwal incident 11
    Red Cross 17
    Afewerk's view of 28
    impotence 47
    Women's Advisory Council 52
    Committee of Thirteen 58
    Eden speaks to 58
    the Emperor addresses 76–7, 172
    Ciano declaration 101
    Union rally (London, 1937) 129

Council resolution 129
and the former German colonies in Africa
    154
Finland joins (1920) 164
expels the Soviet Union 164–5
Lee, Don 61, 70
Leeper, Peter 113
Legion Condor see Condor Legion
Leizaola, Jesús María de (lawyer) 135, 136, 138
Lenin, Vladimir Ilyich 171
Lewin, Ronald 222
Lezama, Basque country 132
Liberia 21
Libya 194
    Italy bombs Senussi Arabs in 13
    Italy seizes 36
    Italian forces mass in 150, 158–9
    GS visits 155–6
    and Mareth Bastion 157
    German influence on 158
Liddell Hart, Captain Basil 124
Lindqvist, Sven: *A History of Bombing* 36, 122
Linklater, Eric
    The Defence of Calais 193
    The Highland Division 193
    The Northern Garrisons 193
Linlithgow, Lord 217
Lints Smith, Mr 98
Liotta, General 98
Little, Brown & Co. 76
Little Gibbi Palace, Addis Ababa 18, 61, 62, 98,
    99, 175, 201–2
Lloyd, Major General W. L. 222, 228, 233
Lloyd George, David 76, 127
London
    GS leaves for Addis Ababa (1935) 13
    and the bombing of Guernica 4
    Yorkshire Post London office 8, 12
    Blitz 172
London, Bishop of 161
London Clinic, Devonshire Place, London 97
Lorenzini, Colonel 198
Louis, Joe 22
Lowenthal (of Reuters) 49
Luftwaffe 52, 80, 114, 115, 176
Lukacs, John: *5 Days in London, May 1940* 171
Lush, Brigadier Maurice 200, 203, 206
    A Life of Service 208
Lutyens, Sir Edwin 220
Luxembourg 170

Maar, Dora 3, 141
Macaulay, Thomas Babington, Baron 93
McDonald, Iverach 147

Macfie, Dr J. W. S. 52, 54, 58
    An Ethiopian Diary 54
Macgregor (ship) 107
Mackenzie, Colin 221, 249
Macmillan, Harold, 1st Earl of Stockton 39
Macmurray, Professor John 109
MacNeice, Louis: *Autumn Journal* vii
MacSweeney, Lieutenant 204, 211
Madagascar 217–18
Madariaga, Salvador de 88
Madrassis 194, 231, 238
Madrid 108, 114, 115, 164
Madros (Armenian driver) 56
Magdala, Ethiopia 9
Magliocco, General 204
Mahara, Ethiopia 50
Mahfud, Ethiopia 56
Mahrattas 194, 197, 238
Mai Ceu, Ethiopia 51
Maillet, André 10
'Major C' (Clively) 175
Majunga, Madagascar 218
Makalle, Ethiopia 49
Makonnen, Bitwoded 50
Makonnen, Ras Tafari *see* Haile Selassie I,
    Emperor
Makonnen, Prince 175
Maktar, Tunisia 159, 176
Malaga, Spain 3
Malaya 187, 217
Malraux, André 129
Mambrini, General 202
Manchester Evening News 124
Manchester Guardian 106, 149
Manchuria 248
Mancini, General 139
Mandel, Georges 161
Mann, Arthur 12
Mannerheim Line 168
Marcus, Harold 214
Mareb River 34
Mareth Bastion, Tunisia 157
Marinetti, Filippo 36
Maritain, Jacques 129
Marks, Sammy 176, 177
Marquina, Basque country 116
Marteartu battalion 110
Martin, Benjamin 63, 99
Martin, Joseph 63, 99
Martin, Kingsley 248–9
Mary, Queen (wife of King George V) 199
Maskal (Feast of the Finding of the True Cross) 183
Maskelyne, Jasper 215–16
Massawa, Eritrea 9, 19

Matthews (padre) 68, 70
Maungdaw, Burma 227, 228, 233
Mauriac, François 129
May (maid) 175
Mayu peninsula 222, 225, 233
Mayu River 225, 229, 233
Melly, Dr John, MC 18, 58, 68, 103, 161
  Esmé in love with 17
  British Ambulance Service in Ethiopia 17–18
  GS meets 17
  GS's opinion of 18
  Red Cross ambulance unit bombed 52
  on the Italo-Ethiopian War 54
  mortally wounded 69
  death and posthumous award 72
  burial 73
Mendigurren, Bruno 92, 93, 131, 132
Mendrakos, George 14
Menelik Girls' School 67
Menelik II, Emperor of Ethiopia 8–11, 14, 18, 33, 51, 212
Messerschmitt Bf 109 fighter plane 115, 118, 158
Mhugs 232
MI3 97
MI5 161, 191, 247
MI6 74
Middle East 160, 190
Middle East GHQ 189, 198, 215
Middle East Intelligence Centre 174
Militär-Wochenblatt (official German army paper) 144
Millán Astray, General José 83, 84
Ministry of Information 193
Ministry of Justice and Culture (Bilbao) 96
Ministry of the Interior (Bilbao) 94
Miró, Joan 141
'Mission 101' (later 'Gideon Force') 174, 188, 189
Mitchison, Naomi: 'Dr A. J. M. Melly' 72
Mockler, Anthony 149
Mogadishu, Somalia 201
Mohammed, Prophet 10
Mohammed Ali's, Addis Ababa 68, 71
Mola, General 104, 108, 110, 111, 112, 123, 128
Mombasa 150, 152
Mon Ciné, Addis Ababa 39, 65, 100, 212
Monks, Noel 193
  meets GS 20
  and Julian 21
  on the horrors of war 41
  on Bolín's cruel streak 86
  on Monnier 111
  and the day of the Guernica raid 115–16, 118, 119–20
  Eyewitness 20, 116

Monnier, Robert ('Jaureghuy') 111–13, 132, 133, 135, 136, 140, 160–63, 186
Montevideo 167
Montezemolo, Generale Alberto Cordero di 208
Montezemolo, Paula di 208
Montgomery, Robert 65
Monzón, Telesforo de 90, 95, 120
Moore, Sir John 172
Moorehead, Alan 179, 181, 203, 241, 250
  African Trilogy: The Desert War 1940-43 198
Moorehead, Caroline: *Dunant's Dream: War, Switzerland and the History of the Red Cross* 54
Moorish infantry 111
Moosa (Ethiopian cook) 29
Moral, Marquis del 142
Moreau, Major Rudolf von 117
Moriatis, Madame 39
Morilla, Father Carlos 108
Morning Post 39
Morocco 13, 79, 80, 83, 126, 156, 157
Morris, Jan 86
Mosley, Leonard 177
Mosley, Sir Oswald 75
Mottistone, Lord 53
Moulin, Jean 129
Mount Agelu, Ethiopia 56
Mount Belaya, Ethiopia 194
Mount Entoto, Ethiopia 14, 43, 102, 203, 209–10
Mount Urkulu, Basque country 113
Moustahil, Ethiopia 29
Mozley, Canon 172
Mukhtar, Omal el 36
Mullah's Fort, Gorahai, Ethiopia 27, 28, 36, 37
Mulugeta, Ras 49–50, 51
Mulugeta, Colonel Tadessa 50, 51
Mumford, Lewis 123
Mundaka estuary 118
Munguia, Basque country 130
Munich Crisis (1938) 152
Museum of Modern Art, New York 142
Mussolini, Benito 140, 177, 189, 193
  and the Abyssinian Dispute 19, 20, 30, 35
  meeting with the ICRC 54
  his overthrow predicted 103
  Hitler visits 148
  proclaims the Italian Empire (1936) 158
mustard gas 36, 40–41, 52–5 (*see also* poison gas)
Muzi Falconi, Alessandro 16, 208
Muzi Falconi, Baron Filippo 15–16, 17, 208
Muzi Falconi, Marion (née Barton) 15–16, 208
Myoksogyangyna, Burma 232

Naga hillmen 224, 229, 237, 238
Nagasaki, Japan 244
Nairobi, Kenya 193
Nalut, Cyrenaica, Libya 158
Nama people 154
Namibia (previously South-West Africa) 148
Napier, General 9
Narvik, Norway 170
Nasibu, Dedjazmatch, Governor of Harar 26
Natal Carbineers 202
National Book Association 153
National government (UK) 46
Nationalists (Spain) 80
    and Nazi Germany 1, 4, 80
    aims 80
    links with Fascist Italy 80
    and *Día de la Raza* 83
    in Toledo 84
    expulsion of GS 85
    keen to control the press 86
    Bolín's complaints 105
    the Nationalist fleet 105
    troops build Vitoria airfield 115
    panicked by reaction to Guernica bombing 126
    blame the victim 126
    Nationalist forces enter Guernica 128, 143, 144
    fall of Bilbao 136
Nazi-Soviet pact (1939) 126, 164
Nazis
    in the Spanish Civil War 1, 3, 4, 104, 168
    across Europe 122
    and evacuations 125
    at 1937 World's Fair 140
    Smuts orders arrests 148
    Axis formed 149
    penetration of South-West Africa 154
    in Tripoli 158
    the threat of Nazism 171
    and Madagascar 218
Nehru Brigade (INA) 231
Neila, Colonel 138
Nelson, Kathleen 17, 54
Nervion River 91, 106, 107, 109, 134, 136
Netherlands 170
New Delhi, India 220
New Gibbi, Addis Ababa 64
New Guinea 231
New Labour 239
New Statesman 72, 248
New Times and Ethiopia News 75
New York City 21, 22, 122, 137, 142, 161
New York Herald Tribune 21
New York Times 1, 30, 34, 71, 72

New Zealand 162, 217
Newton, Joseph 244, 245
Ngjaros, Dr 57
Nigerians 201, 202
Nile Hotel, Wadi Halfa 177
Nile River 8, 43, 174, 177, 179
Noel-Baker, Philip 127, 137, 156, 172
    wins Derby by-election (1936) 76
    friendship with GS 76, 167
    on GS 129, 250
    arranges for the Emperor to meet Butler 173
Noel-Buxton, Lord 18
Non-Intervention Pact 4
Norman, Captain de 57
Normandy (liner) 142
North Africa 155–60, 195, 216
North Bengal, India 237
North Stoneham, England 125
North-West Frontier, India 13
Norway 170
Nosy Bé, Madagascar 218
Nuestra Señora de Begoña church, Bilbao 133
Nur, Ali 11, 24–5, 26, 28, 37, 38, 41
Nurmi, Paavo 167

Oahu, Hawaiian islands 217
Ochandiano, Basque country 127
Office of Press and Propaganda (Spain) 83
Official Secrets Act 175
Ogaden Desert 11, 19, 23–6, 29, 30, 36, 38, 41, 51, 54
Old Castile, Spain 82
Old Delhi, India 220
Olley Air Service, Croydon 79
Olympic Games (1936) 78, 167
Omar, Haji Asfar 23
Onaindía, Canon Alberto 128–9
Operation CANNIBAL 222
Operation Ironclad 218
Operation Magic Fire (*Unternehmen Feuerzauber*) 80
Orford (passenger liner) 75
Oromo people *see* Galla
Orwell, George 5, 87, 93, 122–3
    Homage to Catalonia 124
    'Looking Back on the Spanish War' 125
Ostrich (steamer) 225
Ottoman Empire 36
Ottoman Turks 10
Owens, James 'Jesse' 78
Oxford University 8, 49, 97, 129, 153
    Africa Society 7, 75

Pact of Geneva 47
Padmore, George 22

Page Croft, Sir Henry 143
Paget, General 170
Pagoda War (1885-6) 239
Pakistan 194
Paleologue's garage, Addis Ababa 65, 68
Pankhurst, Dr Richard 214
Pankhurst, Sylvia 75, 173, 214
Papavassiliou, Photis 156
Paramount News 179
Paris
   May Day parades (1937) 3
   Spanish Pavilion, World's Fair 1937
     (*Exposition Internationale des Arts et
     Techniques Appliqués à la Vie Moderne*) 3,
     140
   and the bombing of Guernica 4
   GS stays in (1937) 137, 140, 141
   GS meets Esmé 160
   Ministry of Colonies 160–61
Pasagarri, Basque country 94
Pathans 194
Pathfinders (Hitler Youth) 154
Patriot Resistance in Ethiopia 63, 161, 191, 193,
   202, 208, 209, 211
Pax Romana 160
Pearl Harbor (1941) 216–17, 218
Pedroso y Sturdza, Dolores (Lolita) de 39, 61, 66,
   70
Péman, José María 84
Pennefather-Holland, Captain 24–5
Perera, Enrique 159
Perham, Margery 75
Perkins, Max 130
Perroquet, Addis Ababa, le 31, 39, 212
Peshawar, NW frontier, India 229
Peterson, Lieutenant Colonel A. D. C. 249
Philby, Kim 147
Philippines 83
phosgene gas 13, 52 (*see also* poison gas)
Picasso, Pablo
   appalled by the Spanish Civil War 3
   supports the Spanish Republic 3
   starts to paint *Guernica* 3, 141
   Dream and Lie of Franco 141
   Guernica xiii, 3, 140–42
Pienaar, Brigadier Dan 202
Pietermaritzburg, South Africa 218
Plá y Deniel, Enrique, Bishop of Salamanca 83
Planet News 44
Plate River 167
Platt, Sir William 181, 185, 193, 194, 195, 217, 218, 219
Plymouth, England 176
poison gas 13, 36, 40–1, 46, 50, 52–6, 58, 61–2, 67,
   75, 77, 99, 101

Pokrail, Lok Nat 243
Poland, Germany invades 161
Political Warfare Executive (PWE) 240
Pollard, Major Hugh 79, 126
Ponza (prison island) 204
Port Said, Egypt 13
Porvoo, Finland 168–9
Potez biplane 43–4
Pozuelo, Spain 85
Preston, Paul: *!Comrades!* 88
Prieto, Indalecio 88
Prince of Wales (battleship) 217
Private Eye magazine 39
Profumo, John 39
propaganda 5, 35, 58–9, 74, 80–2, 109, 125–9,
   142–4, 158, 178–80, 182–7, 191–200, 203–6,
   210, 215–17, 221–4, 227–34, 237–40, 249
PSYOPS (Psychological Operations) 5, 179,
   191–2, 198, 200–1, 222–4, 230–3, 239
Puerto Rico 83
Punjabis, Punjab Regiment 66, 194, 228, 231, 238
Pyle, Ernie 160, 172

Radio Sevilla 109
Radio-Club of Portugal 109
Rajputs, Rajputana Rifles 194, 195, 228, 229
Ram, Subadar Richpal 195
Ramillies (battleship) 218
Rangoon, Burma 225
   Memorial 250
Ras Tafari, Crown Prince 199 (*see* Haile Selassie)
Rastafarianism 10, 22
Rathbone, Eleanor 75
Rathedaung, Burma 225, 228, 230
Razor Ridge, Keren 197
Red Cross 17, 36, 42, 47, 48, 50, 56, 65, 100, 101,
   136, 169, 174
Red Sea 8, 9, 13, 19
Reds (Spain) 83, 86, 127, 128, 142
Regia Aeronautica Italiana 46
Reith, Sir John 176
Rennell, Lord 53
Renteria Bridge, Basque country 117, 122
Republican air force (Spain) 93, 106, 109, 118,
   129
Repulse (battlecruiser) 217
Requetés (Carlist militia) 84, 85, 128
Reuters News Agency 1, 16, 22, 34, 38, 40, 49, 64,
   71, 74, 116, 122, 123
Rey, Charles 14
Rheindorf factory, Germany 121, 127
Rhineland 52
Rhodes, Cecil 176
Rice, Archie 161

Richthofen, Manfred, Baron von 114
Richthofen, Generalmajor Wolfram Freiherr
    von 114–15, 121, 123
Rif Mountains, Morocco 79
Right Book Club, The 143
Rimbaud, Arthur 8, 10, 14, 24
Roberts, Andrew: 'Patriotism: The Last Refuge
    of Sir Arthur Bryant' 143
Roberts, Fifi 106, 107, 118
Roberts (of the Foreign Office) 129–30
Roberts, Patrick 71
Roberts, Captain W. H. 106, 107, 118
Robinson, Johannes 22
Rocquefeuille, Comte de 29
Roman Empire 156, 157, 159, 160
Rommel, Erwin 216
Roncesvalles, Pyrenees 87
Roosevelt, President Franklin D. 162, 165, 217
Rothermere, Lord 30
Rotterdam, Holland 123
Rowe and Maw 144, 145
Roy, N. 227, 229
Royal Air Force (RAF) 10, 177, 180, 183, 184–5,
    194, 196
Royal Albert Hall, London 129
Royal Engineers 234
Royal Navy 88, 105, 106, 118, 125, 138, 167, 176,
    181, 217
Royal Scots 236
Royal Welsh Fusiliers, 1st Battalion 234,
    235–6
RSPCA 67
Rufiji River 152
Runeberg, Johann Ludwig 168–9
Rungamuttee Tea Estate 246, 247, 253
Russian Revolution (1917) 164
Russo-Japanese war (1904–5) 216
Ryle, Gilbert 49

Saar Plebiscite 8
Saarbrucken 8
Sabaou Cemetery, Biarritz 103
Said, Bash Shawish (Sergeant Major) 191
St George's Church, Bloomsbury, London 103
St Paul's Cathedral, London 171, 172
St Saviour's Church, East London, South Africa
    250
Salamanca, Spain 104, 126
    Día de la Raza debate (1936) 82–4
    German infantry in 85
Salamanca Press Office 109
Salamanca University 82, 83
Sandford, Colonel Daniel 24, 174, 178, 183, 185,
    188, 191, 200, 207, 210, 214

Sanidad Militar, Bilbao 110
Santa María Church, Durango 108–9
Santa María Church, Guernica 122, 128
Santa Marina, near Bilbao 132
Santa Marina Zar, Basque country 112
Santa Susana nunnery, Bilbao 108
Santander, Spain 93, 136, 138, 148
Santoña, Spain 139
Saunders, Hilary 193
    The Battle of Britain 193
    Bomber Command 193
Savoia-Marchetti SM81 bomber transport plane
    79, 99, 127
Savoy Chapel, London 161
Savoy Grenadiers 99
Savoy Hotel, Beira, Mozambique 219
Sbeitla, Tunisia 159
Sbiba, Tunisia 159
Scandinavia 164–71
Schauman, Eugen 168
Schiaparelli, Elsa 140
Schmidt, Karl Gustav 94
Scotland 170
Second World War (1939–45)
    start of 161–2
    GS reports from three precursor places 5
    GS becomes a soldier (1940) 5
    civilian casualties 122
    Guernica tours USA and Mexico 142
    'phoney war' 160
    first British land offensive 185
    first great Allied victory 193
    first loudspeaker unit used 197–8
    first large-scale opposed landing 218
Selassie (interpreter) 65
Sencourt, Robert (Robert Esmonde Gordon
    George): Spain's Ordeal: A Documented
    History of the Civil War 144
Senussi Arabs 13
Septimius Severus, Emperor of Rome 157
Sert, José Luis 140–41
Seven Seas Spray (ship) 106, 140
Seventh Day Adventist Mission, Dessye 42
Seville, Spain 80
Seyyum, Ras 49
Sfax, Tunisia 156
Shafrazi, Tony 142
Shankalla wilderness, Sudan 191
Shaving Brush hill 230
Sheaf Garth (ship) 107
Sheepshanks, Dick 40
Sheppard, Dick 18
Shelley, Percy Bysshe: Ozymandias 193
Shoa, Ethiopia 44, 59, 102, 103

Shoan plain 56
Shola Mieda, Ethiopia 56
Short Sunderland flying boat 152, 176–7
Siam (later Thailand) 221
Sickle force, Norway 170
Sidi Barrani, Egypt 196
Sidi Bou Zid, Tunisia 159, 160
Sikhs 66, 69, 71, 73, 197, 232
Siliguri, India 237
SIME (Security Intelligence Middle East) 215
Simpson's, Strand, London 78
Simu, Fitorari 37, 41
Sinclair, Sir Archibald 55–6, 106
Singapore 217, 218, 229
Singh, Captain Mohan 231, 232
Slim, General Bill 185, 238
    Defeat into Victory 195
Smallwood, Brigadier 202
Smida, Hamadi 156
Smuts, General J. C. 148, 162, 167, 188
Smyrna, Turkey 68–9, 102
Sobotka, Hans 109
SOE (Special Operations Executive) 188, 215, 217,
    221, 237, 249
SO1 (Propaganda Branch) 215
Somali Muslims 10, 14
Somaliland Camel Corps 182
Somorrostro, Basque country 136
'Sonic Deception' 216
South Africa 22, 146
    GS's background 5–6
    black workers refuse to work on Italian ships
        22
    GS's honeymoon in 146, 161, 162
    Axis threatens 155
    goes into Second World War 162
    apartheid 251
South Africa magazine 248, 250–51
South African Air Force 201
South African Airways 151
South African Division 193
South African Press Association 202
South African Women's Industrial Union 39
South-West Africa (later Namibia) 148, 153, 155
South-West Africa Nazi Party 148
Southampton 125, 166
Southworth, Herbert R. 3
    Guernica! Guernica! A Study of Journalism,
    Diplomacy, Propaganda, and History 126
Soviet Union
    and Spanish press censorship 80
    at 1937 World's Fair 140
    aggression in Finland 164–5
    expelled from the League of Nations 165

Spain
    Nazis field-test *blitzkrieg* 4, 168
    estimated total number of Germans in
        (1936–7) 85
Spanish Civil War 202
    involvement of Nazi Germany 1, 4, 80, 104
    Picasso appalled by 3
    GS travels to (1936) 78
    start of (18 July 1936) 79
    first major airlift of troops 80
    nature of 80
    GS's first experiences of 80–81
    GS expelled from Spain 84–6
    Aguirre on 89
    German efficiency 114
Spanish Foreign Legion 83, 84
Spanish Republic
    Picasso supports 3
    Nazis fight against 4
    Aguirre's reasons for supporting 92
    and the 'Escuadrilla Espana' 129
    and the World's Fair 140–41
Spanish Republican navy 159
Special Air Service (SAS) 215
Spectator 13, 48, 99, 103, 124, 143, 143, 144, 149,
    150
Sperrle, General Hugo ('Sander') 114
SS 154
St-Jean-de-Luz, Basque country 105, 106
Stalin, Joseph 165, 171
Stalingrad, USSR 123
Stanbrook (ship) 107
Standing Committee of Adjustment 248
Star (newspaper) 119
Stather-Hunt, D. W. 143–4
Steer, Barbara Esmé (née Barton; GS's second
    wife) 148, 221, 225, 241
    enjoys socializing 15, 16–17
    appearance 16, 17
    incident with Waugh 31, 39–40
    at Margarita's funeral 103
    marriage to GS 16, 160, 161
    voyage from Cape Town to Southampton
        (1939) 166
    birth of George 171
    hates GS's going to the Sudan 175
    birth of Caroline 218
    and GS's death 247, 248
Steer, Bernard (GS's father) 7, 12, 82, 86, 162, 183,
    229
Steer, Caroline (GS's daughter) 218, 219, 247
Steer, Emma (GS's mother) 12, 38–9, 97, 162
Steer, George Augustine Barton (GS's son) 171,
    172, 219, 242, 247, 253

Steer, George Lowther
  background 6
  childhood 7, 12
  education 7–8, 12, 31, 49, 129, 153, 181
  journalistic apprenticeship 8, 12
  publication of his Guernica report 1–2
  on the Gestapo Special Wanted List 4–5
  appearance 5–6, 20, 35, 40, 137, 152, 161, 183
  personality 5–6, 31–2, 40, 85, 181, 198–9, 248,
    249, 250
  becomes *The Times* Special Correspondent in
    Ethiopia 8
  interviews Haile Selassie 18–19
  Secretary of L'Association de la Presse
    Etrangère 22
  tours the Ogaden 23–30
  relationship with the Emperor 24
  his first book 28
  meets Waugh 30
  in love with Margarita de Herrero 37, 38, 40, 61
  at the British Legation 66–7
  marries Margarita 70–71, 97
  expelled from Ethiopia 14, 74
  meets the Emperor in London 75
  signs publishing contract 76
  first experiences of the Spanish Civil War
    80–81
  expelled from Spain 84–6
  arrival in Bilbao 88, 90–91
  bereaved 96–8
  as historian 93, 108
  actions on the day of the Guernica raid 116–21
  and fall of Bilbao 132–7
  a target for the Catholic Right 144
  sues Sencourt for libel 144–6
  remarries 146, 160, 161
  hepatitis 148
  considers Germany's lost colonies 151–5
  on anti-Semitism 154–5
  on air power 5, 36, 82, 109, 155, 170, 192
  visits Tunisia and Libya (1939) 155–60
  in Scandinavia 164–70
  birth of George 171
  takes the Emperor to the Sudan 175–9
  joins PSYOPS 179
  influence on combat propaganda 239–40
  role in the Ethiopian campaign 179, 180,
    182–7, 191–5
  on Wingate 190
  in Lush's team in Addis Ababa 203–12
  joins SOE 215
  Madagascar operation 217–18
  work in Burma 227–39, 241–5
  last letter to his wife 241–2

  death 244–7
  burial 246–7
  obituaries and assessment 248–51
  writings
  'Abyssinia Today' 149
  'The Abyssinian Adventure' 13
  *The Abyssinian Campaigns: The Official Story
    of the Conquest of Italian East Africa* 193,
    216
  'Addis Ababa - Civilised' 99–103
  'Advance against Basques' 105
  'Bilbao's Last Stand [. . .]' 137
  'The Bombing of Gernika' 144
  'Bombing of Guernica: German Airman's
    Statement' (13 May 1937) 4
  Caesar in Abyssinia 28, 31, 32, 49, 54, 76, 81–2,
    86, 234
  A Date in the Desert 156–60
  'The Ethiopian Tragedy, Final Phase in Addis
    Ababa' 73
  'Germany in Africa' 152
  Into Another Mould [? lost] 242–3
  'Italian Use of Poison Gas' report 55
  Judgment on German Africa 153, 154–5, 156
  Sealed and Delivered 163, 184, 198, 205–6, 214,
    216
  'The Tragedy of Guernica' report (28 April
    1937) 1–2, 3, 4, 121, 123–5, 126, 141
  The Tree of Gernika xiii, 5, 87, 93, 98, 108, 109,
    111, 122, 130, 134, 135, 137–40, 147, 234, 248,
    249
Steer, Margarita *see* Herrero-Steer, Margarita
Stephens, Pembroke 128
Stephenson, Jo 97
Stesso (ship) 107
Stevenson, R. C. 123–4
Stirling, Colonel David 215–16
Stirling, William F. 84–5
Stockholm 167
Stordy, Robert J. 'Wordy' 67
Straits of Gibraltar 79
'strategic bombing' 122, 123 (*see also* aerial
    bombing)
Sudan 150, 153, 156, 174, 175, 178–9, 211, 249
Sudan Defence Force 177, 191, 193
Sudan Frontier Battalion 210
Sudan Interior Mission, Dessye 57
Sudan Survey Department 179
Suez Canal 8, 10, 13, 58, 76, 150
Sufetula, Tunisia 159
Sun Tzu: *The Art of War* 215
Sunday Times 118
Sweden: decision to stay out of the war (1940) 167
Swedish Foreign Ministry 170

Swedish Red Cross 48
Sykes, Christopher: *Orde Wingate* 214–15
Symes, Sir Stewart 177, 178n
    Tour of Duty 178n

Tablet, The (Catholic weekly) 31, 32, 143
Tacitus 114
Taezaz, Dr Lorenzo 22–3, 33, 34, 60, 64, 160, 161,
    162, 175, 179, 184, 210
Taitu, Empress of Ethiopia 14–15
Takazze River 42
Tanahashi, Colonel 234
Tanganyika 152, 153, 155
Tarmaber Pass, Ethiopia 56
Tarr, Jack 230
Tasso, Ligaba 33
Taylor, Captain R. H. R. ('Firkin') 38, 54, 68
Tefere Katama, Ethiopia 25, 28–9
Tembien, Ethiopia 42, 57
Temple Hill, Arakan 230
Tennyson, Alfred: 'Locksley Hall' 45
Terzian, Avedis 207, 211
Terzian, Sarkis 207
Tewodros, Emperor of Ethiopia 9
thermite 121, 144, 172
Thesiger, Wilfred 24, 213
Things to Come (film) 122
Thornhill, Colonel Cudbert 214
Thorpehall (cargo ship) 105
Thurston (ship) 107
Tigre 9, 34
Time and Tide 87
Time magazine 22
Times, The xiii, 8, 49, 248
    GS's reports on Guernica 1, 2, 3–4, 121
    GS as Special Correspondent in Ethiopia 5, 8,
        12–13, 18–19, 30, 44, 55, 73
    Aids to Correspondents booklet 13
    obituary of Sidney Barton 15
    report on the Muzi Falconi shooting 16
    urges GS to go to Dessye 51
    telegram from the Ethiopian Red Cross 52–3
    reports on use of poison gas 55
    tries to get GS re-accredited in Ethiopia 73
    GS's Ethiopian expenses 75–6
    GS as Special Correspondent in Spain 78
    GS's arrangement ends (September 1936) 81
    reports Margarita's death 97
    GS's remuneration 104
    fair coverage of the Spanish Civil War 105
    praises government policy 106
    argument with GS about money and status 146
    reports GS's wedding (1939) 161
    Sandford writes for 174

Times Weekly Edition, The 137
Titulescu, Nicolas 76
To the Four Winds - Lauaxeta (film) 112–13
Tobruk, Libya 158
Tobruz fortress 216
Togoland 155
Toledo, Spain 84, 85
Torrontegui Hotel, Bilbao 92, 96, 109, 111, 112,
    118, 127
Trades Union Congress (TUC) 3
Trajan, Emperor of Rome 159
Tripartite Treaty (1906) 9
Tripoli, Libya 36, 102
Tripoli Grand Prix (1939) 158
Trondheim, Norway 170
Troquard (French intelligence officer) 149
Trotha, General von 154
Truende, Basque country 113
Tsahai-Worek, Princess 52, 53, 59, 76, 161
Tug Argan gap, Somaliland 181
Tuklein Wells, Sudan 185–6
Tunis, Tunisia 157
Tunisia 155, 156, 157, 159, 160, 176, 224

UGT (Union General de Trabajadores) 94, 95, 96
Ullendorff, Professor Edward 77
Umm Idla, Sudan 191, 194
Unamuno, Miguel de 83–4, 138
Union-Castle line 151, 166
United States of America
    reaction to Guernica 4
    Congress 4
    'Appeal to the Conscience of the World' 4
    Pearl Harbor 216–17
    sinks materials into the war 244
Upper Egypt 150
Urkiaga, Esteban ('Lauaxeta') 113, 140
Urrusti, near Bilbao 130
US Pacific fleet 216

Valencia: Cortes 89
Valle, General 53
Vallellano, Countess of 82
van der Post, Laurens 189
Vansittart, Robert 11–12
Varges (cinematographer) 33
Venta de Baños, Spain 82
Verne, Jules 122
Versailles, Treaty of 114
Vickers Valentin transport plane 150, 182
Vickers Vincent light bomber 182, 192
Victoria, Queen, Empress of India etc. 9
Vienna 148, 154
Viipuri (Vyborg), Finland 169, 192

Villa Wahnfried 79
Vinci-Gugluicci (Italian Minister) 33
Vitoria airfield 115, 118
Vizcaya/Bizkaia 89, 90, 108, 133, 249
Vizkargi, Basque country 130

Wadi Halfa, Sudan 177
Wagner, Richard 79, 80
Waldia, Ethiopia 53
Walwal dispute 11–12, 24, 25
War Department (Britain) 161
Warsaw, Poland 123
Waugh, Evelyn
    attitude to GS 5, 31–2
    on Taezaz 22
    works for the *Daily Mail* 30
    meets GS 30
    appearance 30, 31
    review of *Caesar in Abyssinia* 31, 93
    incident with Esmé 31, 39–40
    on Ethiopians 33
    his baboon 34
    and Germany's lost colonies 153
    Black Mischief 8, 15, 23, 31, 32, 66
    Put Out More Flags 193
    Remote People 32
    Scoop 31, 32, 34, 39, 40
    Waugh in Abyssinia 32
Wavell, Major General Archibald 114, 173–4, 188,
    189, 190, 194, 213, 225
Webbe Shebeli valley, Ethiopia 28, 51
Wellington, Arthur Wellesley, 1st Duke of 90,
    92
Wellington College 175
Wells, H. G.
    The Outline of History 204
    Things to Come 122
    The War in the Air 122
West, Rebecca 4–5
West Yorkshire Regiment 194, 197
Western Desert 216
Westminster Abbey, London 124
Wetherall, Major General 202
Whiteheads Grove, Chelsea (No. 7) 173
Who's Who 5
Wienholt, Senator Arnold 'Rocky' 174
    'Unconquerable Ethiopia' 174

Williams, Eric 22
Williams, Lieutenant Colonel Humphrey 234,
    235, 236–7
Wilson (commander, D Company IRWF) 35
Wilson, Captain E. T. C. 182
Winchester, Bishop of 3–4
Winchester, Dean of 103
Winchester College 7, 12, 31, 97, 153, 250
Wingate, Major Orde 189–91, 193, 194, 200–201,
    207, 209, 213–15, 248
Wodaju (cook) 66
Wolfe, Charles 172
Wollega, Ethiopia 204
Wollegas 50
Wollo, Ethiopia 43, 44, 49
Woo, Mr (translator) 230
Woods, Donald 12
Wooha-Boha 61
Worcestershire 194
Workneh, Elizabeth 204, 211, 212
Workneh, Sarah 212
Worku, Lij 23
World's Fair (1937) 3, 140–1
World Trade Center, New York City 122
Worq, Tafere 161
Wright, Armin 96
Wright (at Bank of Ethiopia) 33
Wright, Erica 96
Wykehamist, The 12

Xylander, Colonel Rudolf 144

Yates-Brown, Major Francis 137
Yekatit 12 98–9
Yorkshire Post 8, 12, 13, 161, 248, 249
Young Ethiopians 63, 102
yperite gas and liquid 13, 45–6, 52 (*see also*
    poison gas)

Zamudio Brigade HQ 131
Zauditu, Empress of Ethiopia 10, 61, 63, 67
Zeeland, Paul van 76
Zeila, British Somaliland 19
Zelale, Keren 195
Zibist, Ethiopia 183
Zorrilla, José A. 112
Zubelzu, Spain 81